327.1

Gio

I0395925

DISCARD

WOMEN
Essential Voices for the Nuclear Age
ON WAR

Edited by

DANIELA GIOSEFFI

A TOUCHSTONE BOOK

PUBLISHED BY SIMON & SCHUSTER INC.

NEW YORK   LONDON   TORONTO   SYDNEY   TOKYO

Touchstone
Simon & Schuster Building
Rockefeller Center
1230 Avenue of the Americas
New York, New York 10020

Designed by Jeanne Joudry
Manufactured in the United States of America
10 9 8 7 6 5 4 3 2 1
10 9 8 7 6 5 4 3 2 1 Pbk.
Library of Congress Cataloging in Publication Data
Women on war.

  A Touchstone Book
  Bibliography: p.
  1. Women and peace.   I. Gioseffi, Daniela.
JX1965.W4517 1988   327.1'72'088042   88-23961
ISBN 0-671-67157-X
ISBN 0-671-66781-5 Pbk.

Permissions for use of selections appear on pages 370–377.

Gratitude is due to those authors and publishers of selections which were kindly contributed for use. I am grateful to The Ploughshares Fund and Sally Lilienthal for an award/grant which helped with initial compiling costs; to my editor, at Touchstone Books, Carole Hall, for her invaluable guidance; and for the astute advice of my husband, Lionel B. Luttinger. Thanks is due Grace Paley, Milton Kessler, Galway Kinnell, Harriet Zinnes, Yvonne Chism-Peace, Pedro Pietri, Pearl Breskin, Maurice Edwards, Michael Irwin and Philip Appleman for supportive recommendations at the outset.

This book is warmly dedicated to my daughter, Thea; stepdaughters, Amy, Nina, Tanya; sisters, Camille and Lucille; nieces, Dana and Debbie; and my courageous mother, a lively survivor, Josephine Buzevska Gioseffi—and as well to all the women around the world who are so much a part of it and the hope of the future.

Contents

3

CONTENTS

PART II · CAUSES, REALITIES, AND CURES

4

CONTENTS

PART III · VIOLENCE, MOURNING, COURAGE, AND RESISTANCE

CONTENTS

PART IV · HOPE AND SURVIVAL

CONTENTS

Introduction

"You can no more win a war than an earthquake!" said the first woman ever elected to the U.S. Congress, peace activist Jeannette Rankin. Her words resonate truer than ever today. The horror which troubles children's nightmares will not vanish with a minor agreement about intermediate range nuclear missiles such as the 1988 INF Treaty, for even as a few are disarmed, the Center for Defense Information in Washington, D.C., tells us, that many more newer and more destabilizing weapons are manufactured to take their place. Wars both declared and undeclared continue to rage around the globe. Jeannette Rankin's sensibility is needed more than ever.

When Rankin cast her vote in 1917 and again in 1941 against U.S. entry into war, she is said to have wept with passionate conviction. Many have never forgiven her for what to them was a lapse of judgment, just as Cassandra was maligned for displaying emotion. Yet, to weep, even to be hysterical (from the Greek word for "womb"), is to be appropriately human, and therefore *rational* in the deepest sense of the word. Cool logic has brought us to the brink of what disarmament activists call *omnicide*—a word used to designate an act of homicide combined with suicide and even more terrible than the many genocides in our history—*the total and final destruction of all life on earth.*

Both men and women are beginning to understand the importance of a human response like that of Jeannette Rankin, who held her convictions throughout her life and at the age of eighty-eight led a march of women on Washington, in 1968 against the Vietnam War. Many believe that archetypal masculine logic, devoid of feminine feeling, is the dangerous mode of thinking which created our present predicament and which *must* be avoided if we are to survive as a species. More men and women than ever are interested in what women have to say about the most baffling, challenging, and tragic issue facing all of life. As Dorothy Crowfoot Hodgkin, Nobel Prize–winning scientist, explains in these pages: though coolheadedness may be necessary in the laboratory, the scientist must learn to respond with more consideration for the consequences of what is discovered or invented there. The best minds of our time are warning us that the entire race stands at a crossroads and a constructive choice must be made now, or there will be no other choices. Humankind is, indeed, about to destroy itself as a species and to end all of creation as we know it—*or learn to live in peace.*

Women, traditionally, throughout various cultures of the world, have been charged with humanizing society through emotional nurturance, as well as expressiveness—as in conventional feminine mourning and keening over the death of loved ones. This collection, in that tradition, is a multicultural response to the psychic numbing or apathy that many of us have begun to experience as a result of having to live daily with the realization that the next world war might be of such a magnitude as to create a nuclear winter that will end all.

This book is an international sampling of the challenging and moving literature by women on the subject and issues of war. It is intended to inspire empathetic feeling between differing peoples, and peacemaking action. As far as can be determined, it is the first annotated compendium to give interested men and women an opportunity to explore what women have said on this most vital issue of our time. By no means does it suggest that all women are peacemakers and all men warmongers.

A mixture of genres, commentators, activists, scientists, journalists, essayists, storytellers, and poets create a balance of *ethos, logos,* and *pathos.* The result is a deliberate patchwork quilt of forms and cultural outlooks—like those famous peace quilts from Boise, Idaho, made by a variety of craftswomen from around the world—in a spirit of cross-cultural exchange. When the patches are sewn together, they cover the universal theme well.

The pieces are not without humor and irony, too, as Sojourner Truth, a black American suffragist once quipped, with oblique reference to the Eve and Pandora myths of patriarchy: "If the first woman God ever made was strong enough to turn the world upside down, these women together ought to be able to turn it rightside up again." What Sojourner Truth said could well be an inspiring epigram for a compilation such as this. The text, in its four divisions, is a journey from prophecy and warning, finally ending in transcendence and hope as it points the way to survival.

It symbolizes a kind of dialogue across time and national boundaries. Though all wars cannot be included, there is a universal timeliness to the major themes represented here—as, for example, those offered by Gertrude Kolmar, who wrote her poetry in a concentration camp, or by South Korean student, Jong Ji Lee, in jail under the despotic reign of Chun Doo Hwan or Winnie Mandela of South Africa, whose words from prison echo those of a Southern slave beaten by a plantation owner during the aftermath of the Civil War.

Most selections are contemporary, but many reach back to past wars and a few extend to earlier civilizations. For an example, Enheduanna, a Sumerian priestess (c. 2300 B.C.) and the first known poet of history—man or woman—offers a taste of the first war protest poetry ever written. Ch'iu Chin, an eighteenth-century Chinese poet affords an example of a revolutionary hero and resister of cruel colonization which amplifies the feeling expressed by Greek, Central American, Afghan, or Lebanese women of later times. The inclusion of such older works gives resonance to our continuing search for peace and reminds us of our ageless human desire to change from the course of violence as a means to settling disputes.

Part 1, "Prophecies and Warnings," is meant to articulate the vitality and eminence of the book's major themes. Part 2, "Causes, Realities, and Cures," contains rational explanations and ideas for understanding why war persists despite a worldwide desire for harmony and peace among peoples and nations. Economic concepts about the war machine are clarified. The evils of intervention and exploitative colonialism are highlighted. Some of the selections deal with how the enemy is created with semantics and how language is manipulated to continue the arms race. Aspects of xenophobia are addressed, also. Part 3, "Violence, Mourning, Courage, and Resistance," highlights recent wars and war-torn areas of the world. It points repeatedly to follies of past wars and engenders empathy for the victims of violence, and the resultant famines caused by war. To attempt a cleansing of the spirit and set the stage for an age free of the threat of nuclear, chemical, and biological warfare is the function of the last section, Part 4, "Hope and Survival." Here we find a belief in peace as something more tangible than a mere absence of war. This section affirms a love for earth and our roots in nature and offers strategies for disarmament and peace. In closing, a bibliography introduces a wealth of available literature by women on related themes. Also, a resource list of organizations at the back of the volume offers opportunities for active or monetary involvement in the cause. (Notes on authors and selections follow each of the four parts.)

It is hoped that this book will find its way into many languages of the world, helping in some measure to create a spirit of global community, giving women a communal sense of empowerment, an international empathy in their concern for our fragile planet and the future of children everywhere.

The Ploughshares Fund, a peace foundation in California headed by President Sally Lilienthal, has helped with initial compiling costs for this collection, under its Women's Leadership Development Division, noting the desire among women to read what women have done and said in the face of war and in the cause of peace. The history of art, politics, literature, predominantly written by men, has engraved a masculine image of assertive power upon women's minds. This collection is meant to stimulate participation in peacemaking by offering active female role models. It is a text for any reader of either sex as well as women's studies scholars—a book for Feminism 2000, the newest international phase of the still-growing women's movement. More people than ever are aware of the struggles particular to women. This book assures us that many women are assertive and active, linking hands around the planet, doing their best to save the children, as these pages show many women have always done, throughout neglected "herstory."

Having begun this compilation some time before the 1986 International PEN congress in New York—which I attended as a member of American PEN—I was all the more inspired to complete it. That newsmaking congress of writers showed that, once again, the vast accomplishment of women in the fields of literature and intellectual endeavor was undermined, or ignored in popular history. Even after the ardent feminism of the past decade which witnessed the advent of women's studies scholarship throughout some of the developed countries, once again women were made to feel fairly invisible or ineffectual on the male-proposed theme of that congress: "The imagination of the writer versus the imagination of the state." Though some of the finest writers, poets, essayists, intellects, thinkers on this subject have been women, women's voices were rarely quoted and had only a token representation. From Ch'iu Chin to Vittoria Colonna, Nelly Sachs, Gwendolyn Brooks, or Gabriela Mistral, Toni Morrison, Isabel Allende, Claribel Alegría, Natalia Ginzburg, Zoe Karelli, Wisława Szymborska or Nancy Morejón; from Rosa Luxemburg to Jane Addams; from Emma Goldman or La Pasionaria (Dolores Ibarruri) to Helen Caldicott, Randall Forsberg, Winnie Mandela; from Alexandra Kollantai to Olive Schreiner, Meridel Le Sueur, Hannah Arendt, Alva Myrdal, or Petra Kelly, examples can be offered. As herein suggested, a rich literature exists and needs only to be highlighted. These selections show that women are among the world's foremost innovative thinkers and activists, from Nobel Prize winners to resistance fighters, and, in general, profound poets and thinkers on the subject of war. Indeed, this book might be called: "The Feminine Imagination Versus the Irrationality of the Patriarchal State."

As Hannah Arendt says in these pages, there is no cause for war but the most ancient of all, the one, in fact, that from the beginning of our history has determined the very existence of politics, the cause of freedom versus tyranny. That cause remains, even now, the justification for the so-called Cold War—which rages hot as hell in developing countries of the world where powerful militarists—who gain profits from arms sales to poorer or colonialized nations headed by puppet dictators—send their secret agents to instigate civil strife. It's important to note that Emily Greene Balch, Nobel Peace Prize recipient, was voicing the same concerns about intervention in Haiti in 1925, as many peace activists with the International War Resisters League, or the Women's International League for Peace and Freedom are today.

Everywhere, throughout history and today—in the name of freedom—innocent people are tyrannized, tortured, starved, exiled from their homes or murdered. Right or Left rhetoric rots in the mouths of the over one hundred million who have been killed by wars in this century alone. Angelica Balabanoff, a friend of John Reed and an idealistic socialist—who worked untiringly in the international peace movement—wrote: "History has been falsified without shame by the Fascists and, unfortunately, also, by the Bolsheviks. The truth was never more necessary than it is today!"

Whether the women herein write of the massacre of Jews, Poles, Africans, Armenians, Indians, Vietnamese, Holocaust victim or Hiroshima victim, it is the same nightmare of history from which we must awaken. Always the war horrors are accompanied by women's stories of courage, comforting love, resistance, and transcendence. These, too, are the subjects of this collection. Whether we read of medieval inquisitions in which witches—mostly women—were burned by religious zealots, Nero's Praetorian Guard or Mao Tse-tung's Red Guard, the Hitlers or Stalins in our history earn the same infamy. No nation is free of ancient tribal blood rivalries or the guilt of wars. Overwhelmingly, war has been initiated by powerful leaders who hold military might. Always, the common people even more than their leaders are victims of war, as the poem by a Romanian writer, Ileana Malancioui, titled "Antigone" reminds us.

Indeed, wars continue to be the dominant mode of the twentieth century as we approach the year 2000, even though the threat of total annihilation has outmoded all ideologies and justifications for war. There are many means and ways to solutions of conflict and to disarmament agreements in our sophisticated times. Science has made nuclear disarmament completely verifiable by technologies of various kinds and combinations.

Still, since the end of World War II, over 150 wars, declared and undeclared, have wrought misery and massacre throughout the world. The irony remains that while wars and revolutions are fought in the name of freedom versus tyranny, all of us are hostages to the greatest tyranny civilization has ever known. The final nuclear, biological, or chemical sword of Damocles hangs over all of us, while many are oblivious to the precariousness with which it is poised, or duped by shallow talk or shows of disarmament. If that final sword falls it means death to us and to all we love, our children and our children's children, our music and poetry and art, along with the magnificent snow leopard, and blue heron, death to the giant sequoia, red rose, purple lotus and black orchid, death to all the wondrous creation pulsing from what may be the only blue teardrop of human life and laughter afloat in cold dark space.

Rosa Luxemburg's essay on militarized economies clearly explains how our demise will not be in the cause of freedom, but military profiteering, just as in Germany where she was murdered for her Cassandra prophecies. What she had to say is very much the same as what the U.S. Center for Defense Information in Washington, D.C., is telling us today. Like Eisenhower and Einstein, it warns us that the military has taken over the world economy to a profoundly destructive extent. Accidental nuclear war is now a grave possibility. Still, we are living in relative apathy even with the facts known—as missile reaction time has grown exceedingly short and small tactical weapons or cruise missiles with the blast power of sixteen Hiroshima bombs each continue to proliferate. While the extent of the overkill capabilities of nuclear forces poised on the earth boggles the mind, the neutral outer space surrounding our fragile planet is now threatened with the proliferation of first-strike nuclear weaponry, too. Yet, the U.S. nuclear air force during the last decade swept into action more than three times on Red Alert and all because of the failure of a twenty-nine-cent computer chip, a fact reported even in *The New York Times*.

Maria Montessori, Italian educator, observed long ago, "The people of the world who profess to want to get rid of war as the worst of scourges are, nevertheless, the very ones who concur in the arming and starting of wars." People, perhaps especially women, need to feel empowered to make a difference. Hopefully, this book offers a sense of that empowerment. An excerpt by Petra Kelly of West Germany has documented, as have many other essays by experts, that fallible computers and men—sometimes found to be on drugs or dealing them—hold our futures in their hands. But even as she warns us that the world expenditure on the arms race is now estimated by the United Nations to be well over a thousand million dollars per day, she tells us of a growing network of women who are asserting themselves in the international peace movement and the camaraderie among them which she senses in her global travels.

Many of us who have not experienced the direct devastation of war in our daily lives need to understand that war's realities are all around us. Increased military spending, the experts on the arms race tell us, has lowered the standards of living for billions of people around the globe, but by far the largest percentage of people living below the poverty line is found among families headed by single women—and their numbers are steadily increasing for reasons shown by the writers in this text. The horrendous increase in poverty around the world—especially among women—has been paralleled by the largest "peacetime" military buildup in history. Militarism creates misery everywhere, but women are especially hard hit by its economic violence.

Even those of us who seem to live in peace in developed countries suffer from nuclearized and militarized economies. Scientists tell us that one out of four of us will die of cancer, and the increase in this disease is a direct result of the military and chemical industries that are poisoning our air and waters and destroying our environment, as Dara Janekovic, Yugoslavian journalist, explains.

Where people escape being killed by bombs or bullets, they may not escape famine or disease which follow alongside of war. In countries not seemingly involved in war, people are deprived in various ways of resources, both material and human, which are absorbed by military activities. World economists explain that the Japanese economy and educational system are thriving in a good measure because Japan has not indulged in military development since World War II. This fact dramatizes how other nations have been devastated by their military-industrial barons. Worldwide military expenditures are estimated to amount to more than $900 billion per year. In Britain, for example, it costs nearly two million pounds to train a fighter pilot, the Pledge for Peace in London tells us. The Council for Economic Priorities in the United States shows that, on the average, it costs about the same to arm and train one soldier as it does to educate eighty children, to build one modern bomber as it did to wipe out smallpox over a ten-year period, to launch the latest nuclear missile submarine as it does to build 450,000 homes for the poor. The entire food stamp program to help feed hungry people in the United States does not cost the markup overhead—just the overhead—on one nuclear bomber.

Who sets such priorities? In the United States where there exists one of the strongest feminist movements in history, there are only two women senators and twenty-three congresswomen and few people of color among the hundreds of men running the government on "The Hill." Men hold almost all electoral or appointed positions of power around the world. In the politburos of Eastern-bloc countries, there are nearly no women. A generation of women still living now in developed countries only acquired the right to vote within their own lifetimes. In developing countries—according to United Nations statistics—a huge majority of women still have no voice in the political arena of their lands. Only in a few Scandinavian countries do women have a fair measure of political power. Overwhelmingly, men hold the political power and corporate executiveships making decisions about national priorities for all of us. Most often those charged with such decisions are the last to suffer the deprivation and devastation caused by them.

The few corporate executives or party bureaucrats who profit from this status quo, have now—according to the Union of Concerned Scientists and *The Bulletin of Atomic Scientists*—stockpiled the explosive power for over fifty tons of TNT in nuclear weapons for every human on the globe. Their priorities are destroying the earth and consuming vital resources that belong to all—especially the children—with an insane *overkill*. It is now estimated by United Nations sources that there are more than 50,000 nuclear warheads in the world. The total explosive power of the world stock of nuclear weapons is about equal to one million Hiroshima bombs, each of which has a yield of thirteen kilotons. (A kiloton is equal to a thousand tons of a conventional high-explosive like TNT.) It appears that men as stubborn as Sophocle's King Creon are unwisely deciding the fate of all—including *themselves* and *their* children.

"Where are the women" at the summit talks of our fate? is a question posed by Betty Lall, named by UNESCO as one of the world's three leading women experts on arms control. "It is an interesting fact that women have been shunted aside when high-level discussions turn to issues of armaments, especially interesting since women have been at the forefront as activists where nuclear arms control is concerned," she tells us.

Christa Wolf, an East German writer, points out that many who are very skeptical concerning the survival of the race have a conviction that nations and their economies can be governed only by competition rather than cooperation. Though this fact goes uncontested, the people who are sure we'll be unable to solve critical life problems do not bring themselves to reflect on the relationship that exists between the arms race and patriarchal structures of thought and government. Wolf notes, too, that even the youthful Japanese of today have little sense of the suffering of Hiroshima victims, like those represented here.

The reality or memory of the suffering of war is absent from the lives of many people in developed countries and that, also, is a raison d'être of this collection, to create a global communality concerning past and present wars in the light of our universal fate. As Simone Weil wrote in Paris during World War II, "Pain and suffering are a kind of currency passed from hand to hand until they reach someone who receives them but does not pass them on." Käthe Kollwitz, the great German artist whose drawings provide division for the thematically arranged sections of this book, who portrayed real women, not modish models, in the struggles of war, possessed just such empathy. Her graphics portray the universal woman.

Our Soviet sisters, included along with some of their great poets like

19

Anna Akhmatova, agree that since women are more concerned with the task of birthing and nurturing the human race more than the arms race, an exchange among women of the world, of their own thoughts, writings, and peace initiatives, could serve to encourage them to continue to speak out and act for the salvation of life. As Virginia Woolf once wrote, ". . . the outsider will say I have no country. As a woman, my country is the world." Still, an American, Dorothy Day, makes us wonder in irony when she writes: "We are quite literally a nation which is in the process of committing suicide in the hope that then the Russians will not be able to murder it." One can easily imagine a Russian woman saying something quite similar.

There are areas of the world, like Syria, Turkey, Indonesia, parts of Africa, where serious war crimes have or are taking place, but from which little written or translated information is readily available. Such areas are not deliberately neglected, but not easily represented. Though every country and culture could not be represented, these explanations of the ways and means to peace, exchanged among women of the world, offer communion for those who understand and inspiration for those who wish to avert psychic numbing. They can be added to by any given culture. They offer an opportunity to hear feminine wisdom to the many men who want to listen.

Voices of mothers, daughters, and sisters of earth need to be heeded as much as the maligned but clairvoyant Cassandra, or Aeschylus's "Suppliant Women" at the dawn of Western civilization, needed to be heard. "Surely the earth can be saved by all the people who insist on love," Alice Walker has written. May her conviction prove true as women everywhere link hands in a chorus of life.

Daniela Gioseffi
June 6, 1988, New York

The four illustrations used in this text are by the highly esteemed and world renowned German artist, Käthe Kollwitz (1867–1945). More than any other artist of this century, she was concerned with expressing the need for social justice among the poor, the laborers, and the sufferers of war. No one has more poignantly and profoundly portrayed the grief of parents who lose their sons and daughters to the violence and famine caused by war. For use of the illustrations, the following credits are due:

Seed for Sowing Shall Not Be Milled, 1942,
courtesy of The Galerie St. Etienne, New York City, lithograph on ivory woven paper;
Woman Meditating I, 1920,

courtesy of The National Gallery of Art, Rosenwald Collection, Washington, D.C., lithograph;
Death Seizes a Woman, 1934,
courtesy of The Galerie St. Etienne, New York City, lithograph, signed; Plate 4 from the *Death* cycle;
No More War, 1924,
courtesy of The National Gallery of Art, Rosenwald Collection, Washington, D.C., lithograph retouched with lithograph crayon.

PART I

Prophecies and Warnings

I'm certain that if . . . women in every country would clearly express their conviction, they would find that they spoke not for themselves alone, but for those men for whom war has been a laceration—an abdication of the spirit.

—JANE ADDAMS (U.S.A.)

Where are your husbands, your brothers, your sons? Why must they destroy one another and all that they (and we) have created? Who benefits by this bloody nightmare? Only a minority of war profiteers. . . . Since the men cannot speak, you must. Working women of the warring countries, unite!

—ANGELICA BALABANOFF (UKRAINIAN RUSSIA)

Seed for Sowing Shall Not Be Milled, 1942, **by Käthe Kollwitz**

BELLA AKHMADULINA (U.S.S.R.)

WORDS SPOKEN BY PASTERNAK DURING A BOMBING

In olden times—in forever—
What then was I, a cloud, a star?
Unawakened yet by love,
A mountain stone, transparent as water?

Summoned from eternity by desire,
I was torn from darkness and born.
As a man, now, I'm a singing dome,
Round and inexplicable as a hull.
I've experience now and aptitude in art.
That day I implored: Oh earth!
Give me shelter, even the smallest bush
to forgive and shade me!

There in the sky, the bombsight shone
intractable so that I could taste
the vulnerability of a speck of creation
held in its target line.

I'm on my knees in doom up to my waist.
I writhe in quicksand, breathless:
Oh, crazed boy, wake up!
Don't sight me in your fateful line!

I'm a man, a valuable nugget
Lies in my soul. But, I don't want to glow,
And gleam—I'm a mountain stone,
Worn and smooth, desiring invisibility!

The steady roaring faded;
The bush breathed and grew and I sighed
Beneath it. The merciless modern angel
Flew away, loathing my inconsequence.

Into this world of new senses,
Where things turn golden with light,
Where things sing and sparkle, I bore my body,
an intimate and breakable thing.

I wept, feeling one with all that lives,
breathing, pulsing, alive.

Oh my supplication, lowly, but still lofty,
I repeat your gentle whisper.

Death, I've seen your blank,
Lonely features and carried myself
Away from them as a strange child
Who hardly looked like myself.

I'm not begging for a long life!
But, as in that hour in gray silence,
For some human flamelike unfolding
that accidentally lived in me.

It survived, and above the water
I stood for a long, long time, tired.
I wished to be a cloud, a star,
A mountain stone—transparent as water.

(*Translated by Daniela Gioseffi with Sophia Buzevska*)

HANNAH ARENDT   (GERMANY/U.S.A.)

FREEDOM SLOGANEERING AS AN EXCUSE FOR WAR

. . . The notion that aggression is a crime and that wars can be justified only if they ward off aggression or prevent it, acquired its practical and even theoretical significance only after the First World War had demonstrated the horribly destructive potential of warfare under conditions of modern technology. . . . Perhaps it is because of the noticeable absence of the freedom argument (throughout earlier history as a justification for war) that we have this curiously jarring sentiment whenever we hear it introduced into the debate of the war question today. To sound off with a cheerful "give me liberty or give me death" sort of argument in the face of the unprecedented and inconceivable potential of destruction in nuclear warfare is not even hollow; it is downright ridiculous. Indeed it seems so obvious that it is a very different thing to risk one's own life for the life and freedom of one's country and one's posterity from risking the very existence of the human species for the same purpose that it is difficult not to suspect the defenders of the "better dead than red" . . . slogans of bad faith. Which of course is not to say that

25

the reverse, "better red than dead," has any more to recommend itself;
when an old truth ceases to be applicable, it does not become any truer
by being stood on its head. As a matter of fact, to the extent that the
discussion of the war question today is conducted in these terms, it is
easy to detect a mental reservation on both sides. . . . It is important to
remember that the idea of freedom was introduced into the debate of
the war question only after it had become quite obvious that we had
reached a state of technical development where the means of destruction
were such as to excuse their rational use. In other worlds, freedom has
appeared in this debate like a deus ex machina to justify what on rational grounds has become unjustifiable. Is it too much to read into
current rather hopeless confusion of issues and arguments a hopeful
indication that a profound change in international relations may be
about to occur, namely, the disappearance of war from the scene of
politics even without a radical transformation of international relations
and without an inner change of men's hearts and minds? Could it not
be that our present perplexity in this matter indicates our lack of preparedness for a disappearance of war, our inability to think in terms of
foreign policy without having in mind this "continuation with other
means" as a last resort? . . . It is as though the nuclear armament race
has turned into some sort of tentative warfare in which the opponents
demonstrated to each other the destructiveness of the weapons in their
possession; . . . it is always possible that this deadly game of ifs and
whens may suddenly turn into the real thing.

ALENKA BERMÚDEZ (CHILE / GUATEMALA)

GUATEMALA, YOUR BLOOD

> ". . . why doesn't your poetry
> talk to us about dreams, leaves,
> the huge volcanos of your native land?
>
> Come look at the blood in the streets."
>
> —PABLO NERUDA

Where is the word that will fill in for hunger
and what name can you give to this daily wanting

how to describe the empty table the abysmal eyes
little bellies swollen   foreheads deformed
by weights   the endless burden of centuries
horizons of smoke   burned-up mattresses
no frying pan
scarcity in the stew that's left over because of scarcity
what substantive to use
how to name a finger cut off to get the insurance
what adjective for the holocaust
in what tense do you conjugate the verb to kill
what predicate what future what pluperfect

and when they plunder the roots and change the course of rivers
and they inundate the riverbeds with poison and everything
dies everything dies
when the sap in the trees is threatened crouching hidden
crazy annihilated   what participle will come to the rescue
and seeing that death doesn't have gender or case
that it installs itself multiplies and scatters itself
indiscriminate unlimited specialized and computed
which quartet or triplet will it fit into
in which precious alexandrine
ineffable hendecasyllabic mysterious elegy of nothingness

I reserve the right to use the Spanish word
to tell you: death to death
and victory to life
and combat and battle and machetes to life
and courage and tenderness to life
I reserve the right of the precisely exact
Spanish word
to name death and to name life
as long as the blood holds itself suspended
in our trees.

(Translated by Sara Miles)

Rosalie Bertell (u.s.a./canada)

OMNICIDE: THE PROPHETIC REALITY
OF SPECIES DEATH

The acceptance of the fact of one's personal death is mitigated by experienced continuity with both the past and the future. For adults, this continuity is most obviously linked with biological parenting, but it also occurs because of human memory, culture, literature and scientific endeavors. One can continue to affect history even after one's death. . . . Personal death is natural, although it may be premature . . . or violent as happens in war. The concept of species annihilation, on the other hand, means a relatively swift (on the scale of civilization), deliberately induced end to history, culture, science, biological reproduction and memory. It is more akin to suicide or murder than to natural death process. It is very difficult to comprehend omnicide, but it may be possible to discern the preparations for omnicide and prevent its happening.

The closest analogous human act which we can find in history on which to ground our thoughts about omnicide would be genocide, the deliberate ending of family lines. Hitler deliberately set out to annihilate all Jewish men and women and children, so that they and their offspring would disappear from history. Hitler also tried so to decimate Poland that it would be lost as a nation and culture, and its surviving people reduced to slave labor. Hitler did not declare war, however, against the earth: plants and animals, air, water and food. It was the Second Indochina War in Vietnam which first witnessed the extensive wartime use of technological power to devastate the living environment of earth. . . . The Jewish and Polish people condemned to death by authorities within the Third Reich were carefully "managed" and deceived, so that they would co-operate with the death plans, at least until it was too late to save themselves. . . . It is important to examine . . . the misrepresentation of "outside" reality as the precursor of genocide. It will give us clues to understanding omnicide in its early stages.

LADY BORTON (U.S.A.)

WARS PAST AND WARS PRESENT

Two movie projectors run in my head. The dominant one rolls out the sights and sounds and smells of the present in powerful color. The other projects cracked images from the past in faint black and white. Recently I was sitting in a restaurant, listening to a friend's story, when the projectors changed dominance.

The aroma of eggplant Parmesan filled the restaurant. A candle threw flickering light over our booth in the corner. Robert was telling his tale of hunting Vietcong at night in the Mekong Delta when that black-and-white movie in my mind took over.

As Robert spoke, I could hear the put-put of his Navy patrol boat in the ominous silence of the Mekong, I could hear rifle fire and smell the acrid gunpowder. I could see the stubs of defoliated palm trees silhouetted against an exploding sky.

"We'd sprayed every leaf," Robert was saying. His beard was touched with silver. Wrinkles edged his eyes. "The VC still hid."

I glanced away, my eye catching my own image in the mirror behind Robert. The brocade decor of the restaurant dissolved. Instead, I saw myself standing once again in the specimen room of a hospital outside Ho Chi Minh City, formerly Saigon. It was 1983. The smell of formaldehyde tinged the air. In the dim light I could make out glass crocks lining each wall, floor to ceiling, wall to wall, row upon gray row.

Each crock cradled a full-term baby. One infant had four arms, another a bowl in place of her cranium, a third a face on his abdomen, a fourth his navel protruding from his forehead. All the babies had been born in the early 1980's to women from provinces heavily sprayed with Agent Orange.

A Vietnamese doctor opened the wooden shutters. Sunlight flowed in transforming the crocks with their silver liquid into mirrors that shimmered, row upon row. I shrank back. In each mirror I could see that I remained my normal self.

"We called in air strikes," Robert said, punching his palm with his fist. The waiter set down cream and sugar. He poured coffee. The rich aroma of espresso floated over the restaurant. My lapse had been momentary. Its images receded once more into memory.

Vietnam memories can be strident. Often, they defy words, blocking communication and tangling with a comfortable Western life style. Sometimes they lie silent, reflecting our collective reluctance to place politics aside and address the continuing human effects of the war.

Psychologists have given names—"Vietnam syndrome," "flashback," "post-traumatic stress syndrome"—to the experience of that second movie projector's dominating conscious reality. Such terms make the phenomenon sound foreign, as if we must know war to experience the disorienting ambush of memory.

Anyone who has spent extended time in another culture returns home to the emotional unrest of double images running simultaneously. And those who have always lived here have at some time felt overwhelmed. We've all felt haunted by the death of a relationship, the loss of a child. We can all be surprised when our inner life spins unexpectedly outward.

I learn through experience to control those moments. It's easy enough in my own home to avoid known stimuli, like mirrors. In a restaurant or a friend's house, I have learned to choose a place briskly before I'm the last one seated. I settle down with the mirrors behind me, the way a combat veteran may sit with a wall at his back, his face toward the unpredictable entrance.

Other stimuli are less easily subdued. One recent evening I stopped by the local supermarket. The crowds in the aisles were intimidating. I felt besieged by displays of color, distracted by the smells of pizza, baking bread and budding roses. I pushed my cart past banks of broccoli and cabbages. When I reached for a head of lettuce, an automatic freshener nozzle sprayed my wrist.

That second movie projector in my mind shifted on screen. Suddenly I was back pushing a cart of protein supplements through a refugee camp. It was the late 60's, and I was visiting a Red Cross project in the central highlands of Vietnam. The refugees were preliterate tribespeople who had lived in huts of leaves, hunting and raising their food by slash-and-burn agriculture. Now they camped in tents surrounded by barbed wire.

The sun beat down on the tents. The heavy canvas gave off an odor like hot road tar, clogging my throat. The open latrines buzzed with flies. I passed three children hunkering in the brazen light. Their eyes were glazed, beyond begging. It was too quiet for so many people.

I paused near a woman doing fine embroidering in red and blue and orange. Her bare breasts trembled every time she pulled the needle through the black cloth. A girl of 2 lay next to the woman, naked in the dirt. The girl's dark hair was touched with orange, a symptom of advanced malnutrition. With her bloated belly, she looked like a butternut squash cast out on a compost pile. I pushed on with my cart of supplements, knowing that within hours the child would be dead. In a supermarket, I see that child as I push my cart past tiers of choices. Her face takes over cans of baby formula and boxes of cereal.

Of course, Vietnam has peace. Now, Vietnamese have enough to eat. But still, the intrusion of this outdated memory is instructive. It reminds me that what I witnessed years ago still exists, but elsewhere: in Nicaragua, Gaza, Afghanistan, Ethiopia. Memory can still jar the protective routine of my easy life style.

I've never lived in a house with a television, except for one year. That was in 1967. I was in my mid-20's. Every evening I watched the war on the news. Vietnamese refugees, their faces contorted, their voices anguished, streamed across that flickering blue screen into my living room. Their cries haunted me during the day and stayed with me deep into the night.

The job I took with the Quakers in Quang Ngai, a dusty South Vietnamese town swollen with refugees, included a program that made artificial arms and legs for civilian amputees. I remember one family, a widow and her two sons. The woman's name meant "springtime." She was my age, then 28. One of her sons, age 10, was a paraplegic. The other boy, a toddler, had plump legs peppered with shrapnel. The same mine that wounded the boys had turned Springtime into a double amputee.

During the flood season, I moved this family back into the refugee camp. There was no driving in. I started carrying the older boy, the paraplegic. The water swirled around my thighs. I left him with his grandmother and went back for the younger boy and then for his mother.

I carried Springtime on my hips the way she'd been carrying her sons when she stepped on the mine. Her stumps felt like flippers around my waist. With my bare feet, I felt beneath the water for the path along the paddy dike. I could smell my own sweat. I tried not to let my shortness of breath show. Springtime played with my hair. She drew a coppery ringlet out to its full length and laughed when it sprang back.

Springtime's mother and the two boys watched us from their tin hut. But the distance to them was too great. I had to ease Springtime down into the water that covered the paddy dike. Breathing hard, I sat next to her. Side by side, we rested on the dike, laughing as the brown water lapped around our waists.

I never saw the boat people exodus on television. However, I saw part of that story in person. I remember standing on the jetty of Bidong Island, the largest refugee camp in Malaysia for Vietnamese boat people. It was 1980. I was the camp's health administrator.

A Vietnamese boat appeared on the horizon. It rode low in the water. As the boat drew closer, I could see people gripping the cabin roof like bees clinging in layers to the face of a hive. Soon I could hear the excited voices.

The boat grazed the jetty. Its hull shivered. The captain, a small man

31

with an ashen face, stepped onto the dock. He said 14 passengers had died en route. Most died of thirst. Some drank sea water. One woman went delirious and threw herself into the sea.

I glanced into the cabin. Fuel cans floated in the bilge water, which smelled of diesel and vomit. A woman with a baby at her breast hunkered in the bilge water. A 6-year-old girl with wispy hair clung to a rib in the hull.

The wispy-haired girl collapsed on the jetty. A Vietnamese man unloading pack rations scooped up the child and ran with her toward the island. I followed.

In the camp hospital, I gave the child sips of water. Her name meant "flower." Vietnamese longshoremen brought in more people on stretchers. And more still. I removed Flower's wet clothes. Her skin was soft and white and wrinkled. Her hair was stiff with salt.

That afternoon I found Flower outside the hospital. She stood watching the cooks serve tea from a steaming vat. The next day when I went to check on her, she was gone. I looked for Flower among the thousands who thronged the camp's paths. I never saw her again.

Luon scratched the inside of a sow's ear. The pigpen was next door to the house where I was staying in a village 75 miles southeast of Hanoi. . . .

"Now that sow over there," Luon said, "the one with the nick on her snout, she'll throw a big litter. Always has anyway." Luon, the veterinarian of the cooperative, was in her mid-40's.

Inside the house, we sat on benches at a wooden table. The afternoon light threw shadows over the grass mat on my board bed. The mosquito net became a filmy canopy.

Luon spoke of her husband, who had gone south over the Ho Chi Minh trail with the North Vietnamese Army. "I received one letter," she said. " 'Work hard at home,' he wrote. 'Take care of our children.'

"Two years after Ky's death, I received a small package. Ky had sent three books so our children could read. If there was a letter, it was lost." She brushed a strand of hair from her eyes. "His bones never came home."

Luon bent her head. Her shoulders quivered. Damp hair curtained her face.

If I were a good journalist, I thought, I'd press Luon for details and raw feelings. The tape recorder hummed. From outside the window came the sound of children's voices and the heavy tread of a water buffalo. I let my hand rest on Luon's shoulder.

"Tell me about your children," I said. "And about the animals."

GWENDOLYN BROOKS (U.S.A.)

THE PROGRESS

And still we wear our uniforms, follow
The cracked cry of the bugles, comb and brush
Our pride and prejudice, doctor the sallow
Initial ardor, wish to keep it fresh.
Still we applaud the President's voice and face.
Still we remark on patriotism, sing,
Salute the flag, thrill heavily, rejoice
For death of men who too saluted, sang.
But inward grows a soberness, an awe,
A fear, a deepening hollow through the cold.
For even if we come out standing up
How shall we smile, congratulate: and how
Settle in chairs? Listen, listen. The step
Of iron feet again.   And again   wild.

HELEN CALDICOTT (AUSTRALIA)

THE END OF THE WORLD COULD STILL COME
NEXT YEAR

Fifty percent of people under the age of thirty believe that nuclear war is going to occur within the next ten years. Yet they do nothing. What has happened to our instinct for survival?

We know about nuclear winter now. We know that possibly a thousand bombs dropped on a hundred cities could cover the earth with a cloud of smoke so thick that it will freeze everything and everybody in the dark, and could be the threshold of planetary extinction. Remember that the United States and the Soviet Union have over 50,000 nuclear weapons. . . . Yet, only 25 percent of the eligible voting public of the United States votes. So, we've got to get out and register people who know the issues and feel an instinct for survival. . . . It's getting more

33

and more out of human control. The computers have been known to fail hundreds of times.

. . . George Kistiakowsky, who was Eisenhower's science advisor and who helped make the first bomb, thinks we'll be lucky to survive until 1990. . . . Prevention of nuclear war is a concern that embraces all people of all beliefs, political persuasions, colors, creeds, and races. . . . It is time for people to rise to their full moral and spiritual height, to take the world on their shoulders, and to say I will save the earth. Each person can be as powerful as the most powerful person who ever lived.

ANN DRUYAN (U.S.A.)

AT GROUND ZERO IN HIROSHIMA . . .

At ground zero in Hiroshima there is a plaque that soothes: "Rest in Peace for It Shall Not Happen Again." The desire to salvage some meaning from such a cataclysm is understandable. However, when we consider the reality of our global situation that reassurance seems the emptiest of promises.

During World War II we murdered fifty million of our own. But, somehow we were left unsatisfied. Before the killing stopped we were already hard at work on streamlining the process. Our knowledge, our genius, and enormous amounts of our wealth were deployed to invent weapons that could transform whole cities into crematoria, whole continents into gas chambers. We pored over the photographs of the immolated and irradiated victims of the thirteen-kiloton Hiroshima bomb and at the very same time that we were lamenting their suffering, we were building those bombs bigger and bigger, all the way up to a sixty-megaton model. Now they come in all sizes and we have fifty thousand of them. Clearly, we are not yet serious about preventing it from happening again.

Despite this, I have hope. I believe I know what we must do. We have to stop letting the boys get away with murder by asserting our equality with them in the governance of this planet. We have to denude violence of its phony glory. We have to expose the delusion of nationalism for what it is, one of the early symptoms of the onset of the mass psychosis of war. We have to know what we are talking about so that no bomb salesman can intimidate us with the jargon of science or technology. We must arouse ourselves from our complacency towards the billion of us who have nothing. We must work for social and economic progress everywhere so that nonviolent avenues to justice remain open.

Can these things be done? As women of this era we have personal experience with the radical change that is possible when the conditions are right and there is a unity of political will. Our liberation gives me reason to believe in humanity's future. We *will* redeem the promise made at ground zero and thereby honor the heroic struggles of the 40,000 generations of life-giving women who came before us.

CAROLYN FORCHÉ (U.S.A.)

LETTERS TO AN OPEN CITY

As a child, I knew the rest of the world through the books I read with my friend under the black locust trees in summer, behind our houses built on the diminishing farmland surrounding Detroit. I knew war from Bill Kennedy's "Show Time" on Canada's channel nine Sunday afternoons: films made in the late forties of Americans fighting the Germans or the Japanese. Our foreign travel was a Sunday crossing of the Ambassador Bridge into Windsor, where my mother window-shopped English china and Irish linen, then treated us to tea and crumpets. Europe was where our grandparents came from, preserved in their radio polka music, their kitchen talk, Slavic language prayer-books and, at times, weeping for family members never seen again. For years my grandmother, Anna, had worked in a needle factory here to earn her father's passage; he was turned away at Ellis Island when a sore was discovered on his leg. Europe was not a destination, but a fixed boundary in personal history. The sons and daughters of factory workers could no more hope to travel abroad than my mother could indulge her passion for Wedgwood and lace. These things were not ours. Although my father's hard labor and my student loans had secured for me a university education, I imagined such travel impossible until I was twenty-seven years of age.

The daughter of exiled poet Claribel Alegría convinced me that it was possible; she'd lived all over the world. Maya fingered the blank passport I carried, played old Piaf records for me and shared a sheaf of photographs. In one she is young, waving from a rose-laden balcony in Seville. In the next she gathers her skirt in her hands as it rises in a wind washing the deck of a Mediterranean ferry. Then she lifted her glass to the candlelight. "If you've never been anywhere at all, you must go to Paris. Paris is your city." . . .

I would spend that summer translating the poetry of Claribel Alegría, then living in a stone house called C'an Blau Vell in Deya, a Mallorquin village in a ring of mountains believed by its inhabitants to be one of the spiritual power centers of the earth. . . .

At that time, Claribel had drinks in the afternoons, waiting at the stone ledge of a parted window for mail from her country, which seldom arrived. Latin American exiles passed through her house as summer guests, recounting their experiences in a *salon* held on the terrace as the sun lowered into the Teix. There were Mario Benedetti, Augusto Roa Bastos and the poet Christina Peri-Rossi, who had brought with her a woman friend close to my own age, but wiser in her years. Almost inaudibly, she recounted her arrest in Argentina the preceding year: in the first days of her detention she'd been forced to strip, then stand on a block of ice with her hands pressed to the wall, and was beaten while the ice melted from beneath her. Other guests spoke of the disappearance of their friends and relatives throughout Latin America, of imprisonment, torture and anonymous death. Bougainvillea vines scratched the stone walls as they spoke; glasses were refilled in silence, stray goats clambered up the terraced slopes, their copper bells ringing like the word *thank*. "You cannot understand," Claribel Alegría told me one night in my moonlit guest room. "I am sorry, but you cannot." She left me, walking the corridor between rooms in her robe, a spectre, the ghost of herself.

In the privileged world of that Mediterranean resort island, I learned of the suffering world of El Salvador's provinces. Within a year, at the invitation of Claribel's family, I would see for myself. Here, down impassable roads during the rainy season, in cardboard and scrap lumber shacks beside open sewage, in the midst of malaria and hunger, was where most of the world actually lived.

. . . During my last week in Beirut (in February 1984), under the worst bombardment of that winter, I met with a Lebanese poet in the darkened lobby of the Commodore Hotel. His worry beads clicked through his fingers as he told me that there weren't any poets in Beirut. "They've all left," he said, "—except me, and I don't write poems anymore."

Leaving him, I walked the streets of the Hamra district, icy with the green glass of blown shop windows, the air laced with smoke and cordite. Balcony railings corkscrewed from the pocked walls. Militiamen cradled their AK-47s and kept watch. Here and there a child ran from doorway to doorway with a stack of pita bread. If Deya is a spiritual power center, Beirut is a center of death, abandoned by poets. . . . When one writes "about" the sufferings of others, the attempt is often fettered by one's conscious, if well-meaning, intentions. What then does a poet from the privileged world do? If he or she is fortunate, guides emerge to compensate for privileged but inadequate education—in my case, the victims of my country's military interventions. Such guides are often unaware of the role they play in the privileged poet's life. In England I came upon a tattered paperback authored collectively by something called "The School of the Barbiana": "In Africa, in Asia, in Latin America, in southern Italy, in the hills, in the fields, even in the cities, millions of children are waiting to be made equal. Shy, like me, stupid, like Sandro: lazy, like Gianna. The best of humanity." These guides offer rice, tortillas, boiled water, a place to squat, a hammock, a method of killing mosquitos with herbal smoke and leeches with a struck match: a view of life from the opposite bank of humanity. If the poet is lucky, something of what they offer slips into the soul. But to write of such things? There are a few words from Anton Chekhov, in which we might take little solace: "When you portray the unfortunate and the down-and-out and wish to move your reader to pity, try to be colder. It will give a kind of backdrop to their grief, make it stand out more. All your heroes weep, and you sigh with them. Yes, be cold."

I am in the Palais de Tokyo in Paris, looking at photographs taken by Sebastião Salgado in the Sahel, the southern Sahara, during the last few years. Here are the long processions of exodus from hunger, bones shining through flesh, the dead wrapped in wheat-flour sacks from the Federal Republic of Germany; here the flattened bags of intravenous fluids glowing in morning camp light; there the corpse of an infant stuffed into a trouser leg. The living walk over the parched ground, clothed in what will become their burial shrouds. The Parisians who have come to look at these photographs are elegantly dressed, and stand in small animated groups, waving lit cigarettes. Salgado stands on the periphery, watching the Parisians.

In a clinic on the outskirts of Alexandra township in Johannesburg, there is a room, cheerfully decorated with children's drawings, where European, American and white South African doctors bend over the emaciated bodies of infants, each with a needle in its scalp, receiving the precious, silvery drips of glucose. The police entered the clinic this morning, demanding the records of patients who had been treated during the last few nights of violence. There is a rumor that the people in the township believe that the doctors surrendered the records willingly, in collaboration with the police, and because of this it is possible that the clinic will be fire-bombed soon. After assuring me that the police had in fact forced their way into the files, the doctors explained the procedure of Oral Irrigation Therapy to me, a method by which the dehydrated children can be revived without the paraphernalia of Western medical technology: a liter of boiled water, a pinch of salt, a fistful of sugar, mixed and given with a spoon. To teach this procedure to every mother in the "Third World" would cost what my countrymen spend on pet food in any given year.

The Alexandra doctors are asked if they are afraid to be here. They gaze in the direction of the questioner, uncomprehendingly. Salgado has taken a photograph of Dr. Luc Van der Verken, bending over a child near death in the village of Gourma-Rharous. It is possible, perhaps, to imagine what she feels, squatting over the living remains on the sand floor of that hut. One could attempt a poem, which might include the boy's bead necklace, the light on the doctor's face. It might have been possible, perhaps, for me to imagine Alexandra Clinic without having gone there. There are photographs, such as Salgado's, to help us with this. But there are things impossible to imagine, and they are also the things most difficult to write about when they are actually seen.

We drive a poorly graded road, the dust blooming red behind our rented car, through rattling peeled stands of eucalyptus to the "homeland" Bophuthatswana. We are destined for the village Maboloka, a sprawling refuge dump of humanity, old people and children, sheltered in breeze-block, mud and tin, with a water spigot every few kilometers. They have been put here to die, not mercifully but slowly, of hunger, tuberculosis, dysentery.

A few days earlier, while attempting to visit striking miners at one of Gencor's platinum mines, we'd met a young man from this village, I will call him Michael. We had first seen him in the distance walking the shoulder of the mining company road, a figure moving with the burden of a duffel sack over his shoulder, hesitating, glancing in the direction of the three mine police positioned between him and us, then walking again but more slowly and with visible wariness. The mine police had taken shade under a roadside tree and as we drove past, we saw their rifles first, leaning against its trunk and wedged in its branches, then the men, who brandished sjamboks, whipping the earth with them as they waited for this young man. A little further on, we rolled the window down, and asked Michael if he wanted a ride. After turning to look back toward the distant mine, then ahead to the police, he climbed into the back of the car and whispered, "Pretoria, but any distance will be fine." Making a U-turn, we drove toward the city. "I'm a journalist," my husband said to relieve him. He accepted a Coke. "I've been fired. Twenty thousand of us were fired this afternoon." Several busses packed with miners passed us, and as we drove through their red tunnels of dust, Michael explained that he hadn't wanted to get on the bus, hadn't known where he'd be taken, and preferred, himself, to walk, and then he talked a little about the strike, his life in the mines, his ninety Rand a week (then forty-seven dollars) for sometimes fifteen-hour days, and when he learned we were from America, he talked more animatedly, finally suggesting that we couldn't know life in South Africa if we always stayed in the cities and urban townships. "You have to go to the countryside. Soweto will seem like paradise compared to that. . . ."

My liberal education, for which my father so dearly paid, had left me unprepared for the world I encountered beyond the borders of relative privilege. . . . There had been no study of power, of hunger and homelessness, no study of authoritarian "democracies" or the development of suicidal arsenals. Privilege was never questioned. My education had breathed freely upon any burning desire to visit the cathedrals of Europe, but even then, had I cared to notice, half the world had been abandoned. In handing me my diploma, the president of my university was handing me only a fragment of the map, a part substituted for the whole. . . .

There are poets (Emily Dickinson comes to mind) who, in their brilliance and inner wealth, find it possible to write in isolation, parting the same curtain for a lifetime. I am not one of these. In the window of my earlier life, it is often night, night and winter, a glass steamed with my own breath, and in rubbing it clear I see only my own reflection.

. . .

We spent that winter in South Africa, the most evil and ignoble place we had known. We lived in the white suburbs of Johannesburg, banal, lifeless and stinking of mock orange. To visit the black areas, it was necessary to practice subterfuge, sneaking through back roads without police permits in the company of those who knew these routes. Police permits were impossible to obtain. We crossed back and forth the bridges between comfort and want. The guides emerged again, willing to risk a roadblock, a security check, arrest. They took us calmly past burning wreckage, and through gangs of boys waiting with bricks in their hands. Without weapons, they are given to killing collaborators and informers with whatever is at hand. Such men and women are made to drink oil, or they are ringed in old rubber tires (a "necklace") and set alight. These are the tactics of desperation. During the stoning of an informer, my husband found his camera too heavy to lift, and could not bring himself to record another death, only to find his work published as evidence of "black-on-black violence." We found ourselves unable to withstand the heavy state surveillance. In the end, we kept our curtains drawn, talked in whispers in our house, trusted few people and spoke openly only in our car. Restrictions on our movements intensified. For a brief time, I was able to work with the Soweto parents of detained children, who wanted information about the proper ways to contact and work with international human rights organizations. My husband resorted to hiding his cameras under his clothes, and passing me the exposed film, which I kept in my underwear. These would not appear in the press, however. The media had begun to respect South Africa's ban on visual documentation of unrest. Those who defied the ban found their employees deported.

Sensing that our stay would be shortened, we traveled internally as much as we could, talked to as many people, and with terrible inadequacy addressed their curiosity about struggles for human justice in other parts of the world. In return, we were given glimpses through the fog of our unwitting connivance. While driving near Cape Town, one of our guides began pointing out the geological features of the dry scrub land. "You see nothing from here, yes? Only emptiness. Dry scrub. It's true: from the highway, you see nothing. But let me show you what is happening here." He motioned us to turn onto a dirt road, and after driving perhaps a half mile beyond the desolate rise, we saw it: Kayaliche, a new "re-settlement camp." As far as the eye could see, there were latrines, built some ten feet apart, row upon row, of gray cinderblock like a massive graveyard. "We have to be quick," he said, "no one is allowed here." Climbing to the roof of one latrine, Harry did his best to photograph this vast sweep with a wide-angle lens. "The people are living at Crossroads* now, but any day an excuse will be made. Crossroads will burn and those that are left are going to be moved here. They'll be given platforms and tents beside each of these toilets, a quarter of a million people, each family a toilet and a tent which will be taken away when the authorities think they've had time enough to build their own make-shift houses. Nobody will be able to leave." Hurrying us back to the car, he asked, "What does this look like to you? To me, it looks like the concentration camp it was meant to be."

Despite the claims of the South African and American governments, and the efforts of "eminent persons" to effect change in that country, we perceived a long hopelessness, and the perfection of a diabolical system of social control. "If you understand that," our guide said, "then you understand that the struggle here is not about the issue of public toilets." The townships, squatters' camps and "homelands" are fenced

* See MacKay, p. 224.

off from the rest of the country, with single roads and single railroad tracks leading to and from them. This reminded us, unnervingly, of another place, another time. Our decision was that we could not remain there nor would we be permitted to remain. Such work as we had naively planned, while of little importance from the beginning, had become completely superfluous.

When we arrived in Europe for the birth of our son, we wept with relief. . . . We rented the atelier beside Simone de Beauvoir's, over-looking the cemetery of Montparnasse, where Baudelaire is laid to rest, with Saint-Saëns, Jean-Paul Sartre, Julio Cortazar and also Pierre Le-roux, who invented the word *socialism*. The days were still *gray, half-discarded,* but on that first morning, as we walked to Le Saint-Claire for a meal, we found ourselves overcome. The burden of months of surveillance had been lifted, but our guides were far from us, living a life the rest of the world sanctions but cannot imagine. We had come to one of the last "open cities" of the world, as poet Lynne McMahon has written. In a few weeks, President Reagan would order the bombing of Libya, as if bombing that city would halt the activities of desperate people, and the radiation of Chernobyl's burning reactor would waft over Europe. For now we had reached an oasis of tranquility for the birth of our son, and the work that we imagined lay before us. But what sort of work? I thought perhaps that here, in Paris, it would be possible to write poetry again, and then, after a time, we'd return to America to discover at home what we had wandered the world to learn. As was expected, our applications to the South African government for return visas were denied.

I opened the windows to the spring wind, the scent of narcissus from the graves. Yes, it is possible to work here. From the Hôtel du Quai Voltaire, on Monday, June 3, 1907, Rilke wrote: ". . . to see and to work—how different they are here. . . . All of the things of the past rearrange themselves, line up in rows, as if someone were standing there giving out orders; and whatever is present is utterly and urgently present, as if prostrate on its knees and praying for you. . . ."

Here, Soweto is present, San Vincente, Beirut. This year, the world expenditure for arms has exceeded the total income of the poorer half of humanity. Kremlinologist Victor Zorza, a correspondent for *The Washington Post,* no longer believes that the East-West conflict poses "as serious a threat to humanity as the despair of the world's poor." Whether or not this is so, Zorza has abandoned his life in Washington for a remote village in the Himalayas, to report on the lives of its villagers. "After all," he says, "that is how most people in the world live; it is Americans who are peculiar." So it is as likely that the twentieth-century human condition is understood in a hovel on the outskirts of Jakarta as in Paris or New York. There are, then, two human worlds and the bridges between them are burning.

DARA JANEKOVIC (YUGOSLAVIA)

WORLD WAR III IS HERE IN OUR BODIES

"The unleashed power of the atom has changed everything except our modes of thinking, and thus, we drift toward unparalleled catastrophe. . . . Remove the danger; aim it on time in another direction! That is the most urgent problem of our times. . . ."

Many years ago, words to that effect were pronounced by one of the greatest minds of our century, a man whose formula in 1905 began the atomic age. As a leading American scientist, he advised, and cautioned in vain against nuclear weaponry. No one, it seems, heeded his warning. After all that he had given mankind', Einstein died, disillusioned and unhappy.

Atomic weaponry and the development of the arms race continued on its disastrous course as Einstein had predicted. In spite of the tragedies of Hiroshima and Nagasaki, in spite of, for an example, *The Happy Dragon* misfortune, the fishing boat that was devoured by atomic dust, in spite of the horrors that befell its crew, in spite of what was written—the new terrible and unbelievable truth: Strontium 90 is in our milk, vegetables, fish, and is present, also, in the *human organism*.

The results of nuclear tests and monitoring radioactive particles in atmosphere have been devastating. Responsible scientists tell us the facts and admit the horror that awaits present and future generations, if nuclear proliferation continues on its escalating course. . . .

Each year, 150,000 people of the globe die from leukemia. Thousands of cases are the result of strontium 90 in our bodies and environment. All of us already carry more strontium 90 in our bodies than we should. This is the result of atomic experiments. . . .

Each new experiment will not only increase the number of victims, but will have great consequences for future generations. In years to come, more than 500,000 children will be born with a variety of birth defects. . . . There are no remedies in medicine for the resulting miseries of mankind. . . .

Warnings from the scientific community have been numerous . . . "The only way to survival of the race and the planet is to stop all nuclear testing now!"

Professor Pauling, the American scientist and Nobel Prize winner for chemistry, has appealed to the governments of many nations. Because of the profound and uncertain effects of contemporary testing and the disastrous results of the use of nuclear weaponry for present and future generations, he called for the stoppage of all testing and experimentation with nuclear weaponry and detonations. Soon afterwards, due to his declaration, he was summoned for questioning by the American Senate Commission. . . . He has been intrepid before the Senate investigations. . . .

The response to his petition and appeal for signatures from leaders of the scientific community was immediate and nearly unanimous. Many endorsements arrived from all around the world. The most prominent scientists of forty-four countries, some 9,235 accomplished individuals, signed Pauling's petition. Thirty-six winners of Nobel Prizes were among them, including Albert Schweitzer and Lord John Boyd Orr, Nobel Peace Prize winners; and the famous British philosopher Bertrand Russell; French scientist, Frédéric Joliot-Curie; the United States, Harold Urey; U.S.S.R., Nikolai Semenov; German, Otto Hahn; eight Nobel Prize winning chemists; eight such physicists; and thirteen who had won the prize for physiology and medicine, as well, were among them.

The petition included a call for an immediate and abrupt halt to the nuclear arms race. Every experiment with nuclear bomb detonations widens and increases the quantity of radioactive particles in the atmosphere, and this will have catastrophic consequences if it continues. Human health, especially for future generations, in terms of birth defects and genetic mutations will occur with increasing frequency. . . .

(Translated from Croatian by Ivana Spalatin,
and adapted by Daniela Gioseffi)

LILLIAM JIMÉNEZ (EL SALVADOR)

TO THE SOLDIERS OF EL SALVADOR WHO FROM 1931 TO 1980 HAVE RULED THE COUNTRY THROUGH A MILITARY DICTATORSHIP

All flesh and bone are thus betrayed,
these sons of dogs who cover life with tar
attempting to darken the Sun.

Look at them standing before History
the universal truth,
before the living and the dead
who speak from the graves and attest to their deeds.

Behind their uniforms
thousands of skeletons are crying
who are calmly awaiting with hope their appointed hour.
There is a chill that causes the earth to tremble
and frightens the birds from the forest.

The military men
are a sophism and simultaneously a dialect,
products without reason of the reason of class.
They are men
without authentic manhood.

But tomorrow
Even without desiring it,
they will have to see what must be seen.
They will have to pay
for the horrible fate of each victim,
for all the lips they silenced,
for all the dreams they ripped out of our breasts.

Tomorrow, in the center of their eyes,
the coffins will open up.
They will see face to face
all those whom they have assassinated,
all the luminous immortal fallen.

The thousands and thousands of tortured
and slain
will rise as a rising tide against them.

(Translated by Mary McAnally)

ERICA JONG (U.S.A.)

LAST FLASH

Sometimes I think
of how you are hardly
alive,
of how we are all
hardly
alive,

dodging bullets,
dodging raindrops,
skidding on the ice
of Connecticut
winters,
narrowly missing
death
by botulism,
death in its
rattling can,
death by jaw,
death by womb, by cock,
death by
telepathy.

When I think of
your nuclear dreams
& the way you fuck—
head turned sideways
as if you saw
the Last Flash
(& were shielding
your eyes

with me)—
I think
that we are all

marked
beyond repair
by the notion
that even death
can die,
& that our children
will not know
the unutterable joy
of burying
their parents.

I bury you.
You bury me.
Our ages do not
matter—
since I am
life to you,
love, mother,
aunt & anodyne,
poet, playwright,
repairer, sharer
of your most secret
self.

& what are you
to me?
Son & brother
that I never
had—
clandestine Claudius,
hamstrung Hamlet,
mescaline Malvolio?
What I want
to tell you

is that
I love you.

Impermanent
as we are,
may you
love me.

Darlene Keju-Johnson (Marshall Islands: Bikini, Rongelap, Utirik, Kwajalein)

NUCLEAR BOMB TESTING ON HUMAN GUINEA PIGS

One important date that I never forget was in the year 1946. In that year the navy official from the U.S. government came to Bikini Island. He came and told the chief Juda—and I quote—"We are testing these bombs for the good of mankind, and to end all world wars."

In 1946 very few of us Marshallese spoke English or even understood it. The chief could not understand what it all meant, but there was one word that stuck in his mind and that was "mankind." The only reason why he knows the word "mankind" is because it is in the Bible. So he looked at the man, the navy official, and he says, "If it is in the name of God, I am willing to let my people go."

When the navy official came, it was too late. There were already thousands of soldiers and scientists on the atoll and hundreds of airplanes and ships in the Bikini lagoon. They were ready to conduct the tests. The Bikinians had no choice but to leave their islands, and they have never returned. The navy official did not tell the chief that the Bikinians would not see their home again. Today Bikini is off limits for 30,000 years. In other words Bikini will not be safe for these Bikinian people ever again.

The Bikinians were promised that the United States only wanted their islands for a short time. The chief thought maybe a short time is next week, maybe next month. So they moved to Rongerik.

Rongerik is a sandbar island. There are no resources on it. It was too poor to feed the people. We live on our oceans—it's like our supermarket—and from our land we get breadfruit and other foods. But on Rongerik there was nothing. The United States put the Bikinians on this island and left them there. After a year they sent a military medical official to see how they were. When he got there he found out that they were starving. Imagine; move someone else from their own home, by your power. Dump them on a little sand. And don't even bother to go back and see how they are doing for a year.

The people of Bikini have been moved, or relocated, three times. The people of Enewetak Atoll were also relocated. You cannot imagine the psychological problems that people have to go through because of relocation.

In 1954 the United States exploded a hydrogen bomb, code named BRAVO, on Bikini. It was more than 1,000 times stronger than the Hiroshima bomb. The Marshallese were never told about this bomb.

We were never even warned that this blast was about to happen on our islands. Instead we experienced white fallout. The people were frightened by the fallout. The southern area of our islands turned yellow. And the children played in it. But when the fallout went on their skins, it burnt them. People were vomiting.

The people of Rongelap and Utirik were not picked up until three days after the explosion. It was horrible. Some American soldiers came and said, "Get ready. Jump in the ocean and get on the boat because we are leaving. Don't bring any belongings. Just go in the water." That's your home and you have to decide, with your husband and children, whether you are going to leave or not: But there was no time. People had to run fast. There was no boat to get the people, not even the children and the old people, to the ship. People had to swim with their children. It was very rough. When they got to the ship each family was given one blanket. Some families had 10 or 12 children, and they had to share one blanket.

They were taken to Kwajalein. It took one night to get there. They didn't even give people a change of clothing, so it meant they had to sleep in their contaminated clothing all the way. You imagine. They are burnt, they are vomiting. When they got to Kwajalein they were given soap and were told to wash in the lagoon. The soap and salt water was supposed to wash off the radiation. They were not told what had happened, why it had happened, what was wrong with them. Their hair was falling out, fingernails were falling off . . . but they were never told why.

The people of Rongelap and Utirik were on Kwajalein for three months before they were moved again. The people of Utirik went back to their contaminated island. The people of Rongelap didn't return to Rongelap for three years: it was too contaminated.

Twenty-eight American men who were on Rongerik monitoring the tests and the crew of a nearby Japanese fishing boat were also contaminated. We are in touch with one of these men who were studying the test. He has told us that the United States knew that the wind was blowing towards islands where people lived, but that they went ahead and tested anyway. It was not a mistake. It is interesting that the United States government moved the Marshallese in the 1940s when the small bombs were being tested, and then when the biggest bomb ever was tested the Marshallese were not even warned. This is why we believe that we have been used as guinea pigs.

Since the testing there has been a tremendous increase in health problems. The biggest problem we have now, especially among women and children, is cancers. We have cancers in the breast. We have tumour cancers. The women have cancers in their private places. Children are being deformed. I saw a child from Rongelap. It is an infant. Its feet are like clubs. And another child whose hands are like nothing at all. It is mentally retarded. Some of the children suffer growth retardation.

Now we have this problem of what we call "jellyfish babies." These babies are born like jellyfish. They have no eyes. They have no heads. They have no arms. They have no legs. They do not shape like human beings at all. But they are being born on the labour table. The most colourful, ugly things you have ever seen. Some of them have hairs on them. And they breathe. This ugly "thing" only lives for a few hours. When they die they are buried right away. A lot of times they don't allow the mother to see this kind of baby because she'll go crazy. It is too inhumane.

Many women today are frightened of having these "jellyfish babies." I have had two tumours taken out of me recently and I fear that if I have children they will be "jellyfish babies" also. These babies are being born not only on the radioactive islands but now throughout the 35 atolls and five islands of the Marshalls. I've interviewed hundreds of Marshallese women in the northern islands and this is their story I am telling you. The health problems are on the increase. They have not stopped.

It is not just the people who have been affected but also our environment. . . .

The United States is only leasing the islands but can you imagine if it owned them? That is why in 1982 the people of Kwajalein decided to take direct action. They sailed in to take over eleven off-limits islands and lived there for four months. A thousand people. They were saying to the United States, "You are not going to treat us like second-class citizens in our own islands!" They shut the base down. The missile testing was stopped.

The United States government, after all these years, has never conducted an epidemiological survey. The Department of Energy sends their medical team. But they will only go to the two islands that the United States recognises as affected by the fallout from the 1954 bomb— Rongelap and Utirik. But there are many others. And it is interesting that they will not check the children. They will only check those people who were on Rongelap and Utirik in 1954. . . .

Marshallese are fed up with the DOE and the United States government. We are asking for an independent radiological survey. We want to do it outside of the United States government.

This is what happened with the Rongelap people. They said, "We have had enough! You are not going to treat us like animals, like nothing at all! We are moving." So they moved from Rongelap with the Greenpeace ship, *Rainbow Warrior*. The whole island, 350 people, moved to live on Mejato, which is a small island in Kwajalein Atoll. Kwajalein landowners gave them that island. But the United States wouldn't help. Instead they did a campaign to discredit the Rongelapese.

By doing this the Rongelap people said that they don't want to be part of this whole nuclear craziness. And that their bottom line is, "We care about our children's future." Because they know that they are contaminated. They had to come to a very hard decision. Leaving your island in the Marshalls is not easy. So they decided that their children came first. They know they'll be dying out soon. They are dying now—slowly.

We are only small—very few thousand people out there on tiny islands, but we are doing our part to stop this nuclear madness. And although we are few we have done it! Which means you can do it too! But we need your support. We must come together to save this world for our children and the future generations to come.

MAXINE KUMIN (U.S.A.)

THE NIGHTMARE FACTORY

these are the dream machines
the dream machines
they put black ants in your bed
silverfish in your ears
they raise your father's corpse

they stick his bones in your sleep
or his stem or all thirty-six
of his stainless steel teeth
they line them up
like the best orchestra seats

these are the nightmare tools
down the assembly line
they send an ocean of feces
you swim in and wake from
with blood on your tongue
they build blind sockets
of subways and mine pits

for you to stop in
the walls slick as laundry soap
swelling and shrinking

these are the presses
they hum in nine languages
sing to the orphans
who eat pins for supper
the whole map of europe
hears the computers click
shunting the trains you take
onto dead sidings
under a sky that is
packed full of blackbirds

night after night in
the bowels of good citizens
nazis and cossacks ride
klansmen and judases
postmen with babies
stuffed in their mailsacks
and for east asians
battalions of giants
dressed in g i fatigues
ears full of bayonets

here on the drawing board
fingers and noses
leak from the air brush
maggots lie under
if i should die before
if i should die
in the back room
stacked up in smooth boxes
like soapflakes or tunafish
wait the undreamt of

BETTY LALL (U.S.A.)

THE NUCLEAR THREAT: A WOMAN'S PERSPECTIVE

Where are the women? It is an interesting fact that women have been shunted aside when high-level discussions turn to issues of armament—especially interesting since women have been at the forefront as activists where nuclear arms control is concerned. Yet when push comes to shove, we are the ones being shoved—away from the negotiating table.

For many months the United States and the Soviet Union have been negotiating on three separate armament issues, but on the large negotiating teams of each side, there were no women at the policy level. At the Summit meeting last October [1986] one female policy maker appeared from the U.S., Ambassador Rozanne Ridgway, Assistant Secretary of State for Europe and Canadian Affairs. There was none from the Soviet Union.

Why? After all, women represent over half the populations of these two large, heavily armed and mutually hostile powers. Can it be men are afraid of us? Afraid that women might be less inhibited in overcoming almost 70 years of mutual hostility and suspicion and be willing to negotiate reductions in our nuclear arsenals? Afraid that we would opt to cooperate peacefully to avoid the possibility of a world-wide holocaust?

President Reagan's Chief of Staff, Donald Regan, puts down women by claiming we are not interested or knowledgeable about ways to avoid war and achieve a more stable peace. He told the press at the close of the Summit conference: "They're not going to understand missile throw-weights or what's happening in Afghanistan or what is happening in human rights. Some women will, but most women . . . believe me, your readers for the most part if you took a poll . . . would rather read the human interest stuff of what happened."

Women care deeply about preserving the values that are fundamental to the achievement of a more peaceful, secure, and just world, but we have not been given effective opportunities to inject our views into policy-making decisions. We have not been given choices.

Considering the facts, our participation certainly couldn't hurt.

In the past 13 years, not a single arms control agreement between the Soviet Union and the United States has been ratified by our government though there have been three important ones signed: the SALT II Treaty, the Threshold Nuclear Test Ban Treaty, and the Treaty on Underground Nuclear Peaceful Explosions. A fourth, a Comprehensive Test Ban Treaty, was in the final stages of negotiation before being abandoned by the United States.

Why do we tolerate our government spending so much of our money for destruction—over 300 billion dollars this year alone? Both sides insist on utilizing at least half of their best scientific and engineering talent to develop, test and produce weapons. Since 200 to 500 strategic nuclear warheads are enough to destroy most of the population and industry of each side, why are billions of dollars and rubles spent to produce over 10,000 such warheads each? Why don't we complain that we are borrowing far into the future, saddling generations to come with this enormous Federal debt, to wage a wasteful and dangerous military competition with the Soviet Union?

The answer in part stems from the fact that we tend to trust the pronouncements of our government in Washington—a government that is populated predominantly by white males. When they describe our main adversary in the worst possible terms, we believe our leaders and tend not to question their "facts" or their judgment—to say nothing of whether or not our President and his advisers are telling us the full story.

It is a mad mad race. And it can be stopped; but not unless women are able to participate along with men. Women and men generally are socialized differently. There is no question that throughout history, with a few exceptions, it has been men not women who prepare for and wage wars.

In this nuclear age, we women have been frightened by our respective governments whose leaders control most of the information about the intentions and capabilities of the adversary. If we thought the other side genuinely wanted to reach agreements to stop building stockpiles, would we agree to support the expenditure of hundreds of billions each year for weapons and preparation for war? Did Soviet leader Mikhail Gorbachev stop the testing of nuclear weapons and anti-satellite weapons because he wanted to lull the United States into a trap or because he decided this might improve chances of reaching an agreement for both sides to stop the arms race? Wouldn't our two countries be more secure if we stopped testing these weapons?

Despite the claim of the White House, data available from the U.S. Department of Energy and the Swedish National Defense Institute show that there was no sudden acceleration of Soviet nuclear tests in the months before the Soviet leader announced a unilateral Soviet moratorium and invited the United States to follow.

The Republican Chairman of the Senate Intelligence Committee, David Durenberger of Minnesota, remarked: "If the United States and the Soviet Union could not test their nuclear devices, neither country could make potentially destabilizing qualitative improvements in their nuclear weapons . . . A comprehensive test ban treaty would stop menacing Soviet developments while preserving the technological edge the

United States enjoys in their nuclear warheads" (*Bulletin of the Atomic Scientist,* October, 1985, page 9).

Should we believe our present President who claims such agreements cannot be verified or should we believe our past arms control negotiators who, under both Republican and Democratic Presidents, negotiated for such agreements? When we have such enormous overkill in nuclear weapons and their means of delivery, can't we afford to strengthen our national security by making the sensible decision toward a more stable and peaceful world, to take a small but crucial step by reaching a modest agreement? Must we not consider such steps, not for ourselves alone, but on behalf of those who one day will be in our shoes?

If we are not a part of policy-making decisions, what can women do? We can speak out and know that we are not alone. There are millions waiting for our courage.

The most significant area in need of progress in limiting nuclear weapons concerns the effort to prevent a new round of the arms race in space. *Gorbachev has proposed that the United States and the Soviet Union agree not to attempt to develop and deploy a ballistic missile defense system in space.* If the United States could agree to this, the Soviets indicate a willingness to agree to deep cuts (along with the United States) in strategic offensive nuclear weapons, such as the U.S. MX missile and the Soviet SS18 missiles.

The United States position has been against limiting the development of a system (called the Strategic Defense Initiative or "Star Wars") that might have some capability to defend a part of the U.S. strategic nuclear arsenal against a Soviet attack. It would not be able to defend cities or populations.

The benefits of both sides stopping the "Star Wars" effort would be incalculable. The construction of the entire "Star Wars" system is estimated to cost the United States hundreds of billions of dollars.

Most of the funds appropriated by Congress for the "Star Wars" effort (several billions have already been appropriated but not yet spent) could be used to reduce the deficit and also to fund some of the important domestic programs that have been cut or wiped out in order to give priority to the military. Child care programs, assistance to women living in poverty, counseling and part-time jobs for disadvantaged youth, housing for the elderly poor and the homeless, and better health care for the working poor are among the worthy programs starved by the Reagan Administration and Congress so that the arms race can be waged relentlessly.

Women can especially appreciate that national security is much more than raising and equipping military forces or developing and deploying large-scale nuclear weapons poised for instant attack. The strength of the economy, the degree of our social cohesion and domestic tranquility as a people, as well as relations with our allies in Europe and many other parts of the world are extremely important.

To define national security this way does not mean weakness. Women recognize that weakness cannot be tolerated when a well-armed adversary exists. But overarming and refusal to negotiate seriously, and trying to out-spend the opponent will be counterproductive in the long run and could lead to disaster.

Women participating actively in the national debate, using both knowledge and common sense, can make the difference in whether the United States moves safely toward arms control or dangerously toward the development of new threatening and destabilizing weapons.

The time for women to speak up is *now* and for the future and beyond. Otherwise, in the not-too-distant future, there may be no one left to speak at all.

TAT'YANA MAMONOVA (U.S.S.R.)

WOMEN'S ACTIVE ROLE

I think woman is altruistic. She gives life and appreciates life. That's one of my main concepts. I think the woman is organically against war, for example, and nuclear and chemical destruction, and she can really save the world if she is permitted to play an active role in government in different countries, the Soviet Union among them.

LENORE MARSHALL (U.S.A.)

POLITICAL ACTIVISM AND ART

O why do we write? For fame? for power? prestige? Sometimes, whether in love, in hate, in compulsion, there should still be a further reason. What are we trying to do in this world? The serious writer wants to impose his order on chaos. He has a direction, a goal, to give shape, to form an entity which is his, which represents himself. But today what order is possible? Is it realistic to believe we can shape this chaos, is it honest to set out as though what we have to say will bring clarity or hope or change, do we dare to believe or pretend that our word will be significant, faced as we are by unmanageable disorder everywhere while the great question, overshadowing all others, is the survival of the human race?

Sometimes there is an agonizing conflict for the writer who takes part in a movement in which [she] believes. . . . One wonders sometimes who one is when one feels torn limb from limb between the inner and outer lives, for one can't help it, if one believes passionately in a thing, one has to commit oneself to it. We hear about searching for our identities these days—identity crisis. Perhaps we now have to have more than one identity or perhaps the different sides really do compose into one. Who are we really? we ask. We would like to pursue a direction that is simple and clear and to arrive at our life's work. But our idea of our self-hood and the fact of it are complex. What about the writer, the poet and novelist? SANE was born in my living room in 1957. That is what I think of when I talk about political matters, of the poet (or artist) as peace worker or of the writer's divided life or the divided writer's life or the writer as activist. SANE started really through a conversation with a friend who was as concerned as I at that time about the madness of the arms race and the growing possibility of the destruction of our civilization. . . . The difference between the period in which we founded SANE and now, between yesterday and today, is that there was very little support for a peace movement then. We were considered kooks, cranks, nuts, Just one step above Commies because, they said if you believed in peace, that could help the enemy, so obviously you couldn't believe in peace.

At any rate, when I asked some of my writer friends to join SANE, or in some way speak out against the arms race or nuclear weapons, they would say to me, your job is to write your books. You shouldn't be engaged in these activities. Start your new novel. Of course, it was just what I was doing and wanted to do all the time. Now there are people everywhere who agree with the peace movement. Formerly there was very little to read on the subject. Now there is a large literature. Now people inform themselves about the issues. In the past, the youth generation was silent. Now there is a youth generation that *leads,* and the best of them—not all by any means—but the best of them are the best young people that we've ever had.

EDNA ST. VINCENT MILLAY (U.S.A.)

O EARTH, UNHAPPY PLANET BORN TO DIE

O Earth, unhappy planet born to die,
Might I your scribe and your confessor be,
What wonders must you not relate to me
Of Man, who when his destiny was high
Strode like the sun into the middle sky
And shone an hour, and who so bright as he,
And like the sun went down into the sea,
Leaving no spark to be remembered by.
But no; you have not learned in all these years
To tell the leopard and the newt apart;
Man, with his singular laughter, his droll tears,
His engines and his conscience and his art,
Made but a simple sound upon your ears:
The patient beating of the animal heart.

MICHELE NAJLIS (NICARAGUA)

THEY FOLLOWED US INTO THE NIGHT

They followed us into the night,
they trapped us,
leaving us no defense
but our hands
united with millions of hands.
We were flogged and made to spit up blood.
Our bodies were filled with electric shocks
and our mouths with lime.
For whole nights
we were left out in the wild,
or thrown into timeless cells.
Our nails were torn out,
our blood
splattered on walls,

even on their faces,
but still,
our hands
are united with millions of hands.

(Translated by Amina Muñoz-Ali)

GRACE PALEY (U.S.A.)

THAT YEAR

In my family
people who are eighty-two were very different
from people who are ninety-two

The eighty-two year old people grew up
      it was 1914
      this is what they knew
      War   World War   War

That's why when they speak to the child
they say
      poor little one . . .

The ninety-two year old people remember
      it was the year 1905
      they went to prison
      they went into exile
      they said   ah   soon
When they speak to the grandchild
they say
      yes   there will be revolution
      then there will be revolution   then
      once more   then the earth itself
      will turn and turn and cry out   oh I
      have been made sick

           then you   my little bud
              must flower and save it

MOLLY PEACOCK (U.S.A.)

AMONG TALL BUILDINGS

And nothing, not even the girl you love
with the mole on her arm, will be left. Huge
trenches will be dug just beyond the stove
the whole northeast corridor will become
and the dead will be piled in each rude gouge,
even that girl whose left ear always sticks
slightly out beyond her hair. To fix
the names of who died on tape won't be done
since they'll dig quick to prevent disease. Nobody
likes to hear this kind of talk. I always
hated to hear it myself until I began
loving the mortar between blocks, that cruddy
pocked cement holding up buildings so a man
and woman can embrace in the maze
of what they've built on the errors of their ways.

NAOMI REPLANSKY (U.S.A.)

MY SPOON WAS LIFTED

My spoon was lifted when the bomb came down
That left no face, no hand, no spoon to hold.
Two hundred thousand died in my hometown.
This came to pass before my soup was cold.

WENDY ROSE (HOPI NATION, U.S.A.)

THE FIFTIES

full of concrete caves
dug by frightened men
who cast searchlights
to restricted city skies
for Russian bombers
sure to come sooner or later,
they said. I was little,
easily fit beneath
my desk at school,
listened to the British teacher
tell of the blitz
with long shudders of her arm
showing how the planes had come
like insects out of Germany.
I looked the part
of a war-humbled refugee,
open-mouthed in the air-raid shelter
and tuning in to Conelrad,
practicing how to die
in a foetal position. 1980 now
and my bones have burrowed
deeply into this world,
my tongue has traveled
its many highways
crossing mountains and seasons
and once again
we drill under tables,
store food and water
in bottles and cans—pure enough
for a century or more
of mutating under the sun.
Once again
we scan our western expanse of sky
not for bombers and Russians
but for a thing more final
than antique atom bombs.
Like earthquakes
crawling up the Richter scale

the ghosts of our future
are unpredictable
and out of control.

This is a weather report:
who knows what will end
in the fury of the storm?

January 1980.
Berkeley.

LIBBY SCHEIER (CANADA)

LOVE & WAR & THE FUTURE & THE MARTIANS

I am thinking tonight about war.
The papers have been talking war for days.
Nuclear war a greater danger than ever.
World a tinderbox. War inevitable.
Third world will trigger war.

I think about you too.
Your length and tenderness.
Your long slim back and how it felt
when I moved my hands from your buttocks
to your shoulders as you crouched on the rug
watching your cat, how the pleasure
sounded in your voice as I moved my hands
from your buttocks to your shoulders.
And I am thinking about my little son,
his beautiful small body and his human decency.
I love him with a strength
I never knew I had.

I go blind.
Everything is black, then white,
then black again. And now grey.
I am inside a body in terrible pain.
My face is black on one side.
The skin on my right arm and hip

and breast are burnt off.
I am inside my pain.
A wild animal howl enters me.
It's not a sound that I make.
Yet I know the sound.
Where do I know it from?

It is my son. My son made strange.
I force my eyelids open.
I see my son lying on the ground.
He makes sounds like a tortured bird.
He is raw and burnt and melted.
How do I even know it is my son?
It doesn't look like him or sound
like him. But I know.

I cannot move, my body is too damaged.
But I watch him and hear him, and I drag
my body over to where he is lying.
I inhale strength from a hovering angel
and place my hands around his neck.
I tighten my grip until the terrible sounds
stop, then lie down next to him.

My sight comes back and I am here again
alone in my bedroom writing in longhand,
red felt pen on white paper.
My son breathes loudly, asleep
in the next room. I go and sit on his bed
and feel his calves and feet.

I pray though I don't know how.
I was raised an atheist.
I think of you, person I don't know so well.
I think of future, how we would like it
to roll off our tongues like honey.
But we don't have this sweetness to look toward.
The future is war and fire and death.

SHARON SPENCER (U.S.A.)

A MAYAN PROPHECY

Eat, let's eat, now we have corn meal!
Drink, let's drink, now we have *prozole*!

The day will come when dust will claim the earth

On that day fire will sear the maize
On that day a big cloud will rise
On that day X-ray radiance
On that day no land to seize
On that day
        tender leaves will burn
        the eyes of the dead will close
        man will resign
On that day
        no more cycles of seasons
        no more wars (there will only be one war)
On that day
        no more birds
        no more animals
        no more people

        no god
        to blame

BERTHA VON SUTTNER (AUSTRIA)

STOCKPILES ARE USED

. . . It remains our clear destiny to strive in every practical way to bring nearer the time when the sword shall not be the arbiter among nations . . . although the supporters of the existing structure of society, which accepts war, come to a peace conference prepared to modify the nature of war, they are basically trying to keep the present system intact. . . . All in all, it seems to me that the great . . . disaster is on the way. If so many seeds have been sown, surely the weeds will sprout up soon and surely so much stockpiled gunpowder will explode.

Wisława Szymborska (Poland)

CHILDREN OF THE EPOCH

We are children of the epoch.
The epoch is political.

All my daily and nightly affairs,
all your daily and nightly affairs,
are political affairs.

Whether you want it or not,
your genes have a political past,
your skin a political tone,
your eyes a political color,
What you say resounds,
what you don't say is also
politically significant.

Even coming through the rye,
you walk with political steps
on political ground.

Apolitical poems are also political,
and in the sky there's a moon
that's no longer moonlike.
To be or not to be, that is a question.
Oh darling, what a question, give a suggestion.
A political question.

You don't have to be human
to acquire a political meaning.
It's enough to be petroleum,
cattle fodder, raw material.
Or just a conference table whose shape
was disputed for months.

In the meantime, people were killed.
Animals died,
houses burned,
fields grew wild,
as in distant
and less political epochs.

(Translated by Austin Flint)

MAJ BRITT THEORIN (SWEDEN)

NEVER BEFORE: A WARNING

Our world has faced many disasters and wars, but never before has the destructive capacity of weapons been so immediate, complete, and universal. Never before has humankind been faced with the real danger of self-extinction. . . . Our ultimate goal is to abolish nuclear weapons. But steps to halt and reverse the nuclear arms race must be taken fully. If a train in full speed runs toward catastrophe, first it has to be stopped and then reversed. Let me give you some examples of urgent steps to be taken. . . . The total prohibition of testing on nuclear weapons is the key issue in every nuclear disarmament process. A comprehensive test ban treaty would be an effective barrier against nuclear weapons improvement and new generations of nuclear weapons. Another important measure for preventing nuclear war would be a declaration by all nuclear powers of no first use of weapons. . . . Of high importance, too, is to prevent the militarization of outer space. Such a militarization would trigger a new spiral in the offensive and defensive arms race. We must ban an arms race where the sky is no longer the limit. . . .

Nations must develop mutual understanding, confidence, and cooperation across ideological and political barriers if the nuclear threat is to be remote. . . . What are we giving our children? It is their future which is at stake. And it is up to us to give them hope and a good world to live in. The work of peace is not reserved for politicians and experts. The work of peace calls for everyone. We must all take a personal responsibility. We must ask ourselves in which way we best can promote peace. It is up to the women. Together we are strong and together we can prevent a nuclear war.

WOMEN FOR A MEANINGFUL SUMMIT
(CORETTA SCOTT KING, BETTY LALL, MAXINE WATERS, CORA WEISS, VIA ARTMANE, ELENA KAMENTSKAYA, MARGARITA MAXIMOVA, GALINA USTINOVA) (U.S.A./U.S.S.R.)

WOMEN'S PEACE PLATFORM FOR THE SUMMIT

We, Women for a Meaningful Summit, support the process of disarmament [currently under way]. . . . However, this [the INF Treaty] is only the first step. We urge that the ABM Treaty [to prohibit nuclear weaponry in space] be strictly observed and that the agreement to reduce strategic weapons (START) be concluded without delay. We are concerned that governments may get bogged down by the type of thinking which still exists in the global war system. We are determined to develop peaceful principles which reflect the interdependence and interrelationship of peoples.

At this moment in history human beings have the distinct opportunity to create a world at peace with justice, nuclear-free and nonviolent, one in which we live without fear of each other.

We seek to reach the most lofty and moral plane that humans are capable of, and:

WE DECLARE THAT
—war is obsolete;
—the existence of nuclear and conventional weapons is not a source of security;
—we are not enemies of one another—our real enemies are hunger, disease, racism, poverty, inequality, injustice and violence.

WE BELIEVE THAT
—only through a concept of partnerships among all nations, small and large, can we confront the major ills of the world;
—systems of war must be dismantled and replaced with systems of peace and justice which can be done only by nonviolent means;
—new political thinking must favor common and comprehensive security, embracing political, economic, military, humanitarian, cultural and environmental spheres;
—no nation has the right to intervene in the internal affairs of other nations;
—the Universal Declaration of Human Rights must be fully implemented;

66

—creative, independent initiatives by citizens are of great significance to the peace process;

—the United Nations, the International Court of Justice and other international bodies designed to resolve conflict through peaceful means, must be strengthened and new international and regional institutions may need to be developed to complement existing ones;

—peace and justice education should be an integral part of all school systems and mass media communications.

WE COMMIT OURSELVES TO

—playing our full and rightful role in the decisions that determine the destinies of all peoples based upon the humane values we all share;

—converting significant amounts of the vast funds and resources spent on the arms race to meet human needs and nurture the health of this planet which together we call our home;

—dedicating our time, our work, our talent, our compassion and intellectual capacities to making our vision become a reality.

SUSAN YANKOWITZ (U.S.A.)

ALARMS

Monologue for Mother Earth

(A hospital room. MOTHER EARTH, a woman with a large maternal bosom made of fruits, wearing a nurse's cap, stands beside a bed. On it, like a patient, sits a miniature tree, a few leaves hanging from its branches. A bright overhead light, like an operating lamp, shines down on them. . . .)

Here is a leaf soon after birth, no longer a bud but not yet distinct. Note its plumpness, the absolutely smooth surface of its skin, the soft green color, the way the edges unfurl ever so slightly, like a baby trying to make a fist. This is one of nature's most common creations, struggling to find its form, to discover its identity, all contained even at this early stage inside its body. Through processes invisible to the naked eye, the leaf breathes and eats and grows and fills out. Music delights it; noise defeats its efforts. Perhaps it laughs or cries or makes merry with the birds; this we do not know. What we can affirm, without doubt, is that

67

nature has created a plan which this tendril is in process of attaining. Were the design unimpeded, our leaf would elongate, its color deepen; it would lose its baby fat, so to speak, and begin to achieve its mature form. In that stage, triumphant, we would see it securely rooted to the branch, fully grown and defined, its flesh supple and firmly etched with lines, like the palm of your hand. . . .

But should the tree receive upon its outstretched branches the effluvia of a radioactive rain, everything alters. The natural growth pattern is speeded up to a startling degree, and the leaf immediately begins to show signs of premature deterioration and decay. Its edges begin to brown and curl inward, like claws; moisture evaporates; the earlier radiance fades; age spots, dark blemishes, discolor its surface, and the entire shape changes, shrinking and shriveling, until the leaf is a miserable twisted and desiccated thing, barely recognizable as its earlier incarnation: brown where the other was green, dried out, stiff where before it contained juice. . . .

The lightest breeze, even one delicate breath, can sever it from its source; your feet, dancing or somber, can unwittingly grind it to oblivion in the earth's sudden graveyard. . . .

The leaf, my friends, is luckier than we are in one respect: it has no foresight and thus does not know its fate. Neither, however, does it have the power to change that fate—as we do.

GUENI ZAIMOF (BULGARIA)

THE STAR OBSCURE

Atrocity . . . And with the star obscure
alone, with no one close, so far the homeland.
My Vladimir? . . . God took him and for sure
the sun got cold forever. In this torment

I'm neither poet, nor a woman, but
blood and tears, scream and hatchets. The air hisses.
My soul in the last minutes still rebuts.
Smashed to bits on the iron curtain.

Notes on Selections and Authors, Part I:

BELLA AKHMADULINA (b. 1937) is considered to be one of the most daring poets writing in the U.S.S.R. She was barred from the Writers' Union for many years for writing poems found to be too personal and superfluous. "The

East is dumb, but the West is deaf," is an aphorism among worldly writers of our time. Though U.S. poets seem free to express radical politics, most of their countrymen do not hear them. To write an intimate love poem rather than a poem of socialist realism in countries like China, on the other hand, is considered a revolutionary act of freedom, but in such countries, poets are carefully listened to, even on television and radio. Akhmadulina, in this poem, took a male persona basing the text on a wartime event of the great poet Pasternak's life.

HANNAH ARENDT (1906–1975), born in Hanover, Germany, was the first woman appointed to a full professorship at Princeton University in 1959. Her status as a major political thinker and a prolific writer was established by her publication of *The Origins of Totalitarianism* in 1951. In that book she examined this century's major forms of Nazism and Communism, attempting to discover their origins in the anti-Semitism and imperialism of the nineteenth century. She served as research director of the Conference on Jewish Relations and executive director of Jewish Cultural Reconstruction after the Holocaust.

ALENKA BERMUDEZ (b. ?) is a native of Santiago, Chile, but moved to her husband's homeland, Guatemala, where she now lives with their children. One of her sons was killed in combat in Guatemala, and she now works in Nicaragua representing the Guatemalan Cultural Workers Association. When she writes of the blood of Guatemala, she is referring to the blood of her dead son, also.

ROSALIE BERTELL (b. 1929) is a renowned biomathematician in the U.S. who has portrayed the reality of species death which would result from a nuclear war, with the term nuclear disarmament workers have come to know as omnicide. Dr. Bertell has spoken and written extensively and served as an expert witness on the biomedical effects of nuclear irradiation. She is Director of the International Institute of Concern for Public Health in Toronto.

LADY BORTON (b. 1942) from 1969 to 1971 lived and worked with the American Friends Service Committee, in Quang Ngai, a Vietnamese province that saw some of the heaviest fighting and civilian and military casualties of the war. Her moving accounts, some of which were serialized in *The New York Times*, speak of the plight of refugees everywhere and the sacrifice of those who devote their lives to rehabilitating and salvaging the broken lives of war. She has written a book, *Sensing the Enemy*, about the Vietnamese boat people and is currently editing a collection, *After Sorrow*, of oral histories by Vietnamese survivors and war resisters. She now lives on a farm in Ohio.

GWENDOLYN BROOKS (b. 1917) is a native of Chicago and a pioneer of the blossoming of black literature in America. She won the Pulitzer Prize for Poetry in 1950 for *Annie Allen*, poems about black life in Chicago. A writer concerned with human rights issues, Brooks has served as a professor or guest writer at many colleges and universities, and edited *Black Position*, a magazine of essays.

HELEN CALDICOTT (b. 1939). No other name has a more familiar ring to antinuclear activists throughout the world today than that of Dr. Caldicott (see p. 362). Lately, she is most concerned with the danger of accidental nuclear war due to high-tech missile launching systems or terrorist acts. The danger continues to escalate unrelieved due to proliferation of new and more destabilizing weapons—despite recent disarmament talks and agreements between the superpowers. Also, corporate accountability is her concern.

ANN DRUYAN (b. 1949) is an author, lecturer, and television and movie producer who is also working to help reverse the nuclear arms race. She was cowriter of the Emmy and Peabody Award–winning television series, "Cosmos," and served as creative director of the NASA project to place a message for possible alien civilizations aboard the *Voyager 1* and *2* interstellar spacecraft. Ms. Druyan played a key role in establishing an American seismic network in the Soviet Union to monitor Soviet compliance with their eighteen-month-long unilateral moratorium on underground nuclear tests, a joint U.S./Soviet scientific study of implementing and verifying massive nuclear disarmament, and a U.S./Soviet project to design a legally and scientifically viable treaty banning chemical and biological warfare. On February 5, 1987, Ms. Druyan was arrested for the third time at the Nevada Test Site while protesting continuing U.S. nuclear testing in the face of a Soviet test moratorium. She has described her actions in "Why We Can't Wait: The Need for a Comprehensive Nuclear Test Ban," a lecture given to the American Public Health Association at Cornell University, and other forums. Ms. Druyan is married to the astronomer Carl Sagan. She has coauthored several books, including *Comet,* and her articles have appeared in numerous periodicals.

CAROLYN FORCHÉ (b. 1950) is a U.S. poet who lives part of the time in France with her husband and son. She has translated a book of Claribel Alegría of El Salvador. Forché was one of the first journalists to report the horrors of the current wars in Central America to North Americans. Her book of poems, *The Country Between Us,* dealt extensively with the sufferings of Salvadorans in the continuing oppression that plagues their small country. These excerpts from a prose journal were written in memory of Terrence Des Pres (1939–1987).

DARA JANEKOVIC (b. 1925) is a prominent Yugoslavian journalist. She fought at the age of sixteen in the movement against Hitler and Fascism during World War II—having lost both her parents by the time she was fifteen years of age. At twenty-five, she began her lifelong career as a political commentator for *Vjesnik* (news), traveling the world for Yugoslavia's leading newspaper. She has published many notable interviews with leading political figures of our time. She has been a UN participant, as well. According to Physicians for Social Responsibility, one out of four U.S. citizens dies of cancer. Many assert the increase is due to the nuclear and chemical industries. Today, the recycling of nuclear waste products for food irradiation is a dangerous means of food preservation newly developed by nuclear industrialists. According to eminent scientists, food irradiation will deposit growing levels of poisonous wastes in our bodies and the land. Janekovic's warning is increasingly relevant. The proven wide-ranging results of accidents like Chernobyl have added to the credibility of her warning. Such facts are documented in publications like *The Bulletin of Atomic Scientists.*

LILLIAM JIMENÉZ (b. ?), a Salvadoran poet, has suffered imprisonment for her political convictions. A journalist who now resides in Mexico, she has published several books of poetry and a treatise on the economic and social realities of her homeland. According to the U.S. Committee in Solidarity with the People of El Salvador, Jiménez' country has experienced the loss of a huge percentage of its population to death squads, terrorism, and the resultant poverty of political turmoil.

ERICA JONG (b. 1942) is a contemporary U.S. poet and novelist of New York who has donated her assistance to antiwar, antinuclear, as well as women's rights causes. Though she has published several books of poetry, she is best known throughout the world for her feminist novel, *Fear of Flying,* which has been translated into numerous languages and published in nearly every major city of the globe.

DARLENE KEJU-JOHNSON (b. *c.*1936) was born on Ebeye Island in the Marshall Islands and grew up on the northern islands which are downwind of Bikini and Eniwetok. A graduate student in public health, she has spoken in many countries on the devastating effects of nuclear testing among the peoples and lands of the Pacific islands. She bears witness to the evacuation of Rongelop and Utirik after the people were contaminated by radioactive fallout from the 1954 explosion of a U.S. hydrogen bomb more than 1,000 times stronger than the Hiroshima bomb.

MAXINE KUMIN (b. 1925), recipient of several literary awards, including the Pulitzer Prize for Poetry, is one of the best known poets of the United States. Her last volume, titled *The Long Approach,* is an elegiac odyssey which takes the reader on a trip around the world through Europe, the Middle East, and Japan as it displays an international conscience deeply concerned with the nuclear threat and omnicide.

BETTY LALL (b. 1926), named by UNESCO as one of the world's three leading women experts on arms control, is a political economist, an urban strategist, and labor educator who has served as director of Urban Affairs and Public Policy Programs at Cornell University in New York. A director for the Arms Control Association, she now works for the Council on Economic Priorities, in New York City. She has been an activist in the causes of women's reproductive and equal-pay-for-equal-labor rights. (See W.M.S. note below.)

TAT'YANA MAMONOVA (*c.*1920), a Russian woman of the Soviet Union, now living in the United States, exhibits the same sensibility as many feminists in the world peace movement. According to Barbara Holland, a scholar/ author of *Soviet Sisterhood,* of the University of Indiana Press, Westerners may be unaware that in 1980, a group of U.S.S.R. feminists demonstrated their political opposition to Soviet involvement in Afghanistan. According to Holland, in the days before Gorbachev's *glasnost,* they were exiled for their protests. U.S. feminists have openly protested their government's military intervention in Vietnam and Central America, as earlier French feminists demonstrated against their government's military intervention in Algeria.

LENORE MARSHALL (b. 1899–1971), an American poet and fiction writer, known for her work in the international peace movement, founded the National Committee for a Sane Nuclear Policy. Popularly known as SANE, it has recently merged with the Nuclear Freeze Campaign established by Randall Forsberg (see p. 171). Marshall, a woman of courageous commitment, founded it in her living room, along with Norman Cousins, an editor and writer, and Clarence Pickett, who was the head of the Quaker Friends Service Committee (descended from the days of Lucretia Mott [see p. 273] and the Anti-Slavery Society.) Marshall's life shows how closely allied the peace movement has always been with the literary community of many countries and how often poets like Akhmatova of Russia (see p. 68) have devoted their efforts to humanistic political activism.

EDNA ST. VINCENT MILLAY (1892–1950) is one of the best-known poets of U.S. literature, and many critics say the finest sonneteer of modern English. Her farm home, Steepletop, in upstate New York, is now a colony devoted to working artists. She publicly protested along with many others the trial and execution of U.S. immigrant labor leader activists, Sacco and Vanzetti. Millay was a strong voice for peace and social justice throughout her life. Her sonnet is from a sequence titled *Epitaph for the Race of Man*—amazingly prophetic considering it was written before our current age of nuclear proliferation and anxiety.

71

MICHELE NAJLIS (b. 1946) is a citizen of Nicaragua. She was one of the founders of a literary-political publication titled *Ventana*. She has published volumes of poetry, titled *El Viento Armado* and *Augurios*. Her poem demonstrates a strong solidarity with the people's revolution. Wherever people are oppressed by unjust governments supported by outside interests, as the Nicaraguans were under Somoza, it is easy to find such prophecies of the future among them. They have lost so many loved ones and known so much suffering that their determination is boundless. History shows that as it is among the Filipino, Afghan, African, or Korean people of today, so it was among American or Russian revolutionaries of yesterday who struggled for self-determination.

GRACE PALEY (b. 1922), an award-winning American writer and educator, is well known as a peace and social justice activist (see p. 176). She was a part of the Women's Pentagon Action, and one of the White House Lawn Eleven. In attempts to prevent violence, she has been arrested many times for nonviolent civil disobedience. She has worked closely with the War Resisters League and many other peace groups committed to the cause of human rights.

MOLLY PEACOCK (b. 1947) is an award-winning poet who lives in New York City. Her book, *Raw Heaven,* was widely applauded throughout the literary community of the United States where she serves on the board of the Poetry Society of America. She has spent several years teaching at the American Friends Quaker School where nonviolence training is a part of all spiritual training. Her poem augments the belief of antinuclear activists throughout the world today, such as Dorothy Rowe (see p. 159) or Rosalie Bertell (see p. 28) who like Jonathan Schell, author of *The Fate of the Earth,* believe in imaginative prophecy as preventive psychology.

NAOMI REPLANSKY (b. 1918) is an accomplished American poet living in New York City. She is a member of the Women's Committee of PEN's American Center. Her imaginative quatrain from *Ring Song* echoes the precarious intensity of Pasternak, portrayed by Akhmadulina, during the threat of a bombing (see p. 24).

WENDY ROSE (b. 1948), author of *The Halfbreed Chronicles* and *Plutonium Vespers,* is poet and artist of the Hopi Nation, a tribe of Native American Indians of the western North American continent. The Hopi are known for their ecological intelligence, gifts for prophecy, and worship of the earth and the Corn Goddess.

LIBBY SCHEIER (b. 1945) is a Canadian citizen who was born and bred in New York City. She has won numerous literary prizes and given several readings of her work on Canadian radio and television. Her collection, *Second Nature,* has won critical acclaim, as did her first book, *The Larger Life.*

SHARON SPENCER (b. ?) is a widely traveled American writer who currently lives in New Jersey. A poet and novelist, as well as a professor who teaches world literature, she has in recent years studied Mayan culture in her journeys through Mexico. Her adaptation is from the words of an ancient Mayan prophet, Chilam Balam.

BERTHA VON SUTTNER (1843–1914) of Austria was the first woman to win the Nobel Peace Prize, in 1905. After a lifetime of hard work and writing on peace activism, after a careful study of history and world politics, and after attendance at numerous world peace conferences throughout Europe, she composed this chilling prophetic warning for our time, just before the outbreak of World War I.

WISŁAWA SZYMBORSKA (b. 1923) is a leading poet of Poland. She was edu-

cated at the Jagiellonian University in Cracow in Polish literature and so-
ciology, and has continued to live in southern Poland since 1945. She is poetry
editor of the prominent weekly journal, *Literary Life,* and has received many
coveted awards for her collection of poems, titled *Salt.* This poem answers all
who suppose it is possible to be apolitical in precarious times like these.

MAJ BRITT THEORIN (b. 1932), a member of the Swedish Parliament, chair
to the Committee on Disarmament at Geneva, has spoken widely and elo-
quently, throughout Europe, on antinuclear themes. She is an international
activist among the nonaligned nations of Scandinavia where more women are
in top-level government positions than in any other area of the globe. Her
words of warning were spoken, in the tradition of Alva Myrdal (see p. 367),
before an international convention of women held by the Center for Defense
Information in Washington, D.C., 1984.

WOMEN FOR A MEANINGFUL SUMMIT (1988 Delegation) U.S.: Coretta
Scott King, head of The Martin Luther King, Jr., Center for Nonviolent
Social Change and cochairwoman of WMS (see p. 173); Betty Lall, Council
on Economic Priorities (see p. 71); Maxine Waters, member of the California State Legislature and WMS board member; Cora Weiss, representative
from SANE/FREEZE International and WMS board member, founder and
director for ten years of The Riverside Church Disarmament Program in
New York. U.S.S.R.: Via Artmane, member of the Supreme Soviet of Latvia
and an artist; Elena Kamenetskaya, a lawyer and researcher with The Institute of State and Law, member of the U.S.S.R. Academy of Sciences; Margarita Maximova, head of the U.S.S.R. delegation, chief of Department of
the Institute of World Economy and International Relations; Galina Usti-
nova, official interpreter for the delegation and a professor. Marguerita Papandreou (see p. 152) of Greece, is the international liaison for WMS and
Anne Allen, of Washington, D.C., is the executive director of WMS, U.S.A.
Sharon Parker, head of the delegation to Moscow and a member of the executive committee of WMS, is chairwoman of the Board of Directors and primary
founder of the National Institute of Color. She is of Eastern Cherokee and
Black American heritage and lives in Washington, D.C. The founding purpose of WMS is to give a voice to women at the peace talks.

SUSAN YANKOWITZ (b. 1941) is a contemporary American playwright and a
graduate of the Yale Drama School. She worked with Joseph Chaikin's Open
Theatre and with him wrote *Terminal* which won her a Drama Desk Award
in 1969. Since that time she has written many plays produced by leading
theaters around the world. The monologue here comes from a play very much
on the theme of global feminism and antinuclear ecology, titled *Alarms,*
which premiered in London. She has published a novel and written a tele-
play on the poet Sylvia Plath for National Public Television, and received a
number of awards including a National Endowment for the Arts grant.

GUENI ZAIMOF (b. 1922), a Bulgarian poet with a degree from the National
Academy of Music in Sofia, is a planetary spirit living in exile from her native land but proud of its cultural accomplishments. She has published many
volumes of verse in Bulgarian, Italian, and English. To present poetry on
themes of world peace, she has attended numerous international conferences.
This verse, from a collection by the same name, explains the pain of the
exiled who live between East and West.

PART II

Causes, Realities, and Cures

I am directing a first call for a public opinion resistance movement to the peace organizations. "Peace" may have become too much of a pious cliché. We must make it into a vigorous movement, anti-war and anti-militarism, by getting public opinion mobilized in all kinds of local groups. People must be made "propaganda proof."

—ALVA MYRDAL (SWEDEN)

I'm disgusted with the hollow talk of disarmament—we put wreaths on the grave of the Unknown Soldier, who's pretty damn well known by now as the symbol of the next war—we will never have peace so long as . . . interlocking munitions interests . . . control governmental parties and influential groups—so long as people go on manufacturing death.

—EDNA ST. VINCENT MILLAY (U.S.A.)

Woman Meditating I, 1920,
by Käthe Kollwitz

KAREN ALKALAY-GUT (ISRAEL)

FRIEND AND FOE

Skyhawks fly over my city
on the way to bomb yours.
We are awakened by the noise
and I fall asleep restlessly
dreaming of you and your daughters.

"If anything happens to my girls,
I'll hold you personally responsible."
April 25, Israel is bombing Beirut.
You and I stick to wine with our
lamb casserole in Cyprus
and discuss politics.

Spinning the dial now—from BBC
to the Israel Army Channel—
I don't know what to believe.
The thin voice of an 18-year-old soldier
telling how a Lebanese
kissed him when he jumped out
of his tank is muddled with the British
accents of the newsmen estimating
half a million homeless
in southern Lebanon.

Minutes after the ceasefire in Beirut
CBS photographs antiaircraft fire
from a small apartment building.
(Is that where you live? Then
who lives with you?) The Skyhawks
go down on the city again.

Friend! My husband is in civil defense,
and my sons are too small for the army. You
have daughters and are old and alcoholic.
We can't fight this war.
But both of us are in it
and responsible.

TO ONE IN BEIRUT

Not a day goes by without my thinking of you . . .
as in a clandestine affair I am reminded
by the newspapers, the sounds in the air,
that you are there, and I in Tel Aviv.

Today brings a letter, postmarked Princeton,
sent through Jounieh to Larnaca on its way here.
You are well, as of the sixteenth of July, 1982,
and today is the 30th. Last night
on the news, we were still pounding the city.

As long as we kept from politics, we were friends
strolling down a sea road of an Austrian town,
shocking the guide with our nationalities
and talking poems, sex, divorce, food, wine.

How our lives would be fine
now, if that were all there was
to talk of. But where we live
we speak only of death and think
of somewhere else.

MAYA ANGELOU (U.S.A.)

AFRICA

Thus she had lain
sugar cane sweet
desert her hair
golden her feet
mountains her breasts
two Niles her tears
Thus she has lain
Black through the years.

Over the wide seas
rime white and cold
brigands ungentled

77

icicle bold
took her young daughters
sold her strong songs
churched her with Jesus
bled her with guns.
Thus she has lain.

Now she is rising
remember her pain
remember the losses
her screams loud and vain
remember her riches
her history slain
now she is striding
although she had lain.

AMERICA

The gold of her promise
    has never been mined

Her borders of justice
    not clearly defined

Her crops of abundance
    the fruit and the grain

Have not fed the hungry
    nor eased that deep pain

Her southern exposure
    black death did befriend

Discover this country
    dead centuries cry

Erect noble tablets
    where none can decry

"She kills her bright future
    and rapes for a sou

Then entraps her children
    with legends untrue."

I beg you

Discover this country.

MILA D. ANGUILAR (PHILIPPINES)

DAMN THE DICTATORSHIP

Damn the U.S.–Marcos dictatorship.
My people starve
while Imelda lives it up with Christina Ford.
Thirty days after San Juanico,
usurped sweat of the Filipino people
rice queues longer than any vaunted
"Seventh longest bridge in the world."

Damn the U.S.–Marcos dictatorship.
My people starve
and all the land's riches off to America and Japan.
Ferdinand kisses the corns of the new U.S. ambassador
while coconuts vanish from the stands,
lapped up by a cabal of compradors
who careen in olive oil while soap prices soar.

Damn the U.S.–Marcos dictatorship.
My people starve
the rice queues lengthen
the prices soar.
While Ferdinand schemes to prolong his reign
at least seven years more,
seven miserable years of civil war.
Damn the U.S.–Marcos dictatorship.
Damn it with a million armalites
to utter destruction.

TO A FOREIGNER

You accuse me of sloganeering
And being unpoetic
By writing lines like
"Damn the U.S.–Marcos dictatorship."

Friend, my reply is
You do not understand
The weight, the ocean depth
Of our class hatred.

Yesterday I heard
A comrade had been ambushed.
One of five bullets
Had smashed through his young heart.

When my ears caught
The uttered syllables of his name
The muscles of my jaw tightened
To a firm trigger squeeze
And the heat of anger exploded
Like bullets out of my eyes.

Have you not heard
What the people do to the traitors
Who betray their precious ones?
They cut them up

Into pieces so small
You could hardly tell
They once had the force
To murder a Red fighter.

You are a foreigner indeed,
Foreign to the rhythm of our struggle.
In the face of class murder,
How can we be lyrical?

ANONYMOUS AFGHAN WOMAN (AFGHANISTAN)

TESTIMONY

Our faces thrust between the bars of the prison gate, we wait, clinging to the cold iron, a silent crowd of women, wondering if we will see our husbands, sons, brothers, again. My son is inside the stone walls with his father for whom he carried his gun. Suddenly the names of the political prisoners are posted. The women's eyes strain in the cold, their sockets as frozen as the ground under the prayer rugs the old men bring to the gates to pray for sons, nephews, grandchildren who are tortured or executed inside the walls, among the many men who chose the freedom of their god or death. I've told no one such blasphemy, but my husband is my only god, my son, my only prince of heaven.

Outside the walls, we wait and wail and hope and a woman screams from behind her veil, seeing that her son's name, and her husband's, too, are there among the executed. We know there are no more men left in her family or she would not be here alone. Only the women who have no men left in their families come to the prison gate alone. I am not so lucky as to know my fate. I am no heroine like Naheed. I carry no flag like Malalai. I'm no poet like Rabia Balkhi. I simply wait. I will return again in the morning to wait and wait . . . my mind hanging from a thread like the rag the old woman makes tearing at her veil as she weeps—exposing her withered face in the madness of grief. We envy her tears, as she knows her fate. While we wait holding our vigil at the cold iron gate.

To find my way through the street, I must pass the old palace again, where the guards are displaying the blood-soaked rugs. They dragged us in from the street to show us where women and children were massacred yesterday by the soldiers. They show us to warn us to behave. I make my way back to the camp where my daughters with mangled frostbitten fingers wait by the gate. These words are useless. I will be dead when you read them. . . . I, a woman who dared to dream of love, of poetry, of a life of reading. I taught myself to read, to write, hour after hour before the firelight. . . . I've decided that when I see my husband's beloved name, my son's among the executed of the prison, I will tear my veil from my face and take my daughters with me into the frozen mountains. We will run and the bullets will fly after us and set us free from this wait to be free.

(Adapted to English by Daniela Gioseffi with Emira Omar)

MARGARET ATWOOD (CANADA)

BREAD

Imagine a piece of bread. You don't have to imagine it, it's right here in the kitchen, on the bread board, in its plastic bag, lying beside the bread knife. The bread knife is an old one you picked up at an auction; it has the word BREAD carved into the wooden handle. You open the bag, pull back the wrapper, cut yourself a slice. You put butter on it, then peanut butter, then honey, and you fold it over. Some of the honey runs out onto your fingers and you lick it off. It takes you about a minute to eat the bread. This bread happens to be brown, but there is also white bread, in the refrigerator, and a heel of rye you got last week, round as a full stomach then, now going mouldy. Occasionally you make bread. You think of it as something relaxing to do with your hands.

*

Imagine a famine. Now imagine a piece of bread. Both of these things are real but you happen to be in the same room with only one of them. Put yourself into a different room, that's what the mind is for. You are now lying on a thin mattress in a hot room. The walls are made of dried earth and your sister, who is younger than you are, is in the room with you. She is starving, her belly is bloated, flies land on her eyes; you brush them off with your hand. You have a cloth too, filthy but damp, and you press it to her lips and forehead. The piece of bread is the bread you've been saving, for days it seems. You are as hungry as she is, but not yet as weak. How long does this take? When will someone come with more bread? You think of going out to see if you might find something that could be eaten, but outside the streets are infested with scavengers and the stink of corpses is everywhere.

Should you share the bread or give the whole piece to your sister? Should you eat the piece of bread yourself? After all, you have a better chance of living, you're stronger. How long does it take to decide?

*

Imagine a prison. There is something you know that you have not yet told. Those in control of the prison know that you know. So do those not in control. If you tell, thirty or forty or a hundred of your friends, your comrades, will be caught and will die. If you refuse to tell, tonight will be like last night. They always choose the night. You don't think about the night however, but about the piece of bread they offered you. How long does it take? The piece of bread was brown and fresh and reminded you of sunlight falling across a wooden floor. It reminded you of a bowl, a yellow bowl that was once in your home. It held apples and pears; it stood on a table you can also remember. It's not the hunger or the pain that is killing you but the absence of the yellow bowl. If you could only hold the bowl in your hands, right here, you could withstand anything, you tell yourself. The bread they offered you is subversive, it's treacherous, it does not mean life.

*

There were once two sisters. One was rich and had no children, the other had five children and was a widow, so poor that she no longer had any food left. She went to her sister and asked her for a mouthful of bread. 'My children are dying,' she said. The rich sister said, 'I do not have enough for myself,' and drove her away from the door. Then the husband of the rich sister came home and wanted to cut himself a piece of bread; but when he made the first cut, out flowed red blood.

Everyone knew what that meant.

This is a traditional German fairy-tale.

*

The loaf of bread I have conjured for you floats about a foot above your kitchen table. The table is normal, there are no trap doors in it. A blue tea towel floats beneath the bread, and there are no strings attaching the cloth to the bread or the bread to the ceiling or the table to the cloth, you've proved it by passing your hand above and below. You didn't touch the bread though. What stopped you? You don't want to know whether the bread is real or whether it's just a hallucination I've somehow duped you into seeing. There's no doubt that you can see the bread, you can even smell it, it smells like yeast, and it looks solid enough, solid as your own arm. But can you trust it? Can you eat it? You don't want to know, imagine that.

GIOCONDA BELLI (NICARAGUA)

THE BLOOD OF OTHERS

I'm reading the poems of the dead,
I who am alive.
I who lived to laugh and cry
and shout *Patria Libre o Morir*
while riding in a truck
the day we reached Managua.

I'm reading the poems of the dead,
watching ants on the grass,

my feet bare,
your hair straight,
back bent over the reunion.

I'm reading the poems of the dead
and feeling that this blood we love each other with
doesn't belong to us.

(*Translated by Elinor Randall*)

CAROL COHN (U.S.A.)

SEX AND DEATH AND THE RATIONAL WORLD OF DEFENSE INTELLECTUALS

My close encounter with nuclear strategic analysis started in the summer of 1984. I was one of 48 college teachers attending a summer workshop on nuclear weapons, strategic doctrine, and arms control that was held at a university containing one of the nation's foremost centers of nuclear strategic studies, and that was cosponsored by another institution. It was taught by some of the most distinguished experts in the field, who have spent decades moving back and forth between academia and governmental positions in Washington. When at the end of the program I was afforded the chance to be a visiting scholar at one of the universities' defense studies center, I jumped at the opportunity.

I spent the next year immersed in the world of defense intellectuals—men (and indeed, they are virtually all men) who, in Thomas Powers's words, "use the concept of deterrence to explain why it is safe to have weapons of a kind and number it is not safe to use." Moving in and out of government, working sometimes as administrative officials or consultants, sometimes in universities and think tanks, they create the theory that underlies U.S. nuclear strategic practice.

My reason for wanting to spend a year among these men was simple, even if the resulting experiences were not. The current nuclear situation is so dangerous and irrational that one is tempted to explain it by positing either insanity or evil in our decision makers. That explanation is, of course, inadequate. My goal was to gain a better understanding of how sane men of goodwill could think and act in ways that lead to what appear to be extremely irrational and immoral results.

84

I attended lectures, listened to arguments, conversed with defense analysts, interviewed graduate students throughout their training, obsessed by the question, "How *can* they think this way?" But as I learned the language, as I became more and more engaged with their information and their arguments, I found that my own thinking was changing, and I had to confront a new question: How can *I* think this way? Thus, my own experience becomes part of the data that I analyze in attempting to understand not only how "they" can think that way, but how any of us can.

This article is the beginning of an analysis of the nature of nuclear strategic thinking, with emphasis on the role of a specialized language that I call "technostrategic." I have come to believe that this language both reflects and shapes the American nuclear strategic project, and that all who are concerned about nuclear weaponry and nuclear war must give careful attention to language—with whom it allows us to communicate and what it allows us to think as well as say.

I had previously encountered in my reading the extraordinary language used to discuss nuclear war, but somehow it was different to hear it spoken. What hits first is the elaborate use of abstraction and euphemism, which allows infinite talk about nuclear holocaust without ever forcing the speaker or enabling the listener to touch the reality behind the words.

Anyone who has seen pictures of Hiroshima burn victims may find it perverse to hear a class of nuclear devices matter-of-factly referred to as "clean bombs." These are weapons which are largely fusion rather than fission and they release a somewhat higher proportion of their energy as prompt radiation, but produce less radioactive fallout than fission bombs of the same yield.

"Clean bombs" may provide the perfect metaphor for the language of defense analysts and arms controllers. This language has enormous destructive power, but without emotional fallout; without the emotional fallout that would result if it were clear one was talking about plans for mass murder, mangled bodies, human suffering. Defense analysts don't talk about incinerating cities: they talk about "countervalue attacks." Human death, in nuclear parlance, is most often referred to as "collateral damage"; for, as one defense analyst said, with just the right touch of irony in his voice and twinkle in his eye, "the Air Force doesn't target people, it targets shoe factories."

Some phrases carry this cleaning up so far as to invert meaning. The MX missile will carry ten warheads, each with the explosive power of 300 to 475 kilotons of TNT: *one* missile the bearer of destruction approximately 250 to 400 times that of the Hiroshima bombing. Ronald

Reagan has christened the MX missile "the Peacekeeper." While this renaming was the object of considerable scorn in the community of defense analysts, some of these very same analysts refer to the MX as a "damage limitation weapon."

Such phrases exemplify the astounding chasm between image and reality that characterizes technostrategic language. They also hint at the terrifying way in which the existence of nuclear devices has distorted our perceptions and redefined the world. "Clean bombs" as a phrase tells us that radioactivity is the only "dirty" part of killing people.

It is hard not to feel that one function of this sanitized abstraction is to deny the uncontrolled messiness of the situations one contemplates creating. So that we not only have clean bombs but also "surgically clean strikes": "counterforce" attacks that can purportedly "take out"—that is, accurately destroy—an opponent's weapons or command centers, without causing significant injury to anything else. The image is unspeakably ludicrous when the surgical tool is not a delicately controlled scalpel but a nuclear warhead.

Feminists have often suggested that an important aspect of the arms race is phallic worship; that "missile envy," to borrow Helen Caldicott's phrase, is a significant motivating force in the nuclear buildup. I have always found this an uncomfortably reductionist explanation and hoped that observing at the center would yield a more complex analysis. Still, I was curious about the extent to which I might find a sexual subtext in the defense professionals' discourse. I was not prepared for what I found.

I think I had naively imagined that I would need to sneak around and eavesdrop on what men said in unguarded moments, using all my cunning to unearth sexual imagery. I had believed that these men would have cleaned up their acts, or that at least at some point in a long talk about "penetration aids," someone would suddenly look up, slightly embarrassed to be caught in such blatant confirmation of feminist analyses.

I was wrong. There was no evidence that such critiques had ever reached the ears, much less the minds, of these men. American military dependence on nuclear weapons was explained as "irresistible, because you get more bang for the buck." Another lecturer solemnly and scientifically announced, "To disarm is to get rid of all your stuff." A professor's explanation of why the MX missile is to be placed in the silos of the newest Minuteman missiles, instead of replacing the older, less accurate missiles, was "because they're in the nicest hole—you're not going to take the nicest missile you have and put it in a crummy hole." Other lectures were filled with discussion of vertical erector launchers, thrust-to-weight ratios, soft lay downs, deep penetration, and the comparative advantages of protracted versus spasm attacks—or what one military adviser to the National Security Council has called "releasing 70 to 80 percent of our megatonnage in one orgasmic whump."[1]

But if the imagery is transparent, its significance may be less so. I do *not* want to assert that it somehow reveals what defense intellectuals are really talking about, or their motivations; individual motives cannot necessarily be read directly from imagery, which originates in a broader cultural context. The history of the atomic bomb project itself is rife with overt images of competitive male sexuality, as is the discourse of the early nuclear physicists, strategists, and members of the Strategic Air Command.[2] Both the military itself and the arms manufacturers are constantly exploiting the phallic imagery and promise of sexual domination that their weapons so conveniently suggest. Consider the following, from the June 1985 issue of *Air Force Magazine:* Emblazoned in bold letters across the top of a two-page advertisement for the AV-8B Harrier II—"Speak Softly and Carry a Big Stick." The copy below boasts "an exceptional thrust-to-weight ratio," and "vectored thrust capability that makes the . . . unique rapid response possible."

Another vivid source of phallic imagery is to be found in descriptions of nuclear blasts themselves. Here, for example, is one by journalist William Laurence, who was brought by the Army Air Corps to witness the Nagasaki bombing.

> Then, just when it appeared as though the thing had settled down into a state of permanence, there came shooting out of the top a giant mushroom that increased the size of the pillar to a total of 45,000 feet. The mushroom top was even more alive than the pillar, seething and boiling in a white fury of creamy foam, sizzling upward and then descending earthward, a thousand geysers rolled into one. It kept struggling in an elementary fury, like a creature in the act of breaking the bonds that held it down.[3]

Given the degree to which it suffuses their world, the fact that defense intellectuals use a lot of sexual imagery is not especially surprising. Nor does it, by itself, constitute grounds for imputing motivation. The interesting issue is not so much the imagery's possible psychodynamic ori-

[1] General William Odom, "C3I and Telecommunications at the Policy Level," incidental paper from a seminar, *Command, Control, Communications and Intelligence* (Cambridge, Mass.: Harvard University Center for Information Policy Research, Spring 1980), p. 5.

[2] See Brian Easlea, *Fathering the Unthinkable: Masculinity, Scientists and the Nuclear Arms Race* (London: Pluto Press, 1983).

[3] William L. Laurence, *Dawn over Zero: The Study of the Atomic Bomb* (London: Museum Press, 1974), pp. 198–99.

gins as how it functions—its role in making the work world of defense intellectuals feel tenable. Several stories illustrate the complexity.

At one point a group of us took a field trip to the New London Navy base where nuclear submarines are home-ported, and to the General Dynamics Electric Boat yards where a new Trident submarine was being constructed. The high point of the trip was a tour of a nuclear-powered submarine. A few at a time, we descended into the long, dark, sleek tube in which men and a nuclear reactor are encased underwater for months at a time. We squeezed through hatches, along neon-lit passages so narrow that we had to turn and press our backs to the walls for anyone to get by. We passed the cramped racks where men sleep, and the red and white signs warning of radioactive materials. When we finally reached the part of the sub where the missiles are housed, the officer accompanying us turned with a grin and asked if we wanted to stick our hands through a hole to "pat the missile." *Pat the missile?*

The image reappeared the next week, when a lecturer scornfully declared that the only real reason for deploying cruise and Pershing II missiles in Western Europe was "so that our allies can pat them." Some months later, another group of us went to be briefed at NORAD (the North American Aerospace Defense Command). On the way back, the Air National Guard plane we were on went to refuel at Offut Air Force Base, the Strategic Air Command headquarters near Omaha, Nebraska. When word leaked out that our landing would be delayed because the new B-1 bomber was in the area, the plane became charged with a tangible excitement that built as we flew in our holding pattern, people craning their necks to try to catch a glimpse of the B-1 in the skies, and climaxed as we touched down on the runway and hurtled past it. Later, when I returned to the center I encountered a man who, unable to go on the trip, said to me enviously, "I hear you got to pat a B-1."

What is all this patting? Patting is an assertion of intimacy, sexual possession, affectionate domination. The thrill and pleasure of "patting the missile" is the proximity of all that phallic power, the possibility of vicariously appropriating it as one's own. But patting is not only an act of sexual intimacy. It is also what one does to babies, small children, the pet dog. The creatures one pats are small, cute, harmless— not terrifyingly destructive. Pat it, and its lethality disappears.

Much of the sexual imagery I heard was rife with the sort of ambiguity suggested by "patting the missiles." The imagery can be construed as a deadly serious display of the connections between masculine sexuality and the arms race. But at the same time, it can also be heard as a way of minimizing the seriousness of militarist endeavors, of denying their deadly consequences. A former Pentagon target analyst, in telling me why he thought plans for "limited nuclear war" were ridiculous, said, "Look, you gotta understand that it's a pissing contest—you gotta expect them to use everything they've got." This image says, most obviously, that this is about competition for manhood, and thus there is tremendous danger. But at the same time it says that the whole thing is not very serious—it is just what little boys or drunk men do.

Sanitized abstraction and sexual imagery, even if disturbing, seemed to fit easily into the masculine world of nuclear war planning. What did not fit was another set of words that evoked images that can only be called domestic.

Nuclear missiles are based in "silos." On a Trident submarine, which carries 24 multiple-warhead nuclear missiles, crew members call the part of the sub where the missiles are lined up in their silos ready for launching "the Christmas tree farm." In the friendly, romantic world of nuclear weaponry, enemies "exchange" warheads; weapons systems can "marry up." "Coupling" is sometimes used to refer to the wiring between mechanisms of warning and response, or to the psychopolitical links between strategic and theater weapons. The pattern in which a MIRVed missile's nuclear warheads land is known as a "footprint." These nuclear explosives are not dropped; a "bus" "delivers" them. These devices are called "reentry vehicles," or "RVs" for short, a term not only totally removed from the reality of a bomb but also resonant with the image of the recreational vehicles of the ideal family vacation.

These domestic images are more than simply one more way to remove oneself from the grisly reality behind the words; ordinary abstraction is adequate to that task. Calling the pattern in which bombs fall a "footprint" almost seems a willful distorting process, a playful, perverse refusal of accountability—because to be accountable to reality is to be unable to do this work.

The images evoked by these words may also be a way to tame the uncontrollable forces of nuclear destruction. Take the fire-breathing dragon under the bed, the one who threatens to incinerate your family, your town, your planet, and turn it into a pet you can pat. Or domestic imagery may simply serve to make everyone more comfortable with what they're doing. "PAL" (permissive action links) is the carefully constructed, friendly acronym for the electronic system designed to prevent the unauthorized firing of nuclear warheads. The president's annual nuclear weapons stockpile memorandum, which outlines both short- and long-range plans for production of new nuclear weapons, is benignly referred to as "the shopping list." The "cookie cutter" is a phrase used to describe a particular model of nuclear attack.

The imagery that domesticates, that humanizes insentient weapons, may also serve, paradoxically, to make it all right to ignore sentient human beings. Perhaps it is possible to spend one's time dreaming up scenarios for the use of massively destructive technology, and to exclude human beings from that technological world, because that world itself now includes the domestic, the human, the warm and playful—the Christmas trees, the RVs, the things one pats affectionately. It is a world that is in some sense complete in itself; it even includes death and loss. The problem is that all things that get "killed" happen to be weapons, not humans. If one of your warheads "kills" another of your warheads, it is "fratricide." There is much concern about "vulnerability" and "survivability," but it is about the vulnerability and survival of weapons systems, rather than people.

Another set of images suggests men's desire to appropriate from women the power of giving life. At Los Alamos, the atomic bomb was referred to as "Oppenheimer's baby"; at Lawrence Livermore, the hydrogen bomb was "Teller's baby," although those who wanted to disparage Teller's contribution claimed he was not the bomb's father but its mother. In this context, the extraordinary names given to the bombs that reduced Hiroshima and Nagasaki to ash and rubble—"Little Boy" and "Fat Man"—may perhaps become intelligible. These ultimate destroyers were the male progeny of the atomic scientists.

The entire history of the bomb project, in fact, seems permeated with imagery that confounds humanity's overwhelming technological power to destroy nature with the power to create: imagery that converts men's destruction into their rebirth. Laurence wrote of the Trinity test of the first atomic bomb: "One felt as though he had been privileged to witness the Birth of the World." In a 1985 interview, General Bruce K. Holloway, the commander in chief of the Strategic Air Command from 1968 to 1972, described a nuclear war as involving "a big bang, like the start of the universe."

Finally, the last thing one might expect to find in a subculture of hard-nosed realism and hyper-rationality is the repeated invocation of religious imagery. And yet, the first atomic bomb test was called Trinity. Seeing it, Robert Oppenheimer thought of Krishna's words to Arjuna in the *Bhagavad Gita:* "I am become death, destroyer of worlds." Defense intellectuals, when challenged on a particular assumption, will often duck out with a casual, "Now you're talking about matters of theology." Perhaps most astonishing of all, the creators of strategic doctrine actually refer to their community as "the nuclear priesthood." It is hard to decide what is most extraordinary about this: the arrogance of the claim, the tacit admission that they really are creators of dogma; or the extraordinary implicit statement about who, or rather what, has become god.

Although I was startled by the combination of dry abstraction and odd imagery that characterizes the language of defense intellectuals, my attention was quickly focused on decoding and learning to speak it. The first task was training the tongue in the articulation of acronyms.

Several years of reading the literature of nuclear weaponry and strategy had not prepared me for the degree to which acronyms littered all conversations, nor for the way in which they are used. Formerly, I had thought of them mainly as utilitarian. They allow you to write or speak faster. They act as a form of abstraction, removing you from the reality behind the words. They restrict communication to the initiated, leaving the rest both uncomprehending and voiceless in the debate.

But being at the center revealed some additional, unexpected dimensions. First, in speaking and hearing, a lot of these terms are very sexy. A small supersonic rocket "designed to penetrate any Soviet air defense" is called a SRAM (for short-range attack missile). Submarine-launched cruise missiles are referred to as "slick'ems" and ground-launched cruise missiles are "glick'ems." Air-launched cruise missiles are magical "alchems."

Other acronyms serve in different ways. The plane in which the president will supposedly be flying around above a nuclear holocaust, receiving intelligence and issuing commands for where to bomb next, is referred to as "Kneecap" (for NEACP—National Emergency Airborne Command Post). Few believe that the president would really have the time to get into it, or that the communications systems would be working if he were in it—hence the edge of derision. But the very ability to make fun of a concept makes it possible to work with it rather than reject it outright.

In other words, what I learned at the program is that talking about nuclear weapons is fun. The words are quick, clean, light; they trip off the tongue. You can reel off dozens of them in seconds, forgetting about how one might interfere with the next, not to mention with the lives beneath them. Nearly everyone I observed—lecturers, students, hawks, doves, men, and women—took pleasure in using the words; some of us spoke with a self-consciously ironic edge, but the pleasure was there nonetheless. Part of the appeal was the thrill of being able to manipulate an arcane language, the power of entering the secret kingdom. But perhaps more important, learning the language gives a sense of control, a feeling of mastery over technology that is finally not controllable but powerful beyond human comprehension. The longer I stayed, the more conversations I participated in, the less I was frightened of nuclear war.

How can learning to speak a language have such a powerful effect? One answer, discussed earlier, is that the language is abstract and sanitized, never giving access to the images of war. But there is more to it than that. The learning process itself removed me from the reality of nuclear war. My energy was focused on the challenge of decoding acronyms, learning new terms, developing competence in the language—not on the weapons and wars behind the words. By the time I was through, I had learned far more than an alternate, if abstract, set of words. The content of what I could talk about was monumentally different.

Consider the following descriptions, in each of which the subject is the aftermath of a nuclear attack:

> Everything was black, had vanished into the black dust, was destroyed. Only the flames that were beginning to lick their way up had any color. From the dust that was like a fog, figures began to loom up, black, hairless, faceless. They screamed with voices that were no longer human. Their screams drowned out the groans rising everywhere from the rubble, groans that seemed to rise from the very earth itself.[4]

> [You have to have ways to maintain communications in a] nuclear environment, a situation bound to include EMP blackout, brute force damage to systems, a heavy jamming environment, and so on.[5]

There is no way to describe the phenomena represented in the first with the language of the second. The passages differ not only in the vividness of their words, but in their content: the first describes the effects of a nuclear blast on human beings; the second describes the impact of a nuclear blast on technical systems designed to secure the "command and control" of nuclear weapons. Both of these differences stem from the difference of perspective: the speaker in the first is a victim of nuclear weapons, the speaker in the second is a user. The speaker in the first is using words to try to name and contain the horror of human suffering all around her; the speaker in the second is using words to insure the possibility of launching the next nuclear attack.

Technostrategic language articulates only the perspective of the users of nuclear weapons, not the victims. Speaking the expert language not only offers distance, a feeling of control, and an alternative focus for one's energies; it also offers escape from thinking of oneself as a victim of nuclear war. No matter what one deeply knows or believes about the likelihood of nuclear war, and no matter what sort of terror or despair the knowledge of nuclear war's reality might inspire, the speakers of technostrategic language are allowed, even forced, to escape that awareness, to escape viewing nuclear war from the position of the victim, by virtue of their linguistic stance.

I suspect that much of the reduced anxiety about nuclear war com-

---

4 Hisako Matsubara, *Cranes at Dusk* (Garden City, N.Y.: Dial Press, 1985).
5 General Robert Rosenberg, "The Influence of Policy Making on C³I," speaking at the Harvard seminar, *Command, Control, Communications and Intelligence*, p. 59.

monly experienced by both new speakers of the language and longtime experts comes from characteristics of the language itself: the distance afforded by its abstraction, the sense of control afforded by mastering it, and the fact that its content and concerns are those of the users rather than the victims. In learning the language, one goes from being the passive, powerless victim to being the competent, wily, powerful purveyor of nuclear threats and nuclear explosive power. The enormous destructive effects of nuclear weapons systems become extensions of the self, rather than threats to it.

It did not take long to learn the language of nuclear war and much of the specialized information it contained. My focus quickly changed from mastering technical information and doctrinal arcana, to an attempt to understand more about how the dogma I was learning was rationalized. Since underlying rationales are rarely discussed in the everyday business of defense planning, I had to start asking more questions. At first, although I was tempted to use my newly acquired proficiency in technostrategic jargon, I vowed to speak English. What I found, however, was that no matter how well informed my questions were, no matter how complex an understanding they were based upon, if I was speaking English rather than expert jargon, the men responded to me as though I were ignorant or simpleminded, or both. A strong distaste for being patronized and a pragmatic streak made my experiment in English short-lived. I adopted the vocabulary, speaking of "escalation dominance," "preemptive strikes," and one of my favorites, "sub-holocaust engagements." This opened my way into long, elaborate discussions that taught me a lot about technostrategic reasoning and how to manipulate it.

But the better I became at this discourse, the more difficult it became to express my own ideas and values. While the language included things I had never been able to speak about before, it radically excluded others. To pick a bald example: the word "peace" is not a part of this discourse. As close as one can come is "strategic stability," a term that refers to a balance of numbers and types of weapons systems—not the political, social, economic, and psychological conditions that "peace" implies. Moreover, to speak the word is to immediately brand oneself as a soft-headed activist instead of a professional to be taken seriously.

If I was unable to speak my concerns in this language, more disturbing still was that I also began to find it harder even to keep them in my own head. No matter how firm my commitment to staying aware of the bloody reality behind the words, over and over I found that I could not keep human lives as my reference point. I found I could go for days speaking about nuclear weapons, without once thinking about the people who would be incinerated by them.

It is tempting to attribute this problem to the words themselves—the abstractness, the euphemisms, the sanitized, friendly, sexy acronyms. Then one would only need to change the words: get the military planners to say "mass murder" instead of "collateral damage," and their thinking would change. The problem, however, is not simply that defense intellectuals use abstract terminology that removes them from the realities of which they speak. There *is* no reality behind the words. Or, rather, the "reality" they speak of is itself a world of abstractions. Deterrence theory, and much of strategic doctrine, was invented to hold together abstractly, its validity judged by internal logic. These abstract systems were developed as a way to make it possible to, in Herman Kahn's phrase, "think about the unthinkable"—not as a way to describe or codify relations on the ground.

So the problem with the idea of "limited nuclear war," for example, is not only that it is a travesty to refer to the death and suffering caused by *any* use of nuclear weapons as "limited," or that "limited nuclear war" is an abstraction that obfuscates the human reality beneath any use of nuclear weapons. It is also that limited nuclear war is itself an abstract conceptual system, designed, embodied, and achieved by computer modeling. In this abstract world, hypothetical, calm, rational actors have sufficient information to know exactly what size nuclear weapon the opponent has used against which targets, and adequate command and control to make sure that their response is precisely equilibrated to the attack. No field commander would use the tactical nuclear weapons at his disposal at the height of a losing battle. Our rational actors would have absolute freedom from emotional response to being attacked, from political pressures from the populace. They would act solely on the basis of a perfectly informed mathematical calculus of megatonnage. To refer to limited nuclear war is to enter a system that is de facto abstract and grotesquely removed from reality. The abstractness of the entire conceptual system makes descriptive language utterly beside the point.

This realization helped make sense of my difficulty in staying connected to concrete lives as well as of some of the bizarre and surreal quality of what people said. But there was still a piece missing. How is it possible, for example, to make sense of the following:

> The strategic stability of regime A is based on the fact that both sides are deprived of any incentive ever to strike first. Since it takes roughly two warheads to destroy one enemy silo, an attacker must expend two of his missiles to destroy one of the enemy's. A first strike disarms the attacker. The aggressor ends up worse off than the aggressed.[6]

[6] Charles Krauthammer, "Will Star Wars Kill Arms Control?" *New Republic,* January 21, 1985, pp. 12–16.

The homeland of "the aggressed" has just been devastated by the explosions of, say, a thousand nuclear bombs, each likely to be at least 10 to 100 times more powerful than the bomb dropped on Hiroshima, and the aggressor, whose homeland is still untounched, "ends up worse off"?

I was only able to make sense of this kind of thinking when I finally asked myself: Who—or what—is the subject? In technostrategic discourse, the reference point is not human beings but the weapons themselves. The aggressor ends up worse off than the aggressed because he has fewer weapons left; any other factors, such as what happened where the weapons landed, are irrelevant to the calculus of gain and loss.

The fact that the subjects of strategic paradigms are weapons has several important implications. First, and perhaps most critically, there is no real way to talk about human death or human societies when you are using a language designed to talk about weapons. Human death simply *is* collateral damage—collateral to the real subject, which is the weapons themselves.

Understanding this also helps explain what was at first so surprising to me: most people who do this work are on the whole nice, even good, men, many with liberal inclinations. While they often identify their motivations as being concern about humans, in their work they enter a language and paradigm that precludes people. Thus, the nature and outcome of their work can utterly contradict their genuine motives for doing it.

In addition, if weapons are the reference point, it becomes in some sense illegitimate to ask the paradigm to reflect human concerns. Questions that break through the numbing language of strategic analysis and raise issues in human terms can be easily dismissed. No one will claim that they are unimportant. But they are inexpert, unprofessional, irrelevant to the business at hand. The discourse among the experts remains hermetically sealed. One can talk about the weapons that are supposed to protect particular peoples and their way of life without actually asking if they are able to do it, or if they are the best way to do it, or whether they may even damage the entities they are supposedly protecting. These are separate questions.

This discourse has become virtually the only response to the question of how to achieve security that is recognized as legitimate. If the discussion of weapons was one competing voice in the discussion, or one that was integrated with others, the fact that the referents of strategic paradigms are only weapons might be of less note. But when we realize that the only language and expertise offered to those interested in pursuing peace refers to nothing but weapons, its limits become staggering. And its entrapping qualities—the way it becomes so hard, once you adopt the language, to stay connected to human concerns—become more comprehensible.

Within a few weeks, what had once been remarkable became unnoticeable. As I learned to speak, my perspective changed. I no longer stood outside the impenetrable wall of technostrategic language and once inside, I could no longer see it. I had not only learned to speak a language: I had started to think in it. Its questions became my questions, its concepts shaped my responses to new ideas. Like the White Queen, I began to believe six impossible things before breakfast—not because I consciously believed, for instance, that a "surgically clean counterforce strike" was really possible, but because some elaborate piece of doctrinal reasoning I used was already predicated on the possibility of those strikes as well as on a host of other impossible things.

My grasp on what I knew as reality seemed to slip. I might get very excited, for example, about a new strategic justification for a no-first-use policy and spend time discussing the ways in which its implications for the U.S. force structure in Western Europe were superior to the older version. After a day or two I would suddenly step back, aghast that I was so involved with the *military* justifications for not using nuclear weapons—as though the moral ones were not enough. What I was actually talking about—the mass incineration of a nuclear attack—was no longer in my head.

Or I might hear some proposals that seemed to me infinitely superior to the usual arms control fare. First I would work out how and why these proposals were better and then ways to counter the arguments against them. Then it might dawn on me that even though these two proposals sounded different, they still shared a host of assumptions that I was not willing to make. I would first feel as though I had achieved a new insight. And then all of a sudden, I would realize that these were things I actually knew before I ever entered this community and had since forgotten. I began to feel that I had fallen down the rabbit hole.

The language issues do not disappear. The seductions of learning and using it remain great, and as the pleasures deepen, so do the dangers. The activity of trying to out-reason nuclear strategists in their own games gets you thinking inside their rules, tacitly accepting the unspoken assumptions of their paradigms.

Yet, the issues of language have now become somewhat less central to me, and my new questions, while still not precisely the questions of an insider, are questions I could not have had without being inside. Many of them are more practical: Which individuals and institutions are actually responsible for the endless "modernization" and proliferation of nuclear weaponry, and what do they gain from it? What role does technostrategic rationality play in their thinking? What would a reasonable, genuinely defensive policy look like? Others are more philosophical, having to do with the nature of the "realism" claimed for the defense intellectuals' mode of thinking and the grounds upon which it can be shown to be spurious. What would an alternative rationality look like?

My own move away from a focus on the language is quite typical. Other recent entrants into this world have commented that while the cold-blooded, abstract discussions are most striking at first, within a short time you get past them and come to see that the language itself is not the problem.

I think it would be a mistake, however, to dismiss these early impressions. While I believe that the language is not the whole problem, it is a significant component and clue. What it reveals is a whole series of culturally grounded and culturally acceptable mechanisms that make it possible to work in institutions that foster the proliferation of nuclear weapons, to plan mass incinerations of millions of human beings for a living. Language that is abstract, sanitized, full of euphemisms; language that is sexy and fun to use; paradigms whose referent is weapons; imagery that domesticates and deflates the forces of mass destruction; imagery that reverses sentient and nonsentient matter, that conflates birth and death, destruction and creation—all of these are part of what makes it possible to be radically removed from the reality of what one is talking about, and from the realities one is creating through the discourse.

Close attention to the language itself also reveals a tantalizing basis on which to challenge the legitimacy of the defense intellectuals' dominance of the discourse on nuclear issues. When defense intellectuals are criticized for the cold-blooded inhumanity of the scenarios they plan, their response is to claim the high ground of rationality. They portray those who are radically opposed to the nuclear status quo as irrational, unrealistic, too emotional—"idealistic activists." But if the smooth, shiny surface of their discourse—its abstraction and technical jargon—appears at first to support these claims, a look below the surface does not. Instead we find strong currents of homoerotic excitement, heterosexual domination, the drive toward competence and mastery, the pleasures of membership in an elite and privileged group, of the ultimate importance and meaning of membership in the priesthood. How is it possible to point to the pursuers of these values, these experiences, as paragons of cool-headed objectivity?

While listening to the language reveals the mechanisms of distancing and denial and the emotional currents embodied in this emphatically male discourse, attention to the experience of learning the language reveals something about how thinking can become more abstract, more focused on parts disembedded from their context, more attentive to the survival of weapons than the survival of human beings.

Because this professional language sets the terms for public debate, many who oppose current nuclear policies choose to learn it. Even if they do not believe that the technical information is very important, some believe it is necessary to master the language simply because it is too difficult to attain public legitimacy without it. But learning the language is a transformative process. You are not simply adding new information, new vocabulary, but entering a mode of thinking not only about nuclear weapons but also about military and political power, and about the relationship between human ends and technological means.

The language and the mode of thinking are not neutral containers of information. They were developed by a specific group of men, trained largely in abstract theoretical mathematics and economics, specifically to make it possible to think rationally about the use of nuclear weapons. That the language is not well suited to do anything but make it possible to think about using nuclear weapons should not be surprising.

Those who find U.S. nuclear policy desperately misguided face a serious quandary. If we refuse to learn the language, we condemn ourselves to being jesters on the sidelines. If we learn and use it, we not only severely limit what we can say but also invite the transformation, the militarization, of our own thinking.

I have no solutions to this dilemma, but I would like to offer a couple of thoughts in an effort to push it a little further—or perhaps even to reformulate its terms. It is important to recognize an assumption implicit in adopting the strategy of learning the language. When we outsiders assume that learning and speaking the language will give us a voice recognized as legitimate and will give us greater political influence, we assume that the language itself actually articulates the criteria and reasoning strategies upon which nuclear weapons development and deployment decisions are made. This is largely an illusion. I suggest that technostrategic discourse functions more as a gloss, as an ideological patina that hides the actual reasons these decisions are made. Rather than informing and shaping decisions, it far more often legitimizes political outcomes that have occurred for utterly different reasons. If this is true, it raises serious questions about the extent of the political returns we might get from using it, and whether they can ever balance out the potential problems and inherent costs.

I believe that those who seek a more just and peaceful world have a dual task before them—a deconstructive project and a reconstructive project that are intimately linked. Deconstruction requires close attention to, and the dismantling of, technostrategic discourse. The dominant voice of militarized masculinity and decontextualized rationality speaks so loudly in our culture that it will remain difficult for any other voices to be heard until that voice loses some of its power to define what we hear and how we name the world.

The reconstructive task is to create compelling alternative visions of possible futures, to recognize and develop alternative conceptions of rationality, to create rich and imaginative alternative voices—diverse voices whose conversations with each other will invent those futures.

JAYNE CORTEZ (U.S.A.)

STOCKPILING

The stockpiling of frozen trees
    in the deep freeze of the earth
The stockpiling of dead animals
    in the exhaust pipes of supersonic rockets
The stockpiling of desiccated plants
    on the death root of an abscessed tooth
The stockpiling of defoliants
    in the pine forest of the skull
The stockpiling of aerosols
    in the pink smoke of a human corpse
Stockpiles
    of agent orange agent blue agent white acids
    burning like the hot hoof of a race horse on
          the tongue
Look at it
    through the anti-bodies in the body
    through the multiple vaccines belching in the
          veins
    through the cross-infection of viruses
          stockpiled
          in the mouth
    through the benzine vapors shooting
          into the muscles of the
          stars
    through the gaseous bowels of military
          fantasies
    through the white radiation of delirious
          dreams
Look

this stockpile marries that stockpile
to mix and release a double stockpile of
fissions
exploding
into the shadows of disappearing space
Global incapacitations
Zero
and boom
This is the nuclear bleach of reality
the inflated thigh of edema
the filthy dampness in the scientific pants
of a peace prize
the final stockpile of flesh dancing in
the terrible whooping cough of the wind
And even if you think you have a shelter
that can survive this stockpiling
of communal graves
tell me
Where are you going
with the sucked liver of mustard flint
the split breath of hydrogen fumes
the navel pit of invisible clams
the biological lung of human fleas
the carcinogenic bladder of sponges
lips made of keloid scars
poems in the numb section of the chromosomes
Just where do you think you're going
with that stockpile of
contaminated stink

Listen
When I think of the tactical missiles plunging
into the rancid goiters of the sun
The artillery shells of wiretapping snakes hissing and
vomiting
into the depths of a colorless sky
The accumulation of fried phosphoric pus graffitied
on the fragile fierceness of the moon
The pestering warheads of death-wings stockpiling
feathers upon feathers
in the brain
And the mass media's larval of lies stockpiled
in the plasma of the ears

And the stockpiling of foreign sap in the fluxes
of the blood
And the stockpiling of shattered spines
in chromium suits
under
polyurethane
sheets
I look at this stockpiling
at this rotting vegetation
and I make myself understand the target
That's why I say I'm into life
preservation of life now
revolutionary change now
before the choking
before the panic
before the penetration
of apathy
rises up
and spits fire
into the toxic tears
of this stockpile

MYRNA CUNNINGHAM (NICARAGUA)

A MISKITO WOMAN OF NICARAGUA TESTIFIES

When I was growing up, my father was a mechanic on a banana company boat. Our contact with the multinationals was one of total dependence: everything we had in our home was purchased at the company store, the companies were managed by Americans; the missionaries were Americans and the hospitals were run by Americans. In the 1930's when the lumber and banana companies left, it became very difficult. . . . The Miskito who lived there never used cash; they had traded their products with the companies and later with the merchants. People lost the habit of eating corn, for example, and began to eat wheat. They traded eggs, chicken, even a cow if they had one, but especially bananas; usually they had to trade more than they should and didn't have enough to eat. More than a decline, there was a total change in habits, in nutrition, especially children's nutrition. There were villages among the Río Coco with malnutrition rates of 90% among children. This began in the 1930's and continued up to the revolution. . . . Before the revolution (against the Somoza dictatorship), there was very little contact with the rest of Nicaragua. During the war, however, there were histories of a Miskito general who fought with Sandino. After the revolution, there were the first contacts with the Sandinistas and the Atlantic Coast Miskito or Indian people. The Atlantic Coast people didn't feel they had won anything because they hadn't been much involved in the fighting and their poverty remained the same. It was a change that was not understood. People from the new Nicaraguan government didn't know how to speak Miskito and knew neither the culture nor the ways of thinking of the Indian people, so the Atlantic Coast people were very suspicious of those who came from Managua. This made it easy for Steadman Fagoth (according to U.S. sources, a chief recipient of CIA funds among the Miskito opposition) to gain control among the villages by telling the people that the new government was . . . against Christianity. The people had been Christianized by the Moravians for 150 years, a very conservative Protestant church. The Bay of Pigs was launched from the Atlantic Coast. People had heard years of bad things about Cuba and had been prepared to fear any Communist government. So when Fagoth started telling them that because of communism they would have to stop being Christians, the people believed it. Fagoth's group also said that if the Sandinistas were removed from the Atlantic Coast, the Americans would help out. As I said before, when there had been jobs in the past, it was with American companies. Americans had run the schools and hospitals. People believed this propaganda because the new government was not able to do all it wanted in a few months. . . . But, during the first years of the revolution, over 20 clinics were built, immunization campaigns were done, and the hospitals were made free. We had to close nine clinics because of attacks and kidnapping of nurses and stealing of supplies. . . . I was kidnapped in . . . 1981, as I was leaving the government hospital in Bilwaskarma with the administrator, a nurse and a driver. . . . We were attacked by armed men, most of whom were Miskito, like us, but one was recognized as an ex-National Guard under Somoza. . . . They tied us up and beat us; when it got dark, the nurse and I were taken into a hut. They started praying and singing religious songs, and raped us. . . . They said that they were proud, that they were sure they would win this Christian war against Communists. . . . We were told that we would be executed on Nicaraguan soil . . . we were raped again. . . . The nurse who was raped still has psychological problems after a year and a half. The administrator of the hospital had several surgeries because he was shot in the legs. . . . With the presence of the missionaries, the multi-nationals, the British colonizers (and the poverty among the people), there was a lot of paternalism on the Atlantic Coast, and the people thought that change would come from the outside. Now they see that this isn't true, that if they want change, they have to work for it, but before, if they wanted change, they couldn't work for it. . . .

DOROTHY DAY (U.S.A.)

THIS FILTHY, ROTTEN SYSTEM

We are quite literally a nation which is in the process of committing suicide in the hope that then the Russians will not be able to murder it. . . . Love is not the bombardment of open cities. Love is not killing. . . . What I want to bring out is how a pebble cast into a pond causes ripples that spread in all directions. And each one of our thoughts, words and deeds is like that. Going to jail for distributing leaflets advocating war tax refusal causes a ripple of thought, of conscience among us all. And of remembrance too. . . . There may be ever improving standards of living in the U.S., with every worker eventually owning his own home and driving his own car; but our modern economy is based on preparation for war. . . . The absolutist begins a work, others take it up and try to spread it. Our problems stem from our acceptance of this filthy, rotten system.

MARGUERITE DURAS (FRANCE)

WE MUST SHARE THE CRIME

There are an awful lot of them. There really are huge numbers of dead. Seven million Jews have been exterminated—transported in cattle cars, then gassed in specially built gas chambers, then burned in specially built ovens. In Paris, people don't talk about the Jews yet. Their infants were handed over to female officials responsible for the strangling of Jewish babies and experts in the art of killing by applying pressure on the carotid arteries. They smile and say it's painless. This new face of death that has been discovered in Germany—organized, rationalized— produces bewilderment before it arouses indignation. You're amazed. How can anyone still be a German? You look for parallels elsewhere and in other times, but there aren't any. Some people will always be overcome by it, inconsolable. One of the greatest civilized nations in the world, the age-long capital of music, has just systematically mur- dered eleven million human beings with the utter efficiency of a state industry. The whole world looks at the mountain, the mass of death dealt by God's creature to his fellows. Someone quotes the name of some German man of letters who's been very upset and become very depressed and to whom these things have given much food for thought. If Nazi crime is not seen in world terms, if it isn't understood collectively, then that man in the concentration camp at Belsen who died alone but with the same collective soul and class awareness that made him undo a bolt on the railroad one night somewhere in Europe, without a leader, without a uniform, without a witness, has been betrayed. If you give a German and not a collective interpretation to the Nazi horror, you reduce the man in Belsen to regional dimensions. The only possible answer to this crime is to turn it into a crime committed by everyone. To share it. Just like the idea of equality and fraternity. In order to bear it, to tolerate the idea of it, we must share the crime.

(Translated by Barbara Bray)

KATHY ENGEL (U.S.A.)

THE HAMPTONS

are like South Africa
all the white people
in their big houses
with the big swimming pools
and the big luscious gardens
and the big tennis courts

and the big telephones
and the big helicopters
and the tuned up bodies
on big diets

and all the black people
mowing the big lawns
and cleaning the big kitchens
and scraping the big gritty potatoes
and cleaning up after the big brats

in the Hamptons
they hate apartheid

this year

over there

ORIANA FALLACI (ITALY)

A MAN

"This is the epoch of the *ism*. Communism, capitalism, marxism, historicism, progressivism, socialism, deviationism, corporativism, unionism, fascism: and nobody notices that every *ism* rhymes with fanaticism. This is the period of the *anti*: anticommunist, anticapitalist, antimarxist, antihistoricist, antiprogressivist, antisocialist, antideviationist, anticorporativist, antiunonist: and nobody notices that every *ist* rhymes with fascist. Nobody says that real fascism consists of being *anti* on principle, out of caprice, denying a priori that in every trend of thought there is something right or something to be used in seeking what is right. It is through locking oneself up in a dogma, in the blind certitude of having gained absolute truth, whether it be the dogma of the virginity of Mary or the dogma of the dictatorship of the proletariat or the dogma of law and order, that the sense or rather the significance of freedom is lost, the only concept that is beyond appeal and beyond debate. The fact is that the word 'freedom' has no synonyms, it has only adjectives or extensions: individual freedom, collective, personal, moral, physical, natural, religious, political, civil, commercial, legal, social, artistic; freedom of expression, of opinion, of worship, of the press, of a strike, of speech, of faith, of conscience. In the final analysis it is the only fanaticism that is acceptable: because without it a man is not a man and thought is not thought.

"Many intellectuals believe that being an intellectual means enunciating ideologies, or developing them, treating them, and then linking them together to interpret life according to formulas and absolute truths. This attitude does not care about reality, man, the intellectuals themselves; in other words they refuse to admit that they themselves are not made only of brain: they also have a heart or something resembling a heart, and an intestine, and a sphincter, therefore feelings and needs alien to the intelligence, not controllable by the intelligence. These intellectuals are not intelligent, they are stupid, and in the final analysis they are not even intellectuals, they are the high priests of an ideology. . . . Conclusion, the great disease of our time is called ideology and the bearers of its infection are the stupid intellectuals, the lay high priests not prepared to admit that life (they call it history) furnishes on its own a way of reshuffling their mental masturbations, and thus proves the artificiality of the dogma. Its fragility, its unreality. If this were not so, why would the Communist regimes repeat the same outrages of the capitalist regimes? . . . 'Organized religions do not answer the needs of modern man, religious pantomimes make no sense in our time, whether they come from the churches, or whether they present themselves with the new or pseudo-new dress of Marxism.' Now listen to this: 'An intelligent man cannot accept an ideology that delivers him over to the state, that considers him the state's passive subject. It is outrageous to speak of men in terms of historic missions, it is dangerous. Because after it has been said with books, it is said with the police: establishing at what time I must or must not go to bed, at what time I may or may not drink a bottle of wine, finally lining me up in Red Square to make me go and kneel before the Holy Sepulcher of Lenin. No, you cannot justify anything at all in the name of logic and of history. It is not logic that makes history!' . . .

"We must, today, ask two questions. Do you or don't you accept, directly or indirectly, being killed or being made the object of violence? Are you or aren't you willing, directly or indirectly, to kill or to use violence? . . .

"I believe in democracy! I fight against tyrants, have you forgotten that? I forbid you, forbid you to confuse me with those wretches who shed blood to apply the ideological formulas of their abstractions! Those fascists dressed in red, these pseudo-revolutionaries! . . . In fact every excess habitually leads to the opposite excess, in seasons as in plants and in bodies, and all the more in government." . . .

RANDALL FORSBERG (U.S.A.)

BEHIND THE FACADE: NUCLEAR WAR
AND THIRD WORLD INTERVENTION

I'm going to talk about the connection between nuclear weapons and intervention and what we can do about both, by means of giving a biography of my own growing understanding of the connection between these areas. At the Stockholm Peace Research Institute I worked with statistics of military spending and military forces. I did detailed studies of the military production complex, what weapons had been developed and produced by the United States and the Soviet Union in the 20th century. As I learned all of this statistical information, it wasn't clear to me what people could do politically. What was even less clear to me was how the continuation of this system could be rationalized by the people on top. That was the state of mind in which I came to MIT in 1974 to do graduate work in political science here, specializing in what they called "defense policy"—what I called "military policy and arms control."

It took me a year to find the answer to the question, why? In fact I learned it one day toward the end of the first year here. During the spring semester I took a different sort of course, in conventional military forces—nonnuclear forces, the Army, the Navy, the Air Force, which as you may know, absorb, together with overhead, about 80% of our military budget and a comparable portion on the Soviet side. Now, this course on conventional military forces was taught by the man who for 20 years wrote the Annual Report of the Secretary of Defense. So this was really the horse's mouth.

The spring course spent a lot of time talking about ground forces in Europe. I had been very interested to learn more or less what I expected from studying in Sweden, that the purpose of these two enormous forces on the two sides was to prepare to fight again a World War II in order to deter World War III from happening. It still seemed as illogical to me as it had ever seemed.

And then the last day of the course we looked at the Navy. At the very end, the last hour of this course, we started talking about aircraft carriers and amphibious assault ships which are large, floating military bases. These aircraft carriers can fight an air war in any part of the world. Amphibious assault ships are large landing docks for ground troops, for Army troops and their tanks and artillery and helicopters— they, too, can float anywhere around the world, so you don't need a base on the ground. We are the only country in the world that has them, and we don't have too many—18 aircraft carriers, about 5 of the very largest amphibious assault ships, and about 20 or 23 of the next larger size. Neither of which has any counterpart in any other country. They're very vulnerable because they're large and they're slow. They're also very vulnerable because the Soviet Union soon after World War II saw the potential offensive power of these floating military bases and developed, not just tens or scores, but hundreds of anti-ship cruise missiles. It was observed that probably we wouldn't want to use these floating bases in a war with the Soviet Union. They could be used, however.

Where have they been used? In Vietnam, in Korea. Where could they be used without the threat of a nuclear attack which would eliminate them very quickly? Not against the Soviet Union, but against Third World countries. Against developing countries that don't have nuclear weapons, that have small military forces. They are very vulnerable and really can't be used against strong opposing forces. But if you send them against an nth-ranked developing country, there they could be used with impunity.

Well, I listened in this class, and I said to the teacher, "These are not for use against the Soviet Union." And he said, "Yes, next question." And I said, "But I thought our military policy was to defend, if not ourselves, at least Europe, or somebody, against the Soviet Union. These weapons are only for us to use against, not a comparable military power but against very weak, little, puny developing countries. We are maintaining very large military forces to intervene unilaterally and impose our will on these weak little countries." He didn't like that.

Well, it took me several years to really understand what was going on in the nuclear arms race. I went back and I looked again at the conventional military forces, and I saw it's not just the aircraft carriers, not just the amphibious assault ships of the Marines, it's the Marines themselves. And the lighter parts of the Army which are today being trained to operate in desert environments: they aren't really being trained to operate in Europe. A large part of our conventional military forces, perhaps 50%, are not even intended ostensibly for our defense. The Soviet Union has no capacity to get to this country with conventional military force. So, no part of American forces has anything to do with the defense of this country. The conventional forces are all for use overseas. The nuclear forces are for revenge. Nuclear weapons can't defend us if the Soviet Union launches an attack. But these conventional forces, to the extent that they are for defense of Europe in the first instance, are only about half of our conventional budget, which means a very large part of our military spending is going to non-defense use of our own military force.

Then I came back to the nuclear forces again. Everyone can see that if all nuclear weapons are about deterring a Soviet nuclear attack on our cities by threatening a retaliatory attack on their cities, we've got 500 times more nuclear weapons than we need to obliterate the major cities in the Soviet Union. So if that's all our nuclear policy is about, which was implicit in the SALT I treaty, then they won't have any rationale for getting any more nuclear weapons and the nuclear arms race, at least, will stop. It didn't stop.

But they did come up against a logical wall for the first time in the postwar period. They couldn't rationalize any new weapons beyond what we already had without explaining that indeed, we had more than enough weapons to obliterate all the cities in the Soviet Union, but that we still needed more because the cities are not really the targets. It's the military forces that are the targets, as they have always been in warfare. With attacking military targets, you have a recipe for a permanent arms race. And James Schlesinger announced in the Annual Reports for fiscal year 1975, in the spring of 1974, that we needed some options.

Now we'd always been acquiring more weapons for options, but we had also had this kind of schizophrenia in Washington and in the arms control community that prevailed for the period from 1960 to 1974. During that time, the official line, in the military under McNamara and in the arms control community, was that our strategic nuclear forces are second-strike forces. Our nuclear forces have no other purpose, and under that rationale, they couldn't make any more nuclear forces. So, James Schlesinger said in 1974, well, actually we don't only want to be able to attack Soviet cities. We would like an option to go after some of the Soviet missiles. And he started then a debate that is still going on today. The debate continues to grow increasingly dangerous as new developments become more and more clear in the intercontinental nuclear forces aimed at pre-emptive, widespread first-strikes against the nuclear forces of intercontinental range and against the command and control systems on the other side.

So, around 1977 or 1978, I began to bring these two things together. I understood that the purpose of our conventional force was not only, perhaps not primarily, defense of ourselves or Europe against the Soviet Union. The probability of war in Europe is very, very low. Roosevelt, Stalin, Churchill and Truman at the end of World War II carved up Europe into spheres of influence which are extremely stable. You stay out of my internal meddling and I'll stay out of your internal meddling.

I saw that this non-defensive use of conventional military force was, in fact, related to the use of nuclear weapons against targets other than cities. What is the reason for using nuclear forces against military targets, if the function of nuclear forces is to prevent an attack on cities?

We don't need nuclear forces aimed at military targets in the Soviet Union; we will increase the likelihood of a Soviet attack on American cities. The chances are it will escalate out of control and we'll all get blown up.

So what was the purpose, then, of our having nuclear forces designed to attack military targets? Well, as I learned more I came upon this area of tactical nuclear warfare and first-use policy. And I said, Ah, the purpose (of having nuclear forces to attack military targets) is to threaten escalation. If we have this war in Europe, of course it's going to be an extremely bloody war and nobody can win—this is just a conventional war. But if we suddenly escalate to a pre-emptive nuclear strike against their forces, maybe we can obliterate them. That's the fuzzy theory behind the first use of nuclear weapons in Europe. And then, of course, if it gets out of control, we can escalate to the next level. Or, if you're a smart general, you might not want to wait until it gets out of control. You might decide to begin, not with an attack on tanks over the next hill, but with an attack on those inter-continental forces that threaten our cities. And while you're at it, at the same time, you might as well attack the forces that could threaten European cities and, indeed, attack as much as you possibly could. Because you might not have another chance.

I saw that escalation has nothing to do with deterring a nuclear attack on cities, it's the opposite. Escalation has to do with conventional warfare, with relating nuclear warfare and conventional warfare. Now I come to the final piece of this story.

If there is not going to be another war in Europe, if it's very stable, and if it's very clear that the spheres of influence are divided up and are not going to go to war, why did they keep improving nuclear capability for escalation, not for a counterforce attack? Where is the area in which this escalatory capability—the ability to escalate to nuclear war from conventional war—will actually come into play?

I came to the conclusion that the only place the new generation of nuclear weapons actually plays a role, an active role in international politics, is in backing up intervention on our part and deterring intervention on the part of the Soviet Union.

Suppose there were no nuclear forces, and there were a civil war in Iran and the United States sent in troops to make sure that the socialist side didn't win. What would prevent the Soviet Union from sending its troops over the border and getting into a direct war with the United States? Nothing would prevent them; they would do that. Suppose that we only had a few nuclear weapons—200 U.S. nuclear weapons on submarines aimed at Soviet cities and 200 nuclear weapons on Soviet submarines aimed at U.S. cities. Would the Soviet Union be able to go into Iran and challenge a U.S. intervention there? Would they be afraid that a direct war between the United States and the Soviet Union, a direct conventional war, might lead to a nuclear holocaust? There would be some fear of that.

The Soviet Union might think, ah, they won't risk it. We'll have a limited war, geographically limited and limited in means. That's what 20th century wars are like. We have limited means and limited goals. There have been no all out wars since World War II: there have been no all out wars since nuclear weapons were invented. We cannot have all out wars any longer. But we can continue to play power politics games with limited war, as long as we keep it appropriately limited.

When territory is claimed by the one that goes in first, or the one that's been there traditionally or the one that *does* care (in Afghanistan, we don't care; it has no value, no geographical value, no resources, no wealth, no military value, nothing), the claimant can take the land. But suppose there is not a balance. There is real nuclear superiority. This is the goal.

The concept of fighting and winning a nuclear war does not make sense anymore. It never did, really, but it was more plausible in the 1940s and early 1950s, when nuclear weapons were not on a five-minute alert, when they couldn't be launched on a few minutes' notice. What general with some shred of rationality would dare launch a pre-emptive strike on the other side's nuclear forces, knowing that unless they decide to sit on their hands, the other side is going to launch their weapons before they're hit? No general.

There is no rationale any longer for developing nuclear weapons designed for a pre-emptive, disarming type, first strike against the other side. Nevertheless, that is exactly what U.S. policy is. We are developing the MX and Trident II in order to obliterate Soviet inter-continental forces. Our new weapons in Europe and our weapons on submarines will help obliterate Soviet intermediate-range forces. We are developing a new generation of tactical nuclear weapons which are aimed at the tactical weapons and conventionl forces on the other side.

What's the theory behind doing that? Suppose that at every level of nuclear warfare, at every amount of weapons or at every geographic range, the United States has the capability to obliterate Soviet nuclear capability, but that the Soviet Union, at best, could only destroy part of our capability. Then we might not merely have a standoff in intervention, we might have a monopoly on intervention. The Soviet Union would know that at every level of escalation of war, we had a significant and obvious advantage. This is the golden era of nuclear superiority that the Reagan Administration longs for, one which can never be recaptured. This is what is driving the nuclear arms race. It has nothing to do with defense, it has little to do with deterrence, except in the sense of deterring their intervention while permitting our own. This is not manufactured, it is not an extreme interpretation. Knowing a little bit about weapons and strategy, you can read this yourself if you read the Annual Report of the Secretary of Defense and you look at the goals of our new nuclear weapons.

NATALIA GINZBURG (ITALY)

THE SON OF MAN

There has been a war and people have seen so many houses reduced to rubble that they no longer feel safe in their own homes which once seemed so quiet and secure. This is something that is incurable and will never be cured no matter how many years go by. True, we have a lamp on the table again, and a little vase of flowers, and pictures of our loved ones, but we can no longer trust any of these things because once, suddenly, we had to leave them behind, or because we have searched through the rubble for them in vain.

It is useless to believe that we could recover from twenty years like those we have been through. Those of us who have been fugitives will never be at peace. A ring at the door-bell in the middle of the night can only mean the word "police" to us. And it is useless for us to tell ourselves over and over again that behind the word "police" there are now friendly faces from whom we can ask for help and protection. This word always fills us with fear and suspicion. When I look at my sleeping children I think with relief that I will not have to wake them and run off into the night. But it is not a deep, lasting relief. It always seems to me that some day or other we shall once again have to get up and run off in the middle of the night, and leave everything—the quiet rooms, our letters, mementoes, clothes—behind us.

Once the experience of evil has been endured it is never forgotten. Someone who has seen a house collapse knows only too clearly what frail things little vases of flowers and pictures and white walls are. He knows only too well what a house is made of. A house is made of bricks and mortar and can collapse. A house is not particularly solid. It can collapse from one moment to the next. Behind the peaceful little vases of flowers, behind the teapots and carpets and waxed floors there is the other true face of a house—the hideous face of a house that has been reduced to rubble.

We shall not get over this war. It is useless to try. We shall never be people who go peacefully about their business, who think and study and manage their lives quietly. Something has happened to us. We shall never be at peace again.

We have seen reality's darkest face, and it no longer horrifies us. And there are still those who complain that writers use bitter, violent language, that they write about cruel, distressing things, that they present reality in the worst possible light.

We cannot lie in our books and we cannot lie in any of the things we do. And perhaps this is the one good thing that has come out of the war. Not to lie, and not to allow others to lie to us. Such is the nature of the young now, of our generation. Those who are older than us are still too fond of falsehoods, of the veils and masks with which they hide reality. Our language saddens and offends them. They do not understand our attitude to reality. We are close to the truth of things. This is the only good the war has given us, but it has given it only to the young. It has given nothing but fear and a sense of insecurity to the old. And we who are young are also afraid, we also feel insecure in our homes, but we are not made defenceless by this fear. We have a toughness and strength which those who are older than us have never known.

For some the war started only with the war, with houses reduced to rubble and with the Germans, but for others it started as long ago as the first years of Fascism, and consequently for them the feeling of insecurity and constant danger is far greater. Danger, the feeling that you must hide, the feeling that—without warning—you will have to leave the warmth of your bed and your house, for many of us all this started many years ago. It crept into our childish games, followed us to our desks at school and taught us to see enemies everywhere. This is how it was for many of us in Italy, and elsewhere, and we believed that one day we would be able to walk without anxiety down the streets of our own cities, but now that we can perhaps walk there without anxiety we realize that we shall never be cured of this sickness. And so we are constantly forced to seek out a new strength, a new toughness with which to face whatever reality may confront us. We have been driven to look for an inward peace which is not the product of carpets and little vases of flowers.

There is no peace for the son of man. The foxes and the wolves have their holes, but the son of man hath not where to lay his head. Our generation is a generation of men. It is not a generation of foxes and wolves. Each of us would dearly like to rest his head somewhere, to have a little warm, dry nest. But there is no peace for the son of man. Each of us at some time in his life has had the illusion that he could sleep somewhere safely, that he could take possession of some certainty, some faith, and there rest his limbs. But all the certainties of the past have been snatched away from us, and faith has never after all been a place for sleeping in.

And we are a people without tears. The things that moved our parents do not move us at all. Our parents and those older than us disapprove of the way we bring up our children. They would like us to lie to our children as they lied to us. They would like our children to play with woolly toys in pretty pink rooms with little trees and rabbits painted on the walls. They would like us to surround their infancy with veils and lies, and carefully hide the truth of things from them. But we cannot do this. We cannot do this to children whom we have woken in the middle of the night and tremblingly dressed in the darkness so that we could flee with them or hide them, or simply because the air-raid sirens were lacerating the skies. We cannot do this to children who have seen terror and horror in our faces. We cannot bring ourselves to tell these children that we found them under cabbages, or that when a person dies he goes on a long journey.

There is an unbridgeable abyss between us and the previous generation. The dangers they lived through were trivial and their houses were rarely reduced to rubble. Earthquakes and fires were not phenomena that happened constantly and to everyone. The women did their knitting and told the cook what to make for lunch and invited their friends to houses that did not collapse. Everyone thought and studied and managed his life quietly. It was a different time and probably very fine in its way. But we are tied to our suffering, and at heart we are glad of our destiny as men.

DANIELA (BUZEVSKA) GIOSEFFI (U.S.A.)

THE EXOTIC ENEMY

We could invent love until the sea closed in. That's all a guy like me was sure of in 1936 in Greenwich Village. Those were gloomy dark years in New York City. My father already knew what Stalin and Hitler were up to, even if a lot of others didn't. Us kids felt a vague threat hanging over us. I dreamed of being a revolutionary poet, when I wasn't dreaming of Molly—my pretty, plump and graceful, Greek-Jewish girlfriend. She had a skinny brother, called "Nebby" who was nervous and decidedly unattractive to females. No one remembered that Nebby didn't get his nomer from "nebbish," but from the first part of his name, Nebekovski. Nebby was always worried about the way he looked because girls paid no attention to him. To become a big hero so the girls would want him, he intended to run away and join the Spanish Loyalist Army—but he was afraid of guns and didn't know a thing about shooting one. Molly made me promise to teach him how.

I was ashamed of any nebbishy guys of my ethnos who were scared of guns, scared of the woods, scared of worms when you took them fishing. Being good at guns and fishing made me very suspect among my friends in the city, but I fared well in the country compared to most of the guys who were studying at Stuyvesant High School. My father, a Turkish Jew, had made a point of teaching me to hunt in the woods and fish. He believed that every man ought to know how to defend himself with a gun. He expected that at any time a workers' revolution or German troops might arrive in New York Harbor.

"Wars are fought to save rich peoples' money! People like us are often killed by their own governments!" my father would bellow. After Stalin's purges were known and after Hitler started World War II, he would say the same thing—with more conviction and even louder oratory. "So, why should only the government soldiers have guns? When the Secret Police come for your family, you got to be ready! When the whole world is one country, one race, one religion, one class, then you can be a pacifist!" He would hold forth as he taught me to aim and fire the rifles he bought me on my birthdays. He gave me two hunting rifles—just like his.

"You always need a spare—just in case—and you hide them in different places—one easy to find, the other impossible! You're not going to be a Socialist like these nebbishes in New York—always expecting a workers' revolution and scared even to kill a chicken! A gun's like a poisonous snake to them! They scream like girls if they only see one. They can't put a worm on a hook without throwing up! What kind of a man is that?"

I felt sorry for Nebby. I always thought of him when my father talked like that. I befriended him—mostly because of his sister, but I called him Nebby, too. He was in no great position to protest anything anyone called him. I was proud, too, of being the tallest guy at Stuyvesant High School—the top public school for science and math in New York City—especially, it seemed to me, taller than the guys who were scared of worms, guns and girls—the ones the German guys who hung around the park drinking beer called "sissies." The Jewish guys to get back at them, called them "Krauts," and "Beer bellies." Then the Germans would retaliate with "Kikes" and "Jewbagels!" Everyone was calling the Italians "guineas," or "greaseballs," the Englishmen, "fruits" or "limeys," and the blacks, "schvartzes" or "niggers." Me? I was called the "Crazy Turk" because I liked guns and hunting. But no one messed with me.

"I'm gonna be a hero when I get back from this war!" Nebby told me. "You'll see! Then all the girls in the Party will love me and pay attention to me."

The main girl who was paying attention to me, and I to her, was Nebby's voluptuous sister Molly. I was crazy about her. She had the exotic looks of her pretty, blond Greek mother who was a nurse, and the brains of her Jewish father—a busy doctor who tended poor people's kids for nothing and taught courses in medicine at New York University. Just like my father did. Molly and I were from a liberal Socialist group that was not at all sexually repressed like most of the other kids at school. Molly's mother had—on the insistence of her father—supplied her with birth control devices. We used to read Emma Goldman's and Margaret Sanger's essays and discuss Free Love as a high and mighty ideal—like Alexandra Kollantai of Russia! Molly and I became totally obsessed with each other. I was in the throes of the hottest love affair I'd known since discovering the difference between men and women. We lived in Washington Square. My father was a physician who had written declamatory articles for Emma Goldman's magazine, *Mother Earth*. He supplied me with all the birth control I needed, too, so I wasn't scared of making girls pregnant or catching diseases like some of the other kids at school. Ours was the only house in the square owned by radicals and we had a tendency to shock the neighborhood. I felt like a man of the world—taking Nebby's sister into the attic of my parents' house as often as I could. Molly and I were living a life of nubile bliss—but Nebby felt very left out of all the fun in our crowd and Molly started distracting me from our lovemaking with worry about him.

"Please help Nebby learn to shoot a gun," she pleaded with me. "I'm afraid he can't defend himself. He swears he's really going to run away to join the Spanish Loyalist Army—and he's threatened to tell my parents all about us cutting school to come up here if I tell on him. I'm worried, because he's never even seen a gun in person for real!"

Molly was absolutely beautiful to me—with her blond curls and the roundest softest silkiest breasts and thighs and orgastic sighs in my universe.

So, I did and it wasn't easy. Nebby tried hard, but he was just too nervous and scared of the thing. It made too big a bang and hurt his skinny shoulder when it kicked back. Whenever we finished practicing with my rifle, he claimed he had a terrible headache and had to rest. Still, I did my best to teach him—poor, haunted, scrawny guy, dying for the girls to notice him, aching to be a big hero with a medal on his chest!

To mine and everyone's surprise, he really disappeared one day, and Molly got a letter from him a few days later saying he'd joined the Spanish Loyalist Army and was about to become a real hero. One night, when Molly was supposed to meet me for a trip to the attic, she called instead. She was crying hysterically.

"I can't see you tonight or ever. I don't want to see *any* boys. We heard today that my brother's dead. I'm going to stay home every night after school to be with my parents, because they are crying all the time. They said I should have told them what Nebby was planning to do. I don't feel like making love anymore—because Nebby never will get to."

I'm telling you this story to make a little memorial to Nebby, I mean, Nevin Nebekovski, because now I'm sixty-six, and I still remember Molly. I remember wanting her for so many years, not being able to have her.

How deep the fascination with the exotic other goes—no sentiment about it—this passion with the blood of the other which stains our hands and tongues—this desire to poke at the fruit until its juices run, to tear the rose from its stem, scatter petals to the wind, to pluck the butterfly's wings for the microscope's lens, to plunge a fist into a teetering tower of bricks, watch the debris sail, explode fireworks until all crumbles to dust and is undone, open to the curious eye. Does this or that creature die as I die, cry as I cry, writhe as I would if my guts were ripped from the walls of my flesh, my ripe heart eaten alive?

Always the probing questions of sacred exploration—as if science can be progress without empathy. Does a penis feel as a clitoris feels? Do slanted eyes see as I see? Is a white or black skin or sin the same as a red one? Is it like me? Does it burn, does it peel, does it boil in oil or reel in pain? The obsession to possess the other so completely that her blood fills the mouth and you eat of her flesh from its bone, and then know if she, if he, feels as you feel, if your world is real.

Maybe, Molly was exotic to me—we were different—she a Greek, me a Turkish Jew, or maybe because she was a blond with pale skin and blue eyes, and I'm an olive-skinned brunet with dark brown ones. Even after I had white hair, she remained a kind of obsession that no woman—not my wife of thirty years—no woman—and I tried many before I got married—could erase. I still have dreams about her.

Her mother decided to go to church again after Nebby, her only son, was killed, and her father, a Socialist, didn't approve. It broke his heart when Molly entered a convent and decided to become a nun. Thank goodness she changed her mind and left the convent for college! Her father, by then, had given up his medical practice here and moved to Israel. A few years later, her mother left the Village to look for him. I heard they got back together again over there, and Molly, when she finished college, joined them in Tel Aviv. That's where she taught school for forty years.

Yes, I'm sixty-six, and I can't forget Molly, and I know now that erotic ideas are like flashy lights turning on in heads that echo from mouths and shine up secret places, and people can be greedy in their groins and ugliness can come even from the beauty of nubile bliss. Sex can be ripped from the blood as if the body were not a house of green moss, a vase of kindness, a space for greed set alight from the dark by the glow of hand on hand.

And there are still the word wounds, like roots of mushroom clouds that could rise from the pockmarked earth: *guinea, dago, spick, nigger, polack, wasp, mick, chink, jap, frog, russkie, red bastard, kike, fag, bitch, macho pig, gimp, dyke!* The stench of flesh could follow the sprayed dust of children's eyes melted from wondering sockets, animal skin, thighs, men's hands, women's sighs roasted in a final feast of fire beasts caught like lemmings in a leap to Armageddon—false resurrection! Word wounds could rise from visions of charred lips, burnt books, paper ashes, crumbled libraries, stones under which plastic pens and computers are fried amidst the last cried words, smoke to pay lip service as all dust unto dust returns. . . .

I'm old enough to know, now, that the head is fickle like history. An orchard, the body is free and soul invents itself in smile and song. I had a letter from Molly. I tried writing to her about a year ago—a love poem of our youth, and she finally answered me.

A letter came in the mail this morning from Tel Aviv. She's been a widow now for three years, like me. She said she's coming to New York to visit her grandson next month and she'll call me. We can have dinner and a talk, she says. She thought of me often through these many years. So many long years ago when we were young! Nebby never got to be a hero—just a casualty of machismo—like me. She's worried, she says, about her grandchildren and the threat of nuclear end. . . . It would be worse than Hitler or Stalin, worse than anything right or left, she says!

Yes, we'll invent love until the sea dries up or tides flood over or the bombs explode human blossoms to dust, and poets are only madmen talking crazy and making sense.

EMMA GOLDMAN (U.S.A./U.S.S.R.)

PATRIOTISM AS A CAUSE OF WAR

. . . What, then, is patriotism? "Patriotism, sir, is the last resort of scoundrels," said Dr. Johnson. Leo Tolstoy, the greatest anti-patriot of our times, defines patriotism as the principle that will justify the training of wholesale murderers; a trade that requires better equipment for the exercise of man-killing than the making of such necessities of life as shoes, clothing, and houses; a trade that guarantees better returns and greater glory than that of the average workingman.

Gustave Hervé, another great anti-patriot, justly calls patriotism a superstition—one far more injurious, brutal, and inhumane than religion. The superstition of religion originated in man's inability to explain natural phenomena. That is, when primitive man heard thunder, or saw the lightning, he could not account for either, and therefore concluded that back of them must be a force in the rain, and in the various other changes in nature. Patriotism, on the other hand, is a superstition artificially created and maintained through a network of lies and falsehoods; a superstition that robs man of his self-respect and dignity, and increases his arrogance and conceit.

Indeed, conceit, arrogance, and egotism are the essentials of patriotism. Let me illustrate. Patriotism assumes that our globe is divided into little spots, each one surrounded by an iron gate. Those who have had the fortune of being born on some particular spot, consider themselves better, nobler, grander, more intelligent than the living beings inhabiting any other spot. . . .

The awful waste that patriotism necessitates ought to be sufficient to cure the man of even average intelligence from this disease. Yet patriotism demands still more. The people are urged to be patriotic and for that luxury they pay, not only by supporting their "defenders," but even by sacrificing their own children. Patriotism requires allegiance to the flag, which means obedience and readiness to kill father, mother, brother, sister.

The usual contention is that we need a standing army to protect the country from foreign invasion. Every intelligent man and woman knows, however, that this is a myth maintained to frighten and coerce the foolish. The governments of the world, knowing each other's interests, do not invade each other. They have learned that they can gain much more by international arbitration of disputes than by war and conquest. Indeed, as Carlyle said, "War is a quarrel between two thieves too cowardly to fight their own battle; therefore they take boys from

one village and another village, stick them into uniforms, equip them
with guns, and let them loose like wild beasts against each other." It
does not require much wisdom to trace every war back to a similar
cause. . . .

NADINE GORDIMER   (SOUTH AFRICA)

BURGER'S DAUGHTER

The voice of Lionel Burger, her father, was being heard in public
for the first time for seven years and for the last time, bearing testimony once and for all. He spoke for an hour. '. . . when as a medical
student tormented not by the suffering I saw around me in hospitals,
but by the subjection and humiliation of human beings in daily life
I had seen around me all my life—a subjection and humiliation of live
people in which, by my silence and political inactivity I myself took
part, with as little say or volition on the victims' side as there was in
the black cadavers, always in good supply, on which I was learning the
intricate wonder of the human body. . . . When I was a student, I
found at last the solution to the terrifying contradiction I had been
aware of since I was a schoolboy expected to have nothing more trou-
bling in my head than my position in the rugby team. I am talking of
the contradiction that my people—the Afrikaner people—and the white
people in general in our country, worship the God of Justice and prac-
tise discrimination on grounds of the colour of skin; profess the compassion of the Son of Man, and deny the humanity of the black people they live among. This contradiction that split the very foundations
of my life, that was making it impossible for me to see myself as a
man among men, with all that implies of consciousness and responsibility—in Marxism I found it was analysed in another way: as forces in
conflict through economic laws. I saw that white Marxists worked side
by side with blacks in an equality that meant taking on the meanest of
tasks—tasks that incurred loss of income and social prestige and the
risk of arrest and imprisonment—as well as sharing policy-making and
leadership. I saw whites prepared to work under blacks. Here was a
possible solution to injustice to be sought outside the awful fallibility
in any self-professed morality I knew. For as a great African leader
who was not a Communist has since said: "The white man's moral
standards in this country can only be judged by the extent to which

he has condemned the majority of its population to serfdom and inferiority."

'. . . The Marxist solution is based on the elimination of contradiction between the form of social control and the economy: my Boer ancestors who trekked to found their agrarian republics, subjecting the indigenous peoples of tribal societies by the force of the musket against the assegai, were now in their turn resisting the economic forces that made their feudalistic form of social control obsolete. The white man had built a society that tried to contain and justify the contradictions of capitalist means of production and feudalist social forms. The resulting devastation I, a privileged young white, had had before my eyes since my birth. Black men, women and children living in the miseries of insecurity, poverty and degradation on the farms where I grew up, and in the "dark Satanic mills" of the industry that bought their labour cheap and disqualified them by colour from organizing themselves or taking part in the successive governments that decreed their lot as eternal inferiors, if not slaves. . . . A change of social control in compatibility with the change in methods of production—known in Marxist language as "revolution"—in this I saw the answer to the racialism that was destroying our country then and—believe me! believe me!—is destroying it even more surely and systematically now. I could not turn away from that tragedy. I cannot now. I took up then the pursuit of the end to racialism and injustice that I have continued and shall continue as long as I live. I say with Luther: Here I stand. *Ich kann nicht anders.*'

'. . . stand before this court accused of acts calculated to overthrow the State and establish a dictatorship of the proletariat in this country. But what we as Communists black and white working in harmony with others who do not share our political philosophy have set our sights on is the national liberation of the African people, and thus the abolishment of discrimination and extension of political rights to all the peoples of this country. . . . That alone has been our aim . . . beyond . . . there are matters the future will settle.

'. . . For nearly thirty years the Communist Party allied itself as a legal organization with the African struggle for black rights and the extension of the franchise to the black majority. When the Communist Party was declared a banned organization, and later formed itself as an underground organization to which I belonged, it continued for more than a decade to take part in the struggle for black advancement by peaceful and non-violent means. . . . At the end of that long, long haul, when the great mass movement of the African National Congress, and other movements, were outlawed; the ears of the government stopped finally against all pleas and demands—what advancement had been granted? What legitimate rights had been recognized, according to the "standards of Western civilization" our white governments have declared themselves dedicated to preserve and perpetuate? Where had so much effort and patience beyond normal endurance found any sign of reasonable recognition of reasonable aspirations? . . . and to this day, the black men who stand trial in this court as I do must ask themselves: why is it no black man has ever had the right of answering, before a black prosecutor, a black judge, to laws in whose drafting and promulgation his own people, the blacks, have had a say?' . . .

'That is my answer to the question this court has asked, and my fellow citizens may be asking of me: how could I, a doctor, sworn to save lives, approve the even accidental risk to human life contained in the sabotage of selected, symbolic targets calculated not to harm people—the tactic to which the banned Congress leaders turned in the creation of Umkhonto we Sizwe, the Spear of the Nation—turned to after three hundred years of repression by white guns and laws, after half a century of white indifference to blacks' reasonably formulated, legitimate aspirations . . . the last resort short of certain bloodshed to which a desperate people turned as a means of drawing attention after everything else had been ignored—'

'My covenant is with the victims of apartheid. The situation in which I find myself changes nothing . . . there will always be those who cannot live with themselves at the expense of fullness of life for others. They know "world history would be very easy to make if the struggle were taken up only on condition of infallibly favourable chances."

'. . . this court has found me guilty on all counts. If I have ever been certain of anything in my life, it is that I acted according to my conscience on all counts. I would be guilty only if I were innocent of working to destroy racism in my country.'

MARGHERITA GUIDACCI (ITALY)

CAIN AND ABEL

Cain said to Abel: "Come with me into the fields."
And when they had walked a little way together,
he fell upon Abel with his cudgel, a thick branch

that had been stripped of leaves, and bristled with sharp knobs.
That was the first weapon, not sophisticated,
yet in itself it already contained
all its descendants: arrows, swords, daggers,
because it was enough to open a way to death.
Guns, bombs, suitcases filled with explosives,
And death appeared upon the earth, descending
along Abel's veins, as life
had descended there from Adam's loins:
the first death on earth, a violent death
that shattered the natural course of things
even before it was established.
Violation preceded order, and Adam,
in the decline that weighed on him
(*morte morieris*), a slow consuming
of his waxen face, in which the flame
paled slowly, saw the younger of his sons
dead suddenly, and wept for the slayer and the slain.

(*Translated by Ruth Feldman*)

JEHAN HELOU (HAIFA, PALESTINE)

THE STRUGGLE OF THE PALESTINIAN PEOPLE FOR PEACE

We are gathered in New York at an international peace conference to support the United Nations Third Special Session on Disarmament. . . .

It is impossible to talk about global nuclear disarmament without taking into account the regional conflicts in Central America, South Africa and the Middle East which threaten world peace and constitute a flashpoint for nuclear confrontation. In the Middle East, and specifically in the West Bank and Gaza, the Palestinian population is engaged in an uprising, now entering its seventh month, against the apartheid-like conditions imposed upon them by a brutal twenty-one years of occupation. The legitimate struggle of Palestinians, armed only with stones, has been met with atrocities that shock and horrify peace-loving people worldwide. Over twelve thousand Palestinians have been imprisoned. The bones of youths have been broken to force them to comply with a policy of force and brutality. Hundreds of Palestinian women have suffered miscarriages as a result of the deadly tear gas made in the U.S. and used by Israeli troops. Over 250 Palestinians have been killed—including a nineteen-year-old boy beaten to death in the Gaza strip yesterday. . . .

The Palestine tragedy does not stop with the situation in the West Bank and Gaza. In Israel, Palestinians are suffering from discrimination and racist practices, not excluding the recent calls by several government officials for mass transfer or expulsion of Palestinians from their ancestral homeland. Palestinians living in refugee camps in Lebanon are subject to daily air raids by fighter jets from Israel. These raids result in the maiming and killing and displacement of thousands of families.

The military establishment which oppresses the Palestinians' legitimate demands also plays a role in supporting and arming the racist apartheid regime in Pretoria and the Contras in Central America. Israel's nuclear capacity of over two hundred warheads and its participation in the so-called Strategic Defense Initiative, better known as Star Wars, is a major obstacle to a nuclear-free zone in the Middle East and to world peace in general.

Israeli military aggression and occupation would not be possible if it were not for the massive aid it receives from the U.S. government. Over four billion a year, or thirteen million a day, since 1967—according to United Nations sources—is sent to Israel while millions in the U.S. are homeless, hungry or unemployed. The . . . daily brutalities committed have horrified all peace-loving people throughout the world—and many Jewish people in particular, both in Israel and the U.S., who continue to speak out against it. We the people of Palestine have been fighting for peace and freedom for more than seventy years, and we ask you to join with our voices in a loud cry for global nuclear disarmament and for a better future for all our children. We call for a banning of all forms of chemical, biological and nuclear warfare, and for democracy for all. We appeal to all to join the campaign for world peace of which our campaign to free the Palestinians from cruel colonializing forces is a crucial part. We appeal to you to support us in our right to self-determination and to our own independent land. . . . We stand united in our quest for justice. (*Excerpts* edited by D. Gioseffi from a 1988 speech)

REYNA HERNÁNDEZ (EL SALVADOR)

YANKEES

Whether they cry
    or not
every day that sees daylight laments
    "The Yankees"
    who come to sit in our parks
    and stink up the place
        with their diseases
They wear big boots
    to kick
a knee-high little country
They come
"immunized"
against everything
except for death.

(Translated by Zoe Anglesey)

HELEN KELLER (U.S.A.)

WE THE PEOPLE . . .

We the people are not free. Our democracy is but a name. We vote? What does that mean? It means that we choose between Tweedledum and Tweedledee. We elect expensive masters to do our work for us, and then blame them because they work for themselves and for their class.

CORETTA SCOTT KING (U.S.A.)

THE JUDGMENT OF HISTORY WILL SHOW

You can't fight poverty and discrimination, you can't provide health, security and decent housing, and you can't have a clean environment in the lengthening shadow of nuclear arsenals. The nuclear arms race creates far-reaching social problems in a number of ways. The judgement of history will show that the massive economic insecurity and the psychological numbing and alienation caused by militarization of commerce and society have had a profound effect upon our lives. The proliferation of nuclear weapons is not only the major threat to the survival of humanity; it is also the primary cause of poverty and economic stagnation around the world. The arms race is a shameful theft of funds from programs that would enrich our planet. Here in America, the cost of one bomber could pay for two fully equipped hospitals. With a serious arms control program (not just shallow treaties for show which allow weapons to continue to proliferate less noticed by the public than before), the nations of the world could apply countless billions of dollars saved to advancing social and economic progress.

The supporters of the nuclear arms race claim that peace can only be achieved through strength. Apparently, they mean an ability to destroy the world an infinite number of times. We must ask just what it is that makes the nation safe and secure. If we ruin our economy to engage in an accelerated arms race, are we really any stronger? When we demoralize and polarize millions of jobless, homeless and impoverished Americans, it seems to me that we are dangerously weak at the very fabric of our society. In this sense, the nuclear arms race breeds insecurity, not strength.

JONG JI LEE (SOUTH KOREA)

LETTER FROM PRISON

Dear Mother,

. . . I'll do the best I can to keep my mind and my body well in these circumstances. I know you would rather I were in school than here.

Now, I'm preparing for the trial that comes up soon. Only five days of waiting left, and after a long time of preparation, I face it without anxiety. I hope that this trial will give us the opportunity to show our goodwill, though I don't think this judge will understand our actions. Our actions must be judged by the people's history of suffering. (Under foreign interventionism, not only American, but Russian, Chinese and Japanese. . . .)

Mother, I think I can understand how the people have been abused and are suffering through so many years of Korean history. I've been reading Jang Kil San and thinking of the slaughter and hopeless tears of our people. Also, I'm thinking of the justice that must come to our small peninsula, our people's Korean home, the hopes and dreams for liberation that have been harbored here, and how regrettable it is that our land has been divided so that brother was made to murder brother by colonial powers who had only their own ambitions in mind—the terrible sorrowful history of the constantly slaughtered and pillaged who have wanted to live in peace and establish their own democracy.

Mother, you must understand the moral duty of your daughter and what she must do in the face of such a horrible situation. I am twenty-four years old, and it is time that I become responsible for my life and for the lives of my people. The moon rises and sets and people are born and die. I don't understand providence, but I know that I want to live in tune with nature and with the beauty of our land. I am one small creature who has received the gift of life and I want to give my life back to life. I won't excuse the tyranny and might that go against nature and destroy life with military machinery and greed. I feel that anyone who witnesses evil behavior must stand up to it, and that only to do so constitutes a meaningful life. That's being human. I must fight for human justice. That's my philosophy. My empathy for life.

I know you're worrying about my trial. We'll be very meditative about our trial. We will transcend it with our purpose for democracy and freedom. Please don't worry. You know I'm proud of you and the other mothers who are courageously encouraging each other to bear their losses in the struggle for democracy for Korea's people. Mom, if you are suffering on my account, please don't! Give thanks for our courage and rest assured that I do what I want to do, until we see each other again, and are united as a family. Say hello to my dear uncle, aunts, brother, sister, brother-in-law and cousins. Give my best wishes to Seung Jae for his graduation and admission to high school. I can remember all the images of home and my room and my things, so comforting. I am thinking deeply about how I should proceed in the future. In an isolated place like this, I contemplate the world very profoundly. I hope you can send me many democratic history books, so that I can avoid angry thoughts, even if it's difficult for you. Please let me know news from the outside. Mother, I send my fondest hopes and love to you and Father.

From your daughter,

Jong Ji Lee

(*Translated by Daniela Gioseffi with Clara Kim*)

DORIS LESSING   (SOUTH AFRICA)

THE CATASTROPHE IN AFGHANISTAN

. . . I had been involved for some years with an organization called Afghan Relief, which had invited me to come from London with a group of filmmakers and journalists to see for myself the conditions of the refugees and the Mujahideen—the "holy warriors." . . . Any Muslim country is difficult for a Westerner. We were fighting them for a thousand years. We are full of ignorance and prejudice, and so are they. It is unfortunate that the West, and particularly America, associates the words "Islam" and "Muslim" with "terrorist" or with Fundamentalist Islam, such as we read about in connection with Khomeini and Qaddafi. This is only one strand of Islam and is not, in my view, the most important—though it may, alas, become the most important. Pakistan is not Fundamentalist, like, say, Iran—not anywhere near. Attitudes toward women, for instance, are not consistent, though I'm told they're hardening. . . . A talented, ambitious, or independent woman—for her it must be hell. Just as it was in Victorian England. A woman journalist, unless she knows the language, faces every kind of difficulty because of the attitudes of the men. But a man journalist cannot meet the women in the refugee camps. The camps and the Mujahideen are what the journalists come for. . . . They have no idea how to present themselves sympathetically to the Westerner, adopting instead all kinds of heroic attitudes, talking about martyrdom, dying for their faith. . . . They have that brand of sardonic humor special to people up against it: black and wry and shocking—like Jewish humor. . . . I spent a couple of days visiting people (Afghan refugees) who had found a niche for themselves in Peshawar. . . . There were two young women and an old woman and many children, all friendly, crowding around on a veranda. You have problems talking with the Mujahideen, because of their determination to present themselves as intrepid and heroic, but with the women, there are no such problems. They tell you at once what it was like—how terrible, how frightening, how they suffered, how they suffer now. They weep; they tell you all the details that journalists long to hear and that are so hard to get from the men. . . . Their village, full of women and children—the men had gone to fight—was bombed by the Russians. "There was nothing left of our village," we were told. "In our family, we kept our stores in a cellar under the house. We went down there and were saved, though the house was bombed over us. There were a hundred . . . [survivors] who came out of the village, and seven from our family, including this child here. . . . There was snow and ice. Many had their feet frozen from frostbite. No water—our children's tongues were swollen from lack of water. It took us two weeks. The Russians bombed us all the way. They dive-bombed us day and night. This girl here . . . was on a horse with a baby under her arm. The airplane came low, and she felt blood running. It was from the baby. She fell off the horse. The baby was dead. Of the hundred who left with us, only ten got through the mountains to Pakistan." . . . It was the old woman who did the talking—crying, laughing, miming the sound of the diving planes, the tanks, gunfire, shells. She was full of life and anger. We all sat there close together, we women with the children and understood each other very well. . . . Suddenly one of us asked, "Tell us about your home in Afghanistan." . . . And now the old woman bursts into tears, forgetting all about the camera, and begins a plaint or a chant like this: "Oh, Afghanistan! Afghanistan is my sweetheart. I long for my home, for my homeland, for my people, for my Afghanistan." . . . The teacher pushes forward a little boy, who has a rough (gun) . . . made of wood. He shoots with it "D-d-d-d!"—and shouts "Freedom and death!" when his father directs him with "Freedom or death!"

ROSA LUXEMBURG (POLAND/GERMANY)

MILITARISM AS A PROVINCE OF ACCUMULATION

Militarism serves a very definite function in the history of capital, accompanying as it does every historical phase of accumulation. In the period of so-called "primitive accumulation," it was a means of conquering the New World and the spice-producing countries of India. Later, it was employed to subjugate modern colonies, to destory the social organizations of non-industrialized societies in order to appropriate and compel their means of production. It was used to introduce commodity trade in countries where the social structure had been unfavorable to it, and to change the natives into a proletariat by forcing them to work for slave wages in their own lands or starve. It is responsible for the creation and expansion of spheres of capital interest for Europeans in non-European regions, for stealing railway monopolies in underdeveloped countries, and for enforcing the claims of superpower governments as benevolent international lenders. Finally, militarism is a weapon in the competitive struggle between nations for areas of underdeveloped or non-industrialized lands.

Also, militarism has still another important function. From the purely economic point of view, it is a pre-eminent means for the realization of surplus value; it is in itself a means of accumulation. In examining the question who should count as a buyer for the mass of products containing the capitalized surplus value, we forever refuse to consider the state and its bureaucrats as consumers. Since the state's income is derivative, bureaucracies were all taken to belong to the special category of those who live from surplus value (or partly on the wage of labor), together with the liberal professions and the various parasites of present-day society: rich tax evaders, kings, dictators, presidents, party chieftains, mercenaries or industrial militarists. . . . When the monies concentrated in national treasuries by taxation are used for the production of armaments, the bill of militarism is paid for mainly by the working classes and the small family farmers.

(Adapted by Daniela Gioseffi with D. Luttinger)

JOANNA MACY (U.S.A.)

DESPAIR AND PERSONAL POWER
IN THE NUCLEAR AGE

We women around the country are going to translate the concerns about preparations for nuclear war into a massive outbreak of sanity in this country.

One is what we've begun to do already—and that's doing our homework. The obscenity of warmaking plans, and our obsession with the addictive military stockpiling are wrapped in a mystique about national security. But we're beginning to understand that it is not complicated. And we're going to expose it. Another dimension of action deals not with facts and figures but with their psychological impact. The very existence of nuclear weapons is an assault on the human psyche. People have massive resistance against painful information, and it's not surprising because it is dealing with the extinction of the species. It's as if our society were under a spell, sleepwalking its way to destruction. Capable of hearing speeches, documents, reports and going on as if they hadn't. People need to get in touch with information they have and are afraid to look at.

Ask questions that invite people to reveal their anxieties, their own concerns, their pain for the world, and hear from themselves their truth. That wakes them up. That releases energy, vision. That is the way we can turn it around.

KAREN MALPEDE (U.S.A.)

A WAY OF LOOKING AT KILLING

. . . There is a way of looking at killing as coming not so much from the wish to make the Other dead, as from the felt need to take power of the Other inside oneself, to be energized, enlivened, one might even say eroticized by it. This was the nature of much animal sacrifice in so-called primitive cultures where people lived closer to the truths of the unconscious than we do now. The sacrifice was made, the blood spilled, so that the "god-like" power of the beast might pass, by way of its eaten flesh, into the body of the ones who had killed it for that purpose. . . .

In one of my plays, *A Monster Has Stolen the Sun*, there is a scene in which a man, put into a deep trance by a midwife, enacts the birth of his own child. The actor did this brilliantly, I thought, miming the growth of his belly, his labor pains, then with great effort pulling the child out from between his legs, biting the umbilical cord and speaking the same awesome feelings, put into verse, I spoke to my own baby daughter when she first appeared to me. Then this man, a king, fantasizes that the world is mocking him for what he's done. He smashes his

131

imagined child on a rock, beats his own chest, screams that he is who he's always been, "a man whose mute and shuttered loins hold fast against unknown, unwanted things." He falls in tears upon the ground. In the working class neighborhood where we live many men are veterans of Viet Nam. We once had a neighbor, Karl, who had been a Green Beret. He had been among the forces sent into Cambodia who were not expected to come out alive, and, in fact, most of his buddies perished there. Toward the end of his tour of duty, he had been sent to massacre a village. A six- or-seven-year-old girl child, whose family had all been killed, reached her hands out to him, touched him and begged him for her life. What fleshly sensation did he feel as he looked into her eyes and spared her? What quickening of heart and mind and soul made him put down his gun? . . .

After that, Karl shot only to miss but he had to endure the accusations of his fellow soldiers who began to call him coward. Returning home a "misfit," no longer able to glorify war or his part in it, he began drinking heavily and roaming the block, offering protection from imagined hoodlums to Burl, myself and others whom he liked. He lived at home with his parents. He had no job and, it seemed, was frightened of and impotent with women. The day our daughter was born, Karl knocked and kicked at the door until we opened it. We weren't ready to have company, my husband, Burl, told him. Karl said he would not leave until he had seen the new-born child. Burl brought the infant to him in his arms and Karl stood over her and wept. "You can make new life," he said to Burl, "and all I've ever done is kill." A month or two later he was dead, of drinking and despair. Having renounced the role of murderer, he knew no choice but to become his own last victim. . . . He [was] . . . captive of the [violent] culture in which he lived. He [had] . . . no other stories [from our history to emulate] unless we begin to dream for him . . . and for and with ourselves, all the alternatives to violent murder and the ensuing violence of revenge. I mean quite literally that we need new rites, new myths, new tales of our beginnings, new stories that speak of new options open to us. The task before us is a task of the imagination, for whatever we are able to imagine we will also be able to become.

LENORE MARSHALL (U.S.A.)

CREATING THE ENEMY WITH A NAME

July 3, 1961 or 1962: Communism
Recently I have been struck by the indiscriminate use of the word
"Communist." It is the easy conviction with which the word is made to
include irrelevancies to which I refer, the application of a stereotype to
wholly inappropriate occasions, which seems to me of consequence
within the negative thinking of our time, yet another part of the psychological climate that is an outgrowth of fear and hate and produces
more fear and more hate, and thus even more international tensions.
The label "Communist" is employed as a facile epithet somewhat as
Boche or Bolshevik were in the past, in connection not with a system
or any specific meaning but in a broad blind weighted sense; it means
Them, not Us. I am of course at present not referring to informed language although there too a tinge at once colors the word because of the
world situation, just as presumably the word "Capitalist" even when
correctly employed has a certain emotional overtone in the Soviet
Union. What must be reckoned with, as well as informed usage, is
the general, the common, the careless tossing off of the word and its
impact upon prejudice within our society, its contribution toward the
difficulties of finding a *modus vivendi* between two systems in a period
of crisis.

"Communist!" an ill-tempered farmer yelled at us: we had driven by
mistake into his private road, having lost our way. "Communist!" a
storekeeper said of country neighbors who wrote letters to the local paper protesting against this or that. "Communist!" said the lady at the
hairdresser's, picking up a pamphlet on disarmament that had been left
among movie magazines. "Communist!" said the teacher to a foreign-
born obstreperous student (I heard all of these); and "He's not a Communist, he's just a bookworm!" said a school boy in defense of an ostra-
cized lone-wolf chum, to his pals on the baseball team.

Well, it's trivia. It would be ridiculous if it weren't also deadly.

There's a sort of boomerang effect: next time these speakers meet the
word in any context it will have become invested with the surplus
meanings of the first time. Even when properly employed it will have
attached to it certain nuances—it will be self-infecting. The snowball effect may thus set the framework for political events: after all, politicians aren't deaf to public opinion. How does one break into such a
self-fulfilling cycle?

In Erich Fromm's book, *Marx's Concept of Man,* he points out Marx's humanist philosophy versus the positivistic-mechanistic thinking of much of social science. "The alternatives for the underdeveloped countries," Fromm says, "are not capitalism and socialism, but totalitarian socialism and Marxist humanist socialism." And again: "I am convinced that only if we understand the real meaning of Marxist thought and hence can differentiate it from Russian and Chinese pseudo-Marxism, will we be able to understand the realities of the present day."

August 10: Aix

I have never before seen a passion so intense as the international hatred here. How fiercely they hate the Germans in this country! Our maid, Clodine, who wept hysterically because her son had been called to the front, remarked that it was a wonderful day, for many Germans had been killed, and the "concierge" muttered that it could have been a few thousand more, while they were at it. They can't seem to realize that the people who are their enemies are human beings also, that those masses of dead soldiers are leaving women who will weep as they do—are leaving lives of usefulness in their blind obedience to the state and in misguided patriotism to it. An enemy can have no feelings, is their firm belief.

MARGARET MEAD (U.S.A.)

FALSE HEROES

The tie-up between proving oneself a man and proving this by a success in organized killing is due to a definition which many societies have made of manliness. And often, even in those societies which counted success in warfare a proof of human worth, strange turns were given to the idea, as when the Plains Indians gave their highest awards to the man who touched a living enemy rather than to the man who brought in a scalp—from a dead enemy—because the latter was less risky. Warfare is just an invention known to the majority of human societies by which they permit their young men either to accumulate prestige or avenge their honor or acquire loot or wives or slaves or grab lands or cattle or appease the blood lust of their gods or the restless souls of the recently dead. It is just an invention, older and more widespread than the jury system, but none the less an invention.

Maire Mhac an tSaoi (ireland)

May we never taste of death nor quit this vale of tears
Until we see the Englishry go begging down the years,
Packs on their backs to earn a penny pay,
In little leaking boots, as we went in our day.

[Folk verse]

HATRED

i

What hatred demands is long suffering and a long fuse,
What hatred demands is the non-recognition and the blindness of
  patience,
What hatred demands is a steady finger on the trigger of the rifle—
And don't fire till you see the whites of their eyes like white-of-egg
  in your sights!

ii

When hatred shall come to flower they will fight on street trenches
And they will spread broken glass in the galloping path of police
  horses—
But in the meantime this hatred makes good manure for a garden
On a sand-bank between two tide-marks—where dwell our wives and
  our children!

Nicholasa Mohr (puerto rico/u.s.a.)

"ONCE UPON A TIME . . ."

Bouncy, bouncy, bally,
My sister's name is Paulie.
She gave me a smack,
I gave her one back.
Bouncy, bouncy, bally.

"Now it's my turn," said another girl. "Give me the ball." She too bounced the ball on the black tar roof of the tenement, throwing her right leg over the ball every third bounce.

> One, two, three a nation
> I received my confirmation
> On the Day of Decoration
> Just before my graduation.
> One, two, three a nation!

"Me now," said the third girl, and took the Spaulding ball, bouncing it the same way.

> Once upon a time
> A baby found a dime.
> The dime turned red,
> And the baby fell down dead!

"Try it the other way," said the first girl. "Let's push in."

They pushed the door, and it opened slightly.

All three girls pushed with all their might, and slowly the door began to open.

"A little more and one of us can slide in and see what's making it get stuck," said the third girl.

The door opened about one and a half feet.

"Good. Let's go in and see what's making it stuck." The first girl slipped through. "Ouch," she said. "There's a man sleeping, I think." She quickly came back out.

"Well?" the second girl asked.

"Me again," said the first girl and, taking the ball, began, "Bouncy, bouncy, bally, My sister's name is . . ."

After she finished, she handed the ball to the second girl, and then the third girl took a turn. They repeated this a few times and decided to stop playing.

"It's too hot up here," said the first girl. "Look, the tar is melting and getting stuck to my shoes."

"Ugh, yeah."

"Let's go."

They walked along the rooftops, going from building to building. Each building was separated from the next by a short wall of painted cement, stretching across the width of the building, no higher than three and a half feet. When they reached each wall the girls climbed over, exploring another rooftop.

"It's too hot out here; let's find a hallway to play in," said the second girl.

"O.K.," agreed the third girl, "but let's get a place where they don't throw us out."

"How about the building over there?" The first girl pointed to a tenement several rooftops away. "Most of them families in that building moved out, so probably no one will hear us."

They headed in that direction, eager to be out of the hot sun.

"I hope the entrance ain't locked," said the third girl.

They climbed the last dividing wall and went straight to the entrance, which jutted out of the rooftop at a slant. The third girl pulled at the large metal door; it wouldn't budge.

"It's locked," she said to her companions.

"Wanna come in and see him?" the first girl replied. "It's dark in there. But it was a man; and he was sleeping real sound. He didn't make no noise when I stepped on him."

"Let's go on in and see," said the third girl.

"What if he should wake up?" asked the second girl.

"We'll run real fast," said the first girl.

"Yeah," said the second girl. "Down the stairs. Otherwise he might catch us on the roof. What do you say? O.K.?"

They agreed and slipped in through the partially opened door. They entered the dark hallway carefully, avoiding the body that lay on the floor between the door and the wall.

"See?" The first girl pointed. "He must be fast asleep."

They concentrated as they stared at the body, trying to make things out. After a while, their eyes adjusted to the dark and he became more visible.

"Oh, look! He's got a jacket, and it's from that club," said the third girl.

He lay curled up, facing the wall; they could see his back clearly. He wore a bright orange jacket. A large picture of the head of a leopard baring its teeth was decaled across the back. Underneath, the words PUERTO RICAN LEOPARDS were stenciled in black.

"It's one of them guys," said the first girl. "You know?" she continued. "He's not moving. Maybe . . . maybe he's dead!"

The girls rushed away from him, going down a few steps into the stairwell.

"What do you think we should do?" asked the second girl.

"Maybe we should find out who he is," the first girl responded.

"He might wake up if we get too near," said the second girl.

They looked at one another and then at the young man. He had not moved and still faced the wall, his body curled up.

"Who's gonna look and see who he is?" asked the first girl.

"Not me."

"Not me."

"Not me neither, then."

They stood silently for a while, and finally the third girl said, "We should go and tell the super of the building."

"That's right. Good idea!"

"I say we should still know who it is," said the first girl. "Let's find out—come on!" She went up the steps.

"Wait," called the second girl. "Be careful; he might wake up."

She stopped and nodded in response, then quickly stepped up to the young man. Leaning over, she looked at his face and ran back to her friends.

"Well, who is it?" they asked.

"It's their leader. You know, that real tough guy. Frankie-Chino!"

"No kidding, him?"

"Wow."

"Yes. And you know," said the first girl, "his eyes are closed . . . and he's not breathing!"

"Really?"

"Honest?"

"Go see for yourself," she told her friends.

"I'm scared he might wake up," said the second girl.

"He won't. He's not breathing," said the first girl.

Holding hands, they went up to him and quickly bent over, looking into his face. They ran back down, a little less scared than before.

"I think he's dead," the second girl said. The third girl nodded in agreement.

"What should we do?" asked the first girl. "I know," she went on, "let's go tell them about it at their clubhouse. It's down in the basement, right next to the candy store on Wales Avenue, off Westchester."

They all looked at each other and shrugged their shoulders.

"Let's do it," said the first girl. "Come on."

"All right."

"Sure."

All three ran down the stairs and out into the street. They hurried, talking in short, anxious sentences, planning how they would tell their story.

"They are real tough guys. Wow, my mother better not find out we went there," said the second girl.

"Oh, we won't tell nobody. It's our secret. Right?"

"Also, we have to promise that we won't let nobody else know . . . about him. Except the Puerto Rican Leopards, of course."

They all promised.

138

They reached Wales Avenue and went down the old tenement steps leading to the basement clubhouse of the Puerto Rican Leopards. They got to the door and knocked; no one answered. They knocked again and again, waiting for a response. After a while, the first girl tried the doorknob; the lock released, and the door opened.

They walked in slowly, entering a large unkempt room that was damp and dark. A studio couch with large holes, where the stuffing spilled out, was against the center wall. Several old rusted metal kitchen chairs were scattered about the room, some overturned. A broken radio was set on two wooden crates. The center of the cement floor was covered by a large piece of broken and peeling linoleum. Dirty paper cups and plates were strewn about. The room looked dusty and neglected.

"Nobody's here," said the second girl.

"It looks deserted," said the third girl.

"Let's get out of here," said the first girl. All three walked out of the dark basement and out into the street. The afternoon sun shone brightly; it was hot and humid.

"Whew," said the first girl, "it was so much more cooler down there."

Slowly, they walked along tossing the ball to one another until they got back to their building.

"What do you think?" asked the second girl. "Should we tell somebody what we seen?"

"I think we should just forget it. That guy was probably sleeping and woke up already," said the third girl.

"Yeah. We better not; then they'll ask us what we was doing up on the roof and all," said the first girl.

"Let's have another game of ball," said the second girl.

"Let me go first," said the third girl. "I was last before."

"O.K."

"All right."

Bouncing the ball and throwing her leg over it on every third bounce, she sang,

> Once upon a time
> A baby found a dime.
> The dime turned red,
> And the baby fell down dead!"

MARIA MONTESSORI (ITALY)

A SCIENCE OF PEACE

It is quite strange . . . that as yet there is no such thing as a science of peace, since the science of war appears to be highly advanced, at least regarding such concrete subjects as armaments and strategy. As a collective human phenomenon, however, even war involves mystery, for all the people of the earth, who profess to be eager to banish war as the worst of scourges, are nonetheless the very ones who concur in the starting of wars and who willingly support armed combat.

BHARATI MUKHERJEE (INDIA/CANADA)

THE COLONIZATION OF THE MIND

In order to be recognized as an India-born Canadian writer, I would have to convert myself into a token figure, write abusively about local racism and make Brown Power fashionable. But I find I cannot yet write about Montreal. It does not engage my passions. It is caught up in passion all its own, it renders the Asian immigrant whose mother tongue is neither French nor English more or less irrelevant. Montreal merely fatigues and disappoints. And so I am a late-blooming colonial who writes in a borrowed language (English). . . .

My Indianness is fragile; it has to be professed and fought for, even though I look so unmistakably Indian. Language transforms our ways of apprehending the world; I fear that my decades-long use of English as a first language has cut me off from my *desh*. . . .

I thought particularly of a temple relief from Deoghar, Bihar (an area crowded with skeletons in maps of global starvation). I had not seen the temple relief itself, only a plate of it in a book about Indian art written by Heinrich Zimmer, whose work had not been brought to my attention as a schoolgirl in Calcutta because the missionary school I attended taught no Indian history, culture, art, or religion.

I was entranced not by craftsmanship but by the inspired and crazy vision, by the enormity of details. Nothing had been excluded. As viewer, I was free to concentrate on a tiny corner of the relief, and read into the shape of a stone eyelid or stone finger human intrigues and emotions. Or I could view the work as a whole, and see it as the story of Divine Creation. For me, it was a reminder that I had almost lost the Hindu instinct for miraculous transformation of the literal. . . .

As a very small child, before I learned to read, I used to listen to my grandmother (my father's mother) reciting ancient stories from the puranas. But after I started missionary school in earnest, the old gods and goddesses and heroes yielded to new ones, Macbeth and Othello, Lord Peter Whimsey and Hercule Poirot. I learned, though never with any ease, to come and go talking of Michelangelo, to applaud wildly after each scene in school productions of *Quality Street*, and to sing discreetly as a member of the chorus in *The Gondoliers*. School exposed me to too much lucidity. Within its missionary compound, multiheaded serpents who were also cosmic oceans and anthropomorphic gods did not stand a chance of survival. My imagination, therefore, created two distinct systems of cartography. There were seas like the Dead Sea which New Testament characters used as a prop to their adventures and which the nuns expected us to locate on blank maps of Asia Minor. And then there were the other seas and oceans, carved in stone on walls of temples, bodies of water that did not look like water at all and which could never be located on maps supplied by the school.

The mind is no more than an instrument of change. My absorptive mind has become treacherous, even sly. It has learned to dissemble and to please. Exquisitely self-conscious by its long training in the West, it has isolated itself from real snakes and real gods. But the snakes and gods remain, waiting to be disturbed during incautious sabbaticals.

I had been away from Calcutta for fourteen years. My parents no longer lived there. . . .

I was born in Ballygunge, a very middle-class neighborhood of Calcutta, and lived the first eight years of my life in a ground-floor flat on a wide street sliced in half by shiny tram tracks. The flat is still rented by my *jethoo;* the tram tracks still shine through the mangy blades of grass in the center of the street; and the trams are still owned by British shareholders most of whom have never seen Calcutta. Ballygunge remains, in these small, personal terms, a stable society. Wars with China and Pakistan, refugee influxes from Assam, Tibet, Bangla Desh, and Bihar, Naxalite political agitations: Nothing has wrenched out of recognizable shape the contours of the block where I grew up. . . .

In those first eight years, though I rarely left Ballygunge, I could not escape the intimations of a complex world just beyond our neighborhood. I saw the sleek white trams (perhaps never sleek nor white) and I associated them with glamour and incredible mobility. My own traveling was limited to trips to the *mamabari* a few blocks away, and to school which was in the no man's land between Ballygunge and the European quarters. . . .

I saw processions of beggars at our front door, even Muslim ones, and it was often the job of us small children to scoop out a measure of rice from a huge drum in my widowed grandmother's vegetarian kitchen and pour it into the beggars' pots. I was too little to lean over the edge of the drum and fill the scoop, and for that I was grateful. The beggars terrified me. I would wait for them to cluster at our front door, but when they were actually there, I would hide behind my older cousin Tulu (now a geneticist in Hamburg), who would issue efficient commands to the beggars to stop fighting among themselves and to hold out their sacks and pots. It is merely a smell that I now recall, not the hungry faces but the smell of starvation and of dying. Later, my mother, a powerful storyteller, told me how millions had died in the 1943 Bengal famine—she did not care about precise statistics, only about passion. . . .

Elizabeth Nunez-Harrell (trinidad/u.s.a.)

CALYPSO WOMAN

Trinidad is so small that if you flew with the crows you could cross it from north to south in less than four hours, from east to west you could cross in less than three. But to the people who live there, the sea and land are varied and mysterious. So mysterious that when Columbus tasted the seawater off the southern coast of the island, he thought he was in the Waters of Paradise. And when he saw the three peaks of the Southern Mountain Range, he was certain that before him rose the symbol of the great mystery of the Roman Catholic Church, the Holy Trinity.

Unwilling to accept the possibility that he had made an error in his sextant reading, Columbus preferred to believe that he had discovered the Truth: The earth was not completely spherical but pear-shaped, and this land he had sighted was the top of the bulge of the pear. The Earthly Paradise of which he had often read and yearned to discover!

How was Columbus to know that it was the Orinoco River, its tremendous energy unspent in its voyage through Venezuela, that gushed into the sea off Trinidad, diluting the salt of the water. Why should he doubt his discovery? "Ah," he must have said, "here is the place that God made for His Paradise on Earth. This land of sweet seawater. This land where God has laid before Man the truth of His Holy Trinity. As these three peaks are in one mountain so are God the Father, Jesus Christ His Son, The Holy Ghost the Spirit of God, all three persons of the one God. This island I will call Trinidad in the name of this divine mystery."

And though surely this island had another name, he was not too wrong to call it that, to see in this island elements of the fantastic, mysteries that could not be pierced by reason. For the island was populated then and was to be populated later by a people who approached life's mysteries not with an intellect disengaged from their oneness with nature, but with minds open to truths whispered to them from the sea, the earth, the animals, the birds, the fish.

To the people who lived on the seacoasts that bordered the island the sea was the most intelligent of beings and she was to be respected, feared and loved. She was not the same on all sides of the island. On one side she could be gentle, her force and strength already spent on the coral reefs a few miles off shore. On the other end she could be ferocious, leaving only the smallest border of sandy beach as she crashed into the rocks that faced her on the shoreline, eroding her way farther inland. Near Icacos Point, on the southwestern tip of Trinidad, where the hills of Venezuela are visible to the naked eye, where the great river Orinoco washes her silt in the brine of the Atlantic, she swirled her current deep, dark and treacherous beneath her surface waters, waiting for the foolish. The people knew about Calypso, who lived there among these currents. Tales of her power reached far inland to the towns in the south.

The story went that long, long ago, as the conquistadors who had plundered the great Indian civilizations of South America navigated their ships northward toward the calm waters of the Caribbean, their arms and necks weighted with the gold, silver, emeralds and rubies that they had ravaged from the Incas and the Aztecs, the holds of their ships loaded with more stolen treasure, Calypso lay there, under the sea, waiting and watching. And when the conquistadors, still hungry for the warmth of the tropical sun, had stretched their bodies on the decks of their ships, sprawled out like dough arranged on trays to be baked, the cunning Calypso rubbed her rounded buttocks against the hulls of their ships and pushed them gently into the waters off Icacos Point.

It was her steel-band music that the conquistadors first heard: "Ping-Pang Ping-Pang Pinkety-Ping-Pang." They raised their heads from the decks of their ships and looked across the sea and saw nothing. But

Calypso beat her pans again: "Ping-Pang Ping-Pang Pinkety-Ping Pang."
And the conquistadors, lured by her music, tasting the promise of warm
thighs and swollen breasts, followed her, plunging their ships through
the waters between Icacos and Venezuela. When they sighted the land
that Columbus had discovered for his people, lust had so etched its
way into their souls, they forgot to look for the currents. Calypso,
knowing that they were hers, raised her head above the water and
shook her nappy hair, sending waves cascading to crash with fatal violence against the sides of the ships, churning the waters white, plum-
meting the sea through her tight curls. The conquistadors had no time
for speech. They grabbed their stolen treasures and locked them in
their arms. But then the current came swiftly up from the ocean floor,
snapped against the prows of their ships and, in one precise, calculated
move, pulled Calypso's prey silently down into the dark depths of the
ocean floor.

The villagers tell that when the bodies of the conquistadors began
to ferment in the bowels of the sea, the current vomited their skeletons, their arms still locked around their treasures, and pitched their
bones against the rocks on the shore.

The Arawaks, the Caribs and the Waraos, who for a time were protected by these waters from the white men who came to plunder, then
took the treasures from these skeletons and buried them inland near
the mountain range, deep in the ground everywhere in the south of
Trinidad. When the stories of El Dorado swept through the Caribbean,
the villagers sat around fires on rainy nights and talked of dreams of
finding buried treasure and living the life of Raleigh.

ALANIS OBAMSAWIN (CANADA)

FREE SPIRITS: ANNALS OF THE
INSURGENT IMAGINATION

I don't know the exact place of my birth. I do know that I was born
around Lebanon, New Hampshire. I lived there for six months, then
my mother returned to her reservation in Canada. I'm from the Abenaki Nation. The word comes from Wamabenaki and means 'People
of Sunrise.' We are eastern woodland Indians. Originally our land was
all of New England. Groups of Abenaki people still live in Vermont

and in Maine. On the reservation in Canada, I lived with my aunt who had six other children. We lived mainly outside, whether it was winter or summer. I was very fortunate to know my aunt and an old man that was my mother's cousin. He told me a lot about the history of our Nation. He also taught me many songs and stories. Those two people gave me something special and strong. It was my best time.

I left the reservation when I was nine. We settled in a small town in Canada. That's where all the problems started. We were the only Indian family there. It was bad. I remember sleep as being my best moments. I had such fantastic dreams about animals and birds. But it was the bad time of my life. I attended a French school in the town's slums. That's when they told me that I was poor, that I was dirty, and that we were savages. The tall lone savage in the back of the classroom. When I grew older, the same people who had beaten me up for years and years all of a sudden started flirting with me. It was strange. It took me a long time to lose the hate. I really had a lot of hate in me. Those memories are in my songs. I started collecting music and singing professionally about twenty-five years ago. I always used to sing. I remember rocking my rocking chair and singing all the time, as a young girl. Later I started singing for friends. But I never had any idea that I would go and sing on the stage in front of other people. . . .

I started writing songs about fifteen years ago. Mainly making sounds of what was happening. What I was seeing at the time, and of the visions and dreams I had. I put them into sounds for singing. I also sing traditional sounds and tell stories and legends. I make songs in Indian, in English and in French. It all depends on how it's speaking to me. . . .

I started making films about twelve years ago. I make mostly documentary films. I've produced several films for children because I feel that's where it all starts. I want our children to know their languages. To know who they are before anything else, before anybody else. If you know who you are, you can stand anywhere in the world and not be afraid. If you're always told that your parents were dirty, ugly and pagans, you know what the hell you think you're going to look like when you look at yourself in the mirror, because you are a reflection of what they told you; and it takes a long time to figure out that it's alright to be what you are, and not what they said about you. It shouldn't take half of your life to figure that out. You should know who you are when you first begin and then deal with the rest of the world. . . .

Sometimes I feel like a bridge. It's good that I have the responsibility of being a producer and director with the National Film Board of Canada. It's good to be in a position of power. It's important. The decisions of what goes into the films comes from us. It doesn't come from the outside. It comes from the people who are in the films and from myself. I can consult with the people who are involved and we can decide together. I'm really a bridge between two worlds. It comes through in my songs, my stories and my film work. I'm a fighter, a free spirit, but to be a free spirit at this time is very painful. You're choked by everything around you. You go outside and you're choked by the pollution. You're choked by the cars. You're choked by the traffic lights. You're choked by the law that tells you what you should be, what you have to be. How can you be free if you have to think of all those things they tell you to be? It puts to sleep what you are.

So to become free you have to fight. You have to fight and there is no war. Your soul, your spirit is wanting to breathe, wanting to express itself but you walk outside and you can forget it. So you have to be damn strong to be able to allow your spirit to live the way it should. You cry all the time. It's like dying and nobody buries you. Your real feelings are constantly being suppressed. You're not even allowed to be a child. Just like when the different tribes signed the treaties and they were told, 'As long as the grass will grow, as long as the water will flow.' The people never knew that the newcomers would be able to turn rivers the other way and pretty soon there would be no grass. No one thought that would happen. So who knows what they will do. All I know is that the power of soul, the spirit and the brain is extraordinary.

I'm sure that long ago all beings were able to communicate without traveling. Communicate through their brains, through their souls, through their visions. People were able to do magic. They didn't have all this shit we have to put up with. That's why they had peace in themselves. They could spend time and become very well educated with what they were—through their brains, through their experiences. They could perform operations. They could cure people. They could bring down good or bad people. They had powers which today cost millions and millions of dollars to have just a tiny bit. People have forgotten this. Thank god there's an underground movement in terms of our religion, in terms of our medicine men and in terms of how it is important to not listen to the threatening force that tries to manipulate you. You have to look at what is, and work from that. In other words, work from inside. Work from your heart, and then you go out. Not out, and then tear up your heart—there's nothing left.

I think the damage done to human beings starts in school. It's the teaching. To be stamped by the title teacher is not a compliment. Some people who have that title take it for granted that they're smarter than other people. They begin to oppress those they feel are inferior, which is a word that came with the newcomers. In our language there is no word to say inferior or superiority or equality because we are equal, it's a known fact. But life has become very complicated since the newcomers came here. And how does your spirit react to it? It's like they're going to bury me tomorrow at five o'clock when the door bell rings. It's painful. You have to be strong to walk through the storm. I know I'm a bridge between two worlds. All I ask is for people to wash their feet before they try to walk on me.

CHAILANG PALACIOS (PACIFIC ISLANDS / MICRONESIA)

THE COLONIZATION OF OUR PACIFIC ISLANDS

Micronesia was colonised by the Spanish in the fifteenth century. When the Spanish soldiers came, so did the missionaries. Hand in hand. They landed in Guam and spread out over the Marianas, then all over Micronesia. The missionaries together with the soldiers began to Christianise our ancestors. They were very scared and ran away—they hadn't seen a white person before. It was hard for us to embrace Christianity. The Spanish missionaries were blessing all the soldiers while the soldiers were cutting my ancestors into half, killing our men, raping our women.

When they arrived we were about 40,000. And we ended up just 4,000 because they killed everyone who didn't want to embrace Christianity, which was the Catholic faith. So the Spanish stayed over 100 years. They came to do good work. And they did it very well, because today we are 97% Catholic.

Another nation came, which is the Germans. Both the Spanish and the Germans came for their economic purposes. The Germans again, the same story—killing our men, raping our women. They took our land. The Germans brought their own missionaries, who tried to teach us the Protestant religion. And this started making us, the indigenous group, fight amongst ourselves over who was more Protestant and who was more Catholic. That is always the way: when white nations come to conquer us, to colonise us, they divide us. And it is still happening. But the Germans didn't stay very long. They took off.

And then there is this nation just like an octopus. The octopus that goes very slowly, very slowly, and suddenly it gets you. That is like the

Japanese. They came and were exactly the same. They want us to join their religion, Buddhism. They liked our islands so much they stayed. They took our land for sugar plantations, for pineapple plantations. They again made my ancestors their slaves, together with the Korean and Okinawa people, paying them five cents for the whole day.

Then the Japanese and the USA sat down planning to have war. We, the Micronesian people, were the victims of that war—World War II. We suffered all over the Marianas. It was heavily damaged because it was a big military place for the Japanese. So, once again, my ancestors suffered.

After stripping them of their culture, their language, their land, the Japanese forced my ancestors up into the mountains. They made us dig a hole just in case the Americans and the Japanese fought. We would be safe in the hole. But it didn't happen like that. It was Sunday morning when the war came. Everyone was far away from their holes, visiting grandparents, relatives, friends. All of a sudden—bombs from the sky and the ocean. The people were crushed fifty to one hundred in one hole because there was no way they could get back to their own place to hide. There was no water for those people. It was so hot, so dark, bombs all over. A lot of people died. Children died because their mothers' breasts dried up. No food.

You have heard it, and I have heard it too, from the older generation: "Oh, we are so grateful that the Americans won the war. They saved us from the communists, from Russia." Yet right after the war the Americans came, like the early missionaries, in the name of God, saying, "We are here to Christianize you, to help you love one another, be in peace." We still have the Bible while the missionaries and their white governments have all the land. . . .

For some years we were "off limits." No one could come in and no one could go out unless you were CIA or military American. The whole reason for that is that the U.S. had planned to take over mainland China. So all these nationalist Chinese were in my islands learning how to fight. In time of peace children would be crying at night: there was big bombing and it could be heard all over the island. And the house started to shake. The only thing I remember is my parents saying, "Pray that there will be no more war." So next day I said, "Why do you pray and say 'No more war'?" And she just held me and said, "Oh, my daughter, I feel so sorry for your generation because probably I will not see the next war. But the next war will be so terrible that you won't need to hide." I think I was only 11 or 12 years old. I looked at her and I didn't understand. Naturally my mother died. She was not an educated woman, but with her terrible memories of World War II she just *connected*. "You won't need to hide." Those were her words. I never forget them. . . .

GRACE PALEY (U.S.A.)

ANXIETY

The young fathers are waiting outside the school. What curly heads! Such graceful brown mustaches. They're sitting on their haunches eating pizza and exchanging information. They're waiting for the 3:00 P.M. bell. It's springtime, the season of first looking out the window. I have a window box of greenhouse marigolds. The young fathers can be seen through the ferny leaves.

The bell rings. The children fall out of school tumbling through the open door. One of the fathers sees his child. A small girl. Is she Chinese? A little. Up u u p, he says and hoists her to his shoulders. U u up says the second father and hoists his little boy. The little boy sits on top of his father's head for a couple of seconds before sliding to his shoulders. Very funny, says the father.

They start off down the street, right under and past my window. The two children are still laughing. They try to whisper a secret. The fathers haven't finished their conversation. The frailer father is a little uncomfortable; his little girl wiggles too much.

Stop it this minute, he says.

Oink, oink, says the little girl.

What'd you say?

Oink oink, she says.

The young father says what! three times. Then he seizes the child, raises her high above his head and sets her hard on her feet.

What'd I do so bad, she says, rubbing her ankle.

Just hold my hand, screams the frail and angry father.

I lean far out the window. Stop! Stop! I cry.

The young father turns, shading his eyes, but sees. What? he says. His friend says, Hey? Who's that? He probably thinks I'm a family friend, a teacher maybe.

Who're you? he says.

I move the pots of marigold aside. Then I'm able to lean on my elbow way out into unshadowed visibility. Once not too long ago the tenements were speckled with women like me in every third window up to the fifth story calling the children from play to receive orders and instruction. This memory enables me to say strictly, Young man I am an older person who feels free because of that to ask questions and give advice.

Oh? he says, laughs with a little embarrassment, says to his friend, Shoot if you will that old grey head. But he's joking I know, because he has established himself, legs apart, hands behind his back, his neck arched to see and hear me out. How old are you, I call. About thirty or so?

Thirty three.

First I want to say you're about a generation ahead of your father in your attitude and behavior towards your child.

Really? Well. Anything else Ma'am?

Son, I said, leaning another two, three dangerous inches toward him. Son, I must tell you that mad men intend to destroy this beautifully made planet. That the imminent murder of our children by these men has got to become a terror and a sorrow to you and starting now it had better interfere with any daily pleasure.

Speech, speech! he shouted.

I waited a minute but he continued to look up. So I said, I can tell by your general appearance and loping walk that you agree with me.

I do, he said, winking at his friend, but turning a serious face to mine, he said again, Yes, yes, I do.

Well, then, why did you become so angry at that little girl whose future is like a film which suddenly cuts to white, Why did you nearly slam this little doomed person to the ground in your uncontrollable anger?

Let's not go too far, said the young father. We could get depressed. She WAS jumping around on my poor back and hollering Oink, oink.

When were you angriest—when she wiggled and jumped or when she said oink?

He scratched his wonderful head of dark well cut hair. I guess when she said oink.

Have you ever said oink oink. Think carefully. Years ago perhaps?

No. Well maybe. Maybe.

Whom did you refer to in this way?

He laughed. He called to his friend, Hey Ken, this old person's got something. The cops. In a demonstration. Oink, oink, he said, remembering, laughing.

The little girl smiled and said Oink oink.

Shut up, he said.

What do you deduce from this?

That I was angry at Rosie because she was dealing with me as though I was a figure of authority and it's not my thing, never has been, never will be.

I could see his happiness, his nice grin as he remembered this.

So, I continued, since those children are such lovely examples of what may well be the last generation of humankind, why don't you start all over again, right from the school door as though none of this had ever happened.

Thank you, said the young father. Thank you. It would be nice to be a horse, he said, grabbing little Rosie's hand. Come on Rosie let's go. I don't have all day.

U up says the first father U up says the second.

Giddap shout the children and the fathers yell Neigh Neigh as horses do. The children kick their father's horsechests screaming giddap giddap and they gallop wildly westward.

I lean way out to cry once more, Be Careful! Stop! But they've gone too far. Oh anyone would love to be a fierce fast horse carrying a beloved beautiful rider, but they are galloping toward one of the most dangerous street corners in the world. And they may live beyond that trisection across other dangerous avenues.

So I must shut the window after patting the April cooled marigolds with their deep smell of summer. Then I sit in the nice light and wonder how to make sure that they gallop safely home through the airy scary dreams of scientists and the bulky dreams of automakers. I wish I could see just how they sit down at their kitchen tables for a healthy snack (orange juice or milk and cookies) before going out into the new spring afternoon to play.

MARGARITA CHANT PAPANDREOU (GREECE/U.S.A.)

CAUSES AND CURES OF ANTI-AMERICANISM

One of the questions I am most frequently asked back in the States is, Why is Greece anti-American? The next two questions are, Will Greece get out of NATO? and Will you keep American bases? In feminist circles there are also queries about our progressive measures toward equality for women. I seldom get questions about socialism in Greece, although if I happen to mention that we have a socialist government, the listener turns pale. No one, however, seems to be interested in our conflicts with Turkey, the Cyprus problem or our peace initiatives.

The questions regarding Greece's intentions toward the North Atlantic Treaty Organization and the U.S. bases seem to reflect a keener awareness of national security issues in the States than existed during the years after World War II. But the one about anti-Americanism comes from the heart; people are pained and puzzled by it. Some time ago Administration officials talked about launching a public relations program to dispel anti-American attitudes in Europe, a truly naïve idea. There are substantial reasons for such attitudes and feelings, and unless those reasons are understood and responded to, no media campaign, no exchange-student program, no cultural or scientific collaboration, will change them.

Anti-Americanism does not mean hostility toward the American people. Nor does it signify dislike of American culture. Blue jeans, rock-and-roll, Big Macs, films and television serials are generally popular and are the United States' best and most powerful ambassadors. They are opposed nowadays, particularly by fundamentalist societies, as symbols of modernity, corruption and cultural intervention, but they are not in any way the cause of anti-American attitudes. Anti-Americanism is most prevalent in the underdeveloped and developing world (not, interestingly enough, in the Eastern bloc countries), where people feel that U.S. economic forces have exploited them, military forces have tried to control them and political forces have supported unpopular, undemocratic establishments.

The Philippines is the most recent example. Washington seems to have supported Ferdinand Marcos because it considered him the most reliable guarantor of the U.S. military bases there. Although intelligence reports must have indicated long ago the existence of the growing nationalist movement and the people's dissatisfaction with Marcos and his corrupt government, U.S. policy-makers seemed unable to decide on a course that would honor the Filipinos' right to determine their own destiny and that would dissociate the Administration from the dictator. As a result, public demonstrations during and after the elections bristled with signs and banners castigating the United States.

In Greece all the goodwill that the United States built up during the war, and immediately afterward with a massive aid program that put the economy back on its feet, was slowly dissipated as the nation became more and more dependent on the United States. Washington collaborated first with the Greek monarchy in deciding domestic political matters, then with the rightist government, in 1961, by recognizing fraudulent elections, and finally with the colonels, in 1967, by accepting and eventually strengthening their seven-year dictatorship.

Anti-Americanism reached its peak in 1974, when the dictatorship of the colonels fell; it has diminished considerably since then, as the Pasok government follows a pro-Greek independent foreign policy that is grudingly accepted by the Reagan Administration. The Greeks watch what the United States does in the rest of the world and draw their own conclusions. During the dictatorial rule in Greece, when the United States was involved in the Vietnam War, a war which pitted a giant industrial military machine against a peasant society, even the colonels found it difficult to give open and enthusiastic support to the American side.

Central Intelligence Agency interventions overseas, support for "friendly" dictators, the overthrow of the Allende government in Chile, Watergate, the efforts to overthrow the Sandinista regime, the nuclear arms buildup—all have served to strengthen the image of the United States as an aggressive, ruthless and unethical nation. For Americans to understand anti-Americanism they must take off their cultural blinders and see their country as others see it. They must recognize that America's vast military and economic power does not give it the right

153

to interfere in other nations' development or to frustrate their efforts to achieve independence. To the contrary, it antagonizes their people.

This does not mean that millions of people in the world would not want to live in America. The American way of life, insofar as it applies to those who live in America, continues to be envied. America still stands for opportunity and individual freedom. It means diversity, natural beauty, creativity, dynamism, vitality. But that is not the point, though it may be why Americans are distressed and puzzled about anti-Americanism. They are so convinced that their society is unique, just and good—and this is a conviction that permeates the consciousness of many who grow up in the United States—that they fail to understand criticism of their government's international actions.

The way to fight anti-Americanism is with an enlightened policy of international relations that would seek to break down the global war system and establish a permanent peace; that would avoid intervention in the affairs of other nations but provide moral support to popular democratic forces; and that would rein in the military industrial complex, which affects so many things—the trade balance, the direction of industrial growth, the choice of technology, the rate at which natural resources are extracted, the status of women, even the culture, values and aspirations of people.

These are not unrealistic proposals. One could make the case that they advance "national security interests." They are unworkable only in that there may not be the kind of leadership in Washington that wants to pursue them or that the vested interests opposing them are too deeply entrenched. But given the situation today—a world economic crisis, social unrest and turmoil, and an arms race that is driving the world toward oblivion—these are the only realistic policies. They will make it possible for the world to see the United States with new eyes.

MARGARET RANDALL   (MEXICO/U.S.A.)

MEMORY SAYS YES

All last week you preened before the mirror
viewing emerging breasts, then covering them
with gauze-thin blouse

and grinning: getting bigger, huh?
The week before you wore army fatigues
leveling breasts and teenage freckles,
tawny fuzz along your legs.
A Woman. Beginning.
Today you don fatigues again.
Today you pack, knapsack and canteen,
lace boots over heavy socks
and answer the call Reagan and Haig have slung
at your 12 years.
Yours and so many others . . .
kids, 14, 15, 18, so many others who will go
and some of them stay, their mothers shouting
before Honduran Embassy: "Give us
our sons' bodies back, give us back their bodies!"
At least that.
All last week you preened before the mirror,
moving loose to new rhythms
long weekend nights, Junior High math. Sunday beach.
Today you went off to the staccato of continuous
        news dispatches
and I, in my trench, carry your young breasts
in my proud lonely eyes.

ROCHELLE RATNER (U.S.A.)

BORDERS

Just before a storm
we sit on the porch.
You have been picking berries.
Soon we will go to dinner.

While the others are inside
I ask you how it felt
to grow up in Berlin
with the Wall dividing you

and in broken English
you try to explain
how you lived in East Berlin
and were on vacation
when it happened

you were among the lucky ones
then a new police force;
though the Wall was unexpected
all the bricks were laid.

You say thank God
there was no fighting—
after the first months, that is

and I thank God
we did not live in the South
where there were riots
and my father would have been
among the first attacked.

I am thinking of Israel,
how what Jews say of Arabs
sounded so familiar,
how what began as pride
got out of hand

and I wonder
whether to tell you this.
Uwe, what I should have said was
the borders are inside us.

ELEANOR ROOSEVELT (U.S.A.)

A CHALLENGE FOR THE WEST

I was oh! so happy when our airplane, flying out of Moscow, touched
down at Copenhagen, the first stop in the non-Communist world on
our way back to the United States. For three weeks in the Soviet Union,
I had felt more than at any time in my life that I was cut off from all
of the outside world. For three weeks, I do not believe I had heard any-

one really laugh on the streets or in a crowd. I had been among hospitable people but they were people who worked hard, who lived under considerable strain and who were tired. It was only after I had landed at Copenhagen and heard laughter and gay talk and saw faces that were unafraid that I realized how different were our two worlds. Suddenly, I could breathe again!

But, as I remarked earlier, I was rather frightened, too, and after I reached home my nagging fear continued. I was—I still am—afraid that Americans and the peoples of the rest of the free world will not understand the nature of the struggle against Communism as exemplified by the Soviet Union. It is urgently important for the sake of our country and our people that we get rid of some of our great misunderstandings and that we see clearly the things that must be done.

We are in a great struggle between two vastly different ways of life. While we must have guns, atomic weapons and missiles for retaliation against aggression, they are not going to win this struggle or prevent a catastrophic world war. Nor is belief in the idea of democracy likely to have great effect in areas where democratic institutions are not established. To overemphasize the importance of military power or to propagate merely the abstract idea of democracy is to miss the point. There is much, much more to be done if Western leadership is to be accepted by the masses of the world's underdeveloped countries, if our way of life and our hard-won freedoms are to survive—or, perhaps, if anything is to survive in the Atomic Age—and flourish. We must provide leadership for free peoples, but we must never forget that in many countries, particularly in Asia and Africa, the freedom that is uppermost in the minds of the people is the freedom to eat.

I think it is time for us Americans to take a good look at ourselves and our shortcomings. We should remember how we achieved the aims of freedom and democracy. We should look back in an effort to gauge how we can best influence the peoples of the world. Perhaps we made the greatest impression on underdeveloped countries in the 1930's when we ourselves were making a tremendous effort to fight our way out of a great economic depression. In that period, we united behind bold ideas and vigorous programs and, as they watched us, many people in far countries of the world began to realize that a government could be intensely interested in the welfare of the individual. They saw what was happening and it gave them hope that it could happen to them, too. That was a generation ago, but again today, it seems to me that it is essential for us to examine carefully our actions as a nation and try to develop a program for the welfare of the individual.

In this connection, I was sometimes astonished during my visit to Russia to see what the Soviet Government had brought about during four decades of Communist dictatorship. Illiteracy, which was once 90 per cent, has been reduced until it is now probably less than 10 per cent. The people have been educated in every field—crafts, arts, professions, sciences—and the government has used the educational system for political purposes, to shape the people to the will of the leadership. Educators are sent where they are most important for the purposes of the government. Doctors are sent where they can be most useful. Workers are sent to distant areas of Asia because new fields must be plowed and crops planted. This is dictatorship and it is hateful; but the results achieved by the Soviet regime are obvious to anyone visiting Russia. The water is pure; the milk is clean; the food supply is increasing; industry has made mighty strides. The people are better off materially each year. They know very little of other countries and they are willing to accept a hard life because of Communist propaganda that unites them in fear of aggression by the United States. Furthermore most of them are sustained by a belief in communistic aims.

In this book I have tried to tell a few of the things I saw and learned in Russia and to show what they mean to the people if we look at the Soviet achievements through Russian eyes. They mean a great deal—hope for a better life—to the Russian masses, and Communist propaganda, deceptive though it is, may make them mean something to the peoples of underdeveloped countries that as yet are uncommitted in the struggle between democracy and Communism. This is why we must realize that we are involved in much more than a military struggle.

The Russians recognize that there are vast masses of people in Asia, Africa and parts of Latin America who are closer to the economic conditions that existed forty years ago in Russia than they are to the conditions that have existed for many years in the United States. The leaders of the Soviets can say to them: "We know your conditions. Our people were once hungry, too, not only for food but for health and education, for knowledge and for hope for the future. Look at what we have done in forty years! Take heart. We can help you."

This is the challenge to democracy. This is the real challenge, and it cannot be met by mere words. We have to show the world by our actions that we live up to the ideals we profess and demonstrate that we can provide all the people in this country with the basic decencies of life, spiritually as well as materially. In the United States we are the showcase for the possibilities inherent in a free world, in democracy. If the lives of our people are not better in terms of basic satisfactions as well as in material ways than the lives of people anywhere in the world, then the uncommitted peoples we need on our side will look for leadership elsewhere. . . .

DOROTHY ROWE (ENGLAND)

WHY IS THERE SO MUCH APPALLING CRUELTY IN THE WORLD?

Why is there so much appalling cruelty in the world? Cruelty is not just to those we call our enemies but cruelty to ourselves and the world we live in. For is it not cruel that we have created for the human race a future which could be as brief as four minutes but will be no longer than 150 years. A nuclear war, triggered by national pride or mere computer failure, could eradicate most of us in four minutes and the rest of us in a nuclear winter and its aftermath. Even if we avoid this, the rate at which we are despoiling the planet, cutting down the trees on which our oxygen supply depends, polluting the oceans, killing the life that exists in our rivers and lakes, disrupting the delicate network of life on earth, means that if we do not come to our senses and seek to preserve rather than destroy, then this planet will be unable to continue to support human life for much longer. Meanwhile, as our population increases so does the devastation by natural disasters, created or aggravated by the stripping of the forests and the poverty which forces more and more people to live in disaster-prone areas. Attempts to relieve or eradicate the problems of poverty and population founder on the rocks of greed, corruption and a system of international banking whose stability is undermined by the massive debts of the Third World countries.

The warnings are there all the time for us to see. The planes fly overhead, the missiles are installed. Our newspapers, radio and television show us in words and pictures what cruelty we inflict on one another, either directly by killing and maiming, or indirectly by allowing such cruelty to continue. Some of us heed these warnings and try, in ways which seem puny and ineffective, to alter the course of human history so that the human race will not only continue to exist but will live with greater love and understanding. However, most of us are ignoring the warnings and go on living our lives as if all is well and life will continue forever on this bountiful planet. But denial of reality, that is, lying to yourself, is the most costly error you can ever make. Reality does not become unreal. You do. Our present world is full of people who are unreal to themselves, who do not know themselves. It is they who will destroy us all.

SOOK LYOL RYU (SOUTH KOREA)

POEM BY A YELLOW WOMAN

When I first saw America,
it was like a huge giant,
and I was like a pygmy woman.
I made a desperate struggle with this giant
not to fall. He whistled merrily, waving his hands.
He was a huge man, but a man like a snake.

Now, here I am in America, where
people drink Coca-Cola, where
people are crazy about Spielberg's silly films, where
people chase endless desires, where
people choose an old anachronistic
movie star as their president, where
people enjoy powerful wealth,
but keep homeless people in the street, where
people shout, "ladies first,"
and don't allow a woman to be president.
Now here I am from the country, where
the people are burning American flags,
singing, "Yankee, go home!"
Now here I am in America, where
most of my yellow people are hungry
for McDonald's and greedy for "Made in U.S.A."
My brother who has a master's degree in English literature
thinks about Norman Mailer's American Dream
while selling fishes and vegetables
to his white neighbors 24 hours a day.
My sister, who liked paintings of
Picasso's Blue Period
is working on a sewing machine, with dyed blond hair.

When colored friends are making a rainbow coalition,
my yellow people wonder whether yellow is on the rainbow.
They think the lighter the skin, the closer to heaven,
the darker the skin, the closer to hell.
They decide yellow is in between.
So they smile at white and frown at black.
They make money in the hope of becoming a majority
and forget about the minority.

Now, here I am torn between
my own self-flattery and my own revolt.
When I think about the Native Americans
who were deprived of their land, my stomach cramps.
When I think about the African slaves
who were stolen from their land, I throw up.

Now here I am in America, where
I develop a serious ulcer, a sickness of wrath.

YOLANDA SANCHEZ (PUERTO RICO)

FIFTY THOUSAND PUERTO RICAN PEOPLE DEMONSTRATE AGAINST U.S. NUCLEAR PROLIFERATION

In August of this year [1984] the Puerto Rican Bar Association released its study on nuclear arms and a review and analysis of the 1967 treaty which attempts to create a nuclear free zone in Latin America and the Caribbean. The treaty resulted from meetings convened by the presidents of Mexico, Bolivia, Brazil, Chile and Ecuador, an international call to action. After four years of meetings and discussions, the treaty was finalized and, at least on paper, created a nuclear free zone covering the Southern Hemisphere. It is our contention that although the United States signed the treaty, it has failed to abide by its terms. Specifically, we find that Puerto Rico has become a major communications and staging area for the United States. A review of the official documents under the Freedom of Information Act proves conclusively that installations are in place on the island, making it a nerve center for United States nuclear policy and response in Central America and the Caribbean.

The Puerto Rican Bar Association study is being politicized. It has become a tool for community education. The issue has suddenly and dramatically become a very real and concrete one. A recent demonstration drew fifty thousand people into the streets. Here, as there, it is a matter of public and community education. The issue is here; the threat is real. Our call to action in the Puerto Rican communities will be based on connecting the lack of needed services to the proliferation of arms.

Olive Schreiner (south africa)

BEARERS OF MEN'S BODIES

There is, perhaps, no *woman*, whether she have borne children, or be merely a potential child-bearer, who could look down on a battlefield covered with the slain, but the thought would rise in her, "So many mothers' sons! So many bodies brought into the world to lie there! So many months of weariness and pain while bones and muscles were shaped within; . . . so many baby mouths drawing life at woman's breasts;—all this, that men might lie with glazed eyeballs and swollen bodies, and fixed, blue, unclosed mouths, and great limbs tossed—this, that an acre of ground might be manured with human flesh!" . . .

In a besieged city, it might well happen that men in the streets might seize upon statues and marble carvings from public buildings and galleries and hurl them in to stop the breaches made in their ramparts by the enemy . . . not valuing them more than if they had been paving stones. But one man could not do this—the sculptor! He, who, though there might be no work of his own chisel among them, yet knew what each of these works of art had cost, knew by experience the long years of struggle and study and the infinitude of toil which had gone to shaping of even one limb, to the carving of even one perfected outline, he could never so use them without thought of care. . . . Men's bodies are our women's works of art. Given to us power to control, we will never carelessly throw them in to fill up the gaps in human relationships made by international ambitions and greeds. . . .

War will pass when intellectual culture and activity have made possible to the female an equal share in the governance of modern national life; it will probably not pass away much sooner; its extinction will not be delayed much longer.

It is especially in the domain of war that we, the bearers of men's bodies, who supply its most valuable munition, who not amid the clamour and ardour of battle, but, singly, and alone, with a three-in-the-morning courage, shed blood and face death that the battle-field may have its food, a food more precious to us than our heart's blood; it is we especially, who in the domain of war, have our word to say, a word no man can say for us. It is our intention to enter into the domain of war and to labour there till in the course of generations we have extinguished it.

JONI SEAGER AND ANN OLSON (CANADA AND U.S.A.)

WOMEN IN THE WORLD

Poverty

Worldwide, the largest poverty groups are, first, women-headed households, and second, the elderly (a greater proportion of whom are women because women live longer than men). Together, these two groups represent on average 70 per cent of the poor in most countries in the world. Poverty is rapidly being feminized. The scattered statistics that are available tell the same story worldwide: in the USA, 78 per cent of all people living in poverty are women or children under the age of 18; in Australia, the proportion is 75 per cent; in Canada, 60 per cent of all women over the age 65 live in poverty. . . .

Refugees

Not only do women comprise the majority of refugees, but they also suffer greater hardships as refugees. Women as refugees are still expected to perform the tasks of childcare, cleaning, cooking and collecting fuel and water, but often without resources. Family survival depends on women's ability to adjust and compensate for impoverishment. Women also suffer considerable abuse. Rape by camp guards, border guards, and other refugees is all too common; the most publicized case of refugee rape is the constant marauding of refugee boats in the China Sea, where it is estimated that over 2400 women have been raped by pirates. . . . Though 80 per cent of the world's refugees are women, and women also represent about 80 per cent of health care workers in refugee camps, they have little control over the administration of camps and little voice in the development of national or international refugee policies. . . .

The Vote

Women are still not fully enfranchised worldwide. Despite growing protests, the Kuwaiti government refuses to grant women the vote. . . . In Bhutan, "a one vote per family" rule means that men almost exclusively claim the right. Hong Kong has property restrictions that prevent some men, and a lot of women, from voting. And in South Africa, black women and men are still denied the vote. . . .

Government

The importance of women's recent gains in political power must be measured against the fact that even in the best cases women represent only about 25 per cent of elected national officials. In many countries women have no share of political power. This is certainly true in all countries ruled by militaries. . . . As of 1985, there were no women in the politburos of Bulgaria, Czechoslovakia, E. Germany, the USSR or Vietnam, and only one woman in the politburos of China, Poland, Romania and Yugoslavia. When women do hold cabinet posts, they are often appointments in areas considered to lie within women's traditional interests—women get appointed to be Ministers of Consumer Affairs, not Ministers of Defence. . . .

LAYLE SILBERT (U.S.A.)

THE ENEMY

the enemy
are imperfect men
often squat
hung with large genitalia
they have aortas too awkward
to pump their off-color blood
well
to the tissues of the brain
to feed & ventilate
the neurons of language & the arts

we are not believers
in their pain

Ruth Sivard (u.s.a.)

WORLDWIDE MILITARY PRIORITIES LEAVE SOCIAL PROGRAMS IN THE DUST

In 1986, the nations of the world spent about $30,000 per soldier in running their military forces. For the education of each school-age child they will allocate an average of $455.

This comparison clearly shows how social programs everywhere take second place to armed might. . . . Militarization has made further inroads into a world economy already overburdened by weapons of mass destruction, poverty and debt. Military forces spent an all-time high of about $900 billion in 1986 . . . about $1.7 million each minute.

. . . Around the world, one adult in three cannot read or write; in developing countries, one person in five is undernourished. And the extra spending needed to make inroads against these problems is small compared to the expense of maintaining standing armies. . . . This year the U.N. stopped a locust plague in Africa at half the cost of an hour's world military outlay, saving enough grain to feed 1.2 million people. The bulk of world armaments spending is done by two nations—the United States and the Soviet Union. Together the superpowers, with less than 11 percent of the world's population, account for 60 percent of the world defense expenditures. . . . But defense spending is increasing fastest in the areas that can least afford it—the third world. Military expenditures by underdeveloped nations have gone up 800 percent since 1960, after adjusting for inflation. . . . Ethiopia, for instance, spent $525 million to buy new arms in 1983. . . .

Marina Tsvetayeva (u.s.s.r.)

VERSES TO CHEKHIA, 1938

They grabbed fast, they grabbed big,
grabbed the mountains and their innards.
They grabbed our coal, and grabbed our steel
from us. They grabbed our lead and crystal.

They grabbed the sugar, and they grabbed the clover.
They grabbed the North and grabbed the West.
They grabbed the hive and grabbed the haystack.
They grabbed the South from us and grabbed the East.

They grabbed Vary and grabbed Tatras.
They grabbed the near at hand and the far off.
But worse than grabbing heaven on earth from us,
they won the fight for our native land.

They stole our bullets from us. They stole our rifles.
They grabbed our minerals and our loved ones, too.
But while our mouths hold spit,
the entire country remains armed.

. . . .

Such weeping now fills our eyes,
crying with anger and passion.
Chekia's weeping.
Spain lying in its own blood,

and what a dark mountain
now shades the earth from light.
Now's the time, now's the time, now's the time
to give the billet back to God.

I decline to exist in the crazy house
of the inhuman.
I decline to go on living
in the marketplace of wolves.

I won't howl,
among the sharks of the field.
I won't swim beneath
the waves of squirming backs.

I have no need of holes for hearing
or seeing eyes.
To your crazed world there's
only one answer: No!

(Translated by Daniela Gioseffi with Sophia Buzevska)

BARBARA TUCHMAN (U.S.A.)

POLITICIANS AND TELEVISION

As the world grows more complex and more in need of expert handling in foreign relations, we must not rest content with persons who merely look good on television. . . . Our electoral choices now become crucial, and one hopes they will be founded on a basis more mature than the televised-TelePrompter-artificial images picked by professional fund raisers and advertising companies. . . . The American people [for one example] in the era of television, are not very smart about their political understanding. What is needed . . . is more political sense. . . .

CHRISTA WOLF (EAST GERMANY)

BREAD AND BOMBS

"Knowledge which has not passed through the senses can produce none but destructive truth" (Leonardo da Vinci). There could truly be a new renaissance of consciousness if this insight were to bear fruit again, after the long dangerous experiment with abstract rationality, which resulted in thinking that everything is a means to an end. What speaks against this possibility? The fact that the senses of many people—through no "fault" of their own—have dried up, and that they are justifiably afraid to reactivate them. . . . What loss would mankind suffer if it were deprived of "European man" as is now being contemplated? What can we plead in our own favor? The fact that it was Europeans who, by subjugating and exploiting other peoples and continents, learned—or confirmed—that consciousness of mastery and race which determined the direction of technological development (including development of weapons technology), as well as the structures of the economy and of nations? The fact that we ourselves brought into the world the forces which threaten us? That the megamachine, in its destructive irrationality, represents the final end product of our culture? . . . On the sixth of August, the anniversay of the day the bomb was dropped on Hiroshima, the American President made the decision

167

to build the neutron bomb; the Secretary of Defense revealed that the first warheads have been mounted and could be in Western Europe in a few hours in case they were needed there. This would be our death sentence, I thought; but what did I really feel? Helplessness. I put breakfast on the table in the yard. Talked with the others. Laughed. . . . On the evening of August 6, a documentary film about a Japanese family in Hiroshima. The wife was pregnant when she was exposed to radiation, gave birth to a handicapped daughter and in 1979 died miserably of the delayed effects: bone cancer. The camera showed the states of disintegration. The husband who is a barber. The face of the helpless daughter, who does little things to help out when her mother can no longer do anything for herself. The doctor who tells the wife that her spine has been "affected." The neighbor woman who comes to visit her regularly. The two women's heartrending goodbye. Every time the sick woman's position is shifted, she has to be afraid that one of her brittle bones will break. Her face weeping. Her emaciated arms, imploring hands. The daughter weeping. She refuses to separate from her dead mother at the funeral. Weeks later she asks to go to the cemetery. Kisses the smooth stone on her mother's grave. A class of schoolchildren who have seen this film are taking an interest in the family's fate. Most young people in Japan know nothing about the effects of Hiroshima.

No document could be more moving. It would not have the slightest effect on those in charge of weapons deployment, even if they should see it. Why not? Would it not, in this case, be better to be moved than to make a move? What if no one who works with weapons would lift a finger anymore? Then they would all be unemployed. So what? you think. Better unemployed than dead. But that is not how they think, for they fear certain societal death more than uncertain physical death. These are what I call false alternatives. Their number is increasing. . . . Discussion with an economic official, likeable man. His feeling that we have "passed the zenith." He feels sorry for those who are young today. Great skepticism regarding the future. But, his conviction that nations and their economy can be governed only by yardsticks of competition and performance remains incontestable. It amazes me, though, that even the realization that we are unable to solve life-critical problems does not bring such people to reflect on the relationship that exists, for example, between the arms race and patriarchal structures of thought and government. . . .

VIRGINIA WOOLF (ENGLAND)

AS A WOMAN, MY COUNTRY IS THE WHOLE WORLD

. . . if you insist upon fighting to protect me, or "our" country, let it be understood, soberly and rationally between us, that you are fighting to gratify a sex instinct which I cannot share; to procure benefits which I have not shared and probably will not share; but not to gratify my instincts, or to protect either myself or my country. For, the outsider will say, in fact, as a woman, I have no country. As a woman I want no country. As a woman, my country is the whole world. . . .

Notes on Selections and Authors, Part II:

KAREN ALKALAY-GUT (b. 1945) lives in Israel where she has taught at the University of Tel Aviv. She was born in London and grew up in the United States. She is the author of books of poetry published in Israel and numerous critical articles published in the United States, Canada, and Great Britain. She has translated plays, stories, and poems from Hebrew into English, and organized and chaired the Association of Writers in English under the auspices of the Federation of Writers in Israel. These poems were written to a Lebanese friend in Beirut during the June 1982 bombings.

MAYA ANGELOU (b. 1928) is a contemporary writer of the United States, best known for her novels, *I Know Why the Caged Bird Sings* and *Gather Together in My Name.* She has authored several volumes of poetry concerned with social injustice. She brings an accessible lyricism to such themes. A member of the American Film Institute, she has written several screenplays and received four honorary degrees from various institutions of higher learning, including Smith College in Northampton, Massachusetts.

MILA D. ANGUILAR (b. 1952) is a Filipino journalist, activist, mother, and poet who on August 6, 1984, was arrested and placed in solitary confinement in a prison in Manila for writing these and other poems. She was thirty-two years of age when she was charged with "subversion and conspiracy to commit rebellion," because of her writing. A committee for her release was formed by the Philippine Research Center in New England—aided by American social justice activists. Since the Filipino revolution, many political prisoners under Marcos were released. According to the latest reports in *The Non-Violent Activist,* many revolutionaries are again in jail under the Aquino government.

AN ANONYMOUS AFGHAN WOMAN who was shot fleeing with her daughters from a prison camp in Kabul scribbled this testimony found in a refugee camp by a journalist who brought it out of the country to be translated. Malalai, mentioned in the prose poem, is a Pushtun woman who carried the

169

Afghan flag through the battle of Maiwand against the occupying British forces in the nineteenth century. She is a heroine, legendary among her people. Rabia Balkhi, mentioned next, is another, a poet and philosopher who died in resistance. Naheed, also mentioned, is a modern heroine, a young schoolgirl who led her classmates in a resistance march against the Russian dictatorship. During the demonstration, Russian soldiers fired at the unarmed schoolgirls and many were martyred. What this Afghan woman writes is very similar *in content* to what the Russian poet Anna Akhmatova wrote in *Requiem*—an eminent internationally known work of literature written in the years of Stalin. Tat'yana Mamonova, Natalya Malakhovskaya, Yuliya Voznesenskaya, Tat'yana Goricheva are among a group of Soviet women who were exiled in 1980 for their part in a protest against their government's interventionary war in Afghanistan. Quoted in a book from Indiana University Press, titled *Soviet Sisterhood,* by Barbara Holland, their appeal said, "Women of Russia! Do not let your husbands and sons become the victims of this bloody slaughter! Explain to them how disgraceful and criminal it is to be the aggressor in a foreign country. . . ." When these Soviet women heard of the young schoolgirls' peaceful demonstration and how it was fired upon by government troops, they issued another statement which acknowledged that the participation of young girls in the resistance struggle was an example of modern women's fight against tyranny around the world.

MARGARET ATWOOD (b. 1939), internationally known Canadian novelist and poet, feminist author of the recently acclaimed, *The Handmaid's Tale,* in her prose poem, helps us to understand the basic desperation and primal reality which can lead to war. She has won many literary prizes.

GIOCONDA BELLI (b. 1948) is a prizewinning Nicaraguan poet who has publblished several books of poems, among them *Linea De Fuego,* for which she won the Casa de las Americas prize—an important literary prize of South and Central America—in 1978, and *Amor Insurrector,* 1984.

CAROL COHN (b. 1951) is a senior research fellow at the Center for Psychological Studies in the Nuclear Age in Cambridge, Massachusetts. She is a research associate in psychiatry at the Harvard Medical School. Previously, she was on the faculty of Seminar College at the New School for Social Research in New York City. She is currently working on a book about the language and thinking of nuclear defense intellectuals, under a Research and Writing Grant from the John D. and Catherine T. MacArthur Foundation. A longer version of this article can be read in the Summer 1987 issue of *Signs: A Journal of Women in Culture and Society* published by the University of Chicago Press.

JAYNE CORTEZ (b. 1936), whom the poet Gwendolyn Brooks has called "energy, a nourishment, a Black Nation song," has written more than five books of poetry, has traveled throughout the United States, West Africa, Europe, and the Caribbean, reciting her work. Born in Arizona, she grew up in California and is currently living in New York City. Her poems have been published in *New Black Voices, Free Spirits, Presence Africaine,* and the *UNESCO Courier.* Her poem is from *Coagulations,* which contains many other poems on the nuclear threat and causes of war.

MYRNA CUNNINGHAM (b. *c.*1941) is a Miskito Indian physician who grew up in Bilwaskarma on the Río Coco dividing Honduras from Nicaragua—an area frequently under siege in the current conflict. She later returned to work in a Moravian hospital there. In 1981, she and other health workers were kidnapped and taken to Honduras by U.S.-sponsored Contras. She and a nurse were raped and beaten while captive and the hospital was vandalized and later closed because of the danger of further attacks. The situation of Miskito Indians amounting to a near genocide, caught between Contras and Sandinistas, shows a similarity with, for example, Ukrainians during World War II caught between Fascism and Communism.

DOROTHY DAY (1897–1980) was an American labor organizer and editor of *The Catholic Worker* who wrote movingly of conditions among the poor and working class. She was instrumental in creating a radical Catholic participation in the nonviolent peace and social justice movement in America—particularly during the Vietnam war protests.

MARGUERITE DURAS (b. 1914) is a contemporary French novelist and author of many internationally known books. She recently wrote of the war crimes of World War II in her critically acclaimed memoir, titled *The War*, about life in Paris during those eventful and trying years. The entire book is an insight into what is often women's lot during times of war, as they wait in tense anxiety in suspended lives for soldiers or loved ones to return from the front lines or from prison camps.

KATHY ENGEL (b. 1955) is a peace and social justice activist who lives in New York City with her husband and child. She is executive director of MADRE, a national friendship association with the women and children of Central America and the Caribbean. She serves on the Advisory Board of SISSA (Sisterhood in Support of Sisters in Southern Africa) and has devoted much of her life to such causes. She was one of the cultural coordinators of the massive June 12, 1982, peace and nuclear disarmament march and rally in New York City which drew well over 800,000 Americans from around the country. Also, she has worked for Mobilization for Survival, a national organization devoted to such issues.

ORIANA FALLACI (b. 1934) of Italy is among the first women to forge a reputation in international journalism. She wrote for many years for the distinguished Milan journal, *L'Europeo*. Her articles have appeared in major periodicals throughout the world and she has achieved many awards for her writing. She is the author of several books, including *The Egotists*, which contains interviews of leading political figures, and *Nothing, and So Be It*, on her experiences as a journalist in Vietnam. These passages are from her historical novel, *A Man*, on the life of a Greek resistance fighter. She speaks through the voice of her hero.

RANDALL FORSBERG (b. 1943), a MacArthur Foundation Fellowship winner, is the founder and director of the Institute for Defense and Disarmament Studies, a nonprofit research and education center in Brookline, Massachusetts. Ms. Forsberg worked at the Stockholm International Peace Research Institute, where she conducted a two-year study of worldwide military research and development programs. From 1972 through 1982, she published what were regarded as the most accurate figures available on the arms race between the superpowers. In 1980, Ms. Forsberg drafted the "Call to Halt the Nuclear Arms Race," which became the manifesto of the Nuclear Freeze Campaign and went on to chair the Freeze Campaign's National Advisory Board. Her article, "A Bi-lateral Nuclear-Weapons Freeze," published in the November 1982 issue of *Scientific American,* now read in the Soviet Union, too, became the main statement of the case for a freeze and was widely distributed throughout the world. The selection here is an edited version of a speech to the first Deadly Connections Conference held at the Massachusetts Institute of Technology, Cambridge.

NATALIA GINZBURG (b. 1916), an internationally known Italian author of several books, including *All My Yesterdays,* and *Family Sayings,* who lives in Rome, escaped to a small village in the Abruzzi to live during World War II. Her husband, a resistance fighter, was imprisoned, tortured, and finally murdered by the Nazis. In this personal essay from a book titled *The Little Virtues,* she explains what it was like to live through that war and the indelible mark it has left on the lives that survived it. Those who live in lands which have not known such torment experience, through such writers, the reality and knowledge that might motivate preventative involvement.

DANIELA GIOSEFFI (b. 1941) is a U.S. poet, novelist, and literary critic, who has been an educator for many years. Her poems, *Eggs in the Lake,* won an award/grant from the National Endowment for the Arts. Her novel, *The Great American Belly,* was published in New York, London, and Zagreb. An international treatise on the woman's dance of birth and life, as counterpart to the male war dance in folk cultures, *Earth Dancing: Mother Nature's Oldest Rite,* is related in theme to *Women on War.* She serves as president of her area chapter of SANE/FREEZE. With fellow workers in the book industry in America, she serves on the board of the *Writers and Publishers Alliance for Nuclear Disarmament* and has won an award from *The Ploughshares Fund,* an independent peace foundation, under the category of Women's Leadership Development. She was active in the civil rights movement in the early 1960s, and has read, taught, and lectured widely throughout the United States and Europe. She is a professor of communication arts and creative writing. As do Nadine Gordimer, Oriana Fallaci, or Bella Akhmadulina (see table of contents), she assumes the male persona for the purpose of her narrative.

EMMA GOLDMAN (1869–1940), born in Russia, immigrated to Rochester, New York, in 1886 and worked there in clothing factories. After a few years, she became active in the anarchist movement and her speeches to improve labor rights, or sweatshop conditions, such as those which still exist in many areas of the world, including the United States, attracted attention throughout North America. She began publication of *Mother Earth,* an anarchist journal for the working classes, was imprisoned for public advocacy of birth control, and later for obstruction of the draft before being deported in 1919 to Russia. She soon left Russia because of her disagreement with the Bolshevik government. Allowed reentry to the United States in 1924, but forced to refrain from public lectures on political issues, she still managed to take an active role in the Spanish Civil War in 1936. A cultured and widely read woman, she published many books, among them *Anarchism and Other Essays,* 1911, from which this excerpt is taken.

NADINE GORDIMER (b. 1923) of South Africa has written extensively on the injustices of her native land. Her many novels are known throughout the world for their concern with human rights and the antiapartheid movement. A chief literary figure of our time and one of the most respected and internationally known writers of today, Gordimer, through the voice of her socialist hero in *Burger's Daughter,* delivers what might be viewed as the most eloquent speech against racism and the injustices of apartheid in contemporary fiction.

MARGHERITA GUIDACCI (b. 1921) is a native of Florence, Italy. She has published several books of poetry and is one of the best-known Italian poets of her generation. On the morning of August 2, 1980, a cartel of international neo-Nazi terrorists deposited a suitcase full of explosives in a corner of the second-class waiting room in the Bologna station. It was vacation time and the station was crowded. There were a great many people killed and wounded. The clock stopped at the moment of the explosion and has been left that way as a memorial. *Morte morieris,* mentioned in the poem, and inscribed on the Bologna Clock Memorial, means "Thou shalt die by death," and is from the biblical story of Cain and Abel.

JEHAN HELOU (b. 1943) was uprooted, with her family, from Haifa, Palestine, in 1948 and has been a refugee in foreign lands ever since. She has been active in the Palestinian struggle since 1967. In 1973, she received a master's degree in political science from the American University of Beirut. She continues to work with the Institute for Palestinian Studies in Lebanon. Her husband, Abou Omar, whom she married in 1972—a professor of political science who graduated from Harvard, and who taught for many years at the University of Seattle—joined the Palestinian struggle and was reported missing in Lebanon in 1976. He also worked for the Institute for Palestinian Studies. Jehan Helou serves as a member of The General Union of Palestinian Women and is Assistant Secretary of the Arab Women's Federation.

REYNA HERNANDEZ (b. 1962) participated, as a teenager, in combat for nine years as an urban and rural guerrilla fighter for her people in El Salvador. She suffered imprisonment for a year, but has more recently been able to resume her studies in Sweden where she now lives. She is one of the many poets of Central America collected by the American poet and peace activist Zoe Anglesey in a bilingual anthology of verse published by Bea Gates of the feminist Granite Press. Both Anglesey and Gates labored hard and long at personal sacrifice to bring these poets' voices to the American people.

HELEN KELLER (1880–1968) was an American author and pioneer educator of the blind who overcame her own severe nonhearing, nonseeing handicaps as a child. With the help of her teacher, Anne Sullivan, she progressed rapidly to graduate with honors from Radcliffe College in 1904. She proceeded to lecture throughout the United States and Europe, raising funds for the education of the blind. Her statement has increased profundity in our time when political experts like Barbara Tuchman (see p. 178), for example, point out that in the United States a multimillion-dollar campaign is required to be elected to the presidency, a governorship, or in many cases, even the Senate or House of Representatives.

CORETTA SCOTT KING (b. 1927), president of the Martin Luther King, Jr., Center for Non-Violent Social Change, is the widowed wife of Dr. King and mother of his children. She often marched side by side with her husband through the years of the civil rights struggle in America and continues to travel and lecture on behalf of the ideals she, herself, has always supported. Her declaration here, from a speech given at an international women's conference sponsored by the Center for Defense Information in Washington, D.C., augments the statistics given by Ruth Sivard, world economist (see p. 177).

JONG JI LEE (b. c.1965) is just one of thousands of young Korean college students who have been jailed for demonstrating against the despotic regime of Chun Doo Hwan, former dictator of South Korea. This letter, written in 1986, is one of hundreds collected into a book published by parents of incarcerated students who spend as much as five years or more in jail while awaiting for nothing more than a protest for a democratic election. The book, titled *Jailed Spirits to Imprisoned Minds,* was banned in South Korea where freedom of speech and the press do not really exist. If we consider that American students often do not exercise the right to vote—less than 50 percent of the voting age population in the United States has ever participated in a presidential election—and juxtapose that fact with what Korean or South African students suffer for the right to vote—we experience, in terms of the meaning of democracy, a terrible and profound irony.

DORIS LESSING (b. 1919) of South Africa is an internationally known writer of conscience. Her recent book on the Afghan crisis, *The Wind Blows Away Our Words,* illustrates how religious beliefs of indigenous peoples can be manipulated by opposing political forces and how interventionism, East and West, reigns with terror and confusion in the lives of innocent civilians, especially powerless women, around the globe. International peace movement leaders remind us that World War III is already being fought everywhere around the world and the danger is that shallow nuclear arms agreements can take our guard away from the volatility of the unrest, giving those in developed nations a false sense of security. Those with the power to make a change toward peace and disarmament, experts warn, must be aware of the constantly suffering populations where the so-called Cold War rages hot as hell in its deadly connection with the nuclear arms race.

ROSA LUXEMBURG (1870–1919) is one of the great figures of the world revolutionary movement. A nonviolent activist, she was born in Russian Poland. She studied law and economics in Zurich, Switzerland, and wrote a doctoral dissertation dealing with the development of industry in Poland. Settling in Germany, she became one of the leading writers and theorists of international socialism in the period preceding World War I. She broke with the Second International early in the war because much of the leadership supported the war effort in their countries at what she felt was the expense of the worker. She joined with Karl Liebknecht, peoples' martyr and founder of the Spartacus League, who was assassinated in 1919 by right-wing militarists. Rosa Luxemburg was murdered soon after by the same faction. This excerpt from her economic treatise, *The Accumulation of Capital,* an explanation of militarized economies, reminds us of South African miners or Central American plantation workers of today. According to such organizations as *The Council on Economic Priorities,* working classes continue to be taxed for their own demise in terms of the constant and hazardous development of chemical, biological, and nuclear warfare.

JOANNA MACY (b. 1929) is the well-known American author and founder of Interhelp, an organization for dealing with despair and the psychological realities of the threat of nuclear annihilation. It is her purpose to help people help themselves out of psychic numbing and despair by involving themselves in positive actions which will help to ensure their future and their children's. These words were spoken at a world peace conference of women in 1985, sponsored by the Center for Defense Information, in Washington, D.C.

KAREN MALPEDE (b. 1945) is a playwright and theater historian. She was cofounder, with Burl Hash, of New Cycle Theatre, a pacifist-feminist theater in Brooklyn, New York. Her plays include, *The End of the War, A Lament for Three Women, Making Peace: A Fantasy, A Monster Has Stolen the Sun,* and *Us.* Her books include *People's Theatre in America, Three Works by the Open Theatre,* and *Women in Theatre: Compassion and Hope.* As an influence on her own work, she has written of the internally known pacifist repertory, the Living Theatre of Judith Malina and Julian Beck. This is an excerpt from a much longer talk given at a Women's Conference on Non-Violence. Malpede expounds on a theme close to many modern playwrights, Luigi Pirandello among them, in *You Are What You Think You Are.*

LENORE MARSHALL (1899–1971) American peace activist, writer, founding member of SANE, who died in 1971 (see p. 71) made this essential observation concerning how hate and fear are engendered for the enemy by the use of what communication experts call "buzz" words—supercharged name calling used to create a stereotyped antagonist. Americans have been taught to hate the person called a Communist, as if communism could not be combined with democracy and freedom as was intended by its chief theorist, Karl Marx, and economic expounder, Rosa Luxemburg. Peace movement leaders East and West explain that it is thoroughly ensconced in the popular American mind with the evils of Stalinism, but need not be so. Much literature has been published by established presses in America, of late, on this point.

MARGARET MEAD (1901–1978) was an internationally known American anthropologist, who was at the beginning of her career a student and collaborator of Ruth Benedict of whom she wrote in *An Anthropologist at Work.* Mead's primary focus was on problems of child rearing, personality, and culture, and her major area of study was the peoples of Oceania. She was active with the World Federation of Mental Health and served as curator of ethnology for the American Museum of Natural History in New York City as well as a professor of anthropology at Columbia University.

MAIRE MHAC AN TSAOI (b. c.1935), also known as Maire Cruise O'Brien, a poet of Ireland, created this poem in her native Irish and then translated it into English. For the epigraph to Maire's poem, one might use one of the quatrains she translated from folk verse by men, under the title, *Poets in*

Adversity, as she takes a male point of view in her own ironic poem, "Hatred."

NICHOLASA MOHR (b. ?) is a prizewinning Puerto Rican–American writer of fiction who has written movingly about life in one of the poorest ghetto neighborhoods of New York, the South Bronx. This story, from her book *El Bronx Remembered,* demonstrates what Catholic socialist and peace activist Dorothy Day meant when she said, "Where the war on poverty ends, gang wars begin."

MARIA MONTESSORI (1870–1952), the renowned early-twentieth-century Italian educator who fostered a system of education still in operation throughout the world today, was also, throughout her life, concerned with the peace and social justice movement.

BHARATI MUKHERJEE (b. 1940) was born in Calcutta, India, and lived fifteen years in Canada after receiving her doctorate in Iowa. She is the author of two novels and two much-praised collections of short stories, *Darkness,* and her latest, *The Middleman and Other Stories.* She now teaches at Queens College and lives in New York City with her husband, Clark Blaise, with whom she has coauthored two nonfiction books.

ELIZABETH NUNEZ-HARRELL (b. 1942) comes from Trinidad. She now teaches at Medgar Evans College in New York City where she is chairperson of the Humanities Division. She is currently working on a book dealing with the American civil rights movement in order to understand how American blacks have dealt with the racism common to her island homeland. Here, in an excerpt from her book, *When Rocks Dance,* she portrays the mythological Calypso woman who fends off colonializing powers of intervention.

ALANIS OBAMSAWIN (b. *c.*1950), an Abenaki Indian woman raised on the Odanak Reserve in Quebec and later in Trois-Rivières, a French Canadian area, now lives in Montreal. She speaks her Native American languages as well as French and English, writing songs and making films about her people. She sees herself as a bridge between the indigenous peoples of her land and the colonialists who have come to dominate the population.

CHAILANG PALACIOS (b. *c.*1933) is a Chamorro woman from Saipan, in the northern Mariana Islands. She is a public health education worker. She traveled to Britain for a month-long tour—to speak out for Women Working for a Nuclear Free and Independent Pacific in March of 1985. As a child, she lived through World War II in the Pacific and has been a local witness to the devastation caused by nuclear testing among her island people.

GRACE PALEY (b. 1922), born Grace Goodside, is an award-winning American writer of fiction and poetry (see p. 72). She is best known for her poignant and humorous short stories about the lives of working-class New Yorkers. Her stories have appeared in three critically acclaimed volumes, *The Little Disturbances of Man, Enormous Changes at the Last Minute,* and *Later the Same Day,* from which this story comes. It illustrates, in a small subtle drama of everyday life, the psychological effect of buzzwords on the unguarded mind and the seeds of anger so basic to the state of war.

MARGARITA CHANT PAPANDREOU (b. 1923), head of World Women Parliamentarians for Peace, combines two cultures, American and Greek. She is the American-born wife of Prime Minister Andreas Papandreou of Greece, and she is president of a mass socialist, feminist organization, the Women's Union of Greece. Author of *Nightmare in Athens,* her keen journalism and written commentaries are known throughout the world.

MARGARET RANDALL (b. 1930) is a North American who has lived in Nicaragua, Cuba, and Mexico and traveled in Vietnam, Peru, and Chile. An international writer who for many years has been concerned with social justice and human rights, she has written with understanding of the plight of women in the countries where she has made her home. Her books on such relevant issues include, *From Witness to Struggle: Christians in the Nicaraguan Revolution; Cuban Women Now; Spirit of the People: Women in Vietnam; Sandino's Daughters; Inside the Nicaraguan Revolution.* She has done a good deal of translation from the Spanish and edited the literary magazine, *El Corno Emplumado.*

ROCHELLE RATNER (b. 1948) lives in New York City where she is a literary critic and executive editor of *American Book Review.* Her many books include *Bobby's Girl,* a novel, and *Practicing to Be a Woman: New and Selected Poems.* As a Jewish-American curious about her grandparents' European roots before World War II, she traveled in England and Israel and wrote poems of her experiences.

ELEANOR ROOSEVELT (1884–1962) married Franklin Delano Roosevelt in 1905, and when he ascended to the presidency, she became one of the most active presidential wives her country ever knew. Devoted to numerous social causes, she worked with many women's organizations active in furthering the rights of minorities and laborers. She traveled widely, lecturing, observing conditions, and promoting good causes. From 1945 to 1953, she served as U.S. delegate to the United Nations, and in 1946, she was made chairperson of the Commission on Human Rights, a subsidiary of the Economic and Social Council. Her tireless dedication to the cause of human welfare and world peace finally won her recognition from her former critics. Among her books are *The Moral Basis of Democracy* (1940) and *On My Own* (1958), concerning her travels in the Soviet Union and other Eastern-bloc nations.

DOROTHY ROWE (b. 1930) of Britain is known worldwide for her psychological writing on the causes of depression in our times. The author of several books, her most recent, *Living with the Bomb: Can We Live Without Enemies?* published in 1985, deals with the question of cruelty and our response to it as well as psychic numbing and apathy in our nuclear age. Her many books and lectures explain how inactivity leads to feelings of powerlessness and depression—where activism in the cause alleviates such feelings.

SOOK LYOL RYU (b. 1954) is a South Korean journalist who was one of hundreds of reporters involved in a free press movement in 1980—later expelled from their jobs as a result of repressive measures taken by the South Korean military regime for total control of the press. She has published poems in English and currently works with the Korean press in New York. She is a member of Korean-American Women-for-Action, a group which has worked to expose the brutality committed on South Korean students who have been beaten, raped, or killed during imprisoned interrogation by government police.

YOLANDA SANCHEZ (b. 1932), president of the National Latinas Caucus, explains how so called Third World women are more and more aware of "the deadly connection," detailed by Randall Forsberg (see p. 171). This is so not only in other countries of the world, but within the boundaries of powerfully developed nations, where the horrors of colonialization reach into the urban ghettos of the world to perpetuate poverty, giving resonance to the peace movements slogan: "Think globally, act locally!" Ms. Sanchez offered these important facts of history in a speech she gave in 1984 in Washington, D.C. An activist in East Harlem, she holds a degree in social science from Columbia University in New York.

OLIVE SCHREINER (1855–1920), South African author and feminist, was born in Cape Colony and spent much of her life working as a governess. She went to England where she published the manuscript of her first acclaimed novel, *The Story of an African Farm,* 1883, under the pseudonym of Ralph Iron. An intense portrayal of two children living in the African plains, it stirred controversy for its feminist and antireligious ideals and its exposure of hypocrisy. In her 1911 book titled *Woman and Labour,* she made this well-known declaration on women as childbearers or givers of life and laboring nurturers who are unfairly devoid of political powers or a say in war.

JONI SEAGER (b. 1954) and ANN OLSON (b. 1952), a Canadian and an American scientist, joined forces in creating a graphic book of facts and statistics, titled *Women in the World.* It displays the limits of women's economic, voting, and political power in the world today.

LAYLE SILBERT (b. ?) is an American poet living in New York City who is a well-known photographer of literary personalities. She has also published a book of short stories, *Imaginary People and Other Strangers.* A member of the PEN Women's Committee, she is a supporter of women's literature. Her ironic poem points to xenophobia as a cause of war.

RUTH SIVARD (b. 1915), an American who is one of the world's leading arms control economists, gave these astounding statistics in her 1987 report, excerpted in an article from the *Christian Science Monitor.* In 1988, the world's military expenditure has grown to an overall figure of $963 billion. A dramatic way of showing such an expenditure is to explain, for an example, that in the United States, the entire Food Stamp Program to feed hungry people does not cost the markup overhead on *one* nuclear bomber.

MARINA TSVETAYEVA (1892–1941) is considered by many to be among the finest poets Russia ever produced. Pasternak, among others, offered praise for her passionate work. She led a tragic life, disrupted by wars and political turmoil, caught between her loyalties to the White Russian Army and the Bolshevik Revolution. She experienced war's resultant poverty and periods of political exile. Though she declared that art for her was apolitical and her pen not capable of enlistment for civic good, she wrote many verses in a spirit of opposition to what Akhmatova, Pasternak, Mandelshtam, or others called "The Terrible Years" of purges under Stalin's dictatorship. She lost her youngest daughter to starvation during the Moscow famine of 1919 and suffered great despair when her husband was accused of being a Soviet agent. Her husband was arrested and shot. Later, her son was killed in the war. Marina was evacuated to Yelabuga. In 1941, in total despair, harassed and destitute, she committed suicide. In this poem, Tsvetayeva is referring to the German invaders and the country we now know as Czechoslovakia, then called "Chekhia" by the Russians.

BARBARA TUCHMAN (b. 1912), noted historian and political commentator, is the American author of a historical analysis of war titled *The March of Folly*. Thinking of the threat of nuclear, biological, and chemical war, the possibility of dire economic slowdown, the rape of environment needed for food and water, increasing chemical pollution, and the necessity for new sources of safe and clean energy, she recently made these comments on the dangers of the American electoral process.

CHRISTA WOLF (b. 1929) is considered one of East Germany's most prominent novelists. Her 1984 book is titled *Cassandra*—after the murdered Greek prophetess who told of the disaster that would befall Troy and whose warnings were wrongly ignored. The book, which connects the current threat of disaster and omnicide with patriarchal structures of government and competitive national economies, has become renowned throughout Europe and among U.S. feminists and activists. This commentary is from the journals or diary which follow upon the novel *Cassandra* and are a part of it. They were written in August of 1981, at about the time of the anniversary of Hiroshima. Her novel, *Divided Heaven* (1963), is known worldwide.

VIRGINIA WOOLF (1882–1941), English novelist and essayist, was a successful innovator of modern fiction. She was a member of the Bloomsbury group, which included Dora Carrington and Lytton Strachey, John Maynard Keynes, E. M. Forster, and others. Author of many books, she wrote two feminist tracts, *A Room of One's Own* (1930) and *Three Guineas* (1938) from which this quotation comes.

PART III

Violence, Mourning, Courage, and Resistance

It is organized violence on the top which creates individual violence at the bottom.

—EMMA GOLDMAN (U.S.S.R./U.S.A.)

. . . to refuse to countenance a war that dares not speak its true name . . . you can no longer mumble the old excuse, "We didn't know"; and now that you do know, can you continue to feign ignorance, or content yourselves with mere token utterance of horrified sympathy?

—SIMONE DE BEAUVOIR (FRANCE)

The victims of twentieth-century premeditated genocide— the Jews, the Gypsies, the Armenians—were murdered in order to fulfill the state's design for a new order. War was used in all cases to transform the nation to correspond to the ruling elite's formula by eliminating groups conceived of as alien, enemies by definition.

—HELEN FEIN (U.S.A.)

Death Seizes a Woman,
1934, by Käthe Kollwitz

JANE ADDAMS (U.S.A.)

WAR IS NOT A NATURAL ACTIVITY

War is not a natural activity for mankind. For the young soldier, war is much more anachronistic than to the elderly statesmen who are primarily responsible for the soldiers' presence in the trenches. . . . We had heard a certain soldier say that it had been difficult to make the bayonet charge . . . unless he had been stimulated; that English soldiers had been given rum before a charge, the Germans ether, and that the French were said to use absinthe. . . .

MONA ELAINE ADILMAN (CANADA)

REFLECTION

We embrace, and when I look in the mirror
I see two lovers in a death camp,
their shattered flesh alive with maggots,
a fierce coupling, acrid with smoke.

(Later, when the child was due,
they tied her legs together,
and the baby's head
burst through her guts.)

Now we rest, quiescent, on the slippery
sheets, and I think of the fetal
fluid that ran from her ruined womb
onto the blood-stained prison floor.

Your white body shines, and staring
through the glass are the eyes
of the slaughtered, their bleached bones
a constellation of charred planets.

Anna Akhmatova (russia)

THE FIRST LONG RANGE ARTILLERY
FIRE ON LENINGRAD

A multicolored crowd streaked about,
and suddenly all was totally changed.
It wasn't the usual city racket.
It came from a strange land.
True, it was akin to some random claps of thunder,
but natural thunder heralds the wetness of fresh water,
    high clouds
to quench the thirst of fields gone dry and parched,
a messenger of blessed rain,
but this was as dry as hell must be.
My distraught senses refused
to believe it, because of the insane
suddenness with which it sounded, swelled and hit,
and how casually it came
to murder my child.

*(Translated by Daniela Gioseffi
with Sophia Buzevska)*

Claribel Alegría (nicaragua/el salvador)

EVASION

for Otto René Castillo

We were discussing Siva
birds
Barthes
you stepped blamelessly
between us
and we kept on talking
suddenly

at a pause
you interrupted the crochet
of our sentences
abruptly
opened the window
and pointed to Claudio
lying in his own blood
there was silence
everything stopped
you closed the blinds
and Graciela
taking up the knitting needles again
announced:
I have to undo a whole row
I slipped two stitches.

(Translated by Lynne Beyer)

ISABEL ALLENDE (CHILE/VENEZUELA)

THE HOUR OF TRUTH

Alba was curled up in the darkness. They had ripped the tape from her eyes and replaced it with a tight bandage. She was afraid. As she recalled her Uncle Nicolás's training, and his warning about the danger of being afraid of fear, she concentrated on trying to control the shaking of her body and shutting her ears to the terrifying sounds that reached her side. She tried to visualize her happiest moments with Miguel, groping for a means to outwit time and find the strength for what she knew lay ahead. She told herself that she had to endure a few hours without her nerves betraying her, until her grandfather was able to set in motion the heavy machinery of his power and influence to get her out of there. She searched her memory for a trip to the coast with Miguel, in autumn, long before the hurricane of events had turned the world upside down, when things were still called by familiar names and words had a single meaning; when people, freedom, and *compañero* were just that—people, freedom, and *compañero*—and had not yet become passwords. She tried to relive that moment—the damp red earth and the intense scent of the pine and eucalyptus forests in which a carpet of dry leaves lay steeping after the long hot summer and where the coppery sunlight filtered down through the treetops. She tried to recall the cold, the silence, and that precious feeling of owning the world, of being twenty years old and having her whole life ahead of her, of making love slowly and calmly, drunk with the scent of the forest and their love, without a past, without suspecting the future, with just the incredible richness of that present moment in which they stared at each other, smelled each other, kissed each other, and explored each other's bodies, wrapped in the whisper of the wind among the trees and the sound of the nearby waves breaking against the rocks at the foot of the cliff, exploding in a crash of pungent surf, and the two of them embracing underneath a single poncho like Siamese twins, laughing and swearing that this would last forever, that they were the only ones in the whole world who had discovered love.

Alba heard the screams, the long moans, and the radio playing full blast. The woods, Miguel, and love were lost in the deep well of her terror and she resigned herself to facing her fate without subterfuge.

She calculated that a whole night and the better part of the following day had passed when the door was finally opened and two men took her from her cell. With insults and threats they led her in to Colonel García, whom she could recognize blindfolded by his habitual cruelty, even before he opened his mouth. She felt his hands take her face, his thick fingers touch her ears and neck.

"Now you're going to tell me where your lover is," he told her. "That will save us both a lot of unpleasantness."

Alba breathed a sigh of relief. That meant they had not arrested Miguel!

"I want to go to the bathroom," Alba said in the strongest voice she could summon up.

"I see you're not planning to cooperate, Alba. That's too bad." García sighed. "The boys will have to do their job. I can't stand in their way."

There was a brief silence and she made a superhuman effort to remember the pine forest and Miguel's love, but her ideas got tangled up and she no longer knew if she was dreaming or where this stench of sweat, excrement, blood, and urine was coming from, or the radio announcer describing some Finnish goals that had nothing to do with her in the middle of other, nearer, more clearly audible shouts. A brutal slap knocked her to the floor. Violent hands lifted her to her feet. Ferocious fingers fastened themselves to her breasts, crushing her nipples. She was completely overcome by fear. Strange voices pressed in on her. She heard Miguel's name but did not know what they were asking her, and kept repeating a monumental *no* while they beat her, manhandled her, pulled off her blouse, and she could no longer think, could only say *no, no,* and *no* and calculate how much longer she could resist before her strength gave out, not knowing this was only the beginning, until she felt herself begin to faint and the men left her alone, lying on the floor, for what seemed to her a very short time.

She soon heard García's voice again and guessed it was his hands that were helping her to her feet, leading her toward a chair, straightening her clothes, and buttoning her blouse.

"My God!" he said. "Look what they've done to you! I warned you, Alba. Try to relax now, I'm going to give you a cup of coffee."

Alba began to cry. The warm liquid brought her back to life, but she could not taste it because when she swallowed it was mixed with blood. García held the cup, guiding it carefully toward her lips like a nurse.

"Do you want a cigarette?"

"I want to go to the bathroom," she said, pronouncing each syllable with difficulty with her swollen lips.

"Of course, Alba. They'll take you to the bathroom and then you can get some rest. I'm your friend. I understand your situation perfectly. You're in love, and that's why you want to protect him. I know you don't have anything to do with the guerrillas. But the boys don't believe me when I tell them. They won't be satisfied until you tell them where Miguel is. Actually they've already got him surrounded. They know exactly where he is. They'll catch him, but they want to be sure that you have nothing to do with the guerrillas. You understand? If you protect him and refuse to talk, they'll continue to suspect you. Tell them what they want to know and then I'll personally escort you home. You'll tell them, right?"

"I want to go to the bathroom," Alba repeated.

"I see you're just as stubborn as your grandfather. All right. You can go to the bathroom. I'm going to give you a chance to think things over," García said.

They took her to a toilet and she was forced to ignore the man who stood beside her, holding on to her arm. After that they returned her to her cell. In the tiny, solitary cube where she was being held, she tried to clarify her thoughts, but she was tortured by the pain of her beating, her thirst, the bandage pressing on her temples, the drone of the radio, the terror of approaching footsteps and her relief when they moved away, the shouts and the orders. She curled up like a fetus on the floor and surrendered to her pain. She remained in that position for hours, perhaps days. A man came twice to take her to the bathroom. He led her to a fetid lavatory where she was unable to wash because there was no water. He allowed her a minute, placing her on the toilet seat next to another person as silent and sluggish as herself. She could not tell if it was a woman or a man. At first she wept, wishing her Uncle Nicolás had given her a special course in how to withstand humiliation, which she found worse than pain, but she finally resigned herself to her own filth and stopped thinking about her unbearable need to wash. They gave her boiled corn, a small piece of chicken, and a bit of ice cream, which she identified by their taste, smell, and temperature, and which she wolfed down with her hands, astonished to be given such luxurious food, unexpected in a place like that. . . .

The third time they took her in to Esteban García, Alba was more prepared, because through the walls of her cell she could hear what was going on in the next room, where they were interrogating other prisoners, and she had no illusions. She did not even try to evoke the woods where she had shared the joy of love.

"Well, Alba, I've given you time to think things over. Now the two of us are going to talk and you're going to tell me where Miguel is and we're going to get this over with quickly," García said.

"I want to go to the bathroom," Alba answered.

"I see you're making fun of me, Alba," he said. "I'm sorry, but we don't have any time to waste."

Alba made no response.

"Take off your clothes!" García ordered in another voice.

She did not obey. They stripped her violently, pulling off her slacks despite her kicking. The memory of her adolescence and Miguel's kiss in the garden gave her the strength of hatred. She struggled against him, until they got tired of beating her and gave her a short break, which she used to invoke the understanding spirits of her grandmother, so that they would help her die. But no one answered her call for help. Two hands lifted her up, and four laid her on a cold, hard metal cot with springs that hurt her back, and bound her wrists and ankles with leather thongs.

"For the last time, Alba. Where is Miguel?" García asked.

She shook her head in silence. They had tied her head down with another thong.

"When you're ready to talk, raise a finger," he said.

Alba heard another voice.

"I'll work the machine," it said.

Then she felt the atrocious pain that coursed through her body, filling it completely, and that she would never forget as long as she lived. She sank into darkness.

"Bastards! I told you to be careful with her!" she heard Esteban García say from far away. She felt them opening her eyelids, but all she saw was a misty brightness. Then she felt a prick in her arm and sank back into unconsciousness.

A century later Alba awoke wet and naked. She did not know if she was bathed with sweat, or water, or urine. She could not move, recalled nothing, and had no idea where she was or what had caused the intense pain that had reduced her to a heap of raw meat. She felt the thirst of the Sahara and called out for water.

"Wait, *compañera*," someone said beside her. "Wait until morning. If you drink water, you'll get convulsions, and you could die."

She opened her eyes. They were no longer bandaged. A vaguely familiar face was leaning over her, and hands were wrapping her in a blanket.

"Do you remember me? I'm Ana Díaz. We went to the university together. Don't you recognize me?"

Alba shook her head, closed her eyes, and surrendered to the sweet illusion of death. But she awakened a few hours later, and when she moved she realized that she ached to the last fiber of her body.

"You'll feel better soon," said a woman who was stroking her face and pushing away the locks of damp hair that hid her eyes. "Don't move, and try to relax. I'll be here next to you. You need to rest."

"What happened?" Alba whispered.

"They really roughed you up, *compañera*," the other woman said sadly.

"Who are you?" Alba asked.

"Ana Díaz. I've been here for a week. They also got my *compañero*, Andrés, but he's still alive. I see him once a day, when they take them to the bathroom."

"Ana Díaz?" Alba murmured.

"That's right. We weren't so close back then, but it's never too late to start. The truth is, you're the last person I expected to meet here, Countess," the woman said gently. "Don't talk now. Try to sleep. That way the time will go faster for you. Your memory will gradually come back. Don't worry. It's because of the electricity."

But Alba was unable to sleep, for the door of her cell opened and a man walked in.

"Put the bandage back on her!" he ordered Ana Díaz.

"Please . . . can't you see how weak she is? Let her rest a little while. . . ."

"Do as I say!"

Ana bent over the cot and put the bandage over her eyes. Then she removed the blanket and tried to dress her, but the guard pulled her away, lifted the prisoner by her arms, and sat her up. Another man came in to help him, and between them they carried her out because

188

she could not walk. Alba was sure that she was dying, if she was not already dead. She could tell they were walking down a hallway in which the sound of their footsteps echoed. She felt a hand on her face, lifting her head.

"You can give her water. Wash her and give her another shot. See if she can swallow some coffee and bring her back to me," García said.

"Do you want us to dress her?"

"No."

Alba was in García's hands a long time. After a few days, he realized she had recognized him, but he did not abandon his precaution of keeping her blindfolded, even when they were alone. Every day new prisoners arrived and others were led away. Alba heard the vehicles, the shouts, and the gate being closed. She tried to keep track of the number of prisoners, but it was almost impossible. Ana Díaz thought there were close to two hundred. García was very busy, but he never let a day go by without seeing Alba, alternating unbridled violence with the pretense that he was her good friend. At times he appeared to be genuinely moved, personally spooning soup into her mouth, but the day he plunged her head into a bucket full of excrement until she fainted from disgust, Alba understood that he was not trying to learn Miguel's true whereabouts but to avenge himself for injuries that had been inflicted on him from birth, and that nothing she could confess would have any effect on her fate as the private prisoner of Colonel García. This allowed her to venture slowly out of the private circle of her terror. Her fear began to ebb and she was able to feel compassion for the others, for those they hung by their arms, for the newcomers, for the man whose shackled legs were run over by a truck. They brought all the prisoners into the courtyard at dawn and forced them to watch, because this was also a personal matter between the colonel and his prisoner. It was the first time Alba had opened her eyes outside the darkness of her cell, and the gentle splendor of the morning and the frost shining on the stones, where puddles of rain had collected overnight, seemed unbearably radiant to her. They dragged the man, who offered no resistance, out into the courtyard. He could not stand, and they left him lying on the ground. The guards had covered their faces with handkerchiefs so no one would ever be able to identify them in the improbable event that circumstances changed. Alba closed her eyes when she heard the truck's engine, but she could not close her ears to the sound of his howl, which stayed in her memory forever. . . .

One day Colonel García was surprised to find himself caressing Alba like a lover and talking to her of his childhood in the country, when he would see her walking hand in hand with her grandfather, dressed in her starched pinafores and with the green halo of her hair, while he, barefoot in the mud, swore that one day he would make her pay for her arrogance and avenge himself for his cursed bastard fate. Rigid and absent, naked and trembling with disgust and cold, Alba neither heard nor felt him, but that crack in his eagerness to torture her sounded an alarm in the colonel's mind. He ordered Alba to be thrown in the doghouse, and furiously prepared to forget that she existed.

The doghouse was a small, sealed cell like a dark, frozen, airless tomb. There were six of them altogether, constructed in an empty water tank especially for punishment. They were used for relatively short stretches of time, because no one could withstand them very long, at most a few days, before beginning to ramble—to lose the sense of things, the meaning of words, and the anxiety of passing time—or simply, beginning to die. At first, huddled in her sepulcher, unable either to stand up or sit down despite her small size, Alba managed to stave off madness. Now that she was alone, she realized how much she needed Ana Díaz. She thought she heard an imperceptible tapping in the distance, as if someone were sending her coded messages from another cell, but she soon stopped paying attention to it because she realized that all attempts at communication were completely hopeless. She gave up, deciding to end this torture once and for all. She stopped eating, and only when her feebleness became too much for her did she take a sip of water. She tried not to breathe or move, and began eagerly to await her death. She stayed like this for a long time. . . . Word went out that she was dying. The guards opened the hatch of the doghouse and lifted her effortlessly, because she was very light. They took her back to Colonel García, whose hatred had returned during these days, but she did not recognize him. She was beyond his power.

(*Translated by Magda Bogin*)

LINDA ANDERSON (NORTHERN IRELAND)

GANG-BANG, ULSTER STYLE

Broken Belfast Street,
Grey and dingy,
Sealed off with barbed wire
To stop murderous neighbours.

You lived in that trap,
Suffocating.
He was in another prison
Called Long Kesh.

> Sleepwalking woman,
> You shuttlecocked
> From jail to jail
> On dutiful visits,
> Your eyes were old
> They did not match
> The bright hair
> That made men watch you
> Avidly.

You met him—
Another starved somnambulist.
Two living corpses clung together,
Thawed each other for a while.
But they found out.
They dragged you to their playroom.
Now you lie limp,
Face down,
Dumped in a ditch.
Routine policemen come
Accustomed, stony-faced.
'Turn her over, see the damage.'

> O, poor adventuress—
> In the name of virtue,
> They cut your flaxen hair,
> Defiled your lovely breasts,
> Before degutting you.

ANONYMOUS ANTIWAR BALLAD (IRELAND)

JOHNNY, I HARDLY KNEW YE

While going the road to sweet Athy, Hurroo! Hurroo!
A stick in my hand and a drop in my eye

A doleful damsel I heard cry:
O Johnny, I hardly knew ye!

Where are your eyes that looked so mild? Hurroo! Hurroo!
When my poor heart you first beguiled?
Why'd you go to war leaving me and the child?
O Johnny, I hardly knew ye!

Where are your legs which used to run? Hurroo! Hurroo!
When first you learned to carry a gun?
I fear your dancing days are done!
O Johnny, I hardly knew ye!

It grieved my heart to see you sail, Hurroo! Hurroo!
To battle and fight and rail, Hurroo! Hurroo!
Like a cod you're doubled up head and tail,
O, Johnny I hardly know ye!

With your guns and drums and drums and guns, Hurroo! Hurroo!
With your guns and drums and drums and guns, Hurroo! Hurroo!
The enemy nearly slew you!
O, Johnny, I hardly knew ye!

(Adapted by Daniela Gioseffi)

MARJORIE APPLEMAN (U.S.A.)

MELTING

Too young, her family said.
Too poor, said his.
The neighbors shook their heads.
(Don't they know
there's a war on?)
But they were together at last,
under their own roof.

They worked hard,
watched each other,
hid their fear, glancing
at the hot sky,

and wove
the beginnings of dreams.

At night
as leaves danced and stars fell
they roused out of pure love
the energy to twine
and melt   together.

They were found like that,
silent in sunlight
beneath the napalmed thatch,
melting   together.

EMILY GREENE BALCH (U.S.A.)

HAITI

Of all the black man's burdens perhaps the most tragic is that the un-
cultivated white man finds him funny. All peoples who have known oppression suffer something of this—the Jew (the most tragic figure in
history), the Irishman, the educated Hindu (compare Kipling's Babus),
but none in such measure as blacks. There are many white men who
conceive of themselves as men of the world who yet find it impossible
to take seriously any man of a darker race than their own.

SIMONE DE BEAUVOIR (FRANCE)

REPORTS FROM THE WORLD
TRIBUNAL ON VIETNAM

. . . Many of the [witnesses'] reports dealt with attacks on civilian
population . . . the physicist exhibited specimens of anti-personnel
bombs . . . and he conclusively proved that they could not be used

against military targets . . . they were made up of a hollow metal shell with little spheres for needles inside. They exploded on hitting the ground, scattering these projectiles with great force; they could do no significant material damage, but they could kill or wound great numbers of people when they went off in all directions in the middle of a market or a village square. These . . . weapons were specially designed for the massacre of under-developed communities: neither the roofs nor the walls of straw huts offered any resistance.

. . . We listened to the evidence of two Vietnamese women who had been tortured. One was . . . a pharmacist well known in Saigon, and this had meant that she was tried before being condemned to life-imprisonment, whereas so many others were executed without any process of law; it was also thanks to her wide-spread reputation that she was released after seven years. In her dark blue velvet national dress she was very beautiful and she spoke with great dignity and restraint. She had been appallingly flogged; her chest and belly had been trampled upon; the soles of her feet had been beaten; she had been subjected to the "trip in the submarine," a variation of the medieval torture of the funnel; she had been hung up by her wrists and one day they had tied her half-naked to a tree swarming with ants whose slightest bite causes intolerable burning pain and swellings. She also described the treatment inflicted upon other victims: when she spoke of the sufferings of one of her uncles her eyes filled with tears. She was sent to the notorious death-camp of Pulo-Condor. . . .

Of all the evidence heard, [a West German doctor gave] . . . the fullest and most satisfactory. He began by describing the appearance of the country seen from a plane—it was like the skin of a smallpox patient: eruptions everywhere, vast areas devastated by chemicals, a landscape of dust and ashes. He told us about the military sweeps and searches—the young men taken off by helicopter to interrogation centers, tortured and flung into prison, where they died. Whole territories were completely emptied of their inhabitants: there were four million "relocated" Vietnamese in the South. Then he spoke of the wounds, the burns and the mutilations inflicted on civilian populations by fragmentation bombs, napalm and phosphorus. The testimony was confirmed by an appalling film . . . unbearable. In a hospital we saw the faces of adults and children literally melted, seared away, by napalm—faces in which the eyes, staring with horror, were the only remaining human features. . . . Big leering Americans killing the little Liberation Front soldiers by kicking them in the genitals, shooting them in the back or neck, or just for laughs, in the anus. And others cheerfully setting fire to straw huts. . . . Our unanimous decision (made by judges from around the world) was that the Americans did make use of forbidden weapons, that they did treat prisoners and civilians in an inhuman manner contrary to the laws of war, and that they were committing the crime of genocide. . . . American opposition to the war increased. With the presidential elections coming closer, many politicians declared themselves in favour of peace. . . .

E. BROWN (U.S.A.)

A CRUEL WHIPPING

"Keep still thar, gals, and don't rattle them cups and sassers so powerful hard."

By this time Lindy had finished the assortment of the silver, and had carefully stowed it away in a willow-basket, ready to be delivered to Miss Jane, and thence consigned to the drawer, where it would remain in *statu quo* until the timely advent of another guest.

"Now," she said, "I am ready to wipe the dishes, while you wash."

Thereupon I handed her a saucer, which, in her carelessness, she let slip from her hand, and it fell upon the floor, and there, with great consternation, I beheld it lying, shattered to fragments. Mr. Peterkin sprang to his feet, glad of an excuse to vent his temper upon some one.

"Which of you cussed wretches did this?"

" 'Twas Ann, master! She let it fall afore I got my hand on it."

Ere I had time to vindicate myself from the charge, his iron arm felled me to the floor, and his hoof-like foot was placed upon my shrinking chest.

"You d—n yallow hussy, does you think I buys such expensive chanyware for you to break up in this ar' way? No, you 'bominable wench, I'll have revenge out of your saffer'n hide. Here, Lindy, fetch me that cowhide."

"Mercy, master, mercy," I cried, when he had removed his foot from my breast, and my breath seemed to come again. "Oh, listen to me; it was not I who broke the saucer, it was only an accident; but oh, in God's name, have mercy on me and Lindy."

"Yes, I'll tache you what marcy is. Here, quick, some of you darkies, bring me a rope and light. I'm goin' to take this gal to the whippin'-post." . . .

With a wild, fiendish grin, he caught me by the hair and swung me round until I half-fainted with pain. . . .

"Now hold yer hands here," he said to me.

For one moment I hesitated. I could not summon courage to offer my hands. It was the only resistance that I had ever dared to make. A severe blow from the overseer's riding-whip reminded me that I was still a slave, and dared have no will save that of my master. This blow, which struck the back of my head, laid me half-lifeless upon the floor. Whilst in this condition old Nace, at the command of his master, bound the rope tightly around my crossed arms and dragged me to the place of torment.

The motion or exertion of being pulled along over the ground restored me to full consciousness. . . . In this state of mind, with a moveless eye I looked upon the whipping-post, which loomed up before me like an ogre.

This was a quadri-lateral post, about eight feet in height, having iron clasps on two opposing sides, in which the wrists and ankles were tightly secured.

"Now, Lindy," cried Jones, "jerk off that gal's rigging, I am anxious to put some marks on her yellow skin."

I knew that resistance was vain; so I submitted to have my clothes torn from my body; for modesty, so much commended in a white woman, is in a negro pronounced affectation.

Jones drew down a huge cow-hide, which he dipped in a barrel of brine that stood near the post.

"I guess this will sting," he said, as he flourished the whip toward me.

"Leave that thin slip on me, Lindy," I ventured to say; for I dreaded the exposure of my person even more than the whipping.

"None of your cussed impedence; strip off naked. What is a nigger's hide more than a hog's?" cried Jones. Lindy and Nace tore the last article of clothing from my back. I felt my soul shiver and shudder at this; but what could I do? . . .

I then submitted to have Nace clasp the iron cuffs around my hands and ankles, and there I stood, a revolting spectacle. With what misery I listened to obscene and ribald jests from my master and his overseer!

"Now, Jones," said Mr. Peterkin, "I want to give that gal the first lick, which will lay the flesh open to the bone."

"Well, Mr. Peterkin, here is the whip; now you can lay on."

"No, confound your whip; I wants that cow-hide, and here, let me dip it well into the brine. I want to give her a real good warmin'; one that she'll 'member for a long time."

During this time I had remained motionless. My heart was lifted to God in silent prayer. Oh, shall I, can I, ever forget that scene? There, in the saintly stillness of the summer night, where the deep, o'ershadowing heavens preached a sermon of peace, there I was loaded with contumely, bound hand and foot in irons, with jeering faces around, vulgar eyes glaring on my uncovered body, and two inhuman men about to lash me to the bone.

The first lick from Mr. Peterkin laid my back open. I writhed, I wrestled; but blow after blow descended, each harder than the preceding one. I shrieked, I screamed, I pleaded, I prayed, but there was no mercy shown me. Mr. Peterkin having fully gratified and quenched his spleen, turned to Mr. Jones, and said, "Now is yer turn; you can beat her as much as you please, only jist leave a bit o' life in her, is all I cares for."

"Yes; I'll not spile her for the market; but I does want to take a little of the d——d pride out of her."

"Now, boys"—for by this time all the slaves on the place, save Aunt Polly, had assembled round the post—"you will see what a true stroke I ken make; but darn my buttons if I doesn't think Mr. Peterkin has drawn all the blood."

So saying, Jones drew back the cow-hide at arms length, and, making a few evolutions with his body, took what he called "sure aim." I closed my eyes in terror. More from the terrible pain, than from the frantic shoutings of the crowd, I knew that Mr. Jones had given a lick that he called "true blue." The exultation of the negroes in Master Jones' triumph was scarcely audible to my ears; for a cold, clammy sensation was stealing over my frame; my breath was growing feebler and feebler, . . . I passed from all consciousness of pain. . . .

Nina Cassian (Romania)

ON A JAPANESE BEACH

—Hiroshima Memento

Blind children are brought to the beach.
They bask in sunlight
and wade in waters.

Sunbeams, like a huge woman hug them,
gentle waves kiss their eyes.
Wind combs their hair.
Sand puts slippers on their feet.

But the colors,
only the colors,

the colors can do nothing for them,
but shimmer from surface to surface,
from sand to sea,
from hands to eyelids,

and the children are orphaned by colors;
and the colors are orphaned by children.

(Translated by Daniela Gioseffi
with the author)

VINNIE-MARIE D'AMBROSIO (U.S.A.)

THE GRAND COMMANDER, 1916

to my grandfather, 1865–1960

In coat of red and gold
he duelled, grandpa
versus the two deserters,
under the shadow of the Alps,
lemon-ices sluicing down
the peaks.
Oh it was no grand opera.
That was no pop gun
that got them at dawn
against the grainy gray wall.

ashen my mama
who shrank at the bang.

EMILY DICKINSON (U.S.A.)

FLAGS VEX A DYING FACE

The world feels dusty
When we stop to die;
We want the dew then,
Honors taste dry.

Flags vex a dying face,
But the least fan
Stirred by a friend's hand
Cools like the rain. . . .

. . . .

ENHEDUANNA (SUMERIA, *c.* 2300 B.C.)

LAMENT TO THE SPIRIT OF WAR

You hack everything down in battle. . . .
You slice away the land and charge
    disguised as a raging storm,
growl as a roaring hurricane,
yell like a tempest yells,
thunder, rage, roar, and drum,
expel evil winds!
Your feet are filled with anxiety!

. . . .

Like a fiery monster you fill the land with poison.
As a rage from the sky,
you growl over the earth,
and trees and bushes collapse before you.
You're like blood rushing down a mountain,
Spirit of hate, greed and anger,
dominator of heaven and earth!
Your fire wafts over our tribe,
mounted on a beast,

with indomitable commands,
you decide all fate.
You triumph over all our rites.
Who can fathom you?

(Adapted to English by Daniela Gioseffi)

ELENI FOURTOUNI (GREECE)

GREEK WOMEN OF THE RESISTANCE

NO TO PARTITION
told by *Maria Karra*

In the summer of 1943, when the Germans gave Macedonia and Thrace
to Bulgaria as a reward for its cooperation with them, the people came
out into the streets in massive demonstrations of protest.

I was living in Athens with my uncle at the time. He felt responsible
for me and, fearing that I would be arrested, did not approve of my
affiliation with EPON. He'd wait up every night until I returned from
our meetings. He always looked worried and sternly warned that one
night they'd bring me home on a stretcher. I was not afraid of the
Germans; they couldn't stop me. But I was afraid of my uncle, who
could. Convincing him to let me go to the EPON meeting on the night
before the demonstration was my most difficult task. His only argument,
which he kept repeating over and over, was that I was a girl. But I
was a very determined girl, and in the end he relented.

July 22, 1943: We met before sunrise at Monastiraki. Everything was
ready—hundreds of handbills and first-aid kits; stretchers folded and
casually tucked under our arms; cardboard megaphones hidden inside
shopping bags. The streets were filled with casual passers-by, who at
the appointed moment poured into Syntagma Square like a human
torrent. We scattered handbills, recited poems, and sang songs of freedom. The crowds marched down Athenas street, declaiming poems and
singing songs with us. Just before we reached Omonia Square the soldiers began to shoot. Someone fell, then another, and another. "Damn
the murderers," a woman shouted. Dozens lay dead or wounded. We
piled the wounded onto the stretchers and rushed them to nearby hospitals. Huge banners unfurled, reading: "Death to Fascism," "Freedom

and Democracy," "Bulgarians, stay out of Greece." On the same streets where thousands of famine victims had fallen in the winter of 1941, on the streets that had echoed with the cries of hungry children, we were now fighting without weapons, without shields, to prevent a much worse catastrophe—our country's death by partition.

At the corner of Panepistimiou and Hippocratous streets, they hit us with artillery. The sound of machine guns . . . a tank coming toward us . . . on Homerou street we met it . . . it began to spout fire . . . shouts of pain . . . the whole street was covered with bodies. A young girl lay crushed at my feet. Her fair skin and blond hair were drenched in blood. Through her torn dress I saw a bullet hole between her breasts, and a bloody mass where her belly had been. Her name was Panayiota Stathopoulou. She was my schoolmate and a member of our group. We saw two Germans photographing her from the tank, laughing. We shook our fists at them. They continued to laugh, pointing their camera at another young woman lying in a pool of blood a few yards away. It was Koula Lili. She had jumped on the tank and kicked the gunner in the face when she saw him pointing the gun at Panayiota. He fired at her with his pistol at the same time as he was machine-gunning Panayiota. He turned and pointed the machine gun at us. We put down the stretchers, joined hands, and stood in front of the tank, guarding the wounded with our bodies. We stared at him until he slowly turned the mouth of the machine gun away from us.

Fearing an even greater demonstration at their funeral, they did not let us bury our friends, and threw thousands of us in prison.

IN THE EASTERN SUBURBS OF ATHENS
told by *Toula Mara-Mihalakea*

In the eastern neighborhoods of Athens, populated mostly by factory workers, resistance broke out as soon as the Germans came. Overnight everyone was ready to fight for freedom, just as they had always fought for bread. And the fight for bread was now more than ever before of the utmost importance. Famine was going to be our most immediate foe. There were shortages in everything. The lines of shoppers, waiting hours for fifty grams of oil, a pound of beans, or a piece of bread, were getting longer every day.

We realized that in order to survive we had to act collectively. Our first successful collective act was to convince the shopkeepers, by persuasion and threats, not to hoard what food supplies there were but to sell them at reasonable prices, saving milk and eggs for families with children.*

* Hoarding was later decreed a crime against Greece, punishable by death.

High school students, ages fourteen to eighteen, inspired by the idea of acting with the adults in planning survival and resistance, were organized into one of the first EPON (United Panhellenic Youth Organization) groups in Athens. Our enthusiasm and energy knew no bounds. We were no longer considered wards of our parents under constant supervision, always having to invent ways to circumvent the restrictions imposed on us to preserve our "good name." For the first time girls our age felt important, capable, indispensable.

By day we were still students and daughters, cramming for Latin and math exams or helping our mothers at home. But at night the streets were ours. We kept the Free Press going. We'd cover the walls of the most remote neighborhoods with resistance slogans, and through improvised loudspeakers our voices resounded throughout the city, urging people not to give in, not to be intimidated, to organize and to resist, to take their fate into their own hands. Like lightning we'd run in and out of coffee shops, distributing our handbills.

Maria, Katerina, and I had been best friends since grammar school. The three of us would go out every night together—one writing, the other holding the can of paint, the third on guard at the corner. As soon as we'd hear her whistle, we'd disappear behind a doorway or down some cellar stairs and wait holding our breath until the sound of the boots of the German patrol had passed. Each time we went out, we knew we could meet death. But we had no fear, no anxiety; nothing could stop us.

In January 1943, I was denounced and arrested by the Security Battalions for anti-national acts.

CHILD CENTERS
told by *Nausika Flenga-Papadaki*

I was eighteen in the winter of 1941. Unable to bear the sight of emaciated children scavenging city garbage cans for something to eat, I discontinued my studies in Athens and returned to Mikro Horio, my village in Evrytania. But famine was not only a city occurrence. Because of the inaccessible terrain, my village and the surrounding ones had escaped the terror of the German occupation and had remained essentially free territory. But the monumental ruggedness that protected them against the enemy also meant a lack of fertile, arable land. The meager harvest from the small, rocky fields provided the average family with bread for about three months.

The major source of income for the area had always been money sent by those who had emigrated—to Australia, America, Africa. As a result, Evrytania, though poor, was in touch with the outside world, and its people had acquired a progressive way of thinking, an openness of mind unlike that in other isolated regions. The German occupation cut off outside income, plunging Evrytania into an economic crisis more desperate than that in the urban centers, where at least one had bread rations. Here, as elsewhere, the children were the first victims of malnutrition. I tried to help by taking whatever food we could spare to a couple of neighboring families who had less than we did, and whose children were slowly and quietly starving. It was not enough. My individual, well-meant efforts could never make any difference. I could not personally reach out to the dozens of starving children dragging themselves in the streets.

Only collective effort could save the children from starvation and disease. In Athens I had seen soup kitchens for children opened and operated by disabled veterans. Why not here, too? The next Sunday, as soon as the service was over, with my heart racing and my throat dry, I gathered my courage, got up, and began to speak. My first incoherent words fortunately went unheard in the initial confusion and shock at my act—it was unheard of for a woman to speak inside a church. But I managed to regain my determination, and my voice commanded the people's attention and touched their hearts. I talked of the danger and explained to them the only way to save the children from extermination, the only way to preserve our new generation of Greeks, our only hope for continuity.

The first meal for the hungry children was ready that night. Everyone with even a morsel to spare contributed. Generosity and co-operation by far surpassed mere human duty. "Save the Children" became an inspiring slogan that transcended politics. The first step was taken that day in establishing the Association for the Protection of Children and the National Solidarity Association.*

VERA GANCHEVA (BULGARIA)

THE NIGHT AFTER THE DAY AFTER

Ninety big metal boxes whose contents were not specified on any one of them were kept in the underground vaults of the United States National Archives until recently. Only certain employees of the Archives

* Both developed into nationwide organizations, serving as lifelines throughout the occupation and the civil war, primarily through the efforts of women.

knew that the boxes had arrived in Washington, D.C., from an Ohio air base and that the strictest ban on their opening and transfer had been imposed. Nevertheless, at the end of 1983, the nature of their contents, which had been kept secret so carefully, was disclosed and became a public secret which reverberated like the thundering echo of a political scandal: the contents of the boxes proved to be a colour documentary film made in Nagasaki the day after that Japanese city had been destroyed by the second American atom bomb (as is known, the first one had been dropped on Hiroshima). Incidentally, the use of the word 'destroyed' would hardly be an apt definition of what had happened—the city had virtually been destroyed, obliterated and wiped out. . . . It seems there is no word fully capturing the devastation imprinted on the film which was 102,000 feet long (the film takes no less than a week to show), a devastation all the more horrifying against the background of a bright-blue sky, a 'Technicolour' sky judging by the perfect quality of the colour. It is not an azure blue but a clinically cold colour, its lack of transparency having the depressing quality of a shroud of death.

All of them, predominantly newsmen and public figures (nobody who left the projection room was what he had been like before viewing the film) who saw the film made during that dreadful August of 1945 by a military filming team on the special order of the Pentagon, never mention that sinister blue colour. The assignment had been formulated without euphemisms or without beating about the bush. It simply stated that a shooting team was to leave for Japan at once to make a film about the situation there before the grass had turned green again. The documentary film about the Devastation and Death which Insanity had sown with its crooked and blood-stained fingers caused a great deal of stir which did not cease and which became as violent as the silence veiling that shattering document had been impenetrable, a document which had been duly sealed in metal boxes and hidden away from the public in inaccessible vaults. A 25-minute-long film which was subsequently shown on American television and in many West European countries alongside with shots from that other film also showed the two survivors of the shooting team. Both of them had been assailed by the incurable "atomic" disease and both had paid with their health and their peace of mind for the discipline with which they had successfully fulfilled the "military" "mission" assigned to them four decades ago. According to their own admission, they had found it difficult to decide what had crushed them more: the skin cancer one of them had developed and the lymphemea the other one had caught, or the ghastly memory of what they had seen in Nagasaki: the blinded faces, the fatally burnt and deformed human bodies, the white bones from which all flesh had fallen off, the bald children, crazed witnesses to the holocaust, who had died a week or two later, the ashes and the dead silence reigning after the fire storm. The dispassionate camera never shook in the hands of the cameramen who were fulfilling a military and not an artistic assignment in which all emotion was deemed undesirable. . . . The power of exposure generated by this film has furnished an even stronger proof of the arguments being used by the champions of the anti-war movement in the United States. . . .

Sandra M. Gilbert (u.s.a.)

THE PARACHUTIST'S WIFE

Six men turned to smoke in the next square
of air, their plane became wind.
You were twentythree. Hands over your ears, a roaring
in your veins, a silence
on the radio.

       Flak
knocked twice at the cockpit,
dull knuckles, thumping:
Let me in,
       let me in.

You knew you had to
give yourself to the sky the way we
give ourselves to music—no knowing
the end of the next bar, no figuring
how the chord will fall.

The clouds were cold, the plane trembled.
You pulled the cord and the chute
"bloomed like God's love," a heavenly
jockstrap anchoring you in air.

You were happy, you say, you were
never happier than that day, falling
into birth: the archaic
blue-green map of Europe glowed below you.

You were going to camp, you were
going to be free of death.
The pull of the harness, the swaying,
the ropes creaking—it was so peaceful up there,

like a page of Greek or
an afternoon in a Zen monastery
or a long slow stroll around
somebody's grandfather's garden.

I'm quiet in my kitchen, I won't
bail out, I don't think it would be the same
for me, I think if I
fell like that the hands of flak
would strip me as I
swung from the finger of God, I'd

offer myself as a bright idea
and a chorus of guns
would stammer holes in my story, nothing

would lift me over the black fangs
of the Alps, I'd dangle
like bait and the savage

map of Europe would eat me up.
I stick like grease to my oven, I wear
a necklace of dust,

my feet root in green stone.
You've forgotten I'm here!
But every morning

there are crystals of ice in my hair
and a winter distance glitters
in the centers of my eyes.

I don't need to stroll through the sky
like a hero:
in my bone cave

I marry the wind.

Rose Graubart (u.s.a.)

NEWS PHOTOS OF BOMBED CHILDREN

As dials turn war comes on—
Imagination wastes no time;
it clubs the facts into mind;
it asks, *who are you?* while this goes on:
Some refuse to speak about it,
but break down over news photos of bombed children.
One cried on the breast of a young criminal,
though she knew the bloody specks in his mind
                might catch in her eyes.

Some repudiate desire,
grabbing the hands of pimps.
People who hate are scared of each other,
and lovers are uneasy together.
In this search of their feelings,
they run out singly.
They catch anyone's hand:
Killers and lovers exchange the sweat of their palms.

Kimiko Hahn (u.s.a.)

THE BATH

—August 6, 1945

Bathing the summer night
off my arms and breasts
I heard a plane
overhead *I heard*
the door rattle
froze
then relaxed
in the cool water

one more moment
one private moment
before waking the children
and mother-in-law,
before the heat
before the midday heat
drenched my spirits again.
I had wanted
to also relax
in thoughts of my husband
when he was drafted
imprisoned—but didn't dare
and rose from the tub,
dried off lightly
and slipped on cotton work pants.
Caution drew me to the window
and there an enormous blossom of fire
a hand changed my life
and made the world shiver—
a light that tore flesh
so it slipped off limbs,
swelled so
no one could recognize
a mother or child
a hand that tore the door open
pushed me on the floor
ripped me up—
I will never have children again
so even today
my hair has not grown back
my teeth still shards
and one eye blind
and it would be easy,
satisfying somehow
to write it off as history
those men are there
each time I close
my one good eye
each time or lay blame
on men or militarists
the children cry out
in my sleep
where they still live

for the sake of a night's rest.
But it isn't air raids
simply
that we survive
but *gold worth its weight*
in blood the coal,
oil, uranium we mine
and drill
yet cannot call our own.
And it would be gratifying
to be called a survivor
I am a survivor
since I live if I didn't wonder
about survival today—
at 55, widowed at 18—
if I didn't feel
the same oppressive August heat
auto parts in South Africa,
Mexico, Alabama,
and shiver not from memory
or terror
but anger that this wounded body
must stand *take a stand*
and cry out
as only a new born baby can cry—
I live, I will live
I will to live
in spite of history
to make history
in my vision of peace—
that morning in the bath
so calm
so much my right
though I cannot return to that moment
I bring these words to you
hoping to hold you
to hold you
and to take hold.

JANA HARRIS (U.S.A.)

DREAM OF THE HAIR BURNING SMELL

the women gather, their dreams
played back again and again:

will the children be heirs
to the cloud passing over

killing everyone?
in the day, her eyes open

one smells her own hair burning,
another says, after the cloud

a flesh-sweat falling
from her face, her arms

her daughter's forehead dissolving
when she awoke, she wondered

how will I kill my little girl?
these dreams, they say

oh, these dreams
of row crop corn smoke stained,

the silks burnt away,
another does not in her dream

see the fire, just
the burning smell of hair

of corn husks, the smell
of the false prophet

is everywhere in their dreams,
in the end, black ash

is what rises up again,
these dreams, they say

oh, these dreams

TOYOMI HASHIMOTO (JAPAN)

HELLISH YEARS AFTER HELLISH DAYS

Though at each anniversary the skies over our city are blue and peaceful, the memory of that day in 1945 still troubles my body and soul.

In spite of the wartime conditions, my husband and our little son and I lived a happy life. Many of our neighbors envied us. On the morning of August 9, 1945, I walked to the gate to see my husband off to work. My three-year-old boy, Takashi, went out to play with some of his little friends. I was alone in the house and relieved that the air-raid alarm had just been lifted.

Then, in the distance I heard an approaching airplane. "Japanese?" I wondered. I stepped outside to see my son running to me, calling, "Airplane! Airplane!" The moment we reentered the house, there was a blinding flash followed by a tremendous explosion. The roof of the house caved in, pinning us under a mountain of debris.

Hours passed. I do not know how many. Then I heard my son crying softly and calling for mother and father. He was alive. I tried to reach for him, but a huge beam immobilized me. I could not break free. Though I screamed for help, no one came. Soon I heard voices calling names of neighbors.

My son was bravely trying to crawl from under a heap of clay that had been one of the walls. His back was turned to me. When he faced me, I saw that his right eye was obliterated with blood. Once again, I tried to move, but the beam would not budge.

I screamed so loud and long that I must have lost my voice. I called to the people I could see scurrying about, but they did not hear me. No one answered until the lady next door finally pulled my son out of the wreckage.

Happy that he was at least temporarily safe, I suddenly became aware of a sharp pain in my breast, left hand, and stomach. With my free right hand I grabbed a piece of roofing tile and scraped away the dirt covering my breast. I could breathe more easily. As I tried again to crawl out, I saw that a huge nail was stuck in my stomach.

"Fire! Fire!" I could hear people shouting around me. It was either break free or burn to death. With a violent wrench, I pulled myself from under the beam. In doing so, I ripped the flesh of my stomach. Blood spurted from an agonizing gash in my body.

I was at last out of the ruined house. Still, my son was nowhere to be seen. Perhaps the kind lady next door had led him to safety. I had to search for him, but I could only limp slowly because of the pain in my stomach.

I decided to go to a nearby hill, which was open and might offer some security. As I crept slowly along, people more seriously injured than I clutched at my feet and pleaded for help and water. Among the piteous cries I heard loud voices shouting, "Leave the old people! Help the children first." I wanted to help, but I was in grave need of assistance myself. All I could do was promise to come back with water, if it was possible.

On my way to the hill, I met a neighbor and friend. Looking long and intently at me, she finally said, "It is Toyomi, isn't it?" I knew that my dress was in tatters and that I was bloody and dirty. But now, stopping to examine myself for the first time, I learned worse. One of my ears had been cut nearly off. It and my whole face were caked with congealed blood.

"Thank heaven you're alive!" I heard a familiar voice saying. Turning, with intense happiness, I saw my husband, who was holding our son in his arms. We climbed to the top of the hill together, walking among countless corpses.

On the hilltop, a kind man gave us bed sheets, candles, sugar, and other useful things. At once we began to try to do something for Takashi, who had lost consciousness. After a while, as we dripped sugar water into his mouth, he awakened.

He had already lost the sight of his right eye. Myriad slivers of glass were embedded in his head, face, body, arms, and legs. An air-raid alarm, still in effect, prohibited lighting candles. In the pitch darkness, my husband and I picked out as many pieces of glass from his body as we could find. So full of life and energy until that moment! Now blind in one eye and covered with blood and dirt! Still he bore everything bravely and only asked, "Am I being a good boy?" Pride at his courage and grief for his pain forced us both to weep quietly.

I made bandages from the bed sheet. Placing some boards over two large rocks, I made us a shelter. We were fortunate to be together. In the dark, we could hear people calling the names of their loved ones. I wondered what had happened to my younger and elder sisters.

The light of dawn showed us a hell. Corpses, some burned to cinders, others only partly roasted, lay everywhere. Barely living, faintly breathing, others rapidly drew toward death. A horrible stench filled the air.

In a few days we were taken to a bomb shelter where, in spite of a food shortage, we managed to live for a month. I was in such pain that it was excruciating to carry my son to the toilet. Nonetheless, he and I went daily to a nearby clinic for treatment. As days passed, my hair began falling; and blood oozed from my gums. My husband was too ill to walk. We began hearing rumors that the bomb that had destroyed Nagasaki was of the same kind as the one that had fallen on Hiroshima.

People who had not been injured in the blast began to die, one after another. We waited for our turns to come.

Near the well from which we had to draw all our water corpses were cremated. On our way to the well, we had to pick a ghoulish way through a field of human bones. Often in the morning there would be a dead body by the well that had not been there the evening before. I wondered who would take care of our corpses when we died.

But we did not die. In September, my two drafted brothers returned from the war. My younger and elder sisters turned up, safe and well. In October, we rented the house in Oura where I live with my family today.

In about a year, I began noticing purple spots on my body. I tired easily and suffered occasional sharp pains in the head. I learned that my white-blood-corpuscle count had dropped drastically. Aware that all these symptoms characterized the atomic diseases, I became apprehensive about my future. My husband was so ill that he could not work. By the time Takashi entered primary school, it was becoming difficult for us to make ends meet. Nor was our son's lot in school easy. Cruel neighborhood children hurt him deeply when they jeered and called him a one-eyed devil.

A single bomb had wrecked a peaceful and happy family. True, my husband had not gone to the battle front, but we were nonetheless as much victims of the war as the survivors of soldiers who had died fighting. The government offered financial assistance to such people, but none to our kind. With rising anger, I often asked myself why they discriminated in this way.

To all these trials was soon added my husband's total desperation and determination to kill himself and our son so that I could try to find some happiness on my own. I had to guard him constantly. Even so, he succeeded in making a number of attempts to strangle himself and our son. When, in 1948, he was taken to the police by a neighbor who found him trying to hang himself in the garden, he collapsed on the floor, crying, "Let me die. I can't stand the agony of living any more."

Since he could not work, I had to support the family by serving in restaurants, nursing the sick, and doing whatever odd jobs I could find. Over the years, my determination to keep on going was strengthened by the births of two more children. Still, sometimes I too weakened and contemplated suicide. My work was arduous, and I was weak. Occasionally I fainted on the job.

But even this was not to be the limit of what I was to witness and endure. In 1952, four months after his birth, I noticed something queer about one of my fourth son's eyes. I took him to an ophthalmologist, who diagnosed the case as cancer of the eye. Very rare. One case in ten thousand. He added that unless the eye was removed at once, the cancer would spread; the eye would eventually pop from its socket; and my son would die, withered like a blasted tree. I was too shocked and terrified to cry.

The same doctor recommended that I take my child to a university hospital for treatment. At first I hesitated. We had no money to pay for such care. But I could not sacrifice my son's life. Resolving to scrape together the funds somehow, I took him to a university clinic where the first doctor's diagnosis was confirmed and where I learned that without immediate surgery there was grave danger that the cancer would spread to the other eye. Even in the light of this knowledge, however, I could not consent to having my child's eye removed.

About fifteen months later, this same child began to cough in an odd way. I wanted to take him to a nearby hospital but could not: I owed them money. Instead, I took him to a smaller hospital some distance from our home. The doctor at first said it was only a neglected cold. But when the child got no better and I took him to the hospital again, I was told that it was diphtheria and that he would have to be hospitalized at once at the Nagasaki Hospital. Where was I to get the money?

I asked my elder brother's wife for aid, but she was too short of funds. Nevertheless, she offered to lend me her own son's health insurance policy. Her boy was three, or about a year and a half younger than my fourth son. Though terrified that our insurance fraud would be discovered, I had no choice but to accept her proposal.

Now my son was able to have good medical treatment. Vaccines were tried for a while, but they soon failed to have effect. The doctor insisted on surgery. Though the operation was a success, it had been necessary to install a respiratory device in my son's throat. The device was covered with thick gauze, which had to be kept constantly moist. If it dried, phlegm would accumulate and strangle the boy. Since there was no money to spend on private nurses, I had to stay by his bedside constantly. My younger sister offered to help me, but a few days of the gruelling routine exhausted her and made her ill. Late at night when the doctor made his rounds, he would try to cheer us: "Keep it up. You're doing a good job."

Finally, my child's condition improved. To my delight, he was to be released from the hospital. The time had come to remove the respiratory device. But the doctor who was in charge made a mistake and cut an artery in the throat. The day before he was to have come home, my son died, strangled on his own blood.

The doctor knelt by the bed, groaning for forgiveness. I blamed him. But recriminations would not bring my boy back to life. I had falsified the insurance papers and had no alternative but to remain silent. Upon arriving in the hospital room, my husband collapsed. Weeping bitterly, he blamed himself for being unable to earn money to support the family.

My fourth son died on May 10, 1945. On the nineteenth of the same month, I was given work as a scrub woman in the university hospital. My pay, five hundred yen a day, was barely enough for survival and left nothing for luxuries. When our eldest son was in the sixth grade, penury threatened to deprive him of the chance to participate in the school excursion marking the end of primary and the beginning of middle school. After consideration of our condition, his school allowed him to go on the trip free of charge. But because of my work, I could not see him off. Our next-door neighbor was kind enough to do it for me.

My happiness at the birth of our fifth son, in June, 1956, was to be short-lived. I had hoped he would be a reincarnation of the baby I had lost. And in the most tragic and ironic way, he inherited the same eye disease that had afflicted his dead elder brother.

Why? My husband was a good, kind, gentle man. No one could speak ill of him. I had done no one wrong. I had always tried to be kind to the weak and the elderly. I was considered an excellent mother and housewife. Why, among my five brothers and sisters, had I been singled out for this suffering? My frequent and repeated prayers at Buddhist temples and Shinto shrines had no effect. The white film covering my son's eye was permanent. So deep was our physical and spiritual desolation at the time that the whole family agreed to commit suicide if it should become necessary to hospitalize this little boy.

My husband did not wait for the rest of us. His final suicide attempt left him ill and broken. Once again, there was no money. I pleaded with municipal officials, telling them how my husband's weakened physical state prohibited his working. I explained his history to them and said that I earned only the smallest income as a scrub woman. Finally, they agreed to provide him free hospital care and to put our family on government relief. Our condition had improved a little. But after about three months in a hospital bed, quietly, peacefully, my husband died in his sleep.

Though we did not know it then, our worst trials were over. My eldest son, limited by partial blindness, could not choose an occupation freely. He apprenticed himself to a shoemaker. I continued to work hard in the hope of providing a better future for the other children. Almost before I knew it, three years had passed; and I had been given a chance to remarry.

My second husband, who is crippled in both legs, is a skilled carver of tortoise-shell ornaments. As my children grew up, they earned money and contributed to the general fund so that little by little we were able to buy electrical appliances and ultimately to live an average family life on my husband's earnings alone.

Takashi, my oldest child, in spite of the loss of an eye, now works for a transport company and is the father of two lovely children. Immediately before he entered primary school, a doctor who gave him a physical examination told me that my fifth son's eye cancer had stabilized and would spread no farther. At the time of writing this, he was a senior in high school.

Though we have suffered, our family has, at least in part, survived. There are many others for whom the atomic-bomb sickness remains a constant source of pain and despair or an ever-present threat. Only people who suffer from this kind of illness can know its full terror. Even doctors do not always diagnose it accurately.

Young people today have been fortunate enough never to experience war. But they must not forget. It is the duty of those of us who have lived through the hells of the atomic bombings and the years of agony following them to proclaim our experiences so that war and its evils can be recognized for what they are and abolished from the earth.

ANNE HÉBERT (FRENCH CANADA)

THE MURDERED CITY

Salt and oil purified the city just as well, since water wasn't safe and recourse to God outdated

We drained the marsh, captured the bird of prey, all wings spread, the most gentle of us swearing he'd put it to sleep, a cross on the door

Of course, the night before, all tears, pain, fear, dream or pity had been purged

The horror of death guiding us, certain images judged malevolent were forbidden at once

Everyone's right hand was flattened against the sky to verify each joint and the bones' precision in the light

For a moment we considered the flash of fire to test certain faces that were too fine, only the fear of fire in the executioner's hair prevented this sacrifice

The children were put to sleep by force, noiselessly.

We erected dogma and morals, and the first season lengthened without passion

A heavy wind crashed down on everything. It was judgment at its own peak growing over us, reigning everywhere

Memories were sifted, all love ruthlessly seized along with all dreamy or insolent memory

For a long time suffering and death seemed conquered. That was a lovely dry country to lie in, watching

Soon boredom bloomed in small green places and threatened to become a wound and gangrene

The youngest girl, brandishing her mourning, hoisted agony up on the highest wall overlooking the earth for all to see

The lust for water became so bitter that tears were invoked as a blessing

The girl screamed that she had neither a heart nor a face and that we'd betrayed her from the start

Chased outside the city walls, late to bloom, abrupt as thirst in her eyrie, she turned around

Behind her the city crumbled, stones, sand, cinders, petals of poppies, vermillion hearts in the wind

Fear in her veins, pity between her hands, in one stroke the girl tested the world's misfortune in her flesh

And discovered her own tender face exploding among tears.

(Translated by Al Poulin, Jr.)

Diana der Hovanessian (armenia/u.s.a.)

SONGS OF BREAD*

You think I wrote from love.
You think I wrote from ease.

* Title of a group of poems written in prison in 1915 by the Armenian poet Daniel Varoujan before his execution.

You imagine me singing as I walked
through wheat praising bread.
You imagine me looking from my window
at my children in the grass, my wife
humming, my dog running, my sun still
warm. But this notebook is drenched
in blood. It is written in blood
in a wagon rolling past yellow, amber,
gold wheat. But in the dark, in
the smell of sweat, urine, vomit.
The song of blue pitchers filled
with sweet milk, the song of silver
fountains welcoming home students,
the song of silo, barn, harvest,
tiller and red soil, all written
in the dark. The Turks allowed it.
What harm in a pen soon to be theirs,
a notebook to be theirs, a coat,
theirs, unless too much blood splattered.
You read and picture me in
a tranquil village, a church, on
the Bosporus, on a hillside, not
in anguish, not in fury, not wrenching
back the dead, holding the sun still
for a few more hours, making bread
out of words. This notebook you ransomed
dear friend, postponed, delayed my storm.
You see only its calm.

AN ARMENIAN LOOKING AT NEWSPHOTOS
OF THE CAMBODIAN DEATHWATCH

My sack of tiny
bones, bird
bones, my baby
with head so large
your thin neck bends,
my flimsy bag of breath,
all my lost cousins
unfed
wearing your pink flesh
like cloth
my pink rag doll
with head that grows

no hair,
eyes that cannot close,
my unborn past,
heaving your dry tears.

JUNE JORDAN (U.S.A.)

MOVING TOWARDS HOME

I do not wish to speak about the bulldozer and the
red dirt
not quite covering all of the arms and legs
Nor do I wish to speak about the nightlong screams
that reached
the observation posts where soldiers lounged about
Nor do I wish to speak about the woman who shoved
her baby
into the stranger's hands before she was led away
Nor do I wish to speak about the father whose sons
were shot
through the head while they slit his own throat before
the eyes
of his wife
Nor do I wish to speak about the army that lit continuous
flares into the darkness so that the others could see
the backs of their victims lined against the wall
Nor do I wish to speak about the piled up bodies and
the stench
that will not float
Nor do I wish to speak about the nurse again and
again raped
before they murdered her on the hospital floor
Nor do I wish to speak about the rattling bullets that
did not
halt on that keening trajectory
Nor do I wish to speak about the pounding on the
doors and
the breaking of windows and the hauling of families into
the world of the dead

I do not wish to speak about the bulldozer and the
red dirt
not quite covering all of the arms and legs
because I do not wish to speak about unspeakable events
that must follow from those who dare
"to purify" a people
those who dare
"to exterminate" a people
those who dare
to describe human beings as "beasts with two legs"
those who dare
"to mop up"
"to tighten the noose"
"to step up the military pressure"
"to ring around" civilian streets with tanks
those who dare
to close universities
to abolish the press
to kill the elected representatives
of the people who refuse to be purified
those are the ones from whom we must redeem
the words of our beginning because I need to speak about home
I need to speak about living room
where the land is not bullied and beaten into
a tombstone
I need to speak about living room
where the talk will take place in my language
I need to speak about living room
where my children will grow without horror
I need to speak about living room where the men
of my family between the ages of six and sixty-five
are not
marched into a roundup that leads to the grave
I need to talk about living room
where I can sit without grief without wailing aloud
for my loved ones
where I must not ask where is Abu Fadi
because he will be there beside me
I need to talk about living room
because I need to talk about home

I was born a Black woman
and now

I am become a Palestinian
against the relentless laughter of evil
there is less and less living room
and where are my loved ones?

It is time to make our way home.

Zoe Karelli (greece)

EXHUMATION*

They made packages of the human presence,
whatever remained of their bodies,
to return them to their native land.
One name, one date
is what is left of the young man who stood
erect, in the light of life, who laughed,
or remained thoughtful, when he was sad.
He may have been insignificant in his life,
he had the idea he could die
for duty.

                                        But life

is so beautiful, beyond
the cruelest struggle
beauty exists that we may live,
in girlhood resembling a flower,
in young manhood a strong tree.

I hesitate, that I am so sad
and I lament the destruction
of human beings. The clank of courage
must be strong to be heard,
for the dead to be put behind us,
for us to cross over the bend.
Brothers, I can tell you
with passion and a loud voice,

---

* A special service that exhumed the dead after World War II, and sent the remains
back to their fatherland.

life invites us to forget
death. (Of others or of our own?)
Let us comprehend submission,
a good solution, for us to know fortitude,
to attempt extra courage
on our march.

                                    I think

of the human presence,
that awakens so much love,
pains and feelings, passions
that is strength and beauty
then remains a faceless shadow.

                        (*Translated by Rae Dalven*)

GERTRUDE KOLMAR (GERMANY*)

MURDER

The murderers are loose! They search the world
All through the night, oh God, all through the night!
To find the fire kindled in me now,
This child so like a light, so still and mild.

They want to put it out. Like pouring ink
Their shadows seep from angled walls;
Like scrawny cats they scuttle
Timidly across the footworn steps.

And I am shackled to my bed
With grating chains all gnawed with rust
That weigh upon me, pitiless and strong,
And bite raw wounds into my helpless arms.

The murderer has come! He wears a hat,
A broad-brimmed hat with towering pointed peak;
Upon his chin sprout tiny golden flames
That dance across my body; it is good . . .

* Gertrude Kolmar, a Jewish-German poet died in a Nazi concentration camp.

His huge nose sniffs about and stretches out
Into a tentacle that wriggles like a rope.
Out of his fingernails crawl yellow maggots,
Saffron seeds that sprinkle down on me

Into my hair and eyes. The tentacle
Gropes for my breasts, at rose-brown nipples,
And I see its white flesh twist into the blackness;
Something sinks upon me, sighs and presses—

I can't go on . . . I can't . . . Oh let the blade strike down
Like a monstrous tooth that flashes from the sky!
Oh crush me! There, where blood-drops fly,
Can you hear it cry, can you hear it?

"Mother!" Oh the stillness . . . In my womb: the axe.
From either side of it break forks of flame.
They meet and fold together now:
My child. Of dark green bronze, so stern and grave.

(Translated by Henry A. Smith)

FOUMIKO KOMETANI (JAPAN/U.S.A.)

AMERICA'S CONCENTRATION CAMPS

In the mid-1950's when I was working in Japan for an American firm, a . . . co-worker one day confronted me as if I were General Tojo or Emperor Hirohito. "Because you started the war," she said indignantly, "we had the most terrible time of it in America. We had to live in concentration camps." It was hard for me to think of anybody spending the war years in North America as having a terrible time. My uncle who was killed in the Philippines certainly had *a terrible time*. . . . I was ignorant of the American concentration camps and the racist war crimes committed against American citizens of Japanese ancestry. More than 110,000 people of Japanese descent on the West Coast, more than 80 percent of them American citizens, were wrenched from their homes and imprisoned in desert wildernesses behind barbed wire with machine gunners facing them. . . . I do not recall the Japanese news media, operating under strict American censorship after the war, ever informing us of any of these facts. . . . I can never forget the shock I felt as I watched the first newsreels showing the German death camps after the war—even in Japan the American censors allowed us to see them. But I must confess I felt small shudders of a similar nature as I turned the pages of *Beyond Words: Images from America's Concentration Camps.*

MARGARET MACKAY (U.S.A.)

WOMEN UNDER APARTHEID

The South African people have waged a long and determined struggle for liberation—and in that struggle, women have played a central role.

African National Congress President Oliver Tambo declared, "In our beleaguered country, the woman's place is in the battlefront of struggle," when he declared 1984 the "Year of the Woman" on behalf of the ANC.

Perhaps the fact that Black women are the most heavily oppressed by the apartheid system—on the basis of their race, their class, and their sex—explains why they have opposed it with such courage and determination. . . .

This system scars the life of every Black South African—but women bear the brunt of it.

Many South African women must struggle alone to support children and aged relatives on the barren reserves, apart from husbands and fathers who have sought work in the cities.

Others, driven by the need to earn a living, must leave their children behind and move illegally to the urban areas in search of work. An intricate series of laws prevents them from settling in the cities. Most women are faced daily with the possibility of being "repatriated" to the area where they were born, or to a "homeland" they have never seen, or removed to resettlement camps.

It is almost impossible for a husband and wife to secure the legal right to live together in an urban area. This is why squatter camps—where Black families live together illegally, risking raids, arrests, and fines—have grown up on the outskirts of many townships, like the famous Crossroads camp outside Cape Town. The apartheid government has been trying to bulldoze the camp since 1977, but the women have courageously and successfully resisted this. . . . At least 18 people were killed and scores were wounded in new government efforts to destroy Crossroads. [See p. 40.]

Black women today make up one-third of the African labor force. Most are limited to low paid, unskilled or semi-skilled work. Even when they do the same work as men, they are discriminated against in pay and working conditions. The average earnings of African women are less than half those of African men, and in 1980 they earned only 8% of the income of white men.

Most Black women work as domestic workers. They receive low wages for unrestricted hours of isolated work, caring for the children of white families while their own children are left behind on the reserves.

Agricultural workers are even more exploited. With the increasing mechanization of South African agriculture, many have been forced off the farms they lived and worked on for decades. Most have become seasonal workers.

They are often paid in kind, rather than cash. Their wages are even lower than those of domestic workers and, like them, they are not covered by minimum wage, unemployment benefits or other forms of social security.

A very small proportion of African women work in industry—concentrated in the clothing, textile, food processing and canning plants, where women's wages are significantly lower than those of men.

Only a handful of women are employed as technicians or professionals, mostly as teachers and nurses. By the mid-1970s, there still was not one African woman lawyer, magistrate, engineer, architect, veterinarian, chemist or pharmacist.

High unemployment has affected Black men and women in all types of work since the early 1970's.

"The women are the most oppressed of the Black majority, and perhaps that explains why women have been so much in the forefront of the liberation struggle," says Nomazizi Sokudela, a member of the Women's Section of the ANC. "It also explains why we have seen the struggle for equality, for women's rights, as an integral part of the national liberation struggle.

"Women's inequality has been imposed by the regime—for example, in laws which make women perpetual minors, unable to engage in contracts, to own or dispose of property, or even to serve as legal guardians of our own children."

One leader in South Africa's liberation struggle was Charlotte Maxeke, a founding member of the ANC, who played an important role in the struggle against the 1913 Land Act and helped found the ANC Women's League in 1913.

In the same period, women resisted government efforts to make them carry passes. Their resistance was so successful that the idea was not raised again until the mid-1950s. . . .

Women also led the massive anti-pass campaigns that erupted across South Africa in the mid-'50s. A UN publication describes some of these courageous actions: "On 9 August 1956, in a protest organized by FSAW (Federation of South African Women), more than 20,000 women came to the Union Buildings in Pretoria to see the Prime Minister. When he refused to see them, they placed petitions with more than 100,000 signatures in his office. . . .

"On the day that passes were to be distributed in Sanderton in southeastern Transvaal, all 914 women who went to protest to the Mayor were arrested for taking part in an illegal procession.

"But the women were undaunted. In July 1957, in Gopane Village in the Baphurutse reserve, some women burned their passes. When 35 women were arrested, 233 more volunteered to be arrested. . . . In June 1957, at Pietersburg in the northern Transvaal, 2,000 women stoned officials who came to register them. . . . In October 1957, in Johannesburg, more than 2,000 were arrested" protesting government efforts to register them.

In the same period, women organized a bus boycott in the Black townships of Alexandria, Sophiatown and Lady Shelburne to protest a fare increase. In mass raids, 6,606 Africans were arrested, and another 7,860 were subpoenaed. But the Africans continued to protest, and after five months the fare increase was rolled back.

A wave of repression swept South Africa after the Sharpeville massacre in 1960. Nomazizi Sokudela points out that many women were arrested and imprisoned or banished.

"When the movement went underground, a lot of women left the country to work in the various structures of the movement in exile, whilst others remained and have worked actively in the underground structures inside the country," she said.

"They have also participated fully in the military wing of the ANC, Umkhonto we Sizwe. Thandi Modise, who was arrested in action, is serving an eight-year sentence in South Africa now.

"Dorothy Nyembe, who finished a 15-year prison term in March 1984, has been outstanding in her courageous participation in the liberation struggle . . . and Lillian Keagile. Now these are women who, on top of being imprisoned, are subjected also to torture and rape." . . .

Nomzamo Winnie Mandela has spent almost all of her adult life under banning orders, in prison, or in banishment, with only one 12-month period of freedom since 1963, and has only enjoyed two years of married life with her husband since their marriage in 1958. Nelson Mandela went underground after the ANC was banned in 1960, was arrested a year later and has been serving a life sentence ever since.

In 1977, she was banished to a "living grave" outside the remote township of Brandfort. Repeated government efforts to convict and imprison her have ended in failure—and brought international attention to her plight.

Winnie Mandela has refused to allow her incarceration in Brandfort to break her spirit, or to undermine her confidence that the future belongs to the South African people.

The women of South Africa continue their struggle in the same determined spirit—by defending the squatter camps, defying mass removals, supporting their children's struggle against "Bantu education."

ILEANA MALANCIOUI (ROMANIA)

ANTIGONE

A frozen mound, white body of a dead man
fallen in hard battle and left above the Earth.
Hungry dogs come to bite the treacherous snow
and another winter comes, too, to take its bite.

Let a pure woman appear to break the command,
to wrench the unbelievable hill from the dogs
and hide it as a dear brother—
while those near her wash their hands of it
and allow her to be buried alive in the earth
clothed in unreal white,

for as the emperor lost his great battle
she wept and buried her frozen mound.

(*Translated by Daniela Gioseffi*)

WINNIE MANDELA (SOUTH AFRICA)

NO HUMAN BEING CAN TAKE SUCH HUMILIATIONS

Detention means that midnight knock when all about you is quiet. It means those blinding torches shone simultaneously through every window of your house before the door is kicked open. It means the exclusive right the Security Branch have to read each and every letter in the house. . . . Ultimately it means your seizure at dawn, dragged away from little children screaming and clinging to your skirt, imploring the white man dragging Mummy away to leave her alone. . . . I was kept in Pretoria Central Prison. My cell had a grille inside, a door in the middle and another grille ouside. From what I had read, I realized that mine must be the death cell. I did not even know I was with other detainees in the cell block. I thought I was alone; for months I didn't know that the whole country had been rounded up. All I could hear was a distant cough and a faint sound of prison doors being locked.

Those first few days are the worst in anyone's life—that uncertainty, the insecurity: there is such a sense of hopelessness, the feeling that this is now the end. The whole thing is calculated to destroy you, not only morally but also physically. You know the enemy could keep you there for five years. You are not in touch with anybody. And in those days all I had in the cells was a sanitary bucket, a plastic bottle which could contain only about three glasses of water, and a mug. . . . During menstruation we only got toilet paper or they would say, "Go use your big fat hands." For a bed there was only a mat and three stinking filthy blankets. I rolled one up for a pillow and slept with the other two. . . . The days and nights became so long I found I was talking to myself. It is deathly quiet—that alone is a torture. You don't know what to do with yourself; you sit down, you stand up, you pace up and down. The cell is so small that you can't even run right round. . . . You find yourself looking for anything in the cells; for instance, I remember how happy I was when I found two ants, how I spent the whole day with these ants, playing with them on my finger and how sad I was when the warders switched off the light. That was during the day, but the building was so old that it was perpetually dark. . . .

At night it was not possible to sleep. . . . We had inspection every day in prison. Two wardresses walk in, they order you to stand up, they take off your clothes. They start by inspecting your shoes as you stand there stark naked. They go through your panties, your bra, they go through every seam of every garment. Then they go through your hair and—of course, they never succeed with me, but with female prisoners it's com-

mon practice—they inspect the vagina. . . . Nothing is more humiliating. And you are all alone in that cell. . . . My interrogation started on a
Monday. And I was only delivered back to the cell on the Saturday
night. They interrogated me for five days and five nights. I remember
that vaguely. During the fifth night I was having these fainting spells
which are very relieving. . . . My whole body was badly swollen, I was
passing blood. . . . You can't eat in such circumstances—food is of no
relevance. The whole experience is so terrible, because I had left little
children at home in bed and I had no idea what had happened to
them. . . . Rita Ndzanga and I were interrogated when they were almost through with the others who had been rounded up. She and I
were both banned people. . . . I was interrogated for hours about
some women we had been helping—they were members of the South
African Federation of Women who had been in prison since 1960.
These women had no visitors—the old tactic, when people were tucked
away in prison, and families were not told which prison they were
in. . . . Rita was tortured very badly, she nearly died. . . . Those were
horrible days. I hate to recall them. And I was already quite sick when
I went to prison. I hadn't been able to sleep at all and in prison it
was the same; sometimes I wasn't able to sleep for twenty-four hours.
To have something to do, I started scraping off the paint from the
wall with my fingernails. . . . I would have been allowed to come out
in the very first month of those seventeen months of solitary confinement if I had agreed to the ludicrous suggestions that were made; that
if I cooperated and allowed my voice to be used over the air to call
upon our African National Congress forces at the border to retreat and
put down their arms and have discussions with the government, I
would be released. . . . They would have flown me by helicopter [to
be reunited with Nelson]. . . . They never gave up—right through my
detention. That's how narrow-minded these people can be. After you've
given the best years of your life to this cause—that they can dream
that your principles can still be for sale! If there weren't people in this
country who would still fight for justice, my fate would have been the
same as that of most blacks in this land. Most blacks in this country
go to jail for nothing; thousands are arrested every day whose only
offense is wanting to live together as a family. . . . When they brought
our food in the morning, it was porridge. (Uncooked and full of bird-
shit from sitting outside the cell.) That was how we knew it was
morning. They would take the (toilet) . . . buckets and bring them
back without even rinsing them, turn the lid upside down, put the
plate of [disgusting] food on that lid and you would just see a white
leg pushing in that [toilet] . . . bucket. . . . I suffered from malnutrition; the complexion becomes sallow, you get bleeding gums from lack

of vitamins; I could not stand, I had fever and blackouts. When we were to be charged in October, I could not appear in court. I had to be taken to the prison hospital. The only time we had some relief was when our complaints were raised in court . . . up to that date [from May to October] we hadn't been [allowed] showering or bathing. . . . They never stop trying to humiliate you. . . . No human being can go on taking those humiliations without reaction. . . . You can't intimidate people like me any more. In 1974, when I was convicted and was serving six months in Kroonstad Prison, I met one of our symbols of resistance, Dorothy Nyembe, a close friend of Nelson's. To be there with a woman who was serving fifteen years as she was, who was as courageous as she was, was a tremendous experience for me. . . . The determination of her. She was already over fifty when I met her! I found her a solid pillar of strength. She had been in prison since 1968, but she was so undaunted. Her spirit was exactly the same as when she went in. She is one of the old heroes, one of the great women who have personally made me what I am. . . .

GABRIELA MISTRAL (CHILE)

FINNISH CHAMPION*

Finnish Champion, you are stretched out
in the burnished light of your final stadium,
red as the pheasant in life and in death,
stitched with wounds, drained as a gargoyle spout
of your blood.
You have fallen in the snows of your childhood,
among blue edges and steely mirrors,
crying No! to the North and the East,
a No! that compresses profusion of snow,
hardens the skis to diamonds,
stops the war tank like a wild boar.
Swimmer, ball-player, runner,
let them burn your name and call you "Finland."
Hallowed be your final course,

---

* During World War II Finland put up amazing resistance to two massive invasions by Russian forces, and despite heavy losses succeeded in retaining her autonomy.

hallowed the meridian that took your body,
hallowed the midnight sin that granted your final
miracle.
You denied the invader the draught of your lakes,
your paths, the life-thread of your reindeer,
the threshold of your home, the cube of your arena,
the rainbow of your Virgins and Christ,
the baptized foreheads of your children.

(Translated by Doris Dana)

Elsa Morante (italy)

SUNDAY EVENING

Through the pain of sick wards
and of all prison walls
of barbed-wire camps, of convicts and their keepers,
of ovens Siberias and slaughter-houses
of marches solitudes drunkenness and suicides
and the leaps of conception
the sickly sweet taste of the seed and the dead,
through the innumerable body of pain
theirs and mine,
today I reject reason, majesty
that denies the last grace,
and I spend my Sunday with madness.
Oh pierced prayer of elevation,
I claim for myself the guilt of the offense
in the vile body.
Stamp your grace
on my ill-grown mind. I receive you.

And the small carnage begins again.
The sweat nausea the cold fleshy fingertips the bones' agony
and the round of wonderful abstractions
in the horror of stripping away flesh.
The usual deadly female peacock called Scheherazade
unfurls her wheel of stabbing pains,

feathers and flowers suddenly petrified
in the giddiness of colors against nature, a lacerating lynching
with sharp stones. No way out.
The range of the limitless is another prison law
more perverse than any limit. But still
beyond a glacial era the daily norm
resurfaces at intervals with its poor domestic face
while the blend of nature's kingdoms
melts the veins in waves like childhood's first menses
until the lymph is burned away. The carnal fever is consumed.
Conscience now is only a moth beating against the deathly dark
seeking a thread of substance. Summer is dead.
Farewell farewell destinations addresses popes bestiaries
and numberings,
Via della Scimmia, Piazza Navona, Avenue of the Americas.
Farewell measures, directions, five senses. Farewell slavish duties
slavish rights slavish judgments.
Take refuge blindly on the other side, hells or limbos, it
doesn't matter,
rather than find yourself back in your disgusting domicile
where you're crushed between walls soiled by painted canvases
recognizable as rags and dust of degraded Sindons.
The floor is a bloody mud boiling again
in the rooms, disintegrating ossuaries, in the last lightning flash
of a misshapen brass plate, where lemons
swell to plastic balls. And from the mirror
with dusty eye-sockets something alien but at the same time
close, intimate, stares at you, dark fish-scale beyond every
incarnation,
that also denies the skeleton and the whole business
of geneses and epiphanies
of tombs and Easters. Don't try the twisted ruinous itinerary
of the stairs, that is for you an ascension of centuries,
and above, below, there is always Hell.
The decayed sky is the low ragged tent
of the earthly leper-house. And the Mozartian flute
is a malign hopping that beats back
all the way into your eye-bulb its trivial mimicry
of an obsessive arithmetic that has no other meaning . . .
No further sky's exposed. The thousand-petaled lotus doesn't open.
You're all there is here. There's nothing else.
Be present at this. And stop calling on
dead lovers, dead mothers.
Stripped bare, poorer still than you, they don't frequent this

or other dimensions. Their final habitation
remains in your memory alone.

Memory memory, house of pain
where through great rooms and deserted galleries
an uproar of loudspeakers keeps repeating
(the mechanism is bewitched) always the bitter point
of the Eli Eli without an answer. The shriek of the boy
who leaps blinded by the sacred evil.
The young assassin raving in the mad dormitory.
The cropped Christian litany in the hospital
storeroom, around the old dead Jewess
who pushed away the cross with her small delirious hands.
WITHOUT THE COMFORTS OF RELIGION. This house is
                                        full of blood,
but the blood itself, all blood, is only spectral vapors
like the mind that bears witness to them.
And when the hour of requiem arrives for you, it will be like
                            this through those cries.

The desecrated Sunday declines now
the plague-moons are already sinking
the thorny hedge buds again, your senses chime in five voices.
Hurry again, hurry to meet your usual poor tomorrows,
your usual death-doomed body.
It's supper-time. Oh hunger for life, feed yourself
again on the daily substance of slaughters.
Be born again to forms to confidences and arbitrary choruses
to consciousness
to health
to the order of dates
to your place.

No Revelation. (Even if the play is illegal,
it always depends on the collective factory of free will).
No sin (The machine designed for torture
isn't guilty of the tortures, oh poor sinners).
And no special grace.
(The only common grace is patience
up to the consummation's amen).
Go away content. Absolved, absolved, though backsliding.
Good evening, good evening.
This Sunday too is over.

(Translated by Ruth Feldman and Brian Swann)

YUNNA PETROVNA MORITZ (U.S.S.R.)

RECOLLECTIONS

From the burning train
Onto the grass
They hurled the children.
I floated
Along a bloody, slippery ditch
Of human entrails, bones.

The pilot who flew over me—
A brown pestilence—
Grimaced and laughed
Like a madman.
He fluttered in his flying trunk
He banked his head into his windshield
I saw the swastika on his arm
And what flowed out of his head.

And I saw too the red circle
Of the locomotive wheel
And out of horror
I didn't have enough hands
To cover my eyes,
Because the locomotive was not moving.

But a bloody fog and fumes
Rose from the wheels whirling in place
And the iron control lever groaned
Like an arm bent into an elbow
Separated from the body
In order to turn the locomotive wheels
Posthumously!

Thus in my fifth year
God sent to me
Salvation and a long road . . .
But horror flowed into my flesh and blood—
And rolls about in me like quicksilver!
And when I fall asleep facing the moon,
So bitterly do I cry in my sleep,
That my tears flow down the wall,
In which I hide my recollection.

(*Translated by Thomas P. Whitney*)

TONI MORRISON (U.S.A.)

SULA

Except for World War II, nothing ever interfered with the celebration of National Suicide Day. It had taken place every January third since 1920, although Shadrack, its founder, was for many years the only cele-brant. Blasted and permanently astonished by the events of 1917, he had returned to Medallion handsome but ravaged, and even the most fastidious people in the town sometimes caught themselves dreaming of what he must have been like a few years back before he went off to war. A young man of hardly twenty, his head full of nothing and his mouth recalling the taste of lipstick, Shadrack had found himself in December, 1917, running with his comrades across a field in France. It was his first encounter with the enemy and he didn't know whether his company was running toward them or away. For several days they had been marching, keeping close to a stream that was frozen at its edges. At one point they crossed it, and no sooner had he stepped foot on the other side than the day was adangle with shouts and explosions. Shell-fire was all around him, and though he knew that this was something called *it*, he could not muster up the proper feeling—the feeling that would accommodate *it*. He expected to be terrified or exhilarated—to feel *something* very strong. In fact, he felt only the bite of a nail in his boot, which pierced the ball of his foot whenever he came down on it. The day was cold enough to make his breath visible, and he wondered for a moment at the purity and whiteness of his own breath among the dirty, gray explosions surrounding him. He ran, bayonet fixed, deep in the great sweep of men flying across this field. Wincing at the pain in his foot, he turned his head a little to the right and saw the face of a soldier near him fly off. Before he could register shock, the rest of the soldier's head disappeared under the inverted soup bowl of his helmet. But stubbornly, taking no direction from the brain, the body of the headless soldier ran on, with energy and grace, ignoring altogether the drip and slide of brain tissue down its back.

When Shadrack opened his eyes he was propped up in a small bed. Be-fore him on a tray was a large tin plate divided into three triangles. In one triangle was rice, in another meat, and in the third stewed toma-toes. A small round depression held a cup of whitish liquid. Shadrack stared at the soft colors that filled these triangles: the lumpy whiteness of rice, the quivering blood tomatoes, the grayish-brown meat. All their repugnance was contained in the neat balance of the triangles—a bal-ance that soothed him, transferred some of its equilibrium to him.

Thus reassured that the white, the red and the brown would stay where they were—would not explode or burst forth from their restricted zones—he suddenly felt hungry and looked around for his hands. His glance was cautious at first, for he had to be very careful—anything could be anywhere. Then he noticed two lumps beneath the beige blanket on either side of his hips. With extreme care he lifted one arm and was relieved to find his hand attached to his wrist. He tried the other and found it also. Slowly he directed one hand toward the cup and, just as he was about to spread his fingers, they began to grow in higgledy-piggledy fashion like Jack's beanstalk all over the tray and the bed. With a shriek he closed his eyes and thrust his huge growing hands under the covers. Once out of sight they seemed to shrink back to their normal size. But the yell had brought a male nurse.

"Private? We're not going to have any trouble today, are we? Are we, Private?"

Shadrack looked up at a balding man dressed in a green-cotton jacket and trousers. His hair was parted low on the right side so that some twenty or thirty yellow hairs could discreetly cover the nakedness of his head.

"Come on. Pick up that spoon. Pick it up, Private. Nobody is going to feed you forever."

Sweat slid from Shadrack's armpits down his sides. He could not bear to see his hands grow again and he was frightened of the voice in the apple-green suit.

"Pick it up, I said. There's no point to this . . ." The nurse reached under the cover for Shadrack's wrist to pull out the monstrous hand. Shadrack jerked it back and overturned the tray. In panic he raised himself to his knees and tried to fling off and away his terrible fingers, but succeeded only in knocking the nurse into the next bed.

When they bound Shadrack into a straitjacket, he was both relieved and grateful, for his hands were at last hidden and confined to whatever size they had attained.

Laced and silent in his small bed, he tried to tie the loose cords in his mind. He wanted desperately to see his own face and connect it with the word "private"—the word the nurse (and the others who helped bind him) had called him. "Private" he thought was something secret, and he wondered why they looked at him and called him a secret. Still, if his hands behaved as they had done, what might he expect from his face? The fear and longing were too much for him, so he began to think of other things. That is, he let his mind slip into whatever cave mouths of memory it chose.

He saw a window that looked out on a river which he knew was full of fish. Someone was speaking softly just outside the door. . . .

Shadrack's earlier violence had coincided with a memorandum from the hospital executive staff in reference to the distribution of patients in high-risk areas. There was clearly a demand for space. The priority or the violence earned Shadrack his release, $217 in cash, a full suit of clothes and copies of very official-looking papers.

When he stepped out of the hospital door the grounds overwhelmed him: the cropped shrubbery, the edged lawns, the undeviating walks. Shadrack looked at the cement stretches: each one leading clearheadedly to some presumably desirable destination. There were no fences, no warnings, no obstacles at all between concrete and green grass, so one could easily ignore the tidy sweep of stone and cut out in another direction—a direction of one's own.

Shadrack stood at the foot of the hospital steps watching the heads of trees tossing ruefully but harmlessly, since their trunks were rooted too deeply in the earth to threaten him. Only the walks made him uneasy. He shifted his weight, wondering how he could get to the gate without stepping on the concrete. While plotting his course—where he would have to leap, where to skirt a clump of bushes—a loud guffaw startled him. Two men were going up the steps. Then he noticed that there were many people about, and that he was just now seeing them, or else they had just materialized. They were thin slips, like paper dolls floating down the walks. Some were seated in chairs with wheels, propelled by other paper figures from behind. All seemed to be smoking, and their arms and legs curved in the breeze. A good high wind would pull them up and away and they would land perhaps among the tops of the trees.

Shadrack took the plunge. Four steps and he was on the grass heading for the gate. He kept his head down to avoid seeing the paper people swerving and bending here and there, and he lost his way. When he looked up, he was standing by a low red building separated from the main building by a covered walkway. From somewhere came a sweetish smell which reminded him of something painful. He looked around for the gate and saw that he had gone directly away from it in his complicated journey over the grass. Just to the left of the low building was a graveled driveway that appeared to lead outside the grounds. He trotted quickly to it and left, at last, a haven of more than a year, only eight days of which he fully recollected.

Once on the road, he headed west. The long stay in the hospital had left him weak—too weak to walk steadily on the gravel shoulders of the road. He shuffled, grew dizzy, stopped for breath, started again, stumbling and sweating but refusing to wipe his temples, still afraid to look at his hands. Passengers in dark, square cars shuttered their eyes at what they took to be a drunken man.

The sun was already directly over his head when he came to a town. A few blocks of shaded streets and he was already at its heart—a pretty, quietly regulated downtown.

Exhausted, his feet clotted with pain, he sat down at the curbside to take off his shoes. He closed his eyes to avoid seeing his hands and fumbled with the laces of the heavy high-topped shoes. The nurse had tied them into a double knot, the way one does for children, and Shadrack, long unaccustomed to the manipulation of intricate things, could not get them loose. Uncoordinated, his fingernails tore away at the knots. He fought a rising hysteria that was not merely anxiety to free his aching feet; his very life depended on the release of the knots. Suddenly without raising his eyelids, he began to cry. Twenty-two years old, weak, hot, frightened, not daring to acknowledge the fact that he didn't even know who or what he was . . . with no past, no language, no tribe, no source, no address book, no comb, no pencil, no clock, no pocket handkerchief, no rug, no bed, no can opener, no faded postcard, no soap, no key, no tobacco pouch, no soiled underwear and nothing nothing nothing to do . . . he was sure of one thing only: the unchecked monstrosity of his hands. He cried soundlessly at the curbside of a small Midwestern town wondering where the window was, and the river, and the soft voices just outside the door. . . .

Through his tears he saw the fingers joining the laces, tentatively at first, then rapidly. The four fingers of each hand fused into the fabric, knotted themselves and zigzagged in and out of the tiny eyeholes.

By the time the police drove up, Shadrack was suffering from a blinding headache, which was not abated by the comfort he felt when the policemen pulled his hands away from what he thought was a permanent entanglement with his shoelaces. They took him to jail, booked him for vagrancy and intoxication, and locked him in a cell. Lying on a cot, Shadrack could only stare helplessly at the wall, so paralyzing was the pain in his head. He lay in this agony for a long while and then realized he was staring at the painted-over letters of a command to fuck himself. He studied the phrase as the pain in his head subsided.

Like moonlight stealing under a window shade an idea insinuated itself: his earlier desire to see his own face. He looked for a mirror; there was none. Finally, keeping his hands carefully behind his back he made his way to the toilet bowl and peeped in. The water was unevenly lit by the sun so he could make nothing out. Returning to his cot he took the blanket and covered his head, rendering the water dark enough to see his reflection. There in the toilet water he saw a grave black face. A black so definite, so unequivocal, it astonished him. He had been harboring a skittish apprehension that he was not real—that he didn't exist at all. But when the blackness greeted him with its indisputable presence, he wanted nothing more. In his joy he took the risk of letting one edge of the blanket drop and glanced at his hands. They were still. Courteously still.

Shadrack rose and returned to the cot, where he fell into the first sleep of his new life. A sleep deeper than the hospital drugs; deeper than the pits of plums, steadier than the condor's wing; more tranquil than the curve of eggs.

The sheriff looked through the bars at the young man with the matted hair. He had read through his prisoner's papers and hailed a farmer. When Shadrack awoke, the sheriff handed him back his papers and escorted him to the back of a wagon. Shadrack got in and in less than three hours he was back in Medallion, for he had been only twenty-two miles from his window, his river, and his soft voices just outside the door.

In the back of the wagon, supported by sacks of squash and hills of pumpkins, Shadrack began a struggle that was to last for twelve days, a struggle to order and focus experience. It had to do with making a place for fear as a way of controlling it. He knew the smell of death and was terrified of it, for he could not anticipate it. It was not death or dying that frightened him, but the unexpectedness of both. In sorting it all out, he hit on the notion that if one day a year were devoted to it, everybody could get it out of the way and the rest of the year would be safe and free. In this manner he instituted National Suicide Day.

HOPE MORRITT (CANADA)

BETWEEN THE CROSSES

Guns were quiet and larks were singing in sunny meadows the day I toured the battlefields of two world wars. I thought of my father—Lieutenant Herbert L. Morritt—a Canadian infantry soldier, wounded in 1917 at Passchendaele. He was only nineteen. I counted the time from then to now . . . sixty-nine years.

As our bus moved through France and Belgium, stopping here, there, I felt my father's presence strongly. In the 1950s, 1960s, and 1970s he had spoken of that science-fiction world of yesterday.

"It was a dirty war—mud and gas and stinking, wet trenches and the dead everywhere."

There were lighter moments when he met a young Irish nurse who took care of him when he fell at Passchendaele. After the war they were married and she came with him to Canada. She had other memories of that holocaust.

"Whole cities were bombed out. The destruction was awful. Soldiers died in my arms. They were so young."

A bearded clerk at the hotel I stayed at in Ostende, Belgium, told me: "We will never forget two world wars. If we forget, we might let it happen again."

It is easy to see the military cemeteries as one travels through Belgium and France. Often they are only square enclosures in a farmer's field, but they are bordered by stone walls or hedges and, at one end, the cross of sacrifice (black, edged with white) stands out boldly. Until you stop and study the row upon row of identical headstones with dates, it's difficult to tell whether the site is a burial ground from the First or Second World War. But, all are given tender loving care by the British War Graves Commission. Flowers bloom on every plot and the grass is like a green, velvet carpet.

Valentine Joe Strudwick, at age fifteen, was the youngest to die on the Western Front in the 1914–18 war. With only six weeks of training, young Strudwick was sent to France in 1915 when he had just turned fourteen. He was badly gassed and was sent home to Dorking, Surrey, to recuperate for three months in the summer of 1916. On recovering, he rejoined his regiment—the 8th Rifle Brigade—and was hit by a German shell the first week that he was back in the lines. Several students from an English public school, who were touring the battlefields the day I was there, stood solemnly around Strudwick's grave. I heard one lad whisper to a friend, "He was just my age."

I saw many graves marked simply, "known only to God," and I learned that the British author, Rudyard Kipling, had penned these words over the grave of an unknown soldier, after traveling hundreds of miles, searching in vain for the grave of his only son, killed in 1916.

The British cemetery at Dunkirk was sun-dappled the day I arrived. I saw people cradling boxes in their arms, and I asked the gardener what they were carrying.

"Polish soil . . . to sprinkle on Polish graves," he said. "They're people from Poland . . . relatives who come here every year."

These war dead were casualties of the evacuation of Dunkirk in 1940, and along with plots belonging to British airmen and Polish airmen, I saw the graves of Canadians.

They're so far from home, was my first thought as I viewed the long rows of white headstones gleaming in the sun, the Royal Canadian Air

240

Force crest on each one stamped with the motto: "Through adversity to the stars."

Perhaps the most poignant moment was when I stood near the Menin Gate, the entrance to the city of Ypres in Belgium which was the site of some of the bloodiest battles of the First World War.

Three buglers from the Ypres Fire Department marched up to the gate at 8 P.M., and all traffic in the city stopped while they sounded the Last Post. Since 1929, except for four years during the Second World War, buglers have sounded this famous call for "Lights out."

A tour guide pointed out the place that Canadian army doctor John McCrae had his frontline dressing station in those First World War years. The station was located at the bottom of a hill, now a grassy knoll, the surrounding sky filled with the gentle songs of larks.

"Casualties literally rolled down the hill into McCrae's dressing station," the tour guide said.

Here, in a narrow bunker, after a friend was killed, McCrae penned his famous lines:

> In Flanders Fields the poppies blow
> Between the crosses, row on row
> That mark our place, and in the sky
> The larks still bravely singing fly
> Scarce heard among the guns below . . .

Remembering that my father had walked this very ground, had marched under the Menin Gate, had lost buddies who were buried in these fields . . . remembering that my mother had known McCrae, had helped him dress wounds . . . this, indeed, was a fitting end for my tour of the battlefields and cemeteries of two world wars.

LUCRETIA MOTT (U.S.A.)

THE TIME HAS NOT COME

. . . we have watched the accounts that have been furnished—some in the daily papers, and some in letters and communications directly to us, and in personal visits, of the cruelty that has been practiced in the South; and those accounts have come to us with the expressed desire that we should keep on and not resign the organization. They have told

that the time has not come, while the slave in so many instances is only
nominally and legally free, while in fact that almost unlimited power
of his oppressor continues; and that in many parts of our Southland
large numbers of families of slaves are still actually held in bondage,
and their labor extorted from them by the lash, as formerly; that while,
so far as the law is concerned, they may no longer be publicly bought
and sold, yet they have been actually sold and transferred from place
to place. All these facts show the necessity of our cause (in the Anti-
Slavery Society) . . . and the need for its continued existence. . . .

TRAN THI NGA (VIETNAM)

VIET MINH

The war between the French and the Viet Minh
came nearer and nearer.
One day, going to school,
I heard an explosion and ran to a ditch
already filled with people.
I lay outside the ditch
watching people run by me
shouting and crying through the smoke.

I did not move until the all-clear signal.
Then I saw people lying on the ground
blood everywhere
hands and legs hanging in a tree.

I yelled and fainted.
When I woke up,
I was in a strange house.
Bao was looking down at me
trying to wipe my face with a handkerchief.

We began to whisper more and more
about arrests.
Many anti-French leaflets
were passed out at school.
Teachers left. My best friend, Dung,
did not come to school.

At first I thought she was sick.
Then I found out she had been arrested.

When friends were arrested,
we were never to speak of that person again.

(With Wendy Wilder Larsen)

FAMINE

Worse for us than the bombs
was the famine.
We had money,
but there was no rice to buy.
People ate grass.
We read that out in the countryside
peasants were stealing from landlords.
Father told us the French and Japanese
had overstocked rice in the warehouses.
Tons and tons of rotted grain
had to be dumped into the Red River.

When Father tried to fire our servants,
they begged to stay.
They had been loyal.
Where would they go?
How could they eat?
In the end he let them stay
gave them what he could.

When Father had his high position
teachers bought him gifts—
baskets of fruit
lichee and longan.
We stored them in giant vases in the hall,
cut the mooncakes into pieces to be eaten later.
Now he ordered us to eat less rice.
We made rice balls from what we saved
to give to the people outside the walls.

One day when I opened the gate
for Father to go out,
there were corpses collapsed against the wall.

I fainted.
Father offered soldiers money to remove the corpses.

Sometimes they took bodies that were still alive.
People would call from the carts,
"Don't take me. Don't take me.
I'm not dead yet."

(With Wendy Wilder Larsen)

SHARON OLDS (U.S.A.)

WHEN

for Martin Garbus

When we are standing in the parking lot
with a gentle sea rain falling on us
you tell me about your client who has been tortured,
in prison, in Chile, his forearm cut off and you
touch your own arm below the elbow, where the
hair springs up in the salt air and the
rain stands in fine drops like a spider's web.
It burns in me to get close to his arm,
my lips on the scarlet at the end of the stub,
my nose near the long wrinkles of scorch
where the iron has been laid down upon the body,
my breast on the blackened skin as if to
take it back into the realm of the human
but of course there is nothing I can do, I can't nurse it or
take its reddened head deep into my sex,
back into the body. I cannot do
anything. All I can do is
tell about it, say *This is the human, the*
clippers, the iron—and this is the human, the
hand, the milk, all I can do is
point out the two paths, we can go down either.

VESNA PARUN (YUGOSLAVIA)

THE WAR

My grandfather sits in front of the house and leaves fall.
He looks at the figs that dry on the stone,
while the sun, very orange, vanishes behind the small vineyards
I remember from childhood.

The voice of my grandfather is golden, like the melody of an old clock,
and his dialect is rich, filled with restlessness.
The legend of "Seven Lean Years" follows right after the "Our Father,"
short and eternal.

One day, there was no more fishing.
Now, there is war.
The enemy surrounds the port for miles around.
The whole tiny island trembles in eclipse.
All her sons disappeared in search of war wages—
a long time ago.
Canada,
Australia . . .
They'll board them next for Japan.
It's possible they'll stay forever with their heads among the bamboo.
This is the second winter that they've marched non-stop.
Even the fish sound gloomy in their chase.
One grandson is fair and good, yet, we'll find him in the snow one day
when the mountains are tired.

The girls sing as they prepare the picnic soup.
The children squat on the floor, very frightened
of the boots of the elegant old man.
One mother thinks of the sons and father who became a Malayan.

Strange, how this family has been scattered over four continents.
These big brawny people sound like children in their letters.

My grandfather stares at the red sun in the vineyard,
worn to silence, because death is near—old fisherman of the sea.
Foreign greed; strange hunger.   Freedom is a bit of breadcrust.

Ah, tell the earth that watermills should run faster!
A storm took away leaves; whatever's right shall be.

So, the young boys die, and the old men warm up their sorrows,
staring at the horizon.

(Translated by Ivana Spalatin and Daniela Gioseffi)

THE BALLAD OF DECEIVED FLOWERS

Goat's blood blossoms on the river banks.
Quiet green fields murmur with sunny sounds of bleating herds.
Boys take off their shoes to avoid treading on tiny daisies.
It's a warm Sunday as swallows arrive from their blue distances.
The spider has spun his white web over the aromatic pinewood.
Who would think of the sorrow of prison rooms or murdered bodies.
The children never believe the earth will swallow the flesh.

There's a black smoke on the horizon: soldiers are marching.
Whose are the red meadows? Whose are those windows shining on the
   hill?
The bells ring all around and echo in the daisies, vibrate in
the purple color glancing from the sun.
Why has the spider made his net, if the army marches on?
Ah brothers, read the sonorous fable of flowery clouds!
In the melted snows, one sees the footsteps of deer and the sounds
of fir trees murmur freely through the mountains.
They say that an evil spirit frightens the moonlight,
that eyes glare reflected from night.

Why don't the boys go home with their toys of bright yarn,
let the bees go from their fake flower targets, let them fly free?
An evil spirit walks in the moonlight.
The boys untie their kites,
the army marches on.

Hundreds of tiny hammers forge golden tulips;
blind larvae anticipate nothing.
Only the child has eyes.
Unhappy child! He will see his father hanged on
the white plum tree in their own garden,
from their own plum tree.

Yesterday, goat's blood blossomed on the banks.
Today the drummer's fire destroyed all of spring.
It's ringing in the silent hills, it's ringing alarm in the flowers,
the gunshot bewilders the squirrels, the boys hurry to the boats
tied at the shore, but guards stop them,
rush into tiny anthills to extinguish the candle.

The hidden torpedos demolished the fishermen.   Nothing
remained under the sun.   Only a few dried-out graves
let their ashes fly unnamed in the wind.   The dead
have poisoned the day.   What can a person do?

A frightened daisy opened horrified eyes to a gunner's boot.
A lamb lost its milk and wanders on the road.
The enemy has arrived and called up troops of defenseless flowers.

(Translated by Ivana Spalatin and Daniela Gioseffi)

Minerva Salado   (Cuba)

REPORT FROM VIETNAM FOR
INTERNATIONAL WOMEN'S DAY

A woman is aflame.
She is twenty-one years old
and her flesh is on fire.
Her womb trembles;
her erect breasts are consumed by fire.
Her hips contort.
The muscles of her thighs boil.
Anh Dai's flesh is ignited by flames,
but she does not burn with passion.
It is napalm.

(Translated by Daniela Gioseffi with Enildo Garcia)

Christian Santos   (Nicaragua)

THEY CARRIED THEIR TRUTH TO THE
DITCH WHERE THEY WERE THROWN

I'm chatting with Pedro
on the patio of my house
"The harvest's going to be good," he tells me, and grasping
                                        some leaves,

he rubs them between his hands, smelling them thoughtfully.
Pedro came here today to install the plumbing—
Pedro, whose own house is of cane and clay
    and has no plumbing, the bathroom of the house
    the mountainside around it—
Pedro, who has never had steady work
and merely follows a rut from here to there
and whose partner Luisa has had ten children with him . . .
    she told him this morning
    that she's pregnant again.
"Six of our children have died on us," he tells me.
"The last two were already good strong boys
and helped around the house, serving meals.
The first was Julio, who went at fourteen years old.
The Guard picked him up in the September uprising.
Teodoro (his friend who got away) told me
they put out Julio's eyes so he wouldn't see who tortured him
and he followed them, blind and spitting, and a corporal
tossed the eyes to the dogs, and the dogs ate them. . . ."
Pedro bows his head (he leans against the lemon tree,
breathes heavily) and then looks up again and goes on:
"Juan, my oldest son, was taken in our neighborhood
and tied so one arm and both legs were broken
    in front of all the neighbors
'You son of a big whore,' they called him,
'if you're going to open your mouth it better be to pray'
                and *wham, wham, wham*
they slammed him in the chest with their gun butts
    until he vomited blood."
Pedro throws down the spray of lemon blossom,
and the grasshoppers fly up, startled,
and with a hoarse voice, he finishes telling me:
"Those boys of mine said nothing.
They carried their truth to the ditch where they were thrown."

          (Translated by Anna Kirwan Vogel and Isabella Halsted)

Sappho (Greece, *c.* 500 B.C.)

TO AN ARMY WIFE IN SARDIS

Some say a cavalry troop,
others say an infantry, and others, still,
will swear that the swift oars

of our sea fleet are the best
sight on dark earth; but I say
that whomever one loves is.

(Adapted to English by Daniela Gioseffi)

Lynne Sharon Schwartz (U.S.A.)

THE SPOILS OF WAR

He always sat in the back row, as far away as he could get: long skinny
body and long face, thin curly hair, dark mustache. Sometimes his
bony shoulders were hunched as he peered down at his notebook lying
open on that bizarre prehensile arm that grows out of college classroom chairs. Or else he leaned way back, the lopsided chair balanced
on two legs and propped against the rear wall, his chest appearing
slightly concave beneath his white shirt, and one narrow leg, in jeans,
elegantly stretched out to rest on a nearby empty chair.

Casual but tense, rather like a male fashion model. Volatile beneath
the calm: someone you would not want to meet on a dark street. His
face was severely impassive in a way that suggested arrogance and scorn.

He must have been about twenty-seven years old, an extremely thin
young man—ascetic, stripped down to the essentials. His body looked
so brittle and so electrically charged that I almost expected crackling
noises when he moved, but in fact he slipped in and out silently, in the
wink of an eye. His whole lanky, scrutinizing demeanor was intimidating. He would have no patience with anything phony, I imagined;
would not suffer fools gladly.

About every fourth or fifth class he was absent, common enough for
evening-session students, who had jobs, families, grown-up lives and

249

responsibilities. I was a trifle relieved at his absences—I could relax—yet I missed him, too. His presence made a definite and compelling statement, but in an unintelligible language. I couldn't interpret him as readily as I could the books on the reading list.

I was hired in the spring of 1970. It was wartime. Students were enraged. When I went for my interview at Hunter College I had to walk past pickets into a building where black flags hung from the windows. I would use the Socratic method, I earnestly told the interviewer, since I believed in the students' innate intelligence. To myself, I vowed I would win their confidence. After all, I was scarcely older than they were and I shared their mood of protest. I would wear jeans to show I was one of them, and even though I had passed thirty and was married and had two children, I would prove that I could be trusted. I was prepared—even eager—for youthful, strident, moral indignation.

Far from strident, he was totally silent, never speaking in class discussions, and I was reluctant to call on him. Since he had a Spanish name, I wondered whether he might have trouble with English. Bureaucratic chaos was the order of the day, with the City University enacting in microcosm the confusion in the nation at large; it was not unusual for barely literate or barely English-speaking students to wind up in an Introduction to Literature class. His silence and his blank arrogant look could simply mean bewilderment. I ought to find out, but I waited.

His first paper was a shocker. I was surprised to receive it at all—I had him pegged as the sullen type who would give up at the first difficult assignment, then complain that college was irrelevant. One the contrary, the paper, formidably intelligent, jarred my view of the fitness of things. It didn't seem possible—no, it didn't seem *right*—that a person so sullen and mute should be so eloquent. Someone must have helped him. The truth would come out in impromptu class papers, and then I would confront him. I bided my time.

After the first exam he tossed his blue book onto my desk, not meeting my eyes, and, wary and feline, glided away, withdrawing into his body as if attempting a disappearing act. The topic he had chosen was the meaning of "the horror" in Joseph Conrad's *Heart of Darkness*, the novella we had spent the first few sessions on.

He compared it to Faulkner's *Intruder in the Dust*. He wrote at length about racial hatred and war and their connection in the dark, unspeakable places in the soul from which both spring, without sentimentality but with a sort of matter-of-fact, old knowledge. He knew Faulkner better than I did; I had to go back and skim *Intruder in the Dust* to understand his exam. I do know that I had never before sat transfixed in disbelief over a student paper.

The next day I called him over after class and asked if he was aware that he had an extraordinary mind. He said, yes, he was. Close up, there was nothing arrogant about him. A bit awkward and shy, yet gracious, with something antique and courtly in his manner.

Why did he never speak in class, I asked.

He didn't like to speak in front of people. His voice and his eye turned evasive, like an adolescent's, as he told me this. Couldn't, in fact. Couldn't speak.

What do you mean, I said. You're not a kid. You have a lot to say. You write like this and you sit in class like a statue? What's it all about?

He was in the war, he said, and he finally looked at my face and spoke like the adult that he was. He was lost for a long time in the jungles of Vietnam, he explained patiently, as if I might not know what Vietnam was, or what a jungle was, or what it was to be lost. And after that, he said, he couldn't. He just found it hard to be with people. To speak to people.

But you're so smart. You could do so much.

I know. He shrugged: a flesh-and-blood version of the rueful, devil-may-care, movie war-hero shrug. Can't be helped.

Anything can be helped, I insisted.

No, he insisted back, quietly. Not after that jungle.

Hunter had a counseling service, free. Go, I pleaded.

He had already gone. They keep asking me questions about my childhood, he said, my relationship with my parents, my toilet training. He grinned quickly, turning it on and off. But it doesn't help. It's none of that. It's from when I was lost in that jungle.

You must work, I said. Don't you have to talk to people when you work?

No, he was a meter man.

A what?

He went around checking on cars, to see if they had overstayed their time at the parking meters.

You can't do that forever, I said. With your brains!

Well, at least he didn't have to talk to people, he said sweetly. For now. Maybe later on he would get braver.

And what would he do if I called on him in class? If I made him talk?

Oh no, don't do that, he said, and flashed the wry grin again. If you did that I'd probably run out of the room.

I never called on him because I didn't want to risk seeing him run out of the room. But at least we stopped being afraid of each other. He gave up his blank look, and occasionally I would glance at his face, to see if I was still making sense or drifting off into some seductive, academic cloud of words.

I thought of him a lot this summer after I saw young men lined up at post offices to register for military service. I thought of him also when I heard Ronald Reagan and John Anderson, on television, solemnly pledge themselves to the defense of this country's shores. No candidate has yet pledged himself to the defense of this country's young men, to "taking every measure necessary" to "insure" that their genius does not turn mute and their very lives become the spoils of war.

OCTOBER, 1980

LESLIE MORMON SILKO (LAGUNA PUEBLO NATION, U.S.A.)

GALLUP, NEW MEXICO

"I remember when we drove through Gallup. I saw Navajos in torn old jackets, standing outside the bars. There were Zunis and Hopis there too, even a few Lagunas. All of them slouched down against the dirty walls of the bars along hiway 66, their eyes staring at the ground like they had forgotten the sun in the sky; or maybe that was the way they dreamed for wine, looking for it somewhere in the mud on the sidewalk. This is us too, I was thinking to myself, these people crouching outside bars like cold flies stuck to the wall."

They parked the truck by the Trailways bus station and walked across the railroad tracks. It was still early in the morning, and the shadows around the warehouses and buildings were long. The streets and sidewalks were empty, and on a Saturday morning in Gallup, Tayo knew what they would see. From the doorway of a second-hand store he could see feet, toes poking through holes in the socks. Someone sleeping off the night before, but without his boots now, because somebody had taken them to trade for a bottle of cheap wine. The guy had his head against the door; his brown face was peaceful and he was snoring loud. Tayo smiled. Gallup was that kind of place, interesting, even funny as long as you were just passing through, the way the white tourists did driving down 66, stopping to buy Indian souvenirs. But if you were an Indian, you attended to business and then left; and you never stayed in that town after dark. That was the warning the old Zunis and Hopis and Navajos gave about Gallup. The safest way is to avoid bad places after dark.

The best time to see them was at dawn because after the sun came up they would be hiding or sleeping inside shelters of old tin, cardboard and scrap wood. The shelters were scattered along the banks of the river. Some of them were in the wide arroyo which the creek cut through Gallup, but the others were in the salt cedar and willow thickets which grew along the stream banks. Twice or three times a year the police and the welfare people made a sweep along the river, arresting the men and women for vagrancy and being drunk in public, and taking the children away to the Home. They were on the Northside of town anyway, Little Africa, where Blacks, Mexicans and Indians lived; and the only white people over there were Slav storekeepers. They came at Gallup Ceremonial time to clean up before the tourists came to town. They talked about sanitation and safety as they dragged the people to the paddy wagons; in July and August, sudden cloudbursts could fill the arroyos with flood water, and wash the shelters away.

They had been born in Gallup. They were the ones with light-colored hair or light eyes; bushy hair and thick lips—the ones the women were ashamed to send home for their families to raise. Those who did not die, grew up by the river, watching their mothers leave at sundown. They learned to listen in the darkness, to the sounds of footsteps and loud laughing, to voices and sounds of wine; to know when the mother was returning with a man. They learned to stand at a distance and see if she would throw them food—so they would go away to eat and not peek through the holes in the rusting tin, at the man spilling wine on himself as he unbuttoned his pants to crawl on top of her.

They found their own places to sleep because the men stayed until dawn. Before they knew how to walk, they learned how to avoid fists and feet.

When she woke up at noontime she would call him to bring her water. The lard pail was almost empty; the water looked rusty. He waited until she crawled to the opening. He watched her throat moving up and down as she drank; he tried to look inside to see if she had brought food, but the sun was high now and the inside of the shelter was in shadow. She dropped the pail when it was empty and crawled back inside. "Muh!" he called to her, because he was hungry and he had found no food that morning. The woman with the reddish color hair, the one who used to feed him, was gone. Her shelter was already torn down, taken away in pieces by others in the arroyo. He had prowled for garbage in the alleys behind the houses, but the older children had already been there. He turned away from the shelter and looked up at the traffic on the bridge. Once he had crawled up there and stood on the bridge, looking down at the shelter, and then around at the street where it crossed the tracks; he could even see downtown. She had taken him with her when he was very small. He remembered the brightness of the sun, the heat, and all the smells of cars and food cooking, the noise, and the people. He remembered the inside, the dark, the coolness, and the music. He laid on his belly with his chin on the wooden floor, and watched the legs and the shoes under the tables, the legs moving across the floor; some moved slowly, some stumbled. He searched the floor until he found a plastic bar straw, and then he played with piles of cigarette butts he had gathered. When he found chewing gum stuck beneath the tables he put it in his mouth and tried to keep it, but he always swallowed it. He could not remember when he first knew that cigarettes would make him vomit if he ate them. He played for hours under the tables, quiet, watching for someone to drop a potato chip bag or a wad of gum. He learned about coins, and searched for them, putting them in his mouth when he found them. Once they had lived somewhere else, a place full of food. He dreamed about that place in the past, and about a red blanket which was warm, and moved rhythmically like breathing.

He got used to her leaving the bar with men, giving somebody a dollar to buy the boy food while she was out. After he ate, he slept under the tables and waited for her to come back. The first time she did not come back, the man who swept floors found him. He did not cry when the man woke him; he did not cry when the police came and tried to ask him his name. He clutched the last piece of bread in his hand and crouched in the corner; he closed his eyes when they reached for him. After a long time, she came for him. She smelled good when she carried him and she spoke softly. But the last time, he remembered the white walls and the rows of cribs. He cried for a long time, standing up in the bed with his chin resting on the top rail. He chewed the paint from the top rail, still crying, but gradually becoming interested in the way the paint peeled off the metal and clung to his front teeth.

When she came for him she smelled different. She smelled like the floors of the room full of cribs, and her long hair had been cut. But she came back for him, and she held him very close.

They stayed in the arroyo after that. The woman with the reddish hair helped them drag twisted pieces of old roof tin from the dump, down the banks of the river to the place the other shacks were, in sight of the bridge. They leaned the tin against the crumbly gray sides of the arroyo. His mother rolled big bricks up from the river bed to hold the pieces of cardboard in place. It was cold then, and when the sun went down they built small fires from broken crates they found in the alleys and with branches they tore from the tamarack and willow. The willows and tamaracks were almost bare then, except for the branches higher than a man could reach. One of the men brought an axe with a broken handle, and the drunks who lived in the arroyo chopped down the tamaracks and willows, laughing and passing a bottle around as they took turns with the axe. The only trees they left were where all the people went. A strong, stinging smell that came from that place. He learned to watch out for shit and in the winter, when it was frozen, he played with it—flipping it around with a willow stick. He did not play with the other children; he ran from them when they approached. They belonged to the woman who stayed under the bridge, with low tin walls to block the west wind. That winter he heard a strange crying sound coming from under the bridge, and he saw the children standing outside the low sides of the shelter, watching. He listened for a long time and watched. The next day it was quiet, and the woman carried a bundle of bloody rags away from the bridge, far away, north toward the hills. Later on he walked the way she had gone, following the arroyo east and then north, where it wound into the pale yellow hills. He found the place, near the side of the arroyo where she had buried the rags in the yellow sand. The sand she had dug with her hands was still damp on the mound. He circled the mound and stared at a faded blue rag partially uncovered, quivering in the wind. It was stiff with a reddish-brown stain. He left that place and he never went back; and late at night when his mother was gone, he cried because he saw the mound of pale yellow sand in a dream.

Damp yellow sand choking him, filling his nostrils first, and then his eyes as he struggled against it, fought to keep his eyes open to see. Sand rippled and swirled in his dream, enclosing his head, yellow sand and shadows filling his mouth, until his body was full and still. He woke up crying, in a shallow hole beside the clay bank, where his mother had thrown the old quilt.

He slept alone while his mother was with the men—the white men with necks and faces bright red from the summertime, Mexican men who came from the section gang boxcars at the railroad, looking for the women who waited around the bridge—the ones who would go down for a half bottle of wine. The black men came from the railroad tracks too, standing on the bridge looking down at them. He did not know if they looked at him or if they were only looking at his mother and the women who lined up beside her, to smile and wave and yell "hey honey" up to the men. The white people who drove by looked straight ahead. But late one afternoon some white men came and called, until the women came out of the lean-tos and then the men yelled at them and threw empty bottles, trying to hit them. The woman with reddish hair threw the bottles back at them, and screamed their own words back to them. The police came. They dragged the people out of their shelters—and they pulled the pieces of tin and cardboard down. The police handcuffed the skinny men with swollen faces; they pushed and kicked them up the crumbling clay sides of the arroyo. They held the women in a circle, while they tried to catch the children who had scattered in all directions when they saw the police coming. The men and the women who were too sickdrunk to stand up were dragged away, one cop on each arm. He hid in the tamaracks, breathing hard, his heart pounding, smelling the shit on his bare feet. The summer heat descended as the sun went higher in the sky, and he watched them lying flat on his belly in the dry leaves of tamarisk that began to itch, and he moved cautiously to scratch his arm and his neck. He watched them tear down the last of the shelters, and they piled the rags and coats they found and sprinkled them with kerosene. Thick black smoke climbed furiously into the cloudless blue sky, hot and windless. He could feel the flies buzzing and crawling around his legs and feet, and he was afraid that the men searching would hear them and find him. But the smell in the remaining grove of tamarack and willow was strong enough to keep them away. The men in dark green coveralls came with steel canisters on their backs and they sprayed the places where the shelters had been; and in the burnt smell of cloth and wood, he could smell the long white halls of the place they kept children. At sundown he woke up and caught sight of the headlights on the traffic across the bridge. He stood up slowly and looked restlessly toward the arroyo banks, thinking about food.

It was a warm night and he wandered for a long time, in the alleys behind the houses, where the dogs barked when he reached into the tin cans. He ate as he made his way back to the arroyo, chewing the soft bone cartilage of pork ribs he found. He saved the bones and sucked them to sleep in the tamaracks and willows. Late in the night he heard voices, men stumbling and falling down the steep crumbling bank into the arroyo, and he could hear bottles rattle together and the sound of corks being pulled from the bottles. They talked loudly in the language his mother spoke to him, and one man sat with his back against the bank and sang songs until the wine was gone.

He crawled deeper into the tamarack bushes, and pulled his knees up to his belly. He looked up at the stars, through the top branches of the willows. He would wait for her, and she would come back to him.

MAVIS SMALLBERG (SOUTH AFRICA)

QUOTE FROM THE BUREAU OF INFORMATION, FROM THE *ARGUS*, AUGUST 27, 1986: "THE SITUATION IN SOWETO IS NOT ABNORMAL"

Everything's normal in Soweto today.
We reasonably killed eleven.
They were making a fuss in the street
You know us,
We don't stand any fuss
Not us
So we typically killed eleven
And wounded an average sixty-two
And you?

Went on a regular patrol to a school.
Some children were breaking a rule.
They burned their identity cards.
White kids don't carry 'em
Don't need to, you know
Black kids don't carry 'em
Don't want to, you know
The whole thing was just about to erupt,
When we routinely went to beat them up.
Cornered a few of 'em and rained down the blows
Split one's head.   She's dead,
But nobody knows.
Naturally the children ran all around
So we just shot down those that we found.
Bullets, birdshot, buckshot,
What the hell?   It's all run-of-the-mill!
Saw this "comrade" walking alone,
Shot him down before he got home.
Ja, he died.
You should've seen the ones that we fried.

What a fire!   What a blaze!
Children crying, people dying.
One woman got shot in the hip
That really shut up her lip!
Now she can't walk.   Mmm, there was some talk.

Ja, the situation in Soweto is not
Abnormal today.

What's abnormal, anyway?
What's monstrous, deviant, abhorrent,
weird about gassing a baby
Shooting a child, raping a mother
or crippling a father?
What's odd about killing the people we fear?
No, the situation in Soweto
is quite normal today.

WISŁAWA SZYMBORSKA (POLAND)

TORTURE

Nothing has changed.
The body feels pain,
has to eat and breathe and sleep,
has thin skin and, just underneath it, blood,
quite a store of teeth and nails,
its bones are brittle, its joints stretchy.
In torture all of it is taken into consideration.

Nothing has changed.
The body trembles as it trembled
before the founding of Rome and after the founding,
in the 20th century before and after Christ.
Torture exists as it existed, only the earth shrank
and whatever happens, it's as if next door.

Nothing has changed.
Only there are more people.
Besides old offences, there appeared new,
real, imaginary, momentary and none,
but the scream with which the body responds
was, is, and always will be a scream of innocence
in the immemorial pitch and scale.

Nothing has changed.
Perhaps only manners, ceremonies, dances.

The gesture of hands shielding the head is the same.
The body writhes, pulls and struggles,
knocked down it falls, doubles up,
turns blue, swells, salivates and bleeds.

Nothing has changed.
Besides the course of borders,
the line of forests, shores, deserts and icebergs.
In these landscapes the soul loiters,
disappears, returns, comes closer, wanders off,
remaining a stranger to itself, elusive,
now sure, now unsure of its own existence,
while the body is and is and is
and has no place to go.

LUISA VALENZUELA (ARGENTINA)

I'M YOUR HORSE IN THE NIGHT

The doorbell rang: three short rings and one long one. That was the signal, and I got up, annoyed and a little frightened; it could be them, and then again, maybe not; at these ungodly hours of the night it could be a trap. I opened the door expecting anything except him, face to face, at last.

He came in quickly and locked the door behind him before embracing me. So much in character, so cautious, first and foremost checking his—our—rear guard. Then he took me in his arms without saying a word, not even holding me too tight but letting all the emotions of our new encounter overflow, telling me so much by merely holding me in his arms and kissing me slowly. I think he never had much faith in words, and there he was, as silent as ever, sending me messages in the form of caresses.

We finally stepped back to look at one another from head to foot, not eye to eye, out of focus. And I was able to say Hello showing scarcely any surprise despite all those months when I had no idea where he could have been, and I was able to say

I thought you were fighting up north
I thought you'd been caught

> I thought you were in hiding
> I thought you'd been tortured and killed
> I thought you were theorizing about the revolution in another country

Just one of many ways to tell him I'd been thinking of him, I hadn't stopped thinking of him or felt as if I'd been betrayed. And there he was, always so goddamn cautious, so much the master of his actions.

"Quiet, Chiquita. You're much better off not knowing what I've been up to."

Then he pulled out his treasures, potential clues that at the time eluded me: a bottle of cachaça and a Gal Costa record. What had he been up to in Brazil? What was he planning to do next? What had brought him back, risking his life, knowing they were after him? Then I stopped asking myself questions (quiet, Chiquita, he'd say). Come here, Chiquita, he was saying, and I chose to let myself sink into the joy of having him back again, trying not to worry. What would happen to us tomorrow, and the days that followed?

Cachaça's a good drink. It goes down and up and down all the right tracks, and then stops to warm up the corners that need it most. Gal Costa's voice is hot, she envelops us in its sound and half-dancing, half-floating, we reach the bed. We lie down and keep on staring deep into each other's eyes, continue caressing each other without allowing ourselves to give in to the pure senses just yet. We continue recognizing, rediscovering each other.

Beto, I say, looking at him. I know that isn't his real name, but it's the only one I can call him out loud. He replies:

"We'll make it someday, Chiquita, but let's not talk now."

It's better that way. Better if he doesn't start talking about how we'll make it someday and ruin the wonder of what we're about to attain right now, the two of us, all alone.

"A noite eu so teu cavalo," Gal Costa suddenly sings from the record player.

"I'm your horse in the night," I translate slowly. And so as to bind him in a spell and stop him from thinking about other things:

"It's a saint's song, like in the *macumba*. Someone who's in a trance says she's the horse of the spirit who's riding her, she's his mount."

"Chiquita, you're always getting carried away with esoteric meanings and witchcraft. You know perfectly well that she isn't talking about spirits. If you're my horse in the night it's because I ride you, like this, see? . . . Like this. . . . That's all."

It was so long, so deep and so insistent, so charged with affection that we ended up exhausted. I fell asleep with him still on top of me.

I'm your horse in the night.

The goddamn phone pulled me out in waves from a deep well. Making an enormous effort to wake up, I walked over to the receiver, thinking it could be Beto, sure, who was no longer by my side, sure, following his inveterate habit of running away while I'm asleep without a word about where he's gone. To protect me, he says.

From the other end of the line, a voice I thought belonged to Andrés— the one we call Andrés—began to tell me:

"They found Beto dead, floating down the river near the other bank. It looks as if they threw him alive out of a chopper. He's all bloated and decomposed after six days in the water, but I'm almost sure it's him."

"No, it can't be Beto," I shouted carelessly. Suddenly the voice no longer sounded like Andrés: it felt foreign, impersonal.

"You think so?"

"Who is this?" Only then did I think to ask. But that very moment they hung up.

Ten, fifteen minutes? How long must I have stayed there staring at the phone like an idiot until the police arrived? I didn't expect them. But, then again, how could I not? Their hands feeling me, their voices insulting and threatening, the house searched, turned inside out. But I already knew. So what did I care if they broke every breakable object and tore apart my dresser?

They wouldn't find a thing. My only real possession was a dream and they can't deprive me of my dreams just like that. My dream the night before, when Beto was there with me and we loved each other. I'd dreamed it, dreamed every bit of it, I was deeply convinced that I'd dreamed it all in the richest detail, even in full color. And dreams are none of the cops' business.

They want reality, tangible facts, the kind I couldn't even begin to give them.

Where is he, you saw him, he was here with you, where did he go? Speak up, or you'll be sorry. Let's hear you sing, bitch, we know he came to see you, where is he, where is he holed up? He's in the city, come on, spill it, we know he came to get you.

I haven't heard a word from him in months. He abandoned me, I haven't heard from him in months. He ran away, went underground. What do I know, he ran off with someone else, he's in another country. What do I know, he abandoned me, I hate him, I know nothing.

(Go ahead, burn me with your cigarettes, kick me all you wish, threaten, go ahead, stick a mouse in me so it'll eat my insides out, pull my nails out, do as you please. Would I make something up for that? Would I tell you he was here when a thousand years ago he left me forever?)

I'm not about to tell them my dreams. Why should they care? I haven't seen that so-called Beto in more than six months, and I loved him. The man simply vanished. I only run into him in my dreams, and they're bad dreams that often become nightmares.

Beto, you know now, if it's true that they killed you, or wherever you may be, Beto, I'm your horse in the night and you can inhabit me whenever you wish, even if I'm behind bars. Beto, now that I'm in jail I know that I dreamed you that night; it was just a dream. And if by some wild chance there's a Gal Costa record and a half-empty bottle of cachaça in my house, I hope they'll forgive me: I will them out of existence.

ALICE WALKER (U.S.A.)

ONLY JUSTICE CAN STOP A CURSE

"To the Man God: O Great One, I have been sorely tried by my enemies and have been blasphemed and lied against. My good thoughts and my honest actions have been turned to bad actions and dishonest ideas. My home has been disrespected, my children have been cursed and ill-treated. My dear ones have been backbitten and their virtue questioned. O Man God, I beg that this that I ask for my enemies shall come to pass:

"That the South wind shall scorch their bodies and make them wither and shall not be tempered to them. That the North wind shall freeze their blood and numb their muscles and that it shall not be tempered to them. That the West wind shall blow away their life's breath and will not leave their hair grow, and that their fingernails shall fall off and their bones shall crumble. That the East wind shall make their minds grow dark, their sight shall fail and their seed dry up so that they shall not multiply.

"I ask that their fathers and mothers from their furthest generation will not intercede for them before the great throne, and the wombs of their women shall not bear fruit except for strangers, and that they shall become extinct. I pray that the children who may come shall be weak of mind and paralyzed of limb and that they themselves shall curse them in their turn for ever turning the

breath of life into their bodies. I pray that disease and death shall be forever with them and that their worldly goods shall not prosper, and that their crops shall not multiply and that their cows, their sheep, and their hogs and all their living beasts shall die of starvation and thirst. I pray that their house shall be unroofed and that the rain, the thunder and lightning shall find the innermost recesses of their home and that the foundation shall crumble and the floods tear it asunder. I pray that the sun shall not shed its rays on them in benevolence, but instead it shall beat down on them and burn them and destroy them. I pray that the moon shall not give them peace, but instead shall deride them and decry them and cause their minds to shrivel. I pray that their friends shall betray them and cause them loss of power, of gold and of silver, and that their enemies shall smite them until they beg for mercy which shall not be given them. I pray that their tongues shall forget how to speak in sweet words, and that it shall be paralyzed and that all about them will be desolation, pestilence and death. O Man God, I ask you for all these things because they have dragged me in the dust and destroyed my good name; broken my heart and caused me to curse the day that I was born. So be it."

This is a curse-prayer that Zora Neale Hurston, novelist and anthropologist, collected in the 1920s. And by then it was already old. I have often marvelled at it. At the precision of its anger, the absoluteness of its bitterness. Its utter hatred of the enemies it condemns. It is a curse-prayer by a person who would readily, almost happily, commit suicide, if it meant her enemies would also die. Horribly.

I am sure it was a woman who first prayed this curse. And I see her—Black, Yellow, Brown or Red, *"aboriginal"* as the Ancients are called in South Africa and Australia and other lands invaded, expropriated and occupied by whites. And I think, with astonishment, that the curse-prayer of this colored woman—starved, enslaved, humiliated and carelessly trampled to death—over centuries, is coming to pass. Indeed, like ancient peoples of color the world over, who have tried to tell the white man of the destruction that would inevitably follow from the uranium mining plunder of their sacred lands, this woman—along with millions and billions of obliterated sisters, brothers, and children—seems to have put such enormous energy into her hope for revenge, that her curse seems close to bringing it about. And it is this hope for revenge, finally, I think, that is at the heart of People of Color's resistance to any antinuclear movement.

In any case, this has been my own problem.

When I have considered the enormity of the white man's crimes against humanity. Against women. Against every living person of color. Against the poor. Against my mother and my father. Against me. . . . When I consider that at this very moment he wishes to take away what little freedom I have died to achieve, through denial of my right to vote. . . . Has already taken away education, medicine, housing and food. . . . That William Shockley is saying at this moment that he will run for the Senate of my country to push his theory that Blacks are genetically inferior and should be sterilized. . . . When I consider that he is, they are, a real and present threat to my life and the life of my daughter, my people, I think—in perfect harmony with my sister of long ago: *Let the earth marinate in poisons. Let the bombs cover the ground like rain. For nothing short of total destruction will ever teach them anything.*

And it would be good, perhaps, to put an end to the species in any case, rather than let white men continue to subjugate it, and continue their lust to dominate, exploit and despoil not just our planet, but the rest of the universe, which is their clear and oft-stated intention, leaving their arrogance and litter not just on the moon, but on everything else they can reach.

If we have any true love for the stars, planets, the rest of Creation, we must do everything we can to keep white men away from them. They who have appointed themselves our representatives to the rest of the universe. They who have never met any new creature without exploiting, abusing or destroying it. They who say we poor and colored and female and elderly blight neighborhoods, while they blight worlds.

What they have done to the Old, they will do to the New.

Under the white man every star would become a South Africa, every planet a Vietnam.

Fatally irradiating ourselves may in fact be the only way to save others from what Earth has already become. And this is a consideration that I believe requires serious thought from every one of us.

However, just as the sun shines on the godly and the ungodly alike, so does nuclear radiation. And with this knowledge it becomes increasingly difficult to embrace the thought of extinction purely for the assumed satisfaction of—from the grave—achieving revenge. Or even of accepting our demise as a planet as a simple and just preventative medicine administered to the Universe. Life is better than death, I believe, if only because it is less boring, and because it has fresh peaches in it. In any case, Earth is my home—though for centuries white people have tried to convince me I have no right to exist, except in the dirtiest, darkest corners of the globe.

So let me tell you: I intend to protect my home. Praying—not a curse—only the hope that my courage will not fail my love. But if by some miracle, and all our struggle, the Earth is spared, only justice to every living thing (and everything is alive) will save humankind.

And we are not saved yet.

Only justice can stop a curse.

SIMONE WEIL (FRANCE)

Pain and suffering are a kind of false currency passed from hand to hand until they reach someone who receives them but does not pass them on.

THE ILIAD: POEM OF FORCE

Might is that which makes a thing of anybody who comes under its sway. When exercised to the full, it makes a thing of man in the most literal sense, for it makes him a corpse. There where someone stood a moment ago, stands no one. . . .

The might which kills outright is an elementary and coarse form of might. How much more varied in its devices; how much more astonishing in its effects is that other which does not kill; or which delays killing. It must surely kill, or it will perhaps kill, or else it is only suspended above him whom it may at any moment destroy. This of all procedures turns a man to stone. From the power to transform him into a thing by killing him there proceeds another power, and much more prodigious, that which makes a thing of him while he still lives. He is living, he has a soul, yet he is a thing. A strange being is that thing which has a soul, and strange the state of that soul. Who knows how often during each instant it must torture and destroy itself in order to confirm? The soul was not made to dwell in a thing; and when forced to it, there is no part of that soul but suffers violence. . . .

A man naked and disarmed upon whom a weapon is directed becomes a corpse before he is touched. Only for a moment still he deliberates, he strives, he hopes. . . . But soon he has understood that the weapon will not turn from him, and though he still breathes, he is only matter, still thinking, he can think of nothing. . . . When a stranger, completely disabled, weak and disarmed, appeals to a warrior, he is not by this act condemned to death; but only an instant of impatience on the part of the warrior suffices to deprive him of life. This is enough to make his flesh lose that principal property of all living tissue. A morsel of living flesh gives evidence of life first of all by reflex, as a frog's leg under electric shock jumps, as the approaching menace of the contact with a horrible thing, or terrifying event, provokes a shudder in no matter what bundle of flesh, nerves and muscles. Alone, the hopeless suppliant does not shudder, does not cringe; he no longer has such license. . . .

At least some suppliants, once exonerated, become again as other men. But there are others, more miserable beings, who without dying have become things for the rest of their lives. In their days is no give and take, no open field, no free road over which anything can pass to or from them. These are not men living harder lives than others, not placed lower socially than others, these are another species, a compromise between a man and a corpse. That a human being should be a thing is, from the point of view of logic, a contradiction; but when the impossible has become a reality, that contradiction is as a rent in the soul. That thing aspires every moment to become a man, a woman, and never at any moment succeeds. This is a death drawn out the length of a life, a life that death has frozen long before extinguishing it. . . .

Such a fate for her child is more frightful to the mother than death itself, the husband wishes to perish before seeing his wife reduced to it. A father calls down all the scourges of heaven upon the army that would subject his daughter to it. But for those upon whom it has fallen, so brutal a destiny wipes out damnations, revolts comparisons, meditations upon the future and the past, almost memory itself. It does not belong to the slave to be faithful to his city or to his dead. . . .

One cannot lose more than the slave loses, he loses all inner life. He only retrieves a little if there should arise an opportunity to change his destiny. Such is the empire of might; it extends as far as the empire of nature. . . .

And as pitilessly as might crushes, so pitilessly it maddens whoever possesses, or believes he possesses it. None can ever truly possess it. The human race is not divided, . . . between the vanquished, the slaves, the suppliants on the one hand, and conquerors and masters on the other. No single man is to be found who is not, at some time, forced to bow beneath might. The soldiers, although free and well-armed, suffer no less outrage. . . .

For violence so crushes whomever it touches that it appears at last external no less to him who dispenses it than to him who endures it. So the idea was born of a destiny beneath which the aggressors and their victims are equally innocent, the victors and the vanquished. . . . The necessity of war that belongs to war is terrible, wholly different from that belonging to peaceful works; the soul only submits to the necessity of war when escape from it is impossible. . . . The man faced by an armed enemy cannot lay down his arms. The mind should be able to contrive an issue; but it has lost all capacity for contriving anything in that direction. It is completely occupied with doing itself violence. Always among men, the intolerable afflictions either of servitude or war endure by force of their own weight, and therefore, from the outside, they seem easy to bear; they last because they rob the resources required to throw them off. . . .

Whoever (like the constantly threatened soldier of the battlefield) has had to mortify, to mutilate in himself all aspiration to live, of him an effort of heart-breaking generosity is required before he can respect the life of another. . . . But how many men do we know in several thousand years of history who have given proof of such divine generosity? It is doubtful whether we could name two or three. In default of such generosity the vanquished soldier is the scourge of nature; possessed by war, he, as much as the slave, although in quite a different way, is become a thing, and words have no more power over him than over inert matter. In contact with might, both the soldier and the slave suffer the inevitable effect, which is to become either deaf or mute. . . . Such is the nature of might. Its power to transform man into a thing is double and it cuts both ways; it petrifies differently but equally the souls of those who suffer it, and of those who wield it. This property of might reaches its highest degree in the midst of combat, at the moment when the tide of battle feels its way toward a decision. The winning of battles is not determined between men who plan and deliberate, who make a resolution and carry it out, but between men drained of these faculties, transformed, fallen to the level either of inert matter, which is all passivity, or to the level of blind forces, which are all momentum. This is the final secret of war.

HARRIET ZINNES (U.S.A.)

WOUNDS

Love is the blood of a deep wound
But it is not the blood bursting from the shock of hand grenades.
Be quiet, heart.   You are only mortal: one single heart among hearts.

You are not a stranger here—you are not in exile.
Your stomach does not swell: you have eaten well today:
Had wine with your dinner, a drink before
And I see you now sipping Cointreau.

What if your face is sad?
And your heart in grief?
Your paltry heart.
So! You have lost your love.
Is it a wound that bleeds
That scars your face
Amputates your leg?
What war is that?   Hm!   A love war!

Shame!
Are you forgetting the blood in Cambodia, South Africa, in Nicaragua?
The bloated bellies in Ethiopia?
The American homeless who may not weep for love?
You who have the luxury of the loss of love
Let the blood of your wounds wash the blood of sufferers.

Ah, love, you are with me now
As I remember exile, famine, war.

Notes on Selections and Authors, Part III:

JANE ADDAMS (see page 361).

MONA ELAINE ADILMAN (b. 1924) is a contemporary poet of Canada who
lives in Montreal. *Piece Work* and *Nighty-Knight* are among her many books
of poems. A writer of international sensibility who has published widely, she
here portrays the guilt of those who live comfortably free from the ravages
of war but suffer conscience.

ANNA AKHMATOVA (1889–1966) is one of the best known and loved of
Russian poets of this century. Born in Odessa, she lived also in the areas of
St. Petersburg and Kiev. In 1911, in Paris, the Italian painter, Modigliani,
did sixteen portraits of her. Her husband, Nikolai Gumilev was executed in
1921. She was silenced as a poet for eighteen years—as were Pasternak and
many of her contemporaries during the reign of Stalin. For a while, she was
restored to the Writers' Union, but in 1946, she was politically attacked and
her son arrested. Finally, her son was released and during her last years, she
was admitted again to the Writers' Union and published. Many younger
poets were among her followers, as for example, Joseph Brodsky. In the
West, she is best known for her long poem *Requiem*. She was given an
honorary degree from Oxford University.

CLARIBEL ALEGRÍA (b. 1924), a native of Nicaragua, grew up in Santa Ana,
El Salvador. She now lives in Managua and Mallorca, and is a prolific and

renowned poet and novelist whose work has been translated and published in New York, London, Paris, and Spain. *Flowers from the Volcano* was translated by the United States poet, Carolyn Forché. Other books include *Poetry Lives* and *Luisa in Reality Land.* She has won many distinguished prizes for her work and is best known in the United States for her much translated poem, "A Small Country," about the suffering in El Salvador.

ISABEL ALLENDE (b. 1942), the critically acclaimed Chilean novelist, worked for many years as a journalist. *The House of the Spirits,* from which this chapter comes, was written, she has said, "to keep alive the memory" of her family and country. It was widely read throughout Europe—even in the days before many Americans became aware of the human rights abuses under the Pinochet regime. Niece of assassinated President Salvador Allende, she now lives in exile in Venezuela and has recently completed a second novel. This translation from the Spanish is by the accomplished American writer, Magda Bogin.

LINDA ANDERSON (b. 1949) is a native of Belfast, Ireland, from a working-class family. She studied French and philosophy at Queens University, and earned a degree in education. In 1972, she went to London, taught French in a boys' school, and worked in libraries and offices. After the publication of her first novel, *To Stay Alive,* 1984, she began working full time as a writer, helped by an Arts Council bursary and an advance from her American publishers. Linda writes that she became "obsessed and distressed by the pain endured by the Northern Irish, seeking to understand it." In 1986, her second novel, *Cuckoo,* was published and she was chosen as one of the Top Ten new authors in a joint W. H. Smith and *Cosmopolitan* promotion.

ANONYMOUS. *Irish Antiwar Ballad in the Voice of a Woman* is an old Irish folk lyric, sung to a tune that was later used for a prowar song, attributed to Patrick Gilmore, a bandmaster of the Union Army during the Civil War. Gilmore claimed he'd heard the tune sung by a slave. Sung with the lyrics: "When Johnny comes marching home again, Hurrah, Hurrah, we'll give him a hearty welcome, then, Hurrah, Hurrah! The men will cheer, the boys will shout, The ladies they will all turn out, And we'll all feel gay When Johnny comes marching home," by the Civil War bandmaster, it was used to rally the army to battle—demonstrating how folk sentiments and melodies have often been co-opted for war propaganda purposes.

MARJORIE APPLEMAN (b. 1938) is an internationally known playwright and a poet, now living on Long Island in New York. Her plays which have received many awards include *Nice Place You Have Here, The Bedroom, Penelope's Odyssey, Fox-Trot on Gardiner's Bay,* and *Seduction Duet.* She has taught playwriting at New York University for many years.

EMILY GREENE BALCH (1867–1961), U.S. winner of the Nobel Prize for Peace in 1946, was the second president of the Women's International League for Peace and Freedom after Jane Addams passed on. She spent over three decades of her life rigorously working for world peace. Like Bertha von Sutter (see p. 72) of Austria and Jane Addams (see p. 268), the two women who preceded her as recipients of that prize, she was too ill by the time the laurels came to attend the ceremony, but she survived to give her Nobel lecture in 1948. It was titled "Toward Human Unity or Beyond Nationalism." This quote from her many writings was found in an obscure book of commentary she assembled after spending time wading waist deep in muddy streams through the jungles of Haiti to gather evidence against U.S. intervention there.

SIMONE DE BEAUVOIR (1908–1986) of France, for her book *The Second Sex,* was and remains the most internationally known of modern feminist writers. She is the author of many philosophical works, including *The Ethics of Ambiguity.* These brief excerpts are from a long chapter in *All Said and Done,* on her participation in the Vietnam Tribunal—a world court trial of the U.S. military, staged by Bertrand Russell, during the Vietnam War and held in Europe.

E. BROWN was a "freed slave" whose testimony, written soon after the Civil War under a pen name, gave just one of many accounts smuggled out of the slave plantations which continued after the end of the Civil War. This account from *The Autobiography of a Female Slave* was written soon after the Emancipation Proclamation.

NINA CASSIAN (b. 1924), one of Romania's leading poets, has published over fifty volumes of poetry, children's verse, translations, and a book of short stories. A political exile, fluent in several European languages, she now makes her home in the United States, where she has taught at New York University and the University of Iowa. Two of her volumes have been translated into English, *Lady of Miracles,* and *Countdown.* She is well known by her people for her protest against the repression of the creative spirit by dictatorship. Eva Fieler, Romanian scholar, was her first U.S. translator.

VINNIE-MARIE D'AMBROSIO is a widely published poet of North America who teaches at Brooklyn College of the City University of New York. Here from her book, *The Life of Touching Mouths,* she recalls her grandfather's involvement in World War I.

EMILY DICKINSON (1830–1886), is an internationally known poet of New England. In the few words so emblematic of her style, in two quatrains she expresses an idea similar to the one written by the world renowned poet of antiquity Sappho, also found in this section. Dickinson is the most celebrated woman poet that U.S. literature has produced. She lived a reclusive life in the small town of Amherst and hardly published a poem during her lifetime. She had no idea of the fame that would befall her work.

ENHEDUANNA was a Sumerian poet/priestess who lived c. 2300 B.C. She is the first known poet, man or woman, of prehistory. Her works come to us preserved on artifact from an ancient civilization and yet they lament the same horrors of war known to all the modern women in this collection. Along with Lady Godiva—whose purpose few remember in that she rode naked on a horse through the town of Coventry to protest her husband's starvation taxation of her people, in the eleventh century A.D.—Enheduanna can be thought of as one of the oldest war protesters in history.

ELENI FOURTOUNI (b. 1933), a native of Greece, has spent much of her adult life in New England. She is a poet as well as a scholar of Greek literature who has collected the oral histories of Greek women into a book, *Greek Women of the Resistance,* which includes her own commentary. She has edited and translated a prizewinning book of Greek women poets. These true stories of war violence, courage, and resistance by women of Greece took place between 1940 and 1950. Fourtouni's own book of poetry is titled *Monovassia.*

VERA GANCHEVA (b. c. 1930), a Bulgarian journalist and commentator who has written and published many articles, lives in Sofia. The following excerpt is taken from her review of a documentary film on the bombing of Nagasaki.

SANDRA MORTOLA GILBERT (b. 1936) is a prizewinning poet and literary critic as well as the first Women's Studies specialist to be given a full professorship by the English Department of Princeton University. As such, she is one of the pioneers in American letters to establish the serious nature of such scholarship. She is the prize-winning author of several books of poetry and criticism and has coedited important anthologies of women's literature.

ROSE GRAUBART (b. 1923) is a North American poet, fiction writer, and accomplished painter who is a member of the artists' community in East Hampton, Long Island. In her books of stories, *Down the American River* and *Surplus Love*, she deals with war themes, as in this poem.

KIMIKO HAHN (b. 1955) is an award-winning American poet who teaches Japanese Aesthetics at the Parsons School of Design in New York City. She coordinates readings for the Chinatown Public Library in a program called "Word of Mouth." In her poem she takes the persona of a Hiroshima survivor.

JANA HARRIS (b. 1947) is an American poet living in Washington, D.C., who has published volumes of verse and fiction which have won critical acclaim. Acutely aware of the nuclear threat, she has sponsored a forum at the Manhattan Theatre Club, where she served as director of Writers in Performance, titled "The Writer's Conscience in the Nuclear Age."

TOYOMI HASHIMOTO (b. c. 1925) is a survivor of the U.S. World War II atomic attacks which killed and maimed many thousands of civilians. This personal account from *Cries for Peace,* an oral history project of Japanese youth, published in Tokyo, is only one of many such testimonies by victims of the atomic bombings of Nagasaki and Hiroshima.

ANNE HEBERT (b. 1916), a celebrated French-Canadian poet who has also written extensively for the stage, film, and television, was born and raised in Saint Catherine, a village twenty miles from Quebec. One of her most common themes is that of the sadness of women repressed by the domestic scene. Here, Anne Hébert, like Elsa Morante (see p. 273) ironically confronts our human history of war and misery.

DIANA DER HOVANESSIAN is an accomplished Armenian-American poet and translator. Winner of the Barcelona Peace prize in 1985 for the first poem presented here, "Songs of Bread," which is the title of a group of poems written in prison in 1915 by the venerable and martyred Armenian poet, Daniel Varoujan, she takes his persona and then goes on to share that empathy with a Cambodian woman.

JUNE JORDAN (b. 1936) is a contemporary Jamaican-American poet and educator who has published several volumes of verse, criticism, political commentary, and essays. Her poetry is acutely involved with the protest against social injustice and her sensibility is politically worldly and international. From her latest volume of verse, *Living Room,* comes this poem in which she voices empathy with a Lebanese woman caught in a bombing attack.

ZOE KARELLI (b. 1901) received the coveted Ouranis Award for her complete works in 1978 and is one of the most respected of Greek poets today. The first woman of letters to be elected to the Academy of Athens in 1982, she coined the *feminine* gender usage of the generic term "man," *e anthropos,* in her work to help to establish the equality of women in literature. Here, translated by Rae Dalven of the United States, she writes of a special service that exhumed the dead after World War II, and sent the remains back to their homes.

GERTRUDE KOLMAR (1894–1943) was a Jewish poet who died in a German concentration camp during World War II. Her courage to go on writing poetry in the midst of profound human suffering, and the volume of poems she produced during her Nazi imprisonment, titled *Dark Soliloquy*, is a tribute to the human spirit.

FOUMIKO KOMETANI, noted Japanese writer now living in the United States, wrote this in reviewing a book of drawings from America's concentration camps for Japanese-Americans, titled, *Beyond Words: Images from America's Concentration Camps.*

MARGARET MACKAY (b. *c.* 1950) is an American journalist who visited South Africa to interview women leaders of the antiapartheid struggle. Here in an article reprinted from *The Peoples' Daily World*, she describes the conditions under which South African women endure the policies of their centuries-old repressive colonial regime.

ILEANA MALANCIOUI (b. 1940) is a Romanian writer and philosopher. She received a doctorate in philosophy from Bucharest University and has worked for Romanian television. She is an editor with the monthly literary magazine *Viata Romaneasca.* One of the most prolific of contemporary Romanian poets, she has published nine volumes of poems since her first in 1967. This poem demonstrates an eternal theme through the use of an ancient story. The mighty emperors and dictators carry on their wars, while the lonely kin struggle to mourn and bury their dead with dignity.

WINNIE MANDELA (b. 1934) of South Africa is designated a "banned" person in her own country. She lives under house arrest and is not allowed to address the public or meet with more than one person at a time. For over twenty years she has endured forced separation from her husband, the imprisoned Nelson Mandela, head of the African National Congress, whom most South Africans consider their true political leader. In this excerpt from her own memoir, *A Part of My Soul Went with Him,* she describes the ordeal of her long imprisonment of 1969 when many people were arrested in nationwide dawn raids under the Anti-Terrorism Act—a law ironically named, as it has terrorized thousands of innocent people simply trying to claim their rights as human beings. Winnie Mandela has been repeatedly arrested and confined and many attempts were made on her life. Her daughter, Zindzi Mandela, has had to appeal to the United Nations to save her mother's life.

GABRIELA MISTRAL (1889–1957), a Chilean schoolteacher born in Vicuña, was the first poet of South America to win the Nobel Prize for Literature (1945). She was fifty-six years old when she made the trip to Stockholm from Petropolis, Brazil. Her passionate poetry had become legendary throughout South America, passed from country to country by word of mouth. She traveled widely: Mexico, the United States, Spain, Switzerland, Italy. In 1926, she came to Paris as the Chilean delegate to the League of Nations Committee for Intellectual Cooperation and was able to promote the works of Latin American authors throughout Europe. In 1951, she served as delegate to the United Nations Commission on the Status of Women and as a member of the Committee for Women's Rights. During her last years, she worked as an adviser to UNESCO. On her tomb, her favorite axiom is transcribed: "What the soul is to the body is what the artist does for her/his people." Here, in commemorating one Finnish hero, she commemorates all who died in the Finnish resistance.

ELSA MORANTE (b. 1918) of Italy is known throughout the Americas and Europe for her novel, *History,* 1974—concerned with ravages of the war years—and has authored many critically acclaimed and prizewinning volumes of fiction, fables, and poems.

YUNNA PETROVNA MORITZ (b. 1937) is an accomplished poet of Russia who recently traveled to New York City to read her poems under the auspices of PEN American Center in a cross-cultural exchange with writers of the Soviet Union. Here in a childhood reminiscence of the war, she is translated by Thomas P. Whitney of the United States. Among her celebrated books of poetry are *On the High Shore, A Conversation About Happiness,* and *Cape of Wishes.*

TONI MORRISON (b. 1931) is the author of *Songs of Solomon* and the 1987 Pulitzer Prize–winning, *Beloved,* among other novels. Winner of the National Book Critics Circle Award for *The Bluest Eye,* she holds the Albert Schweitzer Chair for the Humanities at the State University of New York in Albany. In this excerpt from *Sula,* she tells of an American soldier who survives the carnage of World War I. Shadrack, in his way, is a profound peace activist. Like Brian Wilson, Vietnam veteran who lost his legs trying to stop a shipment of American arms to his country's war in Central America, his apparent "craziness" is a sanity superior to that of the society in which he survives his tribulations.

HOPE MORRITT (b. 1930) is an accomplished Canadian novelist, journalist, historian, and biographer, who lives in Point Edward, Ontario. She attended the University of Ontario and has done postgraduate work in Irish literature in Dublin. This remembrance of her father, a lieutenant in the Canadian infantry during World War I, was written when she visited the row upon row of soldiers' graves in Belgium's battlefields. Morritt has written radio plays for the Canadian Broadcasting Corporation and has had stories read on CBC radio.

LUCRETIA MOTT (1793–1880) was a Quaker and a feminist who worked all her life for the abolition of slavery, the rights of labor, and peace and social justice. Like Harriet Tubman, she aided fugitive slaves who fled north and in 1833 organized the Philadelphia Female Anti-Slavery Society. When women were excluded as delegates from the World Anti-slavery Convention in London in 1840, she organized, with Elizabeth Cady Stanton, the first women's rights convention in the United States, in 1848 at Seneca Falls, New York. Her husband, James Mott, also a Quaker, was her constant companion in the antislavery cause and the struggle for women's suffrage. After the Civil War and the Emancipation Proclamation, some were ready to disband the Anti-Slavery Society, but Lucretia Mott spoke out against its disbanding, as here, knowing that the suffering of black people had far from ended.

TRAN THI NGA (b. 1927) is a contemporary Vietnamese poet/novelist who lived through the war years in her shattered country. A bookkeeper in her husband's firm in Saigon, she met Wendy Wilder Larsen, an American teacher who traveled with her journalist husband to Vietnam to live and teach there during the war. The two women, fleeing the fall of Saigon, were reunited in New York after the war. They collaborated on a critically acclaimed book, *Shallow Graves: Two Women and Vietnam,* which tells with startling clarity and insight, the devastating effects of war on those who do not fight on the battlefields.

SHARON OLDS (b. 1942), one of the finest poets living in North America today, is the author of several books and articles, among them *Satan Says.* She has taught creative writing at many colleges, universities, and conferences throughout the United States. She lives in New York City. *The Gold Cell* is her latest book.

VESNA PARUN (b. 1922) is a celebrated Yugoslavian poet. She has published numerous volumes of poems widely read throughout her native land. From a collected volume of her works published in Zagreb, this poem concerns how the young men are sent off to die while old men, and the women are left to wait for their return. Her war poems contrast the peace of what life could be with the chaos of war.

MINERVA SALADO (b. 1944) is a contemporary Cuban poet who is also a journalist. She graduated from the University of Havana with a degree in journalism. Her first book, *At the Closing,* won the Premio David Prize, a top literary award of her country. Minerva Salado has been a correspondent for many international journals and published other critically acclaimed books of poetry since her first.

CHRISTIAN SANTOS (b. 1941) is a poet of Nicaragua who has been published in the United States and Italy. Her poems have been presented in a collection titled *Nicaragua in Revolution: The Poets Speak,* edited by Marc Zimmerman of the United States. Through the experience of one Nicaraguan worker, she portrays the horror of war so commonplace in the lives of Central Americans today.

SAPPHO (*c.* 6th cent. B.C.), famed poet of ancient Greece, though separated from Emily Dickinson by thousands of years of history, offers the same universal truth to end the violence and suffering of war. Compare her quatrain with Dickinson's found earlier in this section. Sappho, native of the island of Lesbos, was a priestess of Aphrodite, Goddess of Love and Kindness, to whom she wrote songs of praise. Her works—destroyed by the Church during the Dark Ages—survive in only about 1,100 lines, but we know that she wrote the mostly widely sung and recited lyrics of her day.

LYNNE SHARON SCHWARTZ (b. 1939) is the award-winning U.S. author of three novels: *Disturbances in the Field, Balancing Acts,* and *Rough Strife;* and two collections of short stories, *Acquainted with the Night,* and *The Melting Pot and Other Stories.* Recipient of National Endowment and Guggenheim fellowships, she is also an educator. Her personal account is the result of a teaching experience during the Vietnam war years at Hunter College in New York City where she lives.

LESLIE MORMON SILKO (b. 1948) is a Native American writer of mixed ancestry who was raised among the Laguna tribe of New Mexico. She has traveled the United States giving readings and teaching creative writing and is best known for her novel, *Ceremony,* which deals with antinuclear themes, as well as her long prophetic poem/chant about the end of the world derived from the folk literature of her people. Here she portrays the plight of disenfranchised indigenous women and their children the world over.

MAVIS SMALLBERG (b. 1945) is a poet and devoted teacher who lives in South Africa. Here she contrasts what the government newspapers report with the realities faced by her people. Her works have appeared in small underground journals published by groups of resisters and are banned in her own country.

WISŁAWA SZYMBORSKA (see pp. 72–73).

LUISA VALENZUELA (b. 1938), the well-known Argentinian, published her first novel, *Hay que sonreir,* when she was only twenty, and at twenty-one, she formed her first collection of short stories. Since then, she has written for numerous journals and published a number of other books. In 1976, the American reading public began to know her work with the publication of *Clara.* Julio Cortazar has said of her: "A woman deeply anchored in her conditions; she is conscious of the still horrible discriminations of our continent, yet she is filled with a joy of life which enables her to surpass the first stages of protest and supervaluation of her sex, taking a legitimate place of equality with any writer in the world of letters. To read her is to enter fully into reality. . . ." This short story, translated into English by Deborah Bonner, is only one of many war themes from her latest North American publication, *Other Weapons*, concerning the violence and subjugation experienced by women of South and Central America.

ALICE WALKER (b. 1944) is the renowned author of *The Color Purple*, which became an award-winning Hollywood movie viewed by millions around the globe. She has received both Guggenheim and National Endowment Award fellowships and a prize from the National Institute of Arts and Letters for her writing. Her poems *Revolutionary Petunias* and *In Love and Trouble*, along with novels like *Meridian*, have established her as one of North America's leading poet/novelists. She credits the celebrated black-American writer and folklorist, ZORA NEALE HURSTON (1901–1960). Hurston was a pioneering American novelist and anthropologist of her people. During the 1920s she traveled through the southern United States collecting black folk tales, for blacks everywhere have always been rich in their own literature—often in the oral tradition—even if whites are only beginning to discover that richness as they are discovering, too, the wealth of Native American cultural wisdom and art nearly lost to us through genocide. This "curse," paraphrased here and blended with oaths from other folk literature, was found by Hurston in her travels and resurrected by the work and efforts of Alice Walker. Walker is a supporter of many humane causes, including several organizations in the peace and social justice movement.

SIMONE WEIL (1909–1943), French by birth, Jewish by heritage, Catholic by conviction, stood in her beliefs outside of organized religions. She earned top honors in her studies, but left her work as a teacher to labor in factories among the working classes. Born into a comfortable family, she risked everything to fight in the Spanish Civil War and later for the Free French. As George A. Panichas, the scholar who has collected and edited her writings, has said, "She confronted the rootlessness of modern man and the death of the spirit in an age of materialism. Her vision was radical. . . . She has come to be increasingly recognized as the greatest ethical writer of this century." Her world-renowned essay, *The Iliad: Poem of Force*, is said to explain the nature of violence in war better than anything else written on the subject. These excerpts are extracted to be pure Weil, deliberately devoid of quotes from the great Homer.

HARRIET ZINNES is an accomplished poet of the United States who has lived in Switzerland as a visiting professor at the University of Geneva. A widely published critic, translator from the French of Jacques Prevert's *Blood and Feathers*, and a fiction writer, she is also a professor at Queens College of the City University of New York. The author of five volumes of poems, her latest book is a collection of short stories titled *Lover*.

PART IV

Hope and Survival

It has been women's task throughout history to go on be-lieving in life when there was almost no hope. If we are united, we may be able to produce a world in which our chil-dren and other people's children can be safe.

—MARGARET MEAD (U.S.A.)

I want that there should be a belief, a faith in the possi-bility of removing mountains to the side of right. If we be-lieve that war is wrong, as everyone must, then we ought to believe that by proper efforts on our part, it may be done away with. . . .

—LUCRETIA MOTT (U.S.A.)

No More War, 1924,
by Käthe Kollwitz

BELLA ABZUG (U.S.A.)

THE ISSUE IS SURVIVAL

Those nuclear weapons are aimed at you and me, our friends, our neighbors, our kids. We have to aim back with votes, with our petitions, with our voices, to tell the people in Congress, in the White House, in the Pentagon, here and in the Soviet Union, and all over the world, that people want to live.

Women can afford to be nonpartisan about peace. We know the difference between national security and a profit-motivated military megalomania that can destroy this world. And that is why, for us, the issue is straightforward. SURVIVAL! I suggest that we demand that half of every delegation to the United Nations consist of women. I would like to suggest that the Arms Control Agency must contain women in negotiating positions. I want to further suggest that we demand a presence of women within the leadership of this country, as well as within the leadership of all other countries.

JANE ADDAMS (U.S.A.)

MATURING CONCEPTS OF PEACE

In my long advocacy of peace, I'd consistently used one line of appeal, contending that peace is no longer an abstract dogma; that a dynamic is found in the internationalism promoted by people of all nations who are determined upon the abolition of degrading poverty, disease and ignorance, with their resulting inefficiency and tragedy. I believe that peace is not merely an absence of war, but the nurture of human life and that in time this nurture will do away with war as a natural process. . . . I was pushed far to the left on the subject of war. . . . That the U.S. has entered the war has not changed my view of the invalidity of war as a method of settlement of social problems a particle, and I can see no reason why one should not say what one believes in time of war as in time of peace. . . . Only in freedom is permanent peace possible. To unite women in all countries who are opposed to any kind of

278

war, exploitation and oppression and who work for universal disarmament and for the solution of conflicts by recognition of human solidarity, by conciliation and arbitration, by world cooperation, and by the establishment of social, political, and economic justice for all without distinction of sex, race, class, or creeds.

Perhaps the one point at which this undertaking is most needed is in regard to our conception of patriotism, which . . . is too much dressed in the trappings of the past and continually carries us back to its beginnings in military prowess and defense. . . . We continue to found our patriotism upon war and to contrast conquest with nurture, militarism with industrialism, calling the latter passive and inert and the former active and aggressive, without really facing the situation as it exists. We tremble before our own convictions and are afraid to find newer manifestations of courage and daring lest we thereby lose the virtues bequeathed to us by war. It is a pitiful acknowledgement that we have lost them already and that we shall have to give up the ways of war, if for no other reason than to preserve the finer spirit of courage . . . it has engendered. . . .

SABILLA ALERMO (ITALY)

YES TO THE EARTH

So shines the Earth in certain mornings' light
with its roses and cypresses
or with its grain and its olives,

so suddenly does it shine on the soul
and isolates it and makes it forget everything
even if an instant earlier the soul
was suffering to the quick or meditating, bitter,

so shines the Earth in certain mornings' light
and in its silence reveals itself,
a marvelous lump spinning from the skies,
and, beautiful in its tragic solitude, so laughs

that the soul, although not asked,
answers, "Yes," "Yes," to the Earth,
to the indifferent Earth "Yes,"

even if in an instant the skies and the roses
and the cypresses should turn dark,
or the labor of living be made more burdensome
and breathing yet more heroic,

"Yes," the subjugated soul answers the Earth,
so does it shine in certain mornings' light,
beautiful over all things and human hope.

(Translated by Muriel Kittel)

SVETLANA ALLILUYEVA (U.S.S.R./U.S.A.)

TWENTY LETTERS TO A FRIEND

. . . Did I know a single person whose life turned out well? It was as though my father [Joseph Stalin] were at the center of a black circle and anyone who ventured inside vanished or perished or was destroyed in one way or another.

He's been gone for ten years now. Both my aunts, Evgenia Alliluyeva, Pavel's widow, and Anna Alliluyeva, Redens's widow and my mother's sister, are back from prison. The Svanidzes' son, who is my age, is back from exile in Kazakhstan. Many people have come back, thousands and thousands who managed somehow to survive. The return of so many people from prison and exile is a great historic turning point. The scale on which the dead have come back to life is difficult to imagine.

In a sense my life, too, couldn't be normal so long as my father was alive. Could I have had as much freedom before as I have now? Could I conceivably have gone any place I wanted to without permission? Could I have met and made friends with anyone I pleased? Could my children have lived freely and without surveillance the way they do now? We can all breathe more freely. It's as though a heavy slab of stone had been lifted from us all. But unfortunately too many things have stayed the same. Russia is too much weighted down by inertia and tradition. The age-old ways of doing things are too strong.

But what is good in Russia is traditional and unchanging, too, even more than what is bad. And perhaps it is this eternal good which gives Russia strength and helps preserve her true self.

Don't ever forget what is good in life. Those of our people who have been through the war and the concentration camps (both German and Soviet), who have known prison both under the Czars and in Soviet times, these people who've seen every horror the twentieth century has unleashed on mankind never forget the kindly faces of childhood. Each of them has small, sunny corners he can remember and draw strength from always, through all of life's sufferings. I can only pity anyone who has nothing of this kind to give him solace. Even those who are callous and cruel retain somewhere, hidden from others, such pockets of memory in the depths of their twisted souls.

The Good always wins out. The Good triumphs over everything, though it frequently happens too late—not before the very best people have perished unjustly, senselessly, without rhyme or reason.

*   *   *   *   *

What sterling, full-blooded people they were, these early knights of the Revolution who carried so much romantic idealism with them to the grave! They were the troubadours, the victims, the blind zealots and the martyrs of the Revolution.

As for those who wanted to set themselves above the Revolution, who wanted to speed up its progress and make tomorrow come today, those who tried to do good by doing evil and make the wheels of time and progress spin faster, have they accomplished what they wanted? Millions were sacrificed senselessly, thousands of talented lives extinguished prematurely. The tale of these losses could not be told in twenty books, never mind twenty letters. Wouldn't it have been better for these people to have gone on serving mankind here on earth rather than have their deaths be the only mark they left in the hearts of men?

History is a stern judge. It's not for me but for history to decide who served the cause of good and who that of vanity and vainglory. I certainly don't have the right.

All I have is my conscience. And conscience tells me that before pointing out the mote in my neighbor's eye I must first see the beam in my own. There's no one, including me, who doesn't have a beam in his own eye.

We are all responsible for everything that happened. Let the judging be done by those who come later, by men and women who didn't know the times and the people we knew. Let it be left to new people to whom these years in Russia will be as remote and inexplicable, as terrible and strange, as the reign of Ivan the Terrible. But I do not think they'll call our era a "progressive" one, or that they'll say it was all for the "good of Russia." Hardly . . .

They will have their say. And what they say will be something new and cogent. Instead of idle whining, they will give voice to a new sense of purpose. They will read through this page in their country's history with a feeling of pain, contrition and bewilderment, and they'll be led by this feeling to live their lives differently.

But I hope they won't forget that what is Good never dies—that it lived on in the hearts of men even in the darkest times and was hidden where no one thought to look for it, that it never died out or disappeared completely.

Everything on our tormented earth that is alive and breathes, that blossoms and bears fruit, lives only by virtue of and in the name of Truth and Good.

(Translated by Priscilla J. McMillan)

Mila D. Anguilar (philippines)

MY SON ASKS

My son asks
how it will be
the New People's Army taking over.

My son,
it will be
the way the Manilans greet their New Year.

I speak not only
of the explosions you can hear
but of the mirth you can smell in the air.

Long before its eve
you will already be hearing
a boom here and a bang there.

But the real rejoicing will come
later, on the new day itself,
when the volleys issue nearer and nearer of each other

until, rising to fever pitch
at the felicitous hour,
the air fills with ceaseless roaring thunder—

the ceaseless roaring thunder
of a million feet marching
through the breathless streets of the city.

And after
the explosions and the cheers have died down
and the smell of gunpowder cleared away, my son,

the nice cup of hot gingertea
and the generous slice of steaming rice cake
lavished by the grateful warm-hearted people.

ANGELICA BALABANOFF (UKRAINIAN RUSSIA)

THE TRUTH WAS NEVER MORE NECESSARY

Today, after twenty years in which the international labour movement has been defeated and dismembered, humanity is again on the verge of self-destruction. The failure to learn the lessons of experience between 1914 and 1922 has led the world to a new cycle of tragedy which today threatens to engulf all of Europe and perhaps America.

I have been an intimate witness of many of these events from their beginnings. I was an active member of the great international movement that collapsed in 1914 and I was one of those who tried to rebuild it and to rally the workers of all countries to an international banner during the World War. I was a leader of Italian Socialism both in its isolated adherence to internationalism and when it became the victim of an infamous betrayal—that of Benito Mussolini. I watched, day by day, the triumph of the new Russia, its energies enriched by the spirit of revolution; I saw its achievements threatened by blockade, starvation, and intervention at the hands of its enemies, and later by the unpardonable mistakes of its friends within and without its borders. Finally, I have known closely and collaborated with the masses of men and women who have been the instruments—and often the victims—of these events, and with the men who most influenced their development—Lenin, Trotsky, Mussolini.

The World War created a rift between the generations which cannot be ignored. The millions who were slaughtered took with them into their graves not only their hopes and sufferings, but the traditions and the knowledge they had inherited and acquired. The physical and moral horrors of our epoch are possible only because of this. The war cancelled a whole period of human progress and the wisdom of its artisans. It made possible a generation that knows nothing of what has gone before—nothing except what its rulers tell it. History has been falsified without shame by the Fascists and, unfortunately, also by the Bolsheviks. The truth was never more necessary than it is today.

Though the movement of which I was a part has been destroyed in half of Europe, not even in this tragic hour do I believe that the work of the generation of revolutionaries to which I belong has been altogether in vain. If there is hope for our civilization beyond the black night of war and totalitarianism, I am convinced that it lies only in the movement to which we—the living and the dead—have given our lives.

Norma Becker (u.s.a.)

STRATEGIES FOR PEACE

In June, 1982 the disarmament movement in the U.S. was able to mobilize over one million people in what has been described as America's single largest peace demonstration. Marching through the streets of Manhattan, a sea of humanity demanded the abolition of nuclear weapons, an end to the arms race, and the funding of human needs.

And while speaker after speaker vigorously condemned an arms race that had gone out of control, there was virtually no mention of the Israeli invasion of Lebanon which had begun the week before. This failure to oppose military intervention made possible by massive U.S. military aid was, in my opinion, an abdication of responsibility. In addition, it was a lost opportunity to raise consciousness and focus the attention of the mass media—which had converged upon New York City from all over the world—on the inevitable consequences and inherent perils of U.S. military/political policy.

So having lamented that error, let us learn from it.

Massive American military build-up and intervention on behalf of foreign right-wing repressive regimes are as inextricably intertwined as the relationship between increased military spending and increased cutbacks in domestic programs. The recent U.S. shipment of 2500 electric cattle prods to South Africa is made possible by the elimination of school-enrichment programs in Harlem.

It is the responsibility of the Peace and Justice movement to constantly emphasize these inter-connections. Human history provides ample testimony that peace is just not possible without justice. And fundamental to any concept of social justice is the affirmation that human rights are our primary value and human welfare our primary goal.

Let's examine what some of the strategic implications of these premises might be for us. First, while some of us choose to work in disarmament organizations, others choose to work in groups seeking economic justice or racial and sexual equality. *But we are part of one movement.*

In this light it seems to me that it is very necessary for us to regard a multi-tactical approach as not only desirable but necessary for a mass heterogeneous society. From legal demonstrations, to non-violent civil disobedience, from draft resistance to teach-ins, from lobbying to letter writing, a multiplicity of forms enables people to move from one level to another. It is essential that we in the movement not trash, put down, or heap scorn or disdain upon forms that do not correspond to the particular one we happen to be pursuing at the moment. . . .

It is a very vital and important form of political struggle. . . . We have to find ways to make foreign policy a community issue. The well-being and survival of every community is now determined more directly by foreign policy decisions than by decisions concerning traffic lights and garbage disposal. Foreign policy decisions cannot be left any longer to the ruling elite and their experts. The link between economic recession and current unemployment, on the one hand, and astronomical appropriations for weapons of mass destruction and subsidies to right-wing regimes, on the other hand, can now be understood more clearly by the average citizen. This opens up all kinds of possibilities to the movement that did not exist at an earlier time. For example, the existing political climate creates the possibility of greater receptivity and responsiveness to such things as the Jobs With Peace Campaign, which can be vigorously pursued in communities throughout the nation. Most communities are hurting badly as a consequence of the military domination of foreign policy. Such things as the peace budget, nuclear-free zones and anti-draft struggles will be met with more positive response. . . . On this whole question of "the Soviet threat," it seems to me we have to find ways and means of transforming the prevailing view of the Russians from "enemies" to co-inhabitants of the planet. And there are ways to do that. There must be massive interpersonal exchange between Americans and Russians from all fields of endeavor, particularly church people, college newspaper editors, members of parent-teacher associations. It has to be on a non-governmental and non-official level, though not to the exclusion of that. What I am projecting is a kind of people's inter-personal exchange. We must invite Soviet citizens to the United States to speak in our neighborhoods, our communities, to our school boards, churches, etc.

Finally, I would like to end with what I believe is our most difficult problem. That is how to get people to move out of a sense of powerlessness and impotency, how to move people—most of whom are not social activists and most of whom, not only in the United States but all over the world, are traditionally concerned with personal matters, personal issues concerning themselves, their loved ones, in a small sphere or circle of social relations. Most human beings do not concern themselves with global strategy, with foreign policy, with trans-national issues, and this is a phenomenon that the movement has always been up against. With time running out we have to look at this existential human phenomenon and begin to examine how to overcome it.

I do not have the answers for this. I know that, commercially, a lot of market research is done on how to get people to buy junk they do not need. This is all behavior management; but on a comparable level what I am talking about is that we need to quickly research and find ways to get people to move out of this behavioral pattern.

What we are saying is that mutual aid and support are essential for human survival on an individual level, and this is true for every member of the species everywhere in the world. We are at a point in human evolution now where human solidarity on a global scale is absolutely vital for the survival of the human species. That is a goal that we have to try to get people to move towards.

ELENA BRUSKOVA (U.S.S.R.)

THE SOVIET PEACE FUND

The Soviet Peace Fund is a mass public organisation founded in 1961 to promote the cause of peace through voluntary donations. The first chairman of the organisation was the famous Soviet writer Boris Polevoy, who was succeeded upon his death by Anatoli Karpov, the former world chess champion.

In accordance with the organisation's charter, the ruling body of the fund, the All-Union Conference, elects a board which oversees the daily business of the Fund. At present this board includes among others the poet Robert Rozhdestvensky, cosmonaut Vladimir Aksyonov, and Rufina Nifontova, the popular actress of stage and screen.

One can donate money to the Soviet Peace Fund simply by going to a savings bank, or sending money to 10 Kropotkinskaya Street, Moscow. Sometimes contributions are sent anonymously, but most often they are signed. The amount of the money donated differs widely. A schoolboy might send a rouble saved from his allowance, five roubles could be sent monthly by a retired woman, and workers from a factory workshop might collectively decide to send a single day's wages, some eight hundred roubles. Author's royalties and work bonuses are sometimes forwarded to the Fund; other people bequeath legacies to it. It has become a tradition in the Soviet Union to organise special performances and concerts, and sponsor exhibition-fairs of painting and sculpture, the profits of which are passed on to the Peace Fund.

Even today in the Soviet Union, it would be difficult to find a family that does not harbour bitter memories of the Second World War. Perhaps this is why there is such a great number of people who have, in one way or another, participated in the work of the Peace Fund through their voluntary donations. Already this number has reached some one hundred million people.

Here we would like to cite some of the letters that often accompany donations sent by Soviet citizens to the Peace Fund. At times they can hardly be called letters, consisting of only a few lines, or even words, or sometimes just a signature. But at other times, pages are received, covered with writing.

"In honour of this day, the birthday of my brother Victor, who died in the Second World War, I pledge that until the end of my life I will every month send part of my pension. Somehow, in some way, I'd like to feel that I'm actively helping to prevent any future wars."

"I'm a mother of three sons. I went through all the hardships of the war: cold, starvation, and bereavement. All the mothers in this world want clear, peaceful skies over their heads, and would like to prevent the deaths of their sons and daughters. On the occasion of this Victory Day, I'm sending my month's pension to the Peace Fund. . . ."

"I'm a veteran of the Second World War, and I cannot help but be involved in the mass peace movement. . . . I was raised in an orphanage, and our government has done a great deal for orphans. This is something I'll always remember. . . ."

"Along with this modest sum of roubles, I am prepared to give my heart and soul to a cause that could prevent the advent of another war.
"An invalid of the Second World War."

"This is my 104th donation. . . ." "I am sending you twenty roubles for starving children in the world." "This is my 27th donation. . . ." "This 170th donation is in memory of my dead brothers, and the others of the twenty million. It is in the name of life. . . ."

Yes, of course, some contributions are for "the victory monument on Poklonnaya Hill in Moscow," "for the business of making peace," "for any goodwill talks that in any way work to rid us of missiles." Perhaps, in memory of the fallen. That is, in memory of those who perished, in the name of those who survived.

"Of course," writes a carpenter from Bukhara, who donated 10,600 roubles to the Peace Fund. *"I could have given my life's savings to my children and grandchildren, of whom I have thirty-six. But I know that they don't need anything, and obtain everything by their own labour. It's not their material comfort that troubles me, but rather their futures. I want them to live on a peaceful earth. I would like to see all the children of our entire planet living under peaceful skies. . . ."*

It seems that to be concerned not for the living standard of one's children, but for their future, requires a lifetime of honest living, and a life so lived cannot help but have an effect on those close to it.

"We, the members of the construction brigade of the Orenburg Drilling Equipment Plant, have decided to forward one day's salary every month to the Peace Fund. And we call on all those who cherish peace on earth to follow our example."
Signed, the brigade foreman, the trade-union representative, a concrete worker, a welder, and a brick layer.

"I'm sixteen years old, and in tenth grade. This five roubles and eighty kopecks is the first money I have ever earned, and I'd like to spend it on something beautiful. And what could possibly be more beautiful than peace?"

"On the occasion of my joining the Komsomol, I'd like, with the permission of my mother, to make a donation to the cause of preserving peace. May everyone live in peace and enjoy life."

"We would like to donate a day's salary from our Komsomol cotton-harvesting brigade at Tashkent school No. 78 to the Peace Fund, in memory of Marat Kasei, Hero of the Soviet Union, who our school is named after. . . ."

It's amazing what a powerful impact an example of a human life may have!

288

"... I want all the children in our world to have both bread and crayons. That is why I am giving away the money that I have long been saving up to buy a camera. ..."

"... We have written protests and held meetings. And now we have decided to make our modest contribution to the cause of peace. This is the money we earned by gathering wild herbs. ...

"Sixth grade pupils."

"... I am a pupil in eighth grade, and have decided to send you fifty roubles I earned in honour of the fortieth anniversary of the Great Victory. I know that the cause of peace is a common cause, and I call upon children and adults alike to fight for peace, happiness, and friendship. ..."

"... We are giving our modest donation on the day of our wedding. This is from newlyweds. ..."

What does a man do when he is happy? When he has to mark a special day that he will remember all his life? How does he engrave this day in his memory? With a party? Or with gifts from relatives? Or a merry holiday with his friends?

We are anxious to celebrate an event in the most memorable way possible. And in our midst, almost unnoticed, there has germinated a new and wonderful ability to show concern for the world beyond one's door, even as a memorable event is taking place right in one's own home.

HELEN CALDICOTT (AUSTRALIA)

ERADICATE NUCLEAR WEAPONS FROM THE FACE OF THE EARTH

... what happened was that at 8:15 A.M. a plane, a single plane appeared overhead, and the Japanese were pleased—they thought the plane had been shot down and the pilot was escaping. Another parachute opened adjacent to the first, and a little boy was reaching up to catch a red dragon fly on his hand against the blue sky ... and there was a blinding flash and he disappeared ... and so did tens of thousands of other human beings. About a hundred thousand people were killed with that bomb . . . the bomb dropped on Hiroshima was equivalent to about 13,000 tons of TNT. That's a small bomb. But let me describe how big that was. The maximum payload any plane could carry during the Second World War was 4 tons of bombs. So they exploded a bomb that was 13,000 tons in a millionth of a second. . . . The hydrogen bomb: some of them are of 20 megatons, that's equivalent to 20 million tons of TNT in one bomb, that's four times the size of all the bombs dropped during the Second World War. They once made a 50 megaton bomb which America blew up in the Pacific, in the South Pacific, and they got such a terrible shock, they never did that again. They could easily make a 100 megaton bomb, they're awfully easy to make. . . . Today, America has . . . enough to overkill every Russian human being over forty times. Russia has enough to overkill every American human being over twenty times. So who's behind? . . . If you think about this in medical terminology, how many times can you kill a human being? And they say—"Oh, Russians ahead." You see the mentality is about at a level of a nine-year-old boy with arrested emotional development. . . . One 20 megaton bomb would create a crater half a mile wide and three hundred feet deep. Everything in that volume would be converted into radio-active fallout, be pulverized; millions of tons of rock would be injected into the stratosphere and troposphere from where it would descend as radioactive fallout. Every person within a radius of six miles from the hypocenter would be vaporized—just turned into gas—as would most buildings. . . . Out to a radius of twenty miles from the hypocenter, most persons would be dead or lethally injured . . . [with] tens of thousands of cases of the most severe burns. . . . Fallout shelters will not help. . . . If you looked at the blast of the flash from forty miles away—just glanced at it—you'd be instantly blinded as the flash would burn the retina of the back of the eye. It would ignite everything that was inflammable within an area of 3,000 square miles; so everything would burn and the fires would coalesce sucking the air in with hurricane force winds to the center of the explosion, and . . . you'd be asphyxiated as the fire would use up all the oxygen. Also, apparently nuclear reactors (plants) are targeted and inside of each reactor is stored as much radiation as would be released by the explosion of 1,000 Hiroshima-sized bombs. . . . Oil refineries are targeted, and so are the large industries, and all airports. . . . In Hiroshima, there was an outside world to come and help—but now there will be nobody. Further, there will be millions of corpses. . . . As the bodies rot and decay, the bacteria, in this . . . breeding place, will multiply rapidly. . . . Then you take the radioactive environment that will become all lethal and virulent: . . . depleted by the effects of radiation . . . we will be susceptible to all the diseases we now medically control, like polio, typhoid, plague, dysentery, hundreds of them. So there will be epidemics of diseases. . . . The ultra violet rays of the sun (without the protective ozone layer) would produce third degree burns and blind every organism on earth . . . (And now there is the knowledge of a nuclear winter, too.) . . . The National Academy of Sciences in a study in 1975 estimated that if both superpowers used only 10 percent of the arsenal of the hydrogen bomb, . . . it could destroy 50 to 80 percent of the ozone layer in the northern hemisphere. . . . Some doctors think that if only 80 percent of the ozone layer is destroyed, it could blind every organism on earth. And people would die—the survivors would die of synergistic combinations of starvation, thirst, radiation sickness, epidemics and infections, sunburn blindness and grief. . . . As Nikita Khrushchev said, "In the event of a nuclear war, the living would envy the dead."

. . . Now you will say, well what can I do? [One] . . . thing I did was to start the Women's Party for Survival, because, as I [travel] talking about this, very often, it's the women who cry. Now I'm not excluding all mothering men. But, you know, women are very passionate, in fact, they very often drive men crazy because they're so passionate and emotional. It's appropriate to be emotional. Often, when I lay out the effects of nuclear war, the person interviewing me on television will say: "Aren't you being a bit emotional?"

You can understand that that's a crazy remark to make. It's like . . . if I have two parents in my office, and I tell them that their child has leukemia and explain the prognosis, and they show no emotional response . . . I would get them a psychiatrist. It's appropriate to be passionate about our survival.

When I had my first baby, I knew I'd die to save that life. Now I had never felt like that about any other human life before, it was a profound revelation for me. If we can mobilize that instinct that women have to save their babies, across the world, we may survive. So I started the Women's Party for Survival and we're having a march on Mother's Day in Washington, wearing our Sunday best, even Republican ladies, everybody . . . because this is a very conservative issue. The ultimate *conservative* issue. . . . The baby is our symbol . . . we thought of an action called Babies Against the Pentagon and that abbreviates to BAP. What we can do, when the Senate is debating the arms race, is to release hundreds of naked toddlers into the Senate chamber.

. . . We're on a terminally ill planet, you know that, and we are about to destroy ourselves. . . . What I'm really saying to you is that if you love this planet, and I'm deeply in love with it, and you watch the spring come and you watch the magnolias flower and the wisteria come out, and you smell a rose—you will realize that you're going to have to change the priorities of your life—if you love this planet.

After World War II, America took the initiative and quickly converted its economy to peacetime uses. . . . The American corporations that are involved in the arms race are run by very intelligent people who will quickly perceive that the people of America will not allow the wartime economic system to continue. . . . They will put their heads together and will be motivated to design equipment that will be used to the benefit of people both in the United States and internationally.

The world urgently needs adequate production and equitable distribution of food. It needs vast production of medicines and vaccines, and redistribution of medical expertise and medical supplies to the millions of suffering people in the Third World. Adequate distribution of birth-control techniques is required to prevent an increase in global population growth from 4.5 billion now to 6 billion in 2000. Reforestation of many areas of the world is a mandatory priority, since trees currently are used to provide fuel for the poor countries, and trees recycle carbon dioxide to produce oxygen. The riches of the sea must be equitably distributed among all nations of the earth and must not be mined only by those few Western nations that currently possess the technology and expertise to do so. All the world's natural resources must be shared and used for the benefit of the family of man and not hoarded and wasted on production of weapons. Millions of the world's people must be delivered from their situation of illiteracy and poverty—a vicious cycle that perpetuates endemic overpopulation and hunger.

The air and water of . . . large parts of the world are fast becoming irretrievably polluted with carcinogenic and mutagenic poisons produced by industry to make profits. There are 4.5 million known toxic chemicals, and 375,000 new ones are produced annually. Most have never been adequately tested for carcinogenicity, and most are released to the environment, often illegally. Many of these chemicals are by-products of industries that produce plastic throwaway materials we don't need (and, of course, weaponry).

. . . [the U.S.] needs to tighten its belt. My husband and I visited Cuba . . . before the revolution, malaria, hookworm, tuberculosis, and gastrointestinal disease were endemic there. Cuba now has one of the best medical schemes in the world—so good that Dr. Julius Richmond, . . . a Surgeon General of the United States, visited Cuba to develop ideas for America's healthcare system. Prerevolutionary illiteracy was about 40 percent; now it is almost negligible. (There are over 40 million, and some say many more, illiterate people in the U.S.) The education programs are excellent. Nevertheless, life is still spare. There is no choice of clothes in the shops—one type of shoe, one type of trouser . . . and a limited variety of food. The government has helped its people enormously, and the people are grateful. We returned to Christmas in America with the stores just dripping with luxury and affluence. We knew then that if America redefined its priorities, it could help to feed many of the world's people. Americans do not have a God-given right to be the wealthiest people in the world to the detriment of millions of others. These poor countries are now developing their own nuclear weapons, and they are justifiably angry. Who will they drop them on?

Men are very smart—so smart they have learned to destroy themselves. They could with a little effort and ingenuity develop a global economic system (excluding the production and sales of weapons) that would benefit the Western corporations, as well as all the countries of earth. For several years, the Third World has been pleading for such a move, but the selfish Western nations have refused to cooperate or to contemplate ways to alleviate the plight of the poor—(even in their own lands). Yet it is obvious that the global situation is all interconnected and relevant to prevention of nuclear war.

All such a scheme would take is creative initiative with the right motivations. If people see that in the end, they, too, will benefit as wealth is equitably shared around the world, thus making the world a safer place, they will become enthusiastic about such an endeavor. This is not pie-in-the-sky talk; it is pragmatic and ultimately reasonable and rational. It will take place only if the people in the wealthy Western democracies educate themselves about the plight of mankind and decide for their own well-being that they and their politicians will create solutions. . . . Conversion of a corporation from war to peace can be achieved not just by decisions of the corporate heads, but also by initiative from the workers. In England, the Lucas Aerospace Industry used to make parts for missiles. After many years, the workers became concerned with the global implications of their work. They called in some consultants and asked, "With our technical skills, what can we make that would benefit mankind?" So the consultants designed electric cars, dialysis machines, and mass-transit systems. The workers then took these plans to the management and said, "We are not going to make missiles anymore. We are going to make equipment." Management was surprised but was influenced. . . . Other workers and high technologists have begun to leave the military industry because of profound moral concern. They have formed an organization called High Technologists for Social Responsibility. . . .

Some scientists, and their colleagues also, are becoming alarmed about the implications of their occupations. I gave a speech at the

293

American Association for the Advancement of Science meeting . . . and a man named Bill Perry, who was the director of the public relations for Lawrence-Livermore Lab, heard me talk. He was taken aback by the information I presented, even though he worked right in the middle of a weapons organization. . . . He contemplated his dilemma for several months and then decided to leave the lab and work for the passage of the nuclear weapons freeze in California. Rarely have I seen such an elated man. He addressed a large meeting in San Francisco . . . where he recounted the history of his conversion, and he said, "I feel like a clean man." More people need to open up their souls to the truth and develop the courage to do what he did. . . .

The American Catholic bishops have written a pastoral letter (against) nuclear weapons and nuclear war (saying that all Catholics should work for nuclear disarmament): . . . Other churches and Jewish organizations have made similar statements about the total immorality of the preparation for and probability of nuclear war.

Many people are moving toward this ultimate solution. Newsman Walter Cronkite recently told me that for years he has been in favor of unilateral nuclear disarmament. He thinks that America should totally disarm within ten years and some of the money saved should be used to create satellites and communications systems to educate the people of the world about how to live in peace. The money could also be used for food programs and to help the industrial conversion process from weapons to peace. He said that he favors passive resistance—that if tens of thousands of people just sat down in front of the Soviet tanks, what could they do? He said we should make the arms negotiators sit at the table, and stop the clock and lock the door until they achieve appropriate arms reductions. . . .

. . . True happiness lies in helping one another. No other generation has inherited this enormous responsibility. We have been given the privilege of saving all past and all future generations, all animals, all plants. Think of the enormous variety of delicate butterflies, think of the gorgeous birds of the earth, of the endless designs of fish in the sea; think of the beautiful exotic flowers with their gorgeous and seductive perfumes; think of the proud lions and tigers and of the wondrous prehistoric elephants and hippopotamuses; think of what we are about to destroy. . . . Rapid nuclear disarmament is the ultimate issue of preventive medicine. It is the ultimate parenting issue. It is the ultimate Republican and ultimate Democratic and ultimate Socialist issue. It is the ultimate patriotic issue. Above all, it is the ultimate spiritual issue. . . . We are the curators of life on earth; we hold it in the palms of our hands. Can we evolve spiritually and emotionally in time to control the overwhelming evil that our advanced and rational intellect has created? We will know the answer to this question in our lifetime.

. . . Men and women are psychologically and physiologically different. Each has a most important role to play in the world, but unfortunately, women play second fiddle on most occasions. Although American women won the vote sixty-five years ago, they have done virtually nothing with it. There are virtually no women in high office. For various reasons—feelings of inadequacy, lack of knowledge, lack of energy contingent upon childbirth and childrearing—women have stayed in the background while men have made virtually all significant and major decisions. Now the world is ready to blow up. Women are worried, but men still make most of the decisions.

. . . decisions in the United States are made by a small minority—white Anglo-Saxon males, middle-aged and older. Because these people have created such enormous problems . . . we need to examine their psychological pathology. Typically, these men never show emotion, never admit mistakes, and are very dependent upon others of the same sex for peer group approval. They are always sure of themselves; they are always right; and above all, they are always tough and strong. [Some men] . . . suggest that in the nuclear age, these men need to redefine strength and courage for themselves, to become men who have the courage to show weaknesses and fallibilities, to admit mistakes, to show emotions, even to cry when appropriate. It takes extraordinary strength and inner courage for a man to be able to do this. A weak, unattractive man never shows any emotion or even admits to having emotions, never is fallible, never admits to making a mistake, hides behind his defense mechanisms, and builds missiles. One could call this dynamic a case of acute missile envy. Such men, who in fact hold the reins of power in Washington, in the Iron Triangle, and throughout the land and the world are anachronistic in the nuclear age.

A typical woman is very much in touch with her feelings. She cries when necessary and has a strong and reliable intuition. She is not afraid to admit she has made a mistake and generally is interested in life-oriented human dynamics. She innately understands the basic principles of conflict resolution. . . . Women are nurturers. Their bodies are built anatomically and physiologically to nurture life. Not all women can have babies and some do not even desire them, but many have a will to give birth. Mothers or not, most women care deeply about the preservation of life. Women on the whole are more capable of capitulation. . . . One of the reasons women are so allied to the life process is their hormonal constitution. . . . Men on the other hand are men because of their hormonal output of androgen. [A man] . . . is typically more psychologically aggressive than women. Some people contend that this is the result of conditioning. I am sure that some aggressive behavior in men is conditioned, but some must also be hormonally controlled. . . . Some recent work has shown that little boys under the age of six are more aggressive than girls of the same age. . . . Perhaps, the men reading this book will look into their souls and examine the validity of these questions. . . . Individuals face a formidable challenge in the nuclear age because of the survival imperative. They must learn to understand the basic principles that underlie and motivate their behavior and to determine how they can enhance the growth of the positive anima and animus and diminish the negative aspects. . . . Women have a very important role to play in the world today. They must rapidly develop their own power so that they can move out into local, national, and international affairs, using their positive animus to save the children of the country and of the world. Through the women's liberation movement, they have learned that they are as intelligent as men and can be as powerful or more powerful, as the occasion arises. They also have developed a confidence in themselves that is delightful to see. The age of woman has arrived. If we don't stand up and rapidly become elected to the highest offices in the country, changing . . . national policies from those of death to those of life, we will all be exterminated. I don't mean that in doing this, women should abrogate their positive feminine principle of nurturing, loving, and caring, I mean they should tenaciously preserve these values but also learn to find and use their incredible power. The positive feminine principle must become the guiding moral principle in world politics. . . . There is no question that women—who give life, nurture it and comfort it—want to do everything they can to bring about a world that is free from nuclear terror. Every poll taken reinforces the fact that women are overwhelmingly in favor of ending the arms race and bringing about a nuclear freeze. . . . We've got to give a tomorrow back to our children! The nuclear arms race not only instills fear in millions of children, it takes food out of the mouths of millions of others, everywhere in the world . . . the moment of actually "pushing the button" that will send the first live thermonuclear weapons will soon be determined by computers. Computers! Not human beings with feelings and concerns, but computers! Computers that are subject to mechanical failure. . . . One such error a few years ago brought us within 14 minutes of accidental nuclear war. . . . Women and children have been the real victims of the arms race. And we will go on being its victims in increasing numbers unless we fight back. Not physically, but with our voices, our minds and our hearts. Used properly, they can be the world's most potent weapons. If enough of us join together. . . .

. . . Each of us must accept total responsibility for the earth's survival. We are the curators of life on earth, standing at a crossroads in time. We must awake from our false sense of security and commit ourselves to using democracy constructively to save the human species, or our democratic heritage will atrophy and be lost.

CH'IU CHIN (CHINA)

FREE WOMEN BLOOMING LIKE FIELDS OF FLOWERS

How many wise men and heroes
Have survived the dust and dirt of the world?
How many beautiful women have been heroines?
There were the nobel and famous women generals
Ch'in Liang-yu and Shen Yu-yin.

Though tears stained their dresses
Their hearts were full of blood.
The wild strokes of their swords
Whistled like dragons and sobbed with pain.

The perfume of freedom burns my mind
With grief for my country.
When will we ever be cleansed?
Comrades, I say to you,
Spare no effort, struggle unceasingly,
That at last peace may come to our people.
And jewelled dresses and deformed feet
Will be abandoned.
And one day, all under heaven
Will see beautiful free women,
Blooming like fields of flowers,
And bearing brilliant and nobel human beings.

(*Translated by Kenneth Rexroth
and Ling Chung*)

JANE COOPER (U.S.A.)

THE BLUE ANCHOR

The future weighs down on me
just like a wall of light!

All these years
I've lived by necessity.
Now the world shines
like an empty room
clean all the way to the rafters.

The room might be waiting for its first tenants—
a bed, a chair, my old typewriter.

Or it might be Van Gogh's room
at Arles:
so neat, while his eyes grazed among phosphorus.
A blue anchor.

To live in the future
like a survivor!
Not the first step up the beach
but the second
then the third

—never forgetting
the wingprint of the mountain
over the fragile human settlement—

ARGENTINA DALEY (HONDURAS)

ON HEARING PEACE HAS BEEN DECLARED

The war is over. A survivor
I will not pray or sing, join hands
with others and dance, drink wine or fill
my mouth with praise for politicians and kings.

But I will cover my head
with cloth and mourn the multitude
of dead who gather wherever I go,
their cadaverous eyes my memory
their white shapes my shadow at noon.

(Translated by Susana Stettri)

BARBARA DEMING (U.S.A.)

THE CHALLENGE OF NON-VIOLENCE

. . . The challenge of those who believe in non-violent struggle is to learn to be aggressive enough. . . . It is stubborn faith that if, as revolutionaries, we will wage battle without violence, we can remain very much more in control—of ourselves, of the future we hope will issue from it. . . . I have had the dream that women should at last be the ones to truly experiment with non-violent struggle—discover it full force. . . . A liberation movement that is non-violent sets the oppressor free as well as the oppressed.

BARBARA EHRENREICH (U.S.A.)

BLOCKING THE GATES TO HEAVEN

When I was the age my children are now, that is, old enough to know everything but still young enough to be dissatisfied with the limited information available, the night sky meant a lot more than a connect-the-dots lesson in ancient Roman mythology. It was a threshold leading to better worlds, where, according to my monthly *Galaxy* magazine, humanoids of great strength and surpassing intelligence drove about purposefully from star to star. In sci-fi convention, life-forms that hadn't developed space travel were mere prehistory—the horseshoe crabs of the cosmic scene—and something of the humiliation of being stuck on a

299

provincial planet in a galactic backwater has stayed with me ever since. But now, with the prospect of Star Wars, I am beginning to feel claustrophobic. It is bad enough that the heavens are still inaccessible, but they are about to become a "shield," which means, for all practical purposes, a lid.

This is no idle metaphor, for NASA is already so compromised by military priorities that we might never really get off the ground. What was the ill-fated shuttle for, if not to show the Russians that we're honing the capacity to pelt them with warheads from beyond the Van Allen belt? Unfortunately, all the shuttle demonstrated is that NASA (and hence, no doubt, the Pentagon) are still stuck at the balsa wood and airplane glue level of technology, in which the key engineering question is whether part A will stay attached to part B, even in the cold and without a rubber band.

Perhaps, though, in some subtle and unacknowledged way, we've been losing interest in the universe. From an entertainment point of view, the Solar System has been a bust. None of the planets turns out to have any real-estate potential, and most of them are probably even useless for filming *Dune* sequels. We may also be despairing of finding any friends out there, and America badly needs friends, since so many of the ones we have on earth are either bad-tempered tyrants or wealthy vagrants who have been forced to leave the tyrant business. A few years ago, Hollywood promised us a universe populated by short, sensitive fellows who would, at the very least, be ideal companions for single mothers. But the search for extraterrestrial intelligence (SETI, to us insiders) has so far only proved that no matter what you beam up—the Pythagorean theorem, pictures of attractive nude people, etc.—the big 800 number in the sky does not return calls. So, in the cinematic imagination, ET was replaced by a batch of gremlins and ghosts, all of unknown provenance and dubious morality.

It could be, though I hesitate to suggest it, that the universe is simply going out of style. It was big in the '50s, with the likes of Asimov and Clarke promoting it, and before we had fully realized that Einstein was serious about a cosmic speed limit that would put even the nearest star about three light-years away by express flight. Black holes, when they came along in the late 1960s, seemed to solve the problem. If you were willing to forgive them for their shrewlike capacity for guzzling whole nebulae and occasional solid matter like stars and planets, they looked as if they could have been put to use as secret passages through which a crew might burrow from galaxy to galaxy before Alzheimer's set in. Such luminaries of sci-fi and sci-fact as Joan D. Vinge and Carl Sagan have already employed black holes as cosmic mass transit systems; and if you don't mind being chewed down to your bosons and spat out on the other side of creation, I suppose it beats staying at home and watching *Star Trek* reruns.

Recent discoveries, though, may have made us wonder whether it's worth the effort. Just a few months ago there was the unsettling news that the universe has, as a result of explosions subsidiary to the big bang, a "bubble structure"—that is, the galaxies seem to be arrayed on the surface of massive bubbles, more or less like dust specks on beer foam. Now, this is not the kind of thing we were brought up to expect from the universe. A great deal of human tradition and prejudice says that big things are automatically majestic and only small things can be silly. So how are we to comprehend such megascale frivolity? It was hard enough to adjust to a grim and indifferent universe that had some purpose other than giving tips to astrologers. But are we ready for a carbonated universe, potentially as "lite" as a dinner from Lean Cuisine or a *USA Today* story on African starvation?

Another bit of bad PR for the universe was the discovery in January of "bizarre structures"—described as threads, loops, and shells—within our own galaxy. We are not talking about some fuzz left on a telescope lens; the threads alone are 100 light-years long by a light-year wide. There must be an explanation, of course, and astronomers are already blaming the big bang, which started the universe, but it is hard to be filled with reverence toward a firmament filled with objects that look like pasta.

Then there's the big bang itself. If that's how it all started, then we might as well face the fact that what's left out there is a great deal of shrapnel and a whole bunch of cinders (one of which is, fortunately, still hot enough and close enough to be good for tanning). Trying to find some sense and order in this mess may be as futile as trying to understand the culture of Japan from the wreckage of Hiroshima, or trying to reconstruct the economy of Iowa from a bowl of popcorn.

So I can well imagine the top scientists at NASA pouring a rare dollop of gin into their Tang and deciding that the universe no longer has the right stuff. Maybe that was when they decided to drop "manned" space travel in the classic sense and fill the available shuttle seats with women, blacks, Jews, Asians, and members of the traditionally Democratic teachers' union. Maybe, a few dollops later, these same famous scientists decided that the noblest course for "man" would be to emulate that great and witty Engineer who designed the universe (with some help, no doubt, from the likes of Morton Thiokol and Bechtel) and go out with the biggest little bang we can muster. Hence Star Wars, an ingenious, trillion-dollar technology designed to squelch all meaningful arms talks, subvert the space program, and generate the national arrogance required for that essential first strike.

There are still a few of us left, though, who don't feel we're too good for the universe, no matter how much it lets us down. Maybe it isn't a vast demonstration of eternal law and order put up there for our edification. Maybe it's more like a room after an all-night party, strewn with random debris by Someone whose idea of a good time we can never hope to fathom. I'd still like to know, still like to meet whoever's out there, still like to think my descendants won't be stuck here forever, toiling away on a large rock near a small-sized star. And for the time being, when I look up at night, I want to sense the huge, untidy humor of infinity—not a gravestone of our own making pressing down on us.

ORIANA FALLACI (ITALY)

INTERVIEW WITH HISTORY

. . . to the same degree that I do not understand power, I do understand those who oppose power, who criticize power, who contest power, especially those who rebel against power imposed by brutality. I have always looked on disobedience toward the oppressive as the only way to use the miracle of having been born. I have always looked on the silence of those who do not react or who indeed applaud as the real death of a woman or a man. And listen: for me the most beautiful monument to human dignity is still the one I saw on a hill in the Peloponnesus. It was not a statue, it was not a flag, but three letters that in Greek signify *No: oxi*. Men thirsting for freedom had written them among the trees during the Nazi-Fascist occupation, and for thirty years that No had remained there, unfaded by the sun or rain. Then the colonels had obliterated it with a stroke of whitewash. But immediately, almost magically, the sun and rain had dissolved the whitewash. So that day by day the three words reappeared on the surface, stubborn, desperate, indelible.

ANNE FRANK (NETHERLANDS)

ANNE FRANK: THE DIARY OF A YOUNG GIRL

I still believe that people are really good at heart. I simply can't build up my hopes on a foundation consisting of confusion, misery and death. I see the world gradually being turned into a wilderness. I hear the ever approaching thunder, which will destroy us, too. I can feel the sufferings of millions and yet, if I look up into the heavens, I think that it will all come right, that this cruelty too will end, and that peace and tranquility will return again.

MATRICE GRICE (ITALY)

THE MARCH AT COMISO:
THE AIR WAS FILLED WITH OPTIMISM

The events began on 6th March [1983] with a march against sexual violence through the streets of the town and although there was limited support from the women of Comiso, a great many Sicilian women from nearby towns were present. . . .

The following day local women joined debates about how to break down the even greater wall of silence created around issues concerning the construction of the missile base. The morning after these debates, on March 8th, 70 women symbolically blockaded the entrance to the base, spinning a web of wool and singing in Sicilian, Italian, English, German and Dutch. Having gained strength from this action, the same women joined by coachloads from other Sicilian towns, marched through the streets of Comiso that afternoon. The Comiso women were singing and calling to others standing on the pavement or watching from windows and balconies. Many joined us along the march and when we arrived in the main square our number had increased to about 700.

Later that evening a local woman told us, "After these few days together we women of Comiso feel much stronger and better able to convince other women to join us." Nearly all the women participated as individuals and felt personally involved. "We are all beginning to realize that we just cannot delegate such important matters—we have a responsibility for our own lives and those of our children." "We can't leave our future to the mercy of the warmongers." Many women had to go back to their home towns but we arranged to meet again at Easter. The air was full of optimism and we all felt a new energy growing within ourselves. The women who could stay on planned to blockade the future cruise base the following morning. Throughout the previous day there had been a massive police presence but they had not intervened at all; this was not the case on the morning of the 9th. They brutally attacked the women, pulling their hair out at its roots, dragging them by their feet and twisting their arms to prevent them from returning to block the road again.

The women were not to be so easily defeated. Two days later a group of women returned to the base to blockade the entrance yet again. This time the police were even more violent despite the fact that no woman had, during any of the actions, reacted violently or abused the police verbally. The Italian-speaking women asked them not to be violent and explained why they were taking this action. They met with replies such as "Go back to where you belong!" and "What about the Russians?"

Each time there was a long queue of traffic waiting to enter the base the women were dragged and thrown violently from the road and police prevented them from returning by twisting their wrists and placing their feet on them. Once the traffic had gone into the base the women returned to block the entrance.

This was repeated five times during which Katherine Barker of Greenham Common Peace Camp had her wrist broken. The women were finally formally advised they were to be arrested and immediately grabbed and pushed into a police van.

A German woman who was acting as a legal observer and had been writing down details was pushed off her bicycle and taken to the van. Another woman who'd been photographing the incident was also grabbed and two men who were standing at the side of the road were arrested and taken along with the women to the prison in the nearby town of Ragusa.

DOROTHY CROWFOOT HODGKIN (ENGLAND)

STAR WARS CAN'T WORK

. . . I'm against the Strategic Defense Initiative. It is most expensive and it won't work, so it's a total waste of money which is needed elsewhere. I think, if you want to get rid of nuclear weapons, as Reagan says he does, you just get rid of them. You don't have to have all this tremendous apparatus in space. . . . I doubt whether this is necessary to progress. And even though tremendous sums are earmarked for these purposes, the effect is almost always not as significant. The direct route, the route of peaceful research, is more productive. You see this very well in the field in which I'm particularly interested—molecular biology. I mean the enormous list of developments which have been produced by precisely this type of research, and not at such great cost, too. . . .

We had a conference in London just before Christmas 1985 with a number of experts on outer space who came from different countries. They went through the various aspects of what might happen should SDI be realized, and they said it was unlikely this thing would work. And I think we must mobilize experts to influence governments so as to prevent deployment of weapons in space. . . .

LINDA HOGAN (CHICKASAW NATION, U.S.A.)

BLACK HILLS SURVIVAL GATHERING, 1980

Bodies on fire
the monks in orange cloth
sing morning into light.

Men wake on the hill.
Dry grass blows from their hair.
B52's blow over their heads
leaving a cross on the ground.
Air returns to itself and silence.

Rainclouds are disappearing
with fractures of light in the distance.

Fierce gases forming,
the sky bending
where people arrive
on dusty roads that change
matter to energy.

My husband wakes.
My daughter wakes.
Quiet morning, she stands
in a pail of water
naked, reflecting light
and this man I love,
with kind hands
he washes her slim hips,
narrow shoulders, splashes
the skin containing
wind and fragile fire,
the pulse in her wrist.

My other daughter wakes
to comb warm sun across her hair.
While I make coffee I tell her
this is the land of her ancestors,
blood and heart.
Does her hair become a mane
blowing in the electric breeze,
her eyes dilate and darken?

The sun rises on all of them
in the center of light
hills that have no boundary,
the child named Thunder Horse,
the child named Dawn Protector
and the man
whose name would mean home in Navajo.

At ground zero
in the center of light we stand.
Bombs are buried beneath us,
destruction flies overhead.
We are waking
in the expanding light
the sulphur-colored grass.
A red horse standing on a distant ridge
looks like one burned

over Hiroshima,
silent, head hanging in sickness.
But look
she raises her head
and surges toward the bluing sky.

Radiant morning.
The dark tunnels inside us carry life.
Red.
Blue.
The children's dark hair against my breast.
On the burning hills
in flaring orange cloth
men are singing and drumming
Heartbeat.

JESSIE WALLACE HUGHAN (U.S.A.)

THE STRENGTH OF WAR RESISTANCE: PATRIOTISM IN ITS HIGHEST SIGNIFICANCE

When we speak in such tremendous numbers, we are none of us able to visualize what it means—10,000,000 men killed in the Great War. . . . Can you imagine . . . great cities being absolutely desolated—every person killed and lying dead—suffering, calling pitifully for a drink of water. . . . A war is not like an earthquake or a tornado—it is an act of men and women. Wars will cease when men refuse to fight and women refuse to approve and allow. Do not allow people to lead you to think for a moment that war is a necessary institution. . . . The strength of the war resistance movement lies in the singleness of its purpose—the abolition of war by the refusal of men and women to carry it on. Our nation has condemned war . . . there is general agreement among us that the present conflict, if it develops into a World war, will mean the end of civilization. War resisters stand in the minority only because they are ready to carry into action what governments have already accepted in words, and to use all their power as citizens to prevent hysterical officials from plunging their country into certain disaster and destruction.

They base their action, therefore, upon the solid ground of reason,

humanity and patriotism in its highest significance. They stand ready
to obey the law without evasion or subterfuge, up to the point where
that law may direct them to violate the principles of reason, humanity
and patriotism as they understand it. In that case, they know no other
course than that taken by Socrates, who refused to cease serving his
city in the way his conscience directed him, but refused also to evade
the penalty decreed against him by his fellow citizens. . . .

The purpose of war resistance is not merely the satisfaction of the
individual conscience, important as this consideration must be to the
man or woman of integrity. The movement works definitely to prevent
each specific war or to bring it to the speediest possible end; it strives
also to break down the war system and its psychology by building up
in each country an ever stronger minority who refuse unconditionally
their personal support.

PETRA KELLY (WEST GERMANY)

WOMEN AND ECOLOGY

While women have increasingly discovered their own oppression in
Western Europe, in the United States, in Australia and elsewhere, they
have also learned to organise themselves and to speak out against the
oppression of others—particularly the victims of militarisation and
nuclearisation.

There has been much consciousness raising among the new brave
women in a 'brave new world'. Political issues become personal, and
personal issues become political. I have been with many women,
whether I marched alongside them in Sydney or Hiroshima or Whyl,
whether I sat in a tent on a windy Irish day at Carnsore Point, or spoke
to them at the UN Plaza during the Disarmament March, or during my
campaign trail for the European Elections as head of the German
Ecological List.

I have hope for the world, although it is ten minutes before Dooms-
day. Women all over the world are rising up, and infusing the antinuclear and peace movements with a vitality and creativity never seen
before. Women stand up in courtrooms and explain the differences between natural and artificial radiation; they stand up at demonstrations
and non-violent occupations of nuclear sites. They are the genuine
ombudsmen of children to come. Like Dr Helen Caldicott, a children's

doctor from Australia, they firmly believe that each of us must accept total responsibility for the earth's survival.

We are discovering how commercial and military technologies impose unacceptable risks to health and life. To defeat these technologies, we must begin to shape world events.

World expenditure on the arms race is over $1,000 million per day. Countless children are condemned to illiteracy, disease, starvation and death by the massive diversion of resources (natural and human) to the arms race. The cost of one tank would supply equipment for 520 classrooms and the cost of one destroyer could provide electrification for three cities and nineteen rural zones. Women who have opposed the military base enlargement in Larzac, women who do not buy toy guns at Christmas, know that the accumulation of weapons today constitutes much more of a threat than a protection. There had been over 900 nuclear explosions on the surface of the earth by the end of 1978 and it is estimated that the number of soldiers in the world today is twice the number of teachers, doctors and nurses.

Woman must lead the efforts in education for peace awareness, because only she, I feel, can go back to her womb, her roots, her natural rhythms, her inner search for harmony and peace, while men, most of them anyway, are continually bound to their power struggle, the exploitation of nature, and military ego trips. Our timidity must end for the earth has no emergency exit.

The conditions are being created for a police state, centralized uncontrollable energy systems, and increasing mechanization all led by the silicon chip which Japanese manufacturers claim achieves circuits in which there only are thirty failures in one billion hours of operation. Increasing numbers of persons will become unemployed and superfluous—already in 1970, in a report to the World Bank, Robert McNamara spoke of such persons as 'marginal men'. It is estimated that by 1980, there will be one billion of them. The huge corporations that make human beings marginal can sell, make and break governments, and decide whether a non-nuclear nation like Ireland will have to go nuclear. And the same big companies now even begin to dominate the solar industry in the West. According to UN reports, a new form of so-called solar monopoly could mean further Third World dependence on a handful of corporations. Already production of large solar-based electricity generating plants is mainly restricted to gigantic companies like Northrup, McDonnell-Douglas and Mobil Oil. The Ford Motor Corporation, Philips and General Motors dominate small- and medium-sized solar power plants. Firms are attempting to restrict access to this technology—awaiting the time when they need areas of *cheap* labour before moving production out to the Third World.

We are often told, that the experts and the big firms do not know how to deal with the problems which threaten worldwide disaster, 'that all the facts are not in,' that more research must be done, and more reports written. This is simply an excuse for endlessly putting off action. We already know enough to begin to deal with all our major problems: nuclear war, over-population, pollution, hunger, the desolation of the planet, the inequality among peoples. The present crisis is a crisis not of information, but of policy. We cannot cope with all the problems that threaten us, while maximising profits.

As things stand now, the people, especially women and children of the Third World, are to perish first. They have already begun to starve; all that is asked of them is to starve quietly. The plight of women in the Third World is one that touches me deeply. There are now about 100 million children under the age of five always hungry. Each year 15 million children die from infection and malnutrition. There are about 800 million illiterates in the world, nearly two-thirds of them are women.

The number of women unable to read and write is about half a billion. In the Third World, 40–70 per cent of agricultural labour is female—they plant the seed, haul the water, tend the animals, strive to keep their families alive—but all the while they are socially inferior. Men in the Third World are lured into the cities to work for one of the many Western companies or join Third World armies, supplied with guns and tanks sold by the same companies. The women left behind on the land, usually infibulated and circumcised (bodily and sexually mutilated), are not taught the use of new irrigation systems and intermediate small scale alternative technology. Instead they learn to buy Nestle's Lactogen Milk Powder to mix with dirty brown water. The result: many babies die with bloated stomachs. Women in the Third World are further exploited through various forms of prostitution— whether through 'rent-a-wife' schemes, as in Vietnam, or through international finance companies developing hotel brothels and promoting tourism through sexist advertisements.

The developed nations are armed to the teeth and mean not only to hold on to what they have, but to grasp anything they still can. Look at the uranium mines in Namibia, look at what we, the Europeans, are doing to the soul and culture of the Aborigines in Australia; look at the plight of the Navajo Indians in North America dying from radon gases. And as the great famines occur, the grain and other agricultural produce is either rotting away in E E C silos or is fed to cattle to supply the rapidly increasing demand for meat in affluent countries. The suffering people of this world must come together to take control of their lives, to wrest political power from their present masters, who are pushing them towards destruction.

This is also a plea to all women to join those sisters who have already risen up—who have helped to shape the ecological revolution. Together we can overthrow all the imposed structures of domination.

Even in the affluent parts of the world the same patterns of sexual inequality may be seen. Equal pay and equal treatment in all areas of schooling, training, promotion and working conditions have not, in reality, been won. Women in South Italy, and in the West of Ireland lead lives of desperation and humiliation. Battered women and children take refuge from husbands and fathers and women increasingly get cervical cancers and other abnormalities from the Pill of the pharmaceutical giants. Women who stay on hormones poison their cells, saturate their bile and risk birth defects in later children. Every eighth child in Germany is born handicapped in some way.

The story of thalidomide, commercially available for years after it should have been outlawed, is just one of many. The pitiful caricatures of adults, living reminders of an unconcerned pharmacology, show how lethal the policies of male researchers and male politicians have been— industries have falsified data, bought off scientists, posited ridiculous risk-benefit ratios and threshold levels. This has resulted in a cancer rate that qualifies as 'epidemic'. The total economic impact—including health care and lost productivity due to cancer—has been estimated at $25 billion a year.

The earth has been mistreated, and only by restoring a balance, only by living *with* the earth, by employing soft energies and soft technologies can we overcome the violence of patriarchy. Although the masculine ego and capitalist consciousness have made advances in science and technology, they have lost touch with the earth in setting out to conquer nature. The desire for power has left in its wake a terrible path of destruction. There is at the same time a danger of women being seen in the subservient role from which they hope to rise. Some of the ecological, communal and human potential movements are deeply infected by a type of romantic escapism which could all too easily recreate woman's role as the servant of male culture. As an English feminist once said, 'We don't want an ecological society where men build windmills and women silently listen, bake bread and weave rugs.'

In recent years, I have also observed that some women have sought to overcome their inferior role by becoming part of the masculine world (Mrs Thatcher, Indira Gandhi, etc.). When women fight for equal status with men, they run the risk of joining the ranks in times of war. We are so conditioned by masculine values that women often make the mistake of imitating and emulating men at the cost of their own feminism. When I assess the world of male values, it is clear to me that I do not want this kind of 'equality'.

Recent court-martial proceedings in the USA have indicated that a large group of guardsmen responsible for nuclear missiles are using and distributing illegal drugs. Armed guards had used marijuana, cocaine and LSD while on duty and carrying a loaded pistol. Another example of wanton disregard for life is provided by the French electricity generating board, which recently decided to bring into operation two new nuclear power stations while admitting that there are certain cracks in key reactor components. While governments all over the world are faced with escalating nuclear research bills (bills, which private industry will *not* pick up), and while workers repair nuclear accidents with pencils and paper clips (as was recently the case in a nuclear station in Virginia) a young woman is shot dead by the police in an anti-nuclear demonstration in Spain; policemen denounce women as 'whores' during pro-abortion demonstrations and there are still investigations going on to discover what really happened to Karen Silkwood.

. . . the police states foreseen by Orwell—all in the name of secure nuclear societies. Women must lose all fear of speaking up and demanding what is theirs and their children's. Only if we begin to rediscover our own nature, can we discover new ways of wholeness, balance, and decentralisation—can we forge a bond with the Earth and the Moon, living with cooperation, gentleness, non-possessiveness and soft energies.

THE POWER OF NON-VIOLENCE

When we talk of non-violent opposition, we do *not* mean opposition to parliamentary democracy. We mean opposition from *within* parliamentary democracy. Non-violent opposition in no way diminishes or undermines representative democracy, in fact, it strengthens and stabilises it. The will of the electorate is not expressed simply by putting one's mark on a political blank cheque every four years. It is expressed in all kinds of local groups operating outside parliament, in works councils and other self-governing bodies. This is the democratic infrastructure of society. Non-violent opposition is one way, among others, of forming political opinion within that infrastructure.

For example, the American civil rights movement undoubtedly had a great influence on public opinion, and significantly affected attitudes to the law among the American public and legal profession. That movement did not bring governments down; it did not spell the end of parliament or the courts; but it did seek to *change* these bodies. This was only possible because the spectacular non-violent campaigns in the streets were backed up by a much quieter approach in the institutions, the courts, the parliaments, the media and the schools. After all, every victory for the American civil rights movement meant a victory in the courts, in parliament, or in the machinery of government.

Non-violent opposition has nothing to do with passivity, and nothing whatsoever to do with the demeaning experience of injustice and violence. In contrast to violent opposition, non-violent opposition is an expression of spiritual, physical and moral strength. This strength is shown most clearly by consciously and specifically *not doing* anything which could be construed as participating in injustice. This could mean *not* obeying unjustified orders, or *not* holding back in situations where injustice is being meted out to others.

Greenpeace, for example, opposes those people who are bent on destroying our environment, in an open, imaginative and non-violent way. Members of Greenpeace place themselves in the firing-line of the whale-catchers' cannon. They have risked their lives by taking their inflatable dinghies in under the ramps where containers of radioactive nuclear waste are dumped in the sea; they have entered areas where nuclear devices are tested; they have been brought in by the Spanish Navy and have escaped from under their noses, all in the space of a single hectic night.

Another example is the non-violent opposition in Poland. In 1981, at 7.30 every evening, the lights went out all over southeast Poland and no water was used, and entire Polish towns took to the streets. Thousands of people, their children and their dogs flocked into the town centre for about forty minutes each time. This was about the same length of time as the evening news programme on Polish television—which just happened to go out precisely at 7.30. And to emphasise their views about the military bias of the television news, many people living in the town centres put their TV sets in their windows with the screen facing the street. The military authorities had no response to make to this new form of opposition in Poland—tanks were not much use. Peaceful demonstrations—which Solidarity has been calling for in all regions—do not need leaders or detailed preparations. They are not even punishable offences; but they always succeed in putting the security forces on a state of alert. In one primary school in Posen, whole classes refused to accept delivery of parcels from East Germany; in Breslau schoolchildren came to school all dressed in black. In Warsaw, students spent their lunch-hour sitting in the corridors in silence. Solidarity banners suddenly appeared overnight on public buildings. Leaflets came down from on high, or spilt out of the litter bins in public parks. A lot of people have been wearing little coils which are on sale in electrical shops. In Polish, they are called *Opór*—in English, resistors.

Dorothee Sölle, a theologian who is active in the women's peace movement, tells of the American Ploughshares 8 Campaign, in her book *Aufrüstung tötet auch ohne Krieg* (*Weapons kill even without war*). 'The Berrigan brothers, Catholics and pacifists, commit acts of civil disobedience in order to obey God. They destroy equipment and objects which pave the way to destruction in order to protect life.' She is referring to when the Berrigan brothers and eight other activists* entered the General Electric Co. arms factory in Pennsylvania. They pushed past the unarmed guards and got through to the security area where they hammered on the warhead cone of a Mark 12a Intercontinental Ballistic Missile. They also poured blood on drawings, plans and other items to do with arms. Later they were arrested and charged with breaking and entering, trespass, criminal conspiracy, behaviour likely to cause a breach of the peace, creating a disturbance, burglary and inciting behaviour.

Dorothee Sölle goes on to say,

> And while Reagan is giving the green light for mass production of a bomb which kills only people, leaving objects and buildings intact, Daniel Berrigan and his friends are in prison in the cause of human dignity. Perhaps we shall see a time when the prisons are so overcrowded with peace campaigners, that the judges cannot make the love of peace a criminal offence any more, when the generals learn to learn, and the bankers stop recommending arms speculation as the best deal going.

And Ingeborg Drewitz, a sister and a highly regarded writer, has called for a world-wide general strike. However, she is very pessimistic on the point, because she believes that it is easier to imagine the outbreak of a Third (and final) World War than the start of a general strike across the world.

But this possibility was indicated, on a much smaller scale, when in January 1978, the ruler of Bolivia, Banzer, was forced to yield to the pressure of the protest movement, and declare a general amnesty; more than 1300 people had joined the hunger strikes initiated by six miners' wives and their children. In the United States, there were the great non-violent campaigns for black rights, in protest against the Vietnam war, and in defence of a group of dispossessed land workers in California. New ideas on non-violent action in practice have come from workers in Larzac in the South of France, from the zone of resistance around Wyhl, and the action groups in Baden and Alsace.

All these examples show that creative opposition, in the spirit of Martin Luther King and Mahatma Gandhi, is possible. In his 1967 Christmas message, Martin Luther King said, 'Even today, I still dream that one day there will be an end to war and that men will beat their swords into ploughshares and their spears into pruning hooks, that nation shall not lift up a sword against nation, neither shall they learn war any more.' And Cesar Chavez, the leader of the American land workers' movement, has said,

* See Molly Rush, p. 367.

We are convinced that non-violence is more powerful than violence. We are convinced that non-violence supports you if you have a just and moral cause. Non-violence gives the opportunity to stay on the offensive, which is of vital importance to win any contest . . . I don't subscribe to the belief that non-violence is cowardice, as some militant groups are saying. In some instances, non-violence requires more militancy than violence does.

Mahatma Gandhi acted in the unshakable knowledge that you do not arrive at the truth by violence, nor justice by hate, nor peace by hostility. In a world of hate, terror and tactical cunning, he placed his faith in the power of the spirit, and the superior strength of goodness, gentleness and complete truthfulness. The Green party too, should be working for more goodness, gentleness and truthfulness. We must act with our hearts as well as with our heads. Gandhi once said, 'The weapon of satyagraha turns what used to be violence into the reverse. Violence arises at the point when one man imposes his will and another man accepts it. But to refuse to bow to the tyrant's will destroys violence.' Gandhi also said that inner resistance must precede outer resistance; one must resist one's own dishonesty and cowardice, and the lies at the bottom of one's heart.

Non-violent groups and movements all over the world are faced with a dual problem. On the one hand, they are confronted by enormous military and structural violence. On the other, they discover that most people believe that using force is the surest way of getting what you want. But there has been a radical opposition to the logic of violence since the time of Jesus Christ.

The Greens must show how to resolve conflicts by regarding those who resort to violence not as enemies, but as people who must be liberated from their enslavement to violence. Practically every violent conflict or social change has proved that violence unleashes violence in return. Violent revolutions usually only mean a change of personnel at the top; the actual system of violence is only altered, never eliminated as a result.

The so-called enemy should be given the opportunity to rethink, to modify his behaviour, and to appreciate that any action we take is not directed against him as a person, but against the element of violence in his role. In this context, I would support the idea of a dialogue with the police and the armed forces, again as a means of focussing on the person, not his role in society. Calling a policeman a pig means you have already abandoned a non-violent attitude.

Time and time again, we forget all too easily that non-violent action embraces a wide and imaginative range of behaviour, which can always be stepped up. *Legitimate action* provides information on controversial issues by publishing facts that have been suppressed. Such activity includes readers' letters, signing petitions, distributing leaflets, demonstrating and knocking on doors. *Symbolic action* aims to provide slogans which can be easily understood, and which highlight typical aspects of violence in any situation of conflict. Symbolic action points the way for further opposition: vigils, silent marches, fasts, as well as more light-hearted events. Like legitimate action, symbolic action does not generally bring direct pressure to bear on the behaviour of the other side, but it does influence public awareness.

Non-cooperation with violent elements in the social system is a basic premise of non-violence in theory and in practice. This whole concept includes legal methods of objection, such as strikes, boycotts, conscientious objection and non-acceptance of state honours, as well as *civil disobedience*—open infringement of the law on grounds of conscience. Civil disobedience is an escalated form of non-cooperation and direct action; it is the deliberate infringement of unjust laws and regulations. Those who engage in non-violent civil disobedience take full responsibility upon themselves for breaking the law on conscientious grounds. They would rather receive punishment or violence, than become violent themselves, or incur the blame for other people's violence by doing nothing.

Non-violence also means that men are reconciled to themselves, with their own species, with nature and the cosmos. In a deeper sense, disarmament means exposing one's own vulnerability. Martin Luther King's appeal to boycott the buses seemed ridiculous to begin with. Planting saplings at Gorleben also seems ridiculous, given that the bulldozers are ready and waiting to plough up the earth. We are not armed and we make an easy target, but we will not cut ourselves off from life. We have gentleness, force of numbers, freedom from domination on our side, and the solidarity to overcome all divisions. Our motto is, 'Be gentle and subversive'.

VERA KISTIAKOWSKY (U.S.A.)

NO TO WEAPONS IN SPACE

The scenario being proposed to take war into space is the most threatening thing that faces us immediately. And I don't mean threatening in the year 2000. It is threatening now, because it is the most destabilizing. It is an invitation to a preemptive first-strike by the Soviet Union because we will face them with the alternative of hitting us first and being able to damage us, or having us hit them first and their not being able to retaliate effectively. The initial argument given for the Strategic Defense Initiative (more commonly known as Star Wars) was that this would be a total defense of the United States. It would be a defense through which no missiles would come and therefore it would make missiles useless and would make possible a total disarmament. It very rapidly became clear that this was a totally incorrect assessment of the possibility, with the technical difficulties staggering. Richard De Lauer, undersecretary of Defense for Research and Development, has said it will take eight research and development programs, each one at least the size of the Manhattan Project in order to bring the Strategic Defense Initiative into fruition. Also, the president's own committee came back with the assessment that you could not build a system that was perfect. There would, in fact, be a percentage of the missiles that could get through from the Soviet Union. More recent assessments have estimated that from 25% to 60% of the population could be killed by missiles that slipped through.

What, then, is the argument to stop the race into space? The overriding argument is that it will lead into a very real threat of preemptive first-strike and all out nuclear war.

ALEXANDRA KOLLANTAI (U.S.S.R.)

THE LETTERS OF KOLLANTAI

October 6, 1939

My Dear, Dear Friend Ada,

Yesterday, I desired so much to tell you how greatly I value your friendship and how much gratitude I feel for all you've done for me, how very much I've treasured your spiritual harmony and the way we understand each other when we talk of world affairs. . . . Life is beautiful in autumn. . . . what exactly does it promise? Well, the hope that I'll be able to achieve some small task this winter, and help to make some peace in this world so troubled with warring. The best one can say is that there's no stagnation, for that's the worst of all. Dear Ada, didn't you as a child want the world to free itself from all its old traditions? Now the world's in the process of completely remaking itself—isn't that what we wanted when we were young? There's a more intelligent way of solving world problems than by picking up weaponry. Negotiations embodied now in the League of Nations!

I don't know. Perhaps, there'll still be wars—but surely humanity will evolve new methods by which governments can negotiate. And that thought gives me hope. So I'm not pessimistic, you see? I gaze into the future with joy and confidence. Do you understand me, dear Ada? . . . The world never stagnates. It's always reawakening. New forms of life are always appearing. I love to look back now at the path trodden by humanity, or leap forward to the glorious lovely future which humanity will inhabit—spreading its wings and saying, "Joy and happiness for all!"

Your loving friend,

Alexandra

(Translated by Daniela Gioseffi with Sophia Buzevska)

KÄTHE KOLLWITZ (GERMANY)

A NEW IDEA WILL ARISE

. . . each war carries within itself, the war which will answer it. Each war is answered by another war, until everything is destroyed. . . . That is why I'm so wholeheartedly for a radical end to the madness, and why my only hope is in a world socialism. . . . My concept of that . . . what I consider the only possible prerequisite for it. . . . Pacifism simply is not a matter of calm looking on; it is work, hard work . . . those lovely small apples out there . . . everything could be so beautiful if it were not for the insanity of war . . . one day, a new idea will arise and there will be an end of all wars. . . . People will have to work hard for that new state of things, but they will achieve it. . . . At such times when I feel I'm working with an international society opposed to war, I'm filled with a warm sense of contentment. . . .

La Pasionaria (Dolores Ibarruri) (spain)

A NEW BEGINNING

Days and years have passed. The old hatreds have abated, and time has closed the wounds which the war opened in the bodies and consciences of millions of men.

New generations now step into the arena of struggle. And there are those who, not having been in war or lived through war, raise anew the banner of democracy, of liberty and justice, for which the most heroic fighters of our war of liberation gave their blood and their lives.

And when again, in the streets of our cities, young people devote themselves to the future democracy of our country, proclaim their desire to make Spain a free country open to progress, in which civil liberties for all Spaniards and freedom of action of all political groups will be possible, we think that our struggle was not in vain. After the long fascist night, . . . The new generation which grew up muzzled and trussed in the shadow of Franco's prisons rejects the Spain built by the Falange with the aid of foreign bayonets, the Spain built by the Franco dictatorship with blood and mud. The Franco dictatorship acts as a brake and a chain. Its disappearance is a historical necessity.

At the crossroads where the hopes and desires of the new generation meet, there is a signpost marked with a question: "Shall we return to the past?"

In Spain the people have experienced various forms of political bourgeois domination: monarchy, republic, fascist dictatorship. In the crucible of war, men, parties, doctrines, actions and systems have been put to a crucial test.

From this recent, living, tremendously instructive experience an irrefutable conclusion has emerged: Only the forces representing the true interests of the country, that express the currents of social development, and move forward with them can provide a base for the political rebirth, the economic and cultural rebirth of Spain.

Do I mean a Socialist solution? Yes, emphatically yes. Only a Socialist solution can stop the interminable procession of revolutions and counterrevolutions which have been the history of the Spanish state. A Socialist solution in step with the needs and desires of the nation.

And we are not dealing here with a situation that must be forced. If Socialism arises naturally as a stage in the development of society, then the road leading to it is not determined solely by the wills of men. It appears under specific conditions determined by historic causes.

In the past, when capitalism's reign over the world was absolute, the road to Socialism was conceived chiefly in terms of civil wars and violent revolution. But today, there is the possibility of a pacific route, of a democratic road toward Socialism. At times we Communists failed to show the necessary flexibility in the face of positions which we considered harmful to the resistance; or we did not sufficiently criticize or evaluate defeatist attitudes and obscure maneuvers. Nevertheless, not for one moment either then or now have we underestimated the historic and revolutionary importance of the participation of the democratic bourgeoisie in the popular resistance to fascism. . . .

Above all, what the Spanish war conclusively showed was that without the unity of the working class, the leadership of a democratic revolution will inevitably fall into the hands of the bourgeoisie, which will slow down the revolution, will stop it halfway and will even transform it into a weapon against the proletariat.

Franco's victory paralyzed Spain's democratic development. After three long decades of fascist dictatorship, the political and economic problems which have plagued Spain's historical development, and which during the war were just beginning to be solved by the Republican government, are still very much with us—only worse, far more in crying need of solution. The roots of the unity of democratic and working-class forces, of all national sectors desirous of bringing progress to Spain, are still very much alive.

It is the mission of Spain's youth to give impetus to this broad, Spanish unity; to wipe out the past of reaction and backwardness; to wipe out the presence of jails and terrors and corruption.

The youth of Spain are our hope. I am confident that they will take, that they are now taking, the only way that makes heroes of simple men, that makes them builders of a new life, of a new world: the way of struggle for *democracy*, for peace and for Socialism.

FRANCES MOORE LAPPÉ (U.S.A.)

FOR THE FUTURE

. . . Among the most striking changes in the last decade has been the growing popular awareness that we live in a *world* economy guided by corporate entities that span the globe, lacking loyalty to any polity. "Corporate flight" has become almost a household term. The implications are enormous. Gradually, Americans can come to see that as long as people abroad are denied human rights, including the right to organize to protect their interests, any bargaining power Americans have had as workers will continue to erode. . . .

Polls taken in the 1980's, for example, have noted that almost two-thirds of [U.S. citizens] . . . believe that wealth should be more evenly distributed, that upwards of 80% of us agree that every [one] . . . should have the opportunity to work guaranteed as a right. That more than two-thirds of us oppose interventionist U.S. policies in Central America, Apartheid in South Africa, and so on. . . .

We ourselves must believe that those of us working actively for peace and justice are not cursed with the burden of saving the world, but blessed with what many many . . . yearn for—a way to put the seeming insanity of the world to rights so that we can make real choices for change. Our lives must not say: "You must come help us shoulder the mighty burden of making the world better." Instead . . . *We must demonstrate how government can be reclaimed as a vehicle through which we can act on our deepest values, rather than remain an instrument of authoritative (or corrupt) control.* . . .

LOLITA LEBRON (PUERTO RICO)

I HAVE ALL THE PASSION OF LIFE

I have all the passion of life.
I love the sun and the stars
and the seeds.
Everything fascinates me:
water, brooks, groves,
dew and cascades.

I adore looking at the
flowing streams: this clear
proof of beauty;
this joy in my marrow,
in my sight,
this knowing about what's hidden,
and this sensation of seeing
what is clear.

Whoever denies life its joy,
the wealth of its complexity,
its rainbow-like countenance,

its downpour and its universe
of beauty, its generous giving,
the caress, the grain
with fruit and delicacies,
the bud, the flower, pain and
                    laughter;
those who deny life its measure
of joy
are the unseeing ones.
Nor have they drunk from
life's overflowing cup of passion.

I have all the rapture,
the savoring.
That's why they stare and ask:
"Lolita, what do you see of
any beauty?
What do you like? The sky?
These sterile and arid mountains,
these hours so full of ugliness
and injustice,
with endless sighs
and the pushing and the shoving?"

"Why do you sing and laugh, Lolita?
Is your face really lit up
with the joy of life?
Are you mad, Lolita?"

(Translated by Gloria Waldman)

MERIDEL LE SUEUR (U.S.A.)

WOMEN KNOW A LOT OF THINGS

Minneapolis

Women know a lot of things they don't read in the newspapers. It's pretty funny sometimes, how women know a lot of things and nobody can figure out how they know them. I know a Polish woman who works in the stockyards here, and she has been working there for a good many years. She came from Poland when she was a child, came across the vast spaces of America, with blinders on, you might say, and yet she knows more than anybody I know, because she knows what suffering is and she knows that everyone is like herself, throughout the whole world. So she can understand everything that happens, and moving between the shack where she lives on the Mississippi bluffs and the canning department of Armours, she feels the hunger and the suffering of Chinese women and feels as if she is in Flint with the Woman's Brigade.

I was having a cup of coffee with her the day the Woman's Brigade knocked out the windows so the air could get into the factory to the gassed sit-downers and she told about how they were all singing a song we knew:

> "We shall not be moved
> Just like a tree standing by the river
> We shall not be moved."

And how they were all leaning out of the windows singing this song, hundreds of them probably, with machine guns mounted on the buildings opposite and she got up and walked around the little stove that warmed her shack. She couldn't sit still.

"Imagine that," she said. "Can you believe it, them all singing that song, with the guns pointing right at them and the women, scooting in there and smashing those windows. O, say, I woulda like to have been there." And she wasn't in that shack at all, the boundaries of that shack weren't anything.

That's the way it is with women. They don't read about the news. They very often make it. They pick it up at its source, in the human body, in the making of the body, and the feeding and nurturing of it day in and day out. They know how much a body weighs and how much blood and toil goes into the making of even a poor body. Did you ever go into a public clinic to weigh your child? And you feel of him anxiously when you put his clothes on in the morning. You pick him up trying to gauge the weight of his bones and the tiny flesh and you wait for the public nurses to put him on the scales, and you look, you watch her face like an aviator watches the sky, watches an instrument register a number that will mean life and death.

In that body under your hands every day there resides the economy of that world; it tells you of ruthless exploitation, of a mad, vicious class that now cares for nothing in the world but to maintain its stupid life with violence and destruction; it tells you the price of oranges and cod liver oil, of spring lamb, of butter, eggs and milk. You know everything that is happening on the stock exchange. You know what happened to last year's wheat in the drouth, the terrible misuse and destruction of land and crops and human life plowed under. You don't have to read the stock reports in Mr. Hearst's paper. You have the news at its terrible source.

Or what kind of news is it when you see the long, drawn face of your husband coming home from the belt line and the speed up and feel his ribs coming to the surface day after day like the hulk of a ship when the tide is going down?

Or, what price freedom and the American Way so coyly pictured on the billboards, when you go up the dark and secret and dirty stairs to a doctor's office and get a cheap abortion because you can't afford another baby and wait for the fever that takes so many American women, and thank heaven if you come through alive, barely crawling around for months?

A woman knows when she has to go to work and compete with other men, and lower the price of all labor, and when her children go to work, tiny, in the vast lettuce and beet fields of the Imperial Valley and Texas. She knows when she has to be both father and mother, her husband like a fine uncared-for precision machine, worn down in his prime, or eaten by acids in Textile, or turned to stone by Silicosis.

In the deeps of our own country, the deep south, Arkansas and Tennessee and Alabama women are beginning to read the news right. In the center earth of China women who for centuries have been slaves, are lifting their faces from the earth and reading a sign in the skies.

In South America, in the deepest and most inaccessible mountains, a woman walking behind a donkey, or working in the sugar cane, is preparing to vote, if she was asked, the way of her international sisters. It's the same there, wondering if there is enough meal in the sack, if watered thin, for a meal. Anxiously looking at the lank husband's body, the dark quick hungering eyes of children, measuring with eagle eye their appetites, knowing to a grain how much would send them from the table without a roving eye.

Hunger and want and terror are a Braille that hands used to labor, used to tools, and close to sources, can read in any language.

International Woman's Day is the recognition of that mutual knowledge leading to the struggle of women throughout the world.

When we look at Germany and Italy we know that the coming of fascism exploits men and women alike, and takes from woman the painful civic and political gains she has bought with a century of struggle.

This year promises to be a crucial one for women, and one that will unite them in even closer bonds with the international struggle against war and fascism, those twin beasts that threaten our frail security. The cause of women will be the cause of all toiling humanity.

Men and women alike are beginning to know this. No longer does the good union man keep his woman at home to mind the kids. The Woman's Brigade at Flint was an important weapon in the strike. The Woman's Auxiliary came out of the kitchen and fought side by side with the men. This is only a beginning.

Immediate in the struggle in America is the Woman's Charter. This document will draw up a Legislative plan, uniting all women against reaction which strikes at democratic rights and at the labor movement while pushing women back into the dark ages. The basic principles of this Charter are: that women should have full political and civil rights; full opportunity for education; full opportunity for employment according to their individual abilities, and without discrimination because of sex; and security of livelihood, including the safeguarding of motherhood.

This coming year will see the tide of war and fascism rising high, but it will also see the strong and invincible wall of working men and women, locked in strong formation in a party of farmers and workers everywhere, in a Farmer Labor Party, saying with the international workers, in Spain, Russia, China, FASCISM SHALL NOT PASS.

Maria Simarro, one of the young women of the Spain Youth Delegation now touring America, told me that in Spain when they gave the women the vote, everyone was very nervous. Here were thousands of illiterate peasant women, held for many years in medieval ignorance and darkness, kept in subjugation to the Church, to endless toil and childbearing. What would they vote for? How could they understand international problems, the great program of the United Peoples Front of Spain and the world? It was a problem that worried everyone. They held the election in their hands. The Liberal Spanish government was afraid. These newly enfranchised women could turn the tide of the election. They needn't have worried.

The so-called ignorant peasant women of Spain were not ignorant. They voted with their hands, their feet, the knowledge bred and seeped in sun drenched labor, in every bone and muscle, in grief in the night, and terror, of hours of walking behind the plow, their sweat dropping into the furrows, birthing children on straw with only the blessing of the priest to ease the pain.

They voted from this knowledge, solid, with one voice, one body, for the Peoples' Front of Spain, voted for that democracy they later showed themselves ready to defend against the Church and the Landlords.

This is the kind of knowledge the women of 1937 must have. They

325

are no longer negative mourners, weepers at the weeping wall, shrouded in the black of grief and defeat. The old English folk song says, "Men must work, and women must weep. . . ." No longer. The International women of 1937 will protect democracy with their lives, demanding food that can now be so abundantly provided out of the earth's rich land and factory, demanding security for loved ones—standing militant in the wheat fields, at factory gate and bench, raising her cry of—Land . . . Bread . . . and Peace.

DENISE LEVERTOV (U.S.A.)

MAKING PEACE

A voice from the dark called out,
    "The poets must give us
imagination of peace, to oust the intense, familiar
imagination of disaster. Peace, not only
the absence of war."
         But peace, like a poem,
is not there ahead of itself,
can't be imagined before it is made,
can't be known except
in the words of its making,
grammar of justice,
syntax of mutual aid.
         A feeling towards it,
dimly sensing a rhythm, is all we have
until we begin to utter its metaphors,
learning them as we speak.
         A line of peace might appear
if we restructured the sentence our lives are making,
revoked its reaffirmation of profit and power,
questioned our needs, allowed
long pauses. . . .
         A cadence of peace might balance its weight
on that different fulcrum; peace, a presence,
an energy field more intense than war,
might pulse then,

stanza by stanza into the world,
each act of living
one of its words, each word
a vibration of light—facets
of the forming crystal.

WHAT IT COULD BE

Uranium, with which we know
only how to destroy,

lies always under
the most sacred lands—

Australia, Africa, America,
wherever it's found is found an oppressed
ancient people who knew
long before white men found and named it
that there under their feet

under rock, under mountain, deeper
than deepest watersprings, under
the vast deserts familiar
inch by inch to their children

lay a great power.
                    And they knew the folly
of wresting, wrestling, ravaging from the earth
that which it kept
                    so guarded.

Now, now, now at this instant,
men are gouging lumps of that power, that presence,
out of the tortured planet the ancients
say is our mother.
                    Breaking the doors
of her sanctum, tearing the secret
out of her flesh.

But left to lie, its metaphysical weight
might in a million years have proved
benign, its true force being to be
a clue to righteousness—

showing forth
the human power

not to kill, to choose
not to kill: to transcend
the dull force of our weight and will;

that known profound presence, *un*touched
the sign
providing witness,
        occasion,
          ritual
for the continuing act of
*non*violence, of passionate
reverence, active love.

MAIREAD CORRIGAN MAGUIRE (IRELAND)

DEAR SON

Dear Luke,

Today you picked a little yellow rosebud from the garden and carried it in to the house to give it to me. Your little baby face beamed up at me as you gave me the rosebud. What joy that moment held for me—joy knowing how deeply I love you, and then as I went to put the rose in water, I realized it had no stem, and that without water it would never grow from a rosebud into a beautiful full rose, but that soon, all too soon, it would die.

I felt sad for a moment at this thought and as I watched you toddle across the room, I wondered how I might help you, my little rosebud, grow and 'blossom' into manhood. What can I teach you? What can I say to you that will help you to grow up in this 'thorny' world, and yet know peace, joy and happiness, which, dear Luke, are the greatest treasures anyone can possess.

Always know, Luke, that you are deeply loved. You are loved by Daddy and me, and your brothers and sisters. But as you grow up and begin to ask questions for yourself you will know that men and women have a need in their hearts for something more, something deeper than that found even in the very best of human love.

As you walk along a beach at night and listen to the waves lapping gently on the shore, or look up into a night sky at millions of stars, know too that He who created all this, created it for you because HE loves you. You are part of this beautiful creation and you are beautiful, special and unique in this Universe. Love, and believe in yourself, because only then can you love and believe in others.

Luke, do not be afraid to love others unselfishly. Yes, many times you will get your fingers pricked on the thorns of disappointment or rejection, but many more times you will pluck the rose of love and receive great happiness and joy from its sweet scent and colour. Don't be afraid to risk loving and remember that, as the little rosebud needed the water to live, so much more you and I, and all the people of the world need to love and be loved. Know that 'love' is the greatest gift you personally can give to another fellow traveller along the 'thorny' path of life. . . .

With ever so gentle steps, walk side-by-side with all the travellers on this 'thorny' path of life. They will differ from you in colour, creed (there are many paths to God), culture and politics—but above all remember your fellow travellers have the same needs as you. Our common humanity is far more important than any religious or political ideologies. Treat every man and woman justly and gently as you would have them treat you.

In your life Luke, pray to be a 'just' man. Your life is precious and sacred, Luke, and your first right as a human being is your right to your life. So as you would ask natural justice of your fellow travellers in respecting your right to life, then you too must give 'justice' and respect every person's right to life. This means, my little son, that you must never kill another human being.

It will not be easy for you to refuse to kill. Sadly we live in a world where those who refuse to kill and choose to live nonviolent lives are looked upon as naïve or as cowards. Yes, it will take all of your courage to walk unarmed and refuse to hate and kill, in a world which insists that you must have enemies and be prepared to kill them before they kill you.

Stand tall and strong, armed only with love, dear Luke, and refuse to hate, refuse to have enemies, refuse to let Fear master your life. Only love can bring down the barriers of hate and enmity between men and nations. Hate and weapons only fuel the fear and bring closer the day of war.

Let no man plant in your heart the false seed of pride in any country's flag, a seed that produces the flower of narrow nationalism which grows so wildly, trampling and killing all life around it. Remember always, Luke, people are more important than countries.

I would not give one hair of your precious head for any country—you are more important than any country. And if I feel this passionate love for you, and for my other children, Mark, Joanne, Marie Louise and

John, I too feel passionately for the lives of the little children who are mine too, who today die of starvation in Ethiopia; for the little children in Moscow and the little children in New York who are told they must be enemies and may end up someday killing each other—in the name of the 'flag'. Remember, Luke, you have no country. The world is your country. You have not only 2 brothers and 2 sisters but millions of brothers and sisters.

Pray also for the gift of wisdom. It is a wise man who soon comes to know that the human family's real enemies are those of injustice, war, starvation, poverty. But wise men also know that it is only by men becoming different and thinking in new ways, that these things will become different.

When 'human' life is held as so sacred that no one can kill, then justice will reign in people's hearts and in all lands. Wars will be no more. Justice will mean that no man has too much, while some have nothing. Greed and selfishness will turn into feeding the hungry and removing all poverty. It is possible, Luke, to change to this kind of world. You just have to refuse to accept the old ways of 'thinking' and 'doing' things, and begin to 'think' and 'act' in a way more in tune with the magnificent goodness in man. All men know today that killing and starvation are wrong—it is just that not enough are prepared to change themselves and to work on making things different.

And now, my little son, before you fall asleep, let me say the most important thing of all to you. Be happy, be joyous, live every minute of this beautiful gift of life. When suffering comes into your life, and sadly I cannot, much as I would love to, protect you from all suffering, and when you come through the winter of your life, remember that summer will return, the sun will shine again, and the road will be covered in beautiful, oh so very, very beautiful, yellow roses of love.

God bless you and keep you, my little Luke.

Mummy

GOLDA MEIR (ISRAEL)

AN EVOLUTION THAT INCLUDES DEMOCRACY

. . . I'm sure that someday children in school will study the history of the men who made war as you study an absurdity. They'll be astonished, they'll be shocked, just as today we're shocked by cannibalism. Even cannibalism was accepted for a long time as a normal thing. And yet today, at least physically, it is not practiced much any more. We can only arrive at peace . . . through an evolution . . . that includes democracy. . . .

NANCY MOREJÓN (CUBA)

BLACK WOMAN

I can still smell the foam of the sea I was forced to cross.
Neither I nor the ocean remember that night.
But I can't forget the first bird I saw in the distance.
The clouds were high like innocent witnesses.
Perhaps, I haven't forgotten my lost coastline or my
ancestral tongues.
They dragged me here and here I've lived.
And because I was made to work like a beast here,
here I was born again.
I was forced so many times to remember my Mandingo origins.

      I became disobedient.

You, master, bought me in the square.
I embroidered your coat and gave birth to your son,
but my son had no name.
And you, master, died in the arms of an impeccable British
                  Lord.
      I walked far.

This is the land where I suffered the stocks
    and the whip.
This is the land where I flow through many rivers,
    and under its sun planted seed.
This is the land where I harvested
    but reaped no food.

As a home, I had a prison.
I myself carried the stones to build the barracks.
I sang the national anthem composed by your national
                  birds.

      I rebelled.

In this same land, I touched fresh blood and rotting bones
    of others enslaved by this land like me.
And I never again dreamed of the road home to Guinea.
But, was it Guinea? A Benin? Was it Madagascar?
                              Or Cabo Verde?

           I worked even harder.

I composed my own song infused with my African memories.
Here, I built my own world.

           I fled to the mountains.

My true independence was a shelter in the highland jungles,
    where I learned to mount a horse among the soldiers of
                        Maceo's troops.
Only in a century much later,
next to my descendents
from the azure mountain,
           I came down from La Sierra

to be finished with exploiters and usurers,
with generals and slave owners.
Now, I exist: only today do we have and create our own.

           Nothing is alien to us.
Ours is the land!
Ours, the sea and sky!
Ours, the magic of dreams!
I am equal among the people.   Here, I dance with them
beside trees we have planted to share among ourselves,
our communal harvest!
The prodigal wood already resounds!

        (Translated by Daniela Gioseffi with Enildo García)

ALVA MYRDAL (SWEDEN)

PEACE IS OUR ONLY HOPE

The longing for peace is rooted in the hearts of all people. But the
striving, which at present has become insistent, cannot lay claim to
such an ambition as leading the way to eternal peace, or solving all

disputes among nations. The economic and political roots of the conflict are too strong. Nor can it pretend to create a lasting state of harmonious understanding between men. Our immediate goal must be more aimed at preventing what, in the present situation, is the greatest threat to the very survival of mankind, the threat of nuclear weapons. . . . It is not worthy of mankind to give up. We win nothing by doing only wishful thinking. There is always something one can do!

MARGARITA CHANT PAPANDREOU (GREECE/U.S.A.)

GLOBAL FEMINISM FOR THE YEAR 2000

In Greece, in village areas, there were women not long ago who would not sit at the same table with their husbands, but would do the serving and eat later. In those years, many times when I was guest at such a table, I would urge the wife to join us, my feminist inner rage reaching a bursting point. I succeeded once, and then the woman acted so embarrassed that I regretted my pressure. I also worried that subsequently she may have been tongue-lashed or worse for her audacity. Nowadays, with a change in attitudes, this is a dying practice. In fact, to illustrate how far along we've come, last week the Greek parliament passed by a majority vote the law legalizing abortion. This after many years of work by the women's movement. . . .

I am going to argue in my presentation today that the feminist movement in Western democracies is ready *to seek and achieve formal political power*. I say this because (1) we have learned that "ladies" *do become politicians;* politics is no longer only a man's business, (2) we are more educated, (3) we participate to a greater extent in the labor force, and (4) we are having fewer children. In addition, the Movement has matured, and seeking *formal political power* is appropriate following the international efforts of the Decade of Women and the success of the Nairobi Conference. And last, but not least, the Movement *needs* its spokespeople in the formal political structure of all countries.

Now to women in politics—women in power. If we say that politics means an involvement in the public sphere for social, economic or political purposes—either for creating change or for preservation of the status quo, then women have been involved informally for many years and most recently in the large political movement of women's liberation.

333

Despite this involvement, we observe that the system of every country reflects almost exclusively the male vision of how the members of its society should function. This can be said without exception because there is no society in the world which is not patriarchal, which is not male-dominated. In other words, men have produced the kind of society they want and have developed the rules and regulations to maintain the status quo. The role that women have been given in society up to now has little to do with our biology. Decisions were taken long ago that were economic and political, and then an appropriate mythology was produced for our second class status which became embedded deeply in the culture of all societies. In some societies, particularly Western, the myth is that women are weak, emotional and brainless, and have to be cared for and controlled. In other societies, and this is true of many Arab societies, women are viewed as a powerful force for evil, for destruction—and, therefore, must be held back, down, under control. More than a thousand years ago in Greece an entire meeting of the church synod was devoted to the question of whether a woman was a human being or an animal. It was finally settled by vote, and the forces that asserted we belong to the human species won by one vote. It was rather an academic exercise because life did not change for the woman dash human after that historic debate. She was still held down, controlled, enslaved. In all societies she was exploited by the system, either as unpaid labor in the home or as cheap labor in the marketplace. We women have lived for so long in such a different social, economic and cultural world than men that we can only be described as a *dependent culture* within a male system.

This woman's culture has its own norms and standards of behavior which are passed on from generation to generation. In tests on sex differences in values and interests—the same basic results are seen in almost all cultures—women score high on scales for esthetic, social, and religious values. Men get their high marks for politics, economics, and technology. These *socially induced* characteristics make a difference in male and female culture. If society developed the culture which had the *value system* of Women's World—that of non-violence, of caring and nurturing, of non-oppressive personal and institutional relations—well, let's just put it in simple dramatic terms—there *would be food* for the starving Africans; half a million women *would not die* of maternal causes every year, child mortality rates would drop, and there would be resolution of conflict through non-violent means. These so-called feminine values are sorely needed in giving birth to a new ETHOS—a new era. We would be a *much better off world*—and we would be a VIABLE world.

Now I come to a *key question for feminists*. How do we manage from a position of relative powerlessness to change our societies? To realize this vision of the world. How do we manage to make those changes when we are not in positions of power to do so? And, if we need to get into decision-making centers, how do we do that without compromising our own *value system?*

Let me start out by making a few definitions to set the framework for my talk.

I would like to make a distinction among three terms: *sisterhood,* the *women's movement* and *feminism.* Worldwide—or global *sisterhood—* can be defined simply as a concern and a personal care for women as a group all over the map—a compassion, an understanding, an empathy. It is the way in which we relate to each other. We offer each other the love and support that we have been socialized to lavish primarily on husband and children. It is a consciousness that with all the things that divide us—class, religion, color, cultural traditions—we do share things *in common* as a gender group . . . we are the least educated, lowest on the economic pyramid, bear the child-raising and household responsibility, have minimum political and decision-making power in the public sphere, etc.

These are the grounds then for *sisterhood*—our similarities. The *worldwide women's movement* can be considered the organized arm of sisterhood, a loosely networked federation of women's organizations, in resistance to humiliation, inequality and injustice. A *strategy* for this women's movement is where *feminism* comes in. Feminism embodies the awareness of the special oppression and exploitation that all women face as a gender group. Feminism also means the willingness to organize and fight against women's subjugation in society and for the elimination of *sex-based injustice.* Feminists must decide what exactly is wrong, whose fault it is and what should be done to make matters right. Hard decisions have to be made, a political-ideological framework developed, and priorities decided. Above all, *we must have a vision,* an image of the kind of world we would like to live in if we had the power to mold it—a new form of social organization which would create a different kind of society.

The reason I make these distinctions is that the support of women in general under Sisterhood does not mean necessarily the support of all women to political office. In the case of politics, it is not sufficient that the candidate be just a woman; she must be a woman with feminist goals, demands and principles. Women in political positions will be deciding on issues that concern our lives, our children's lives, and the life of society, and their *political orientation* is critical.

Of course, we should realize that at a global level, to support feminism is suspect in many countries—Eastern Europe, the Soviet, Arab countries, dictatorial Latin American countries.

It was suspect in Greece when my family and I returned from six years in exile after the fall of the dictatorship in 1974. The word *feminism* was connected to the well-known simplistic version of bra-burning, hatred of the man, sexual promiscuity, destruction of the home and the family. This version, of course, had been fed to the people not only by a male-dominated society, but also by a junta-controlled press and the ultimate in patriarchal societies—a military dictatorship. When the dictators took over after a coup d'état in April, 1967, one of their *very first acts* was the abolishment of all women's organizations. I always say that this had its bad and its good side: bad because women were not allowed to organize on behalf of their liberation, but good because it demonstrated the *power of women* when organized and the fear that this instilled in a dictatorial regime. Recently, the courageous women of Chile have been demonstrating this power. It is the women who are overthrowing the dictatorships, the oppressive regimes. The brave mothers of the disappeared of Argentina! And, the women of South Africa with the dynamic, committed Winnie Mandela!

So, women in general, but feminists in particular, are seen as a threat to a patriarchal system of power.

Another reason feminism is rejected is that it is perceived by the socialist countries as a reform movement in capitalist societies; that is, it does not challenge the political-economic system on which inequality is based, but merely tries to improve the status of women within the existing capitalist order.

But no matter how you couch the objections to feminism, in political-philosophical terms, in fancy or unfancy language, it is the feminists' insistence on the right of women to develop their full human potential and to have control over their reproductive functions that has offended the patriarchal mentality. Not to mention economic interests that may be hurt by losing female unpaid or poorly paid labor.

One gets tired of all the put-downs of feminism. And women and men who say, "Well, I believe in the same things, but I don't want to be called a feminist." Now, I can say "bull"—and refer to a word I used earlier. Feminism is the most powerful revolutionary force in the world today. Are these reluctant feminists afraid that it is too subversive, too anti-establishment? So be it. As long as we continue to question the givens, as long as we remain the challengers, then we are alive and kicking. All of this is urgently needed in a world that is not working, is dangerously out of control and is losing a sense of what it means to be human. In getting at the heart of sex bias, we are challenging the social fabric of a society, its political orientation and decisions of its political authority. And, we are challenging *all* systems.

What *does* feminism have to say about the burning political, economic, social issues of today? We *do* have another approach. How do feminists look at the armaments race, nuclear power, international relations, development in the Third World, value of women's work, budget allocations of the countries we live in? Don't we have *a new, a different perspective*? An enlarged vision of the human experience?

But, I don't want to dwell on the problems of feminism. I wanted to give a definition and set it in an international context. Feminism exists in other parts of the world and is expanding. But, that's a whole other topic, and an interesting one, which perhaps you can deal with in a workshop on global feminism. Today in discussing *women in politics,* I will be talking about societies like the U.S., Greece, Australia, Argentina, Japan—societies where electoral politics are possible, where the individual is free to organize to achieve power.

Now let's see what we have done so far. We've done a lot in terms of global consciousness-raising. We've accomplished changes in laws. We've eliminated barriers to upward mobility in careers. We have reached higher levels of educational attainment. We've broken into "male" fields. We've hit out at and reduced the stereotyping of women.

We have not yet been able to break into that bastion of male power— the traditional political arena—electoral politics. (You know the statistics in the U.S. In a recent questionnaire by World Priorities, answered by 58 countries on percentages of representation of women in National Legislatures and Executive Cabinets, the U.S. came out 40th on the list, Greece 41st. The countries high on the list were the Nordic countries, where there is a deep feminist consciousness and commitment to social justice.)

From all the indicators of power, we can hardly claim that there has been revolution, although the concept of equality between the sexes *is* revolutionary. It is called the "unfinished revolution."

In order to complete this revolutionary process we must develop a strategy which is concerned with the gaining of power. Generally, we don't like such terms. The word POWER itself sounds too male. Power for us, however, represents the capacity to change, to change ourselves and our environment. We are not interested in exploitative power, but a mutual strengthening. Because of our understanding of the misuse and abuse of power, since 9 times out of 10 we were the unwilling victims, we developed non-hierarchical-type organizations which helped us *individually* to liberate ourselves. That was fine, but not enough. Ultimately, our organizations became strong pressure groups for changes in laws and practices. That was fine, too, but not enough. It was what we've always done. Haven't we always worked behind the scenes to influence those who *hold* the power? In our families with our fathers or our husbands; in the public sphere with our lobbying? I don't want to put this lobbying effort down. It is essential, critical and *must continue.*

Now we must also get into positions, to be an integral part of the decision-making, to decide *ourselves* on an equal basis with men on the direction of our societies.

A problem in gaining power is that the very thing we want to transfer, changing the relation of the genders to political power and reproductive labor, is one of the major obstacles in gaining power. It is very
difficult to organize a campaign, attend meetings, write brochures, read
political theory while washing diapers, dispensing cough syrup, cooking
meals, nursing sick relatives, cleaning house and providing the emotional needs of family members. To mention a few tasks of women.

And, yet we have to do it if we are to make feminist principles a way
of life. I believe that if the Women's Movement is to increase in power,
both as a lobbying force, and for moving its spokespersons into traditional political positions, then it *must become more of a mass movement,* more of a *grass-roots movement.* It means not only getting in
touch with the average woman, the truly dispossessed woman, the ra-
cially discriminated-against woman, the factory worker, but also incor-
porating *her* in the Movement. It means learning from *her* how she
perceives changes that would make her oppression less, her life more
decent—how *she* looks at the struggle for equality—what she likes about
it, what she finds threatening about it.

. . . We have come to accept too readily that a certain percentage of
people will be unemployed, that the right to work is not also a human
right—which means full employment. We forget that that percentage
represents human beings, individual lives—and increasingly with the
feminization of poverty—women's lives. . . .

While I have been dwelling on issues within our countries that seem
to be of more immediate domestic concern, all actions of feminist
organizations have *international meaning.* Feminists throughout the
world watch, study, learn, get ideas from feminist actions in other countries. Because of the key role of the U.S. in the world today, the wom-
en's movement in *this* country takes on special importance. It is impossible for the Movement here not to concern itself with global issues.

On international goals, we have the opportunity to form coalitions
with the peace movement, the ecological movement, the movement
against hunger in the world and others. The peace movement especially is a natural home for feminists; our history confirms this: the Pank-
hursts, the Ashtons, the Schwimmers, the Jane Addams's in the past; recently the Greenham Commons women of Great Britain, women of the
Nordic countries and women here as well have set the example. The
looming threat of nuclear devastation demands our participation in
peace activities, activities for survival. The connection between militarism and sexism is of great concern to us. Patriarchy is a system of

values of competition, aggression, denial of emotion, violence. These values are particularly prevalent in war where the competition is through force, where there are victors and victims, losers and winners. It is a "Weltanschauung"—a *belief* which tries to smother the human capacity to care. We must press the peace movement into asking the question, *"Is peace possible in a patriarchal world?"* This will force peace educators to explore the links between denial of women's rights and the war system, and the dependence that both sexism and militarism have on violence.

We must understand how and why violence has become so much a part of our lives; violence in the home, muggings, rapes in the streets, terrorism throughout the world, confrontation between nations. Have you stopped to think we are really a world at war? The huge international arms traffic, the immense budgets of defense departments, the fleets travelling the world through international waters, the 40 or more local wars that are raging now: *we are on a war system.*

A new mode of thinking—a mode that feminism is in the process of developing—is essential to a world where conflict is solved by nonviolent means. Feminists are trying to transcend the dichotomous thinking that has produced the we–they syndrome that divides and factionalizes the world, which polarizes the world and feeds the war system. Human beings make distinctions between good and evil; *we* being virtuous and noble, *they* being incapable, unreliable, corrupt. In the feminist world of tomorrow all people would have the responsibility to nurture, to build trust, to enhance life, and to participate in political and community affairs.

Women's peace organizations, efforts such as the Women's Coalition for a Meaningful Summit, an ad hoc Committee formed in the U.S. prior to the Geneva Summit, and now continuing its activities in anticipation of the second meeting between Reagan and Gorbachev, are *vital initiatives* by women and need to be supported and internationalized.

Women are not at the peace table. We are not there where our commitment to peace, our capacities to find solutions through dialogue, debate, our sensitivities to human needs, human rights *are sorely needed.* Therefore, we still must pressure—from the outside—for considerable improvement in relations between the super-powers, for a process of confidence—building and trust. Feminists can make clear that one does not have to agree with the political or economic systems of a country in order to like and understand its people. One does not have to assume that one must blast a population off the face of the earth because it has a different cultural value, a different organization of its society.

Also, at the international level, the Movement must get involved in issues of development. For those of us in the privileged Western world, and I use that term to mean that we are better off in both our economic human rights and our political human rights—being aware, of course, of the Third World within advanced cultures—the racial and ethnic minorities, the impoverished female segments, we have an obligation, a moral duty, if you like, to explore what can be done to reduce the enormous gap in wealth between rich and poor nations, and, as concerned women, to give serious attention to the special needs and situations of women in these countries to determine whether development has improved their lot, or worsened it. . . .

I have tried today in a short period of time to cover a vast territory— to describe what broad issues are vital to us, how we must continue to build our movement to strengthen our power to be change-agents and why we must also have our spokespersons in the traditional decision-making political structure.

We are entering a new phase of feminism—call it Grass-Roots Feminism, call it Feminism 2000, call it Global Feminism, call it Life-Preserving Feminism—call it simply New Phase Feminism—whatever it may be, it will make history, as did the First Phase of Modern Feminism. Its horizons are unlimited. Never before have women become probably the *only* salvation for the survival of humanity. . . .

Without dreams, without a vision, there can be no hope, and hope is the essence and motivating force in the cause for social change.

. . . The feminist movement has a vision. We understand, first of all, that we have but one earth, shared by one humanity. This globe is home to all—all people, all life, all laughter, all love, all music, all art. We will make it a woman's world, not in the sense of control, or power, or dominance, but in the sense of the revolutionary vision that we have—a revolution of the human spirit. Those values that we call women-centered values—caring and gentleness, equality, justice, dignity, compassion—will be diffused throughout society. . . .

MURIEL RUKEYSER (U.S.A.)

IT IS THERE

Yes, it is there, the city full of music,
Flute music, sounds of children, voices of poets,
The unknown bird in his long call. The bells of peace.

Essential peace, it sounds across the water
In the long parks where the lovers are walking,
Along the lake with its island and pagoda,
And a boy learning to fish. His father threads the line.
Essential peace, it sounds and it stills. Cockcrow.
It is there, the human place.

On what does it depend, this music, the children's games?
A long tradition of rest? Meditation? What peace is so profound
That it can reach all habitants, all children,
The eyes at worship, the shattered in hospitals?
All voyagers?
              Meditation, yes; but within a tension
Of long resistance to all invasion, all seduction of hate.
Generations of holding to resistance; and within this resistance
Fluid change that can respond, that can show the children
A long future of finding, of responsibility; change within
Change and tension of sharing consciousness
Village to city, city to village, person to person entire
With unchanging cockcrow and unchanging endurance
Under the
              skies of war.

MOLLY RUSH (U.S.A.)

LETTER FROM JAIL

Dear Greg and Bobby,

Please don't think I don't want to be home with you. But you know
how serious a protest* this was. Many people have been encouraged and
moved to think more deeply about nuclear weapons as a result. We have
gotten many letters from all over the country from people writing to
offer their prayers and their support. We hope that what we did will
make some real difference in moving other people to act in protest so
that you and all the children will have a better future. . . .

We did what we did to say that it is wrong, it is a sin, to build those
bombs. I did what I did because I want you to grow up, to live a full

* See the discussion of the Ploughshares & Campaign, p. 314.

341

life, to have children of your own without having to live in fear for their lives—as I live in fear for your life. It is important that we go into court to challenge G.E., the court and the government to see the real issues—the issues of life and death that we face, all of us, even the G.E. employees.

I don't want to be separated from you. I will come home as soon as I can, as soon as I have done what I must do.

All my love,

Mom

NELLY SACHS (GERMANY/SWEDEN)

CHORUS OF THE DEAD

We from the black sun of fear
Holed like sieves—
We dripped from the sweat of death's minute.
Withered on our bodies are the deaths done unto us
Like flowers of the field withered on a hill of sand.
O you who still greet the dust as friend
You who talking sand say to the sand:
I love you.
We say to you.
Torn are the cloaks of the mysterious dust
The air in which we were suffocated,
The fires in which we were burned,
The earth into which our remains were cast.
The water which was beaded with our sweat
Has broken forth with us and begins to gleam.
We are moving past one more star
Into our hidden God.

MACHINES OF WAR

Machines of war set up
here below, night-stained
beneath Sagittarius,
hieroglyph of great preparedness.

And above and below divided
by miles of birth and death
But the arrow of longing
is sharpened by both sides
and the same iron quivers
as preservers of zero hour.

(Translated by Ruth and Matthew Mead)

Eleanor Cutri Smeal (u.s.a.)

A POLITICAL FOCUS ON MILITARY PROFITEERY: THE FIRST STEP TO PEACE

Nowhere have women been more excluded than in the military and foreign affairs. When it comes to the military and questions of nuclear disarmament, the gender gap becomes the gender gulf. I'm coming from the school of hard knocks, rather than from a philosophical standpoint. So my question is, how do you organize this problem? I feel that one of the reasons that people aren't doing something is because they can't figure out what to do. Our first job is to create a political focus in our movement to end the arms race. We have not done this adequately enough. We're talking about public policy. We are not talking about philosophy. And for public policy to change, you've got to get involved with politics. We have to figure out how to get into the hard knock school and fight.

There is a huge profit motive in the arms race. That is what this is all about. When you talk about it to the average person, and you talk about it in terms of money, they understand it a lot more than if we talk about it in terms of philosophy. They understand they're being ripped off. We've got to make this a much more down to earth issue, a much more hard political partisan issue and move our agenda in a way that is organizable.

SAMANTHA SMITH (U.S.A.)

NOTHING COULD BE MORE IMPORTANT

I mean if we could be friends by just getting to know each other better, then what are our countries really arguing about? Nothing could be more important than not having a war if a war would kill everything. . . . People who have been to the Soviet Union know that the Soviet people don't want a war at all, they just want peace, just like the people in the United States. . . .

. . . Sometimes I still worry that the next day will be the last day of the earth. But with more people thinking about the problems of the world, I hope that someday soon we will find the way to world peace. Maybe someone will show us the way.

ANN SNITOW (U.S.A.)

HOLDING THE LINE AT GREENHAM COMMON: BEING JOYOUSLY POLITICAL IN DANGEROUS TIMES [FEB. 1985]

I made my first trip to the women's peace encampment at Greenham Common last May partly to assure myself it was still there. After mass evictions in April, the press had announced with some glee that the continuous vigil at the U.S. cruise missile base was over at last. Certainly on my arrival in the freezing rain there seemed little enough evidence to contradict these reports.

When I reached the prosperous town of Newbury with a friend who had given me a lift from London, we couldn't at first find even the base, which our map said was a misshapen oval just outside the town. How could something nine miles around, bounded by a 10-foot fence, guarded by large contingents of the U.S. Air Force, the Royal Air Force, and the police be so quietly tucked away?

Finally a scrawled woman's symbol painted on the road gave us a clue. We went up to the plateau of land that was once "common" to all. And suddenly, the fence was right in front of us in the fog. The Greenham fence looks very serious—thick wire mesh topped by several feet of rolled barbed wire, all supported at frequent intervals by cement pylons. Ten feet farther inside are more rolls of barbed wire, forming a tangled second barrier rather like those on the battlefields of World War I. Inside the fence, we could just make out—through sheets of wire and rain—concrete runways, small bunkerlike buildings, a treeless wasteland. One structure, rather like a giant, half-buried two-car garage, was, as I learned later, a missile silo.

But there were no women. Here was a gate, certainly, one of the nine where the women live, and before it several little humps of plastic, but the only people on view were a few policemen. A mile farther along and, finally, two women, standing beneath a twisted umbrella that they seemed to be holding more over the struggling fire than themselves. Two smallish women in the rain. Impossible. In silent agreement we drove on to yet another gate with again a huddle of plastic, an extinguished fire, a forlorn dereliction.

I finally understood: this was it. I asked to be dropped off back with those women with the umbrella and the fire. (You can't imagine what a depressing idea this was.) We drove back. I struggled into the waterproof boots my friend had lent me—absolute necessities as I soon discovered—and joined the women.

They were Donna and Maria. They were very, very wet. Maria's face was hidden under her sodden hood, though one could just manage to see she had a bad cold. Donna wished the world to know she was "fed up." Neither was interested in talking much. They seemed faintly aroused to hear that I had just come from New York, but as the day progressed I came to understand their lack of surprise. We stood there in the stinking nowhere and people stopped by in cars, visiting us from all over the world. If Greenham feels like world's end, it is also a mecca, a shrine of the international peace movement.

Inventive, leaderless, a constantly rotating population of women have blocked the smooth functioning of this cruise missile base for three years now. In the great traditions of pacifism, anarchy, and English doggedness in adversity, they have entered the base, blockaded its gates, danced on its missile silos, made a mockery of its security systems, and inspired other people to set up peace camps elsewhere in Britain and all over the world—in Italy, for instance, and Australia, Japan and the United States.

The camps were empty that first day because some of the women were exhausted; some in jail; some in New York suing Ronald Reagan; some at the cruise missile base in Sicily, helping the beleaguered women's peace camp there; some in Holland for a big government vote on NATO. After a few hours, Donna, too, left with one of the circumnavigating cars, off to Reading for a bath and a drink. Maria and I stayed where we were, which proved to be Indigo Gate. (The women have named their homes for the colors of the rainbow.) Although most of the women were gone, the Greenham peace camp was not shut down: at each gate several women were sticking it out in the rain. In fact, you can't really shut Greenham, even if you drag all the women away from all the gates. They come back or they go home, explaining that it hardly matters: "Greenham women are everywhere."

Back in 1981 when I first heard about the women's peace camp at Greenham Common, I was impressed but a little worried, too. Here was a stubborn little band of squatters obstructing business as usual at a huge military base. But the early media reports celebrated these women as orderly housewives and mothers who would never make this vulgar noise just for themselves but were naturally concerned about their children, innocent animals, and growing plants.

My feminist reaction was: not *again*. I had joined the women's liberation movement in 1970 to escape this very myth of the special altruism of women, our innate peacefulness, our handy patience for repetitive tasks, our peculiar endurance—no doubt perfect for sitting numbly in the Greenham mud, babies and arms outstretched, begging men to keep our children safe from nuclear war.

We feminists had argued back then that women's work had to be done by men, too: no more "women only" when it came to emotional generosity or trips to the launderette. We did form women-only groups— an autonomous women's movement—but this was to forge a necessary solidarity for resistance, not to cordon off a magic femaleness as distorted in its way as the old reverence for motherhood. Women have a long history of allowing their own goals to be eclipsed by others, and even feminist groups have often been subsumed by other movements. Given this suspiciously unselfish past, I was uneasy with women-only groups that did not concentrate on overcoming the specific oppression of women.

And why should demilitarization be women's special task? If there's one thing in this world that *won't* discriminate in men's favor, it's a nuclear explosion. Since the army is a dense locale of male symbols, actions, and forms of association, let men sit in the drizzle, I thought; let *them* worry about the children for a change.

But even before going to Greenham I should have known better than to have trusted its media image. If the women were such nice little home birds, what were they doing out in the wild, balking at male authority, refusing to shut up or go back home? I've been to Greenham twice now in the effort to understand why many thousands of women have passed through the camps, why thousands are organized in support groups all over Britain and beyond, why thousands more can be roused to help in emergencies or show up for big actions.

What I discovered has stirred my political imagination more than any activism since that first, intense feminist surge 15 years ago. Though I still have many critical questions about Greenham, I see it as a rich source of fresh thinking about how to be joyously, effectively political in a conservative, dangerous time. Obviously this intense conversion experience is going to take some explaining.

When, in the summer of 1981, a small group of women from Cardiff in Wales decided to use their holidays to take a long walk for peace, they could choose from a startlingly large number of possible destinations. Unobtrusive, varying in size and purpose, more than 100 U.S. military facilities are tucked away in the English countryside, an embarrassment of military sites available for political pilgrimage.

One U.S. base distinguished itself as particularly dreadful. Enormous, centrally located, but quietly carrying on incognito, the site was Greenham Common, outside the town of Newbury, where the U.S. Air Force was then preparing for 96 ground-launched cruise missiles to be deployed in the fall of 1983. The cruise, along with the Pershing II missile, is a centerpiece of NATO's new European arsenal. Because it is small and deployed from mobile launch points on sea or land, and because it flies low, the cruise is hard to detect—transparently a first-strike weapon.

To protest this new step in the arms race, the Welsh women set out to walk 120 miles due east to Newbury, only 60 miles out from London. They were a varied bunch, mostly strangers to each other—36 women from very different class and political backgrounds, four men in support, and a few children. Their nine-day walk, which was ignored by the press, filled them with excitement and energy, and they were greeted warmly in the towns along the way.

By the time they reached Greenham, however, the media silence had become galling. Four women decided to chain themselves to the main gate of the base to force the world to take notice. This act of protest has had children and grandchildren undreamed of by the original, quite humble, and politically inexperienced Greenham marchers. Teachers, farmers, nurses, and—yes—housewives, they had had no intention of *staying* at Greenham. But first the media took their time; then tents had to be set up and people informed. A few days spent in support of the chained women lengthened to a week, then two. Some campers had to leave, but others were just arriving.

The summer days began to give way to the chill damp of English winter. Perhaps it felt callow to give up protesting against nuclear dis-

aster just because the afternoons were drawing in. Gradually, as the
peace camp persisted—a small cluster of tents and caravans at the main
gate of the base—one fact became plain: Greenham was tapping a great,
hidden energy source for protest. There were enough women who were
willing to give bits of time stolen from the work-that-is-never-done to
keep a campfire perpetually burning on Greenham Common.

After initial amusement and tolerance, the missile base took alarm.
Winter came but the women did not go away. On January 20, 1982,
the nearby town of Newbury served notice on the camps of its intention to evict.

If ever the women had considered packing it in, this evidence that
they were a real thorn in the side of the American military and its
English support systems must have clinched matters. Prime Minister
Margaret Thatcher told the world the women were irresponsible; she
didn't like them one bit. The women began telling reporters, "We're
here for as long as it takes"—the "it" left menacingly unspecific. Some
may have meant only the local rejection of U.S. cruise missiles. But
by this time even the opposition Labour party was beginning to consider the far more ambitious goal of unilateral disarmament as a serious
English option.

The long-threatened eviction didn't come until late May 1982, when
the camp was nine months old. By this time the women's community
was firmly entrenched. Individual women came and went, but the camp
endured. The shifting population made even honest generalizations
about the women difficult, while the press had long ended its ro-
mance with docile housewives and now made more insulting efforts to
stereotype them (just middle-class ladies, just lesbians, just green-haired
punks). The women themselves refused self-definition, other than to
say that they were unified by their double commitment—to nonviolence
and to direct action. Since they eschewed leaders as well as generalizations, there was no spokesperson to mediate between the world and the
spontaneous acts of the group.

It is no doubt this very amorphousness that has made evicting the
women so difficult. The police are taught to arrest the ringleader, but
here there is none. Campers evicted from the Common land simply
cross over to Ministry of Transport land, a strip alongside the road, or
to Ministry of Defense Land. Evicted from there, they move back to
council land. Constant evictions—sometimes daily—have become a central, shaping reality of Greenham life. Since no location there is legal,
even the smallest acts of persistence acquire special symbolic weight.
For anyone, just visiting Greenham Common, sitting down on an overturned bucket at a campfire for a chat and tea, is an act of civil disobedience.

348

During my first visit, a two-day stay, I assumed that it was with grisly irony that the women had named the gates the colors of the rainbow. My time at Indigo was absurdly bleak and monochromatic. We struggled to keep the fire going; Maria (who, it turned out, was from Spain) performed a vegetarian miracle on a tiny, precariously tilted grill; we talked to the guards five feet from us on the other side of the fence about war, peace, men, women, weather, money; we slept in an ingenious but soaking handmade teepee, while outside an ever-changing pair of guards patrolled with growling dogs under giant arc lamps, which sizzled in the rain and lit up our dreams.

Greenham seemed mainly a passive test of endurance, though it was obvious, too, that instead of destroying the encampment, the stream of evictions has become a source of solidarity, resistance, and imagination. Where once gardens were planned, now a few flowers grow in a pram, easily rolled away at a moment's notice. Where once elaborate circus tents were pitched, now a cup on a stick holds up a makeshift roof. Those unprepossessing huddles of plastic I saw on my arrival were actually full of women, sheltering from the rain. These "benders" can look squashed and ugly from outside; but the bent branches that support the plastic are often still covered with leaves, making the inside a bower. When the bailiffs come with their big "chompers," they get a pile of soggy polyethylene, while the campers carry their few possessions across the road to safety. As soon as the bulldozers are gone, up go the plastic shelters once more.

Familiar domestic collages of blackened tea kettles, candles, corn flakes, bent spoons, chipped plates (never paper ones) lie around as if the contents of a house had been emptied into the mud, but here the house itself is gone. The women have left privacy and home, and now whatever acts of housekeeping they perform are in the most public of spaces up against the fence or road. Greenham is the ultimate housewife's nightmare: the space that can never be swept clean, ordered, sealed off, or safe. But as the mud blackens hands and the wood smoke permeates clothes and hair, the women of Greenham give up gracefully. (With thick irony I was offered the following suggestions: "Wood smoke is a pretty good deodorant." "Try washing dishes in boiling water; it loosens things up a bit, under the fingernails.")

The evictions have further clarified the situation this is life *in extremis,* life carried on where authority and custom do not mean it to be lived. There is only one source of water for all the camps. Only small and portable Robinson Crusoe contrivances have a chance. Greenham shreds the illusion of permanence and pushes those who live there into a naked, urgent present.

It is hard to imagine a better intellectual forcing ground for people struggling to grasp the full reality of the nuclear threat. Sitting at the fire, we discussed postindustrial society, postimperialist England, whether or not one should eat meat, the boundary between useful and irresponsible technical advances. Strewn around us were mixtures of very old technologies (how to make a fire with nothing but damp wood; how to cook everything on that fire—there is no electricity *anywhere* in the camps; how to build a shelter from bracken) and useful new ones (plastic protects everything; some women have fancy Gore-Tex sleeping bags or jackets because, though waterproof, they "breathe").

I told one woman who has lived at Greenham for two years that sometimes the camps looked to me as if World War III had already happened, as if we were rehearsing for life after the bomb, in a flat landscape where there will probably be plenty of bits of plastic and Velcro, but no clean water, no electricity, nowhere to hide. She looked at me pityingly: "Greenham is a holiday camp next to what things would be like if these bombs go off."

Of course, of course. Still, Greenham is a grim reminder of how much effort the simplest acts of maintenance take once one has removed oneself from the house, the town, the city. People there are experimenting with self-governance in small communities; they are living with less, seeking new definitions of comfort and satisfaction.

Certainly that less is more seemed the message of my first visit. But on my second, Greenham revealed a whole new side, a dramatic richness. I arrived my second time in delicate sunlight for an action called "10 million women for 10 days," timed to coincide with last September's vast NATO maneuvers on the East German–West German border. This time instead of a wasteland I found a carnival, a caldron of direct action, a wildly kinetic place. Circus tents were going up for the ten-day gathering and caravans offered free food. Strings of colorfully dressed women lined the road, walking clockwise and counterclockwise, in the great Greenham round. They had come to act.

Part of what makes the daily exhaustion of Greenham endurable for so many different kinds of women—and in such large numbers—is that contrary to first appearances, the place is a magnificent, exotic stage set for effective political gestures. Unlike the political demonstrations I have known, peace camps are permanent frames that can give form to hundreds of individual acts of resistance. Energy flows like light—because of the immediacy of everything, the constant, imminent possibility for self-expression and group solidarity.

You are not only joining something larger than yourself but something that is continuously, inexorably taking its stand of militant witness and rebuke, even while you're sleeping, even when you're fed up and go off to spend a night in town, even when you're angry, confused, or at political loggerheads with every other woman in the place. Greenham is a springboard from which actions that would usually take months of laborious planning can be dreamed, discussed, and performed between night and morning.

Ideas for Greenham action can come from anywhere—something read in the paper, an image someone shares at the fire—and one such action made Greenham internationally famous, the "embrace the base" demonstration of December 12, 1982. The precipitating image—borrowed from the U.S. Women's Pentagon Action—was of women encircling the fence, surrounding it with feelings of power and love. No one knew if enough women would come to stretch around the nine-mile perimeter, so the nervous few who had set the idea in motion told everyone to bring long scarves to use as connectors, just in case.

Somewhere between 30,000 and 50,000 came, more than enough to embrace the entire round. (Whatever the press says, the women are always uncountable: Greenham has no center, no check-in point, no higher ground for surveying the scene. It is forced—by geography and police—to be scattered; it is elusive and invertebrate by choice.) The women festooned every inch of fence with symbols, paint, messages. To those who were there and the millions more who heard about it, the action seemed a miracle. The next day, 2,000 women blockaded the base, and, two weeks later, on New Year's dawn, 44 climbed the fence and began an hour's dance on the half-completed missile silos.

On the anniversary of "embrace the base" the women tried another, more hostile image of encirclement. Again 50,000 came, this time with mirrors they held up to the fence, reflecting its own dreary reality back on itself. At yet another carefully planned action, the women locked the soldiers inside the base by securing all the gates with heavy-duty bicycle locks. The increasingly frantic soldiers couldn't cut their way out and, finally, had to push one of their own gates down.

But it is a distortion of Greenham activism to mention only these large and well-known events, which required an unusual amount of advance planning. In fact, nothing was more maddening for an old new leftist like me than the effort to figure out where a Greenham action comes from—rather like trying to find out how a drop of dye travels through a gallon of water. Women told me: Well, this one had this idea. And we all had a meeting. (Who is "all"? "Whoever wanted to do an action.") Then some of us didn't like it. And we kept talking about it. We changed it a bit. We agreed to ask all our friends and their friends, by phone, by chain letter. We have a big network.

One of the brilliant structural inventions of the peace movement as a whole is its combination of small affinity groups with large networks. In the small group you are known, valued, listened to. These are the people you choose from the heart, the ones you want next to you if the police get rough. The small group can be relatively homogeneous to start with or it can be a comfortable locus from which shared values and ideas develop over time. Either way, the small group feels like a place you can return to.

But instead of being an isolated enclave, the affinity group is linked to others in an international network, which shares some if not all the small group's goals. The Greenham network includes men as well as women, organized in a number of forms, in ecology groups, local political groups, male support groups, Campaign for Nuclear Disarmament groups. (The Campaign for Nuclear Disarmament is Britain's mass membership organization comparable to the National Mobilization for Survival in the United States.) There are also other active peace camps like the flourishing one at Molesworth (the second English site where cruise missiles are to be deployed), where both men and women are just now getting in gear to resist the pre-cruise renovation. Consensus is often possible in small groups that work together for a long time, while the network operates differently, joining people in coalitions where sharp disagreements are also acknowledged.

Most direct action at Greenham, though, is generated not from the larger network but within small affinity groups. An idea or image travels around the gates like wildfire. "Let's get up at 4:00 A.M. and shake a big stretch of fence down." "Let's have a vigil at the gate at sunset and call the names of the people who wanted to be here but couldn't." "Let's confuse them by blockading the road a mile from the gate and creating such a traffic jam that they can't get to us to arrest us." Once, at Easter: "Let's dress up like furry animals and cover overselves with honey, and break into the base." (No one arrested the women who did this one—maybe because they were too sticky?)

Or take the fence, that always present reminder of an "outside" versus "inside," a raggle-taggle band of colorful women who sing and dance and watch versus a gray-and-brown squad of soldiers who march and drill and watch. My first impression of this fence as something final and authoritative left me entirely unprepared for the women's view of it: they have simply rejected it as a legitimate boundary. Slipping under or cutting doors through the wire, they enter the base constantly, exploring, painting, filching frighteningly bureaucratic memos about nuclear war—symbolically undermining the concept "security." Hundreds have been arrested for criminal damage to the wire, yet women continue to enter the base routinely, in large numbers.

But is Greenham only a place where you can go and feel you've made a difference but really you haven't? . . .

Certainly Greenham's effectiveness is hard to measure. The powers that be—from Margaret Thatcher to NATO and even as far as the Kremlin—profess to be paying no attention to the women, nor to the mass European peace movement in general. But the women don't accept the powers that be, a stance that has earned them a grudging respect among their compatriots.

As early as the 1950s, Winston Churchill warned the British that they were letting their island become an "unsinkable aircraft carrier" for the United States. Successive governments of both parties ignored these warnings, preferring to think of England as maintaining some measure of old empire through its "special relationship" with the world's greatest power.

But, in order to keep up these costly prerogatives, to have an independent nuclear force and colonial clout in farflung places like the Falklands, the British government has allowed its own soil to be colonized. Britain has quietly become a client state. . . .

To turn around an arms race so richly fed by capital investment, a mass movement is essential, but what sort of *mass*? Greenham's effectiveness must be measured not only by the role it plays in mobilizing large numbers but also by the kind of political culture it has to offer those numbers. . . .

I met women of every class and generation, though very few black, Asian, or Indian women make their way there. There were Grannies against Cruise and striking miners' wives; there were a disproportionate number of professionals and intellectuals; there were both straight and lesbian women, with lesbian energy a great source of Greenham vitality and staying power; there were glorious flocks of young girls playing various forms of hooky, casting a cold, clear eye on their dim future in the present English job market. There were genuinely marginal women who would be on the dole, or in mental institutions, or in some other form of big trouble if Greenham weren't there. Greenham is a melting pot, with all the false unities that can imply, but with the potential, too, for a new cosmopolitanism for feminist activism, a direct confrontation with the differences among women.

These women bring to the fire values forged in a variety of movements: they absolutely reject any leadership (like the anarchists, or like the feminist consciousness-raising groups some of them came from); they insist on nonviolence (like the pacifist, Quaker, or other Christian groups some of them came from). They are ecologists, trade unionists, Labour party members, and, frequently, Campaign for Nuclear Disarmament (CND) activists. A wide variety of left politics also fertilizes

Greenham; in England, left paradigms are taken more for granted than in the United States. . . .

The Greenham women I talked to take great pains to point out that the purpose of Greenham is not to exclude men but to include women—at last. Though a few women there might still tell you women are biologically more peaceful than men, this view has been mostly replaced by a far more complex analysis of why women need to break with our old, private complicity with public male violence. No one at Greenham seems to be arguing that the always evolving Greenham value system is inevitably female. The women recognize their continuity with the Quakers, with Gandhi, with the entire pacifist tradition, and with the anarchist critique of the state. At the same time, women, the Greenham campers believe, may have a separate statement to make about violence because we have our own specific history in relation to it. . . .

A whole activist generation is being forged at Greenham, not of age but of shared experience. These women are disobedient, disloyal to civilization, experienced in taking direct action, advanced in their ability to make a wide range of political connections. The movable hearth is their schoolroom, where they piece together a stunning if raffish political patchwork.

Before visiting Greenham, I had feared that its politics would prove simple-minded, that those absolutes, life and death, would have cast more complex social questions in the shade. How, for instance, could the old question What do women want? survive when the subject is Mutual Assured Destruction (MAD, U.S. military slang for nuclear deterrence). As Brenda Whisker wrote in *Breaching the Peace,* an English collection of feminist essays criticizing the women's peace movement, "I think that stopping the holocaust is easier than liberating women." Hard words certainly, but understandable, solidified through bitter experience. While women and children are first, feminism continues to be last. . . .

I wonder if women are having to learn at Greenham—with a difference—what men learn too early and carry too far: the courage to dare, to test reaction, to define oneself *against* others. Nonviolent direct action takes great courage. The big men on their horses or machines are doing as ordered—which is comfortable for them. In contrast, it can be truly terrifying to refuse to do what an angry, pushing policeman tells you to do. For women particularly, such acts are fresh and new and this cutting across the grain of feminine socialization is a favorite,

354

daring sport of the young at the fence. Such initiations give women a revolutionary taste of conflict, lived out fully, in our own persons, with gender no longer a reliable determinant of the rules.

Certainly it is no use for women to turn self-righteous, as I had found myself doing—claiming a higher moral ground than men. On that ground we are admired but ignored. As Dorothy Dinnerstein has argued in *The Mermaid and the Minotaur,* emotional women have traditionally been treated like court jesters that the king keeps around to express his own anxieties—and thus vent them harmlessly. A woman's body lying down in a road in front of a missile launcher has a very different symbolic resonance for everyone from that of a male body in the same position. Greenham's radical feminist critics wonder just what kind of peace a female lying down can bring. Won't men simply allow women to lie in the mud forever because the demonstrators themselves only underline men's concept of what is female (passivity, protest, peace) and what is male (aggression, action, war)?

Before I came to Greenham, I shared these worries. But at Greenham at its best, women's nonviolent direct action becomes not another face of female passivity but a difficult political practice with its own unique discipline. The trick—a hard one—is to skew the dynamics of the old male-female relationships toward new meanings, to interrupt the old conversation between overconfident kings and hysterical, powerless jesters. This will surely include an acknowledgment of our past complicity with men and war making and a dramatization of our new refusal to aid and assist. (I think of a delicious young woman I heard singing out to a group of also very young soldiers: "We don't find you sexy anymore, you know, with your little musket, fife, and drum.")

Perhaps some of the new meanings we need will be found buried in the old ones. If women feel powerless, we can try to share this feeling, to make individual men see that they, too, are relatively powerless in the face of a wildly escalating arms race. Naturally, this is a message men resist, but the women at Greenham are endlessly clever at dramatizing how the army shares their impotence: The army cannot prevent them from getting inside the fence or shaking it down. It cannot prevent them from blockading the gates. It cannot prevent them from returning after each eviction.

Or, rather, it could prevent all this, but only by becoming a visibly brutal force, and this would be another kind of defeat, since the British armed services and police want to maintain their image of patriarchal protectors; they do not want to appear to be batterers of nonviolent women. Greenham women expose the contradictions of gender: by being women they dramatize powerlessness but they also disarm the powerful. . . .

If you decide to visit Greenham, or any of the growing number of permanent peace camps, women-only and mixed, that are springing up in Europe and here in the United States, your experiences will be entirely different from what I have described here. As I write, the Greenham network keeps changing, usually beyond the range of media reports. This very week the death of Greenham was announced once more, but when I called friends they only laughed. "Of course the women are still there." The water situation is desperate and benders have given way to still more primitive plastic shelters, but everyone is "quite cheery."

When I describe Greenham women—their lives in these circumstances—I often get the reaction that they sound like mad idealists detached from a reality principle about what can and cannot be done, and how. In a sense this is true. The women reject power and refuse to study it, at least on its own terms. But the other charge—that they are utopian dreamers who sit around and think about the end of the world while not really living in this one—is far from the mark.

In a piece in the *Times Literary Supplement* last summer, "Why the Peace Movement Is Wrong," the Russian émigré poet Joseph Brodsky charged the peace movement with being a bunch of millenarians waiting for the apocalypse. Certainly there are fascinating parallels between the thinking of the peace women and that of the radical millenarian Protestant sects of the 17th century. Both believe that the soul is the only court that matters, the self the only guide, and that paradise is a humble and realizable goal in England's green and pleasant land. The millenarians offered free food just like the caravans now on the Common: Food, says one sign. Eat till You're Full.

But the women are not sitting in the mud waiting for the end, nor are they—as Brodsky and many others claim—trying to come to terms with their own deaths by imagining that soon the whole world will die. On the contrary, the women make up one of the really active anti-millenarian forces around. President Reagan has told fundamentalist groups that the last trump ending human history might blow at any time now; the women believe that the dreadful sound can be avoided, if only we will stop believing in it.

Greenham women see a kind of fatalism all around them. They, too, have imagined the end, and their own deaths, and have decided that they prefer to die without taking the world with them. Nothing makes them more furious than the apathy in the town of Newbury, where they are often told, "Look, you've got to die anyway. So what difference does it make how you go?" These are the real millenarians, blithely accepting that the end is near.

In contrast, the women look very hardheaded, very pragmatic. They see a big war machine, the biggest the world has known; and, rather than sitting in the cannon's mouth hypnotized, catatonic with fear or denial, they are trying to back away from the danger, step by step. They refuse to be awed or silenced by the war machine. Instead they say calmly that what was built by human beings can be dismantled by them, too. Their logic, clarity, and independence are endlessly refreshing. Where is it written, they ask, that we must destroy ourselves?

SHARON SPENCER (U.S.A.)

INVOCATION TO THE MAYAN MOON GODDESS

Mother of All
without you, we die
without you, we kill, spill blood
our own blood, the blood of others.
Come Quickly.   Come.   Come Quickly.

Mother of All
without you we live by violence
enslaved by the axe and the sacrificial stone
ripping hearts from living bodies
of people like ourselves.

Mother of All,
enslaved by the teachings
of blood-drenched gods
we kill, kill, kill, kill,
people like ourselves.

Mother of All,
we are dying,
caught in the blood cycle,
we kill, we kill other people,
people like us, we kill
the old people, we kill the children,
especially the children, we kill
the young, we kill the husbands
and the wives, we kill the fathers
and mothers of people,

people like ourselves, people
we might have become in another world,
the people, the dead might have become
in a world in which money was respected
not worshipped.   Come.   Come Quickly. Come.

Mother of All, we are dying
of the old laws.   Oh Mother Moon,
give us, we pray, a law to live by.
Come Quickly.   Come.   Come Come.

MOTHER TERESA   (AGNES GONXHA BOJAXHIU) (ALBANIA/YUGOSLAVIA/INDIA)

WORKS OF PEACE

Our poor people are great people, a very lovable people. They don't need our pity and sympathy. They need our understanding and love and they need our respect. We need to tell the poor that they are some-body to us, that they too have been created by the same loving hand of God, to love and be loved. . . . Love cannot remain by itself—it has no meaning. Love has to be put into action and that action is service. . . . All works of love are works of peace.

SOJOURNER TRUTH   (U.S.A.)

WOMEN

Now if the first woman God ever made
was strong enough to turn the world
upside down, these women together ought
to be able to turn it back and get it
rightside up again. . . .

GRACE KENNAN WARNECKE (U.S.A.)

WHAT ABOUT THE RUSSIANS?

What do our children learn about Russia? They see James Bond movies and television thrillers where the Russians are all spies and killers. And recently the American press made quite a brouhaha about the new Soviet mini-series in which American diplomats are spies and villains. I, too, find this alarming but can one say that is very different from what we are producing here?

It is appalling that despite our obsession with the Russians how little most Americans know about them, whereas in every major Soviet city there are schools where the language instruction is in English, and there is extensive study of U.S. society and cultures, including our literature. We should encourage more of our students to study the Russian language, and make more Russian studies available. We should also encourage all Congressional representatives to visit the Soviet Union, and invite Soviet political leaders to visit here.

In this bleak and dangerous time, what we can do to improve the situation is to give Americans a more realistic picture of Soviet life.

JOANNE WOODWARD (U.S.A.)

SEEDS OF PEACE

Without new ideas, new leadership and new action by women, men will go on preparing for the next war because they have always prepared for war.

But women know that the next war will be the end of us, our children and our fragile, beautiful planet. . . .

Our only hope is to prevent that war and the decision on how to do that is too important to be left to the men alone.

. . . This is a war about which women were never consulted. And because we were never consulted, we have no need to defend the decisions or ideas that have produced over 50,000 nuclear warheads. We say "no" to this obscenity. And we say "yes" to fresh ideas and alternatives that people all over the world are coming up with. New ideas that will pull us away from the abyss we are all poised on. . . .

Two thousand years ago a Roman noble said: "If you would have

359

peace, prepare for war." For two thousand years men have been preparing for war—and fighting wars. Women know we are preparing for a war right now. This time a nuclear war in which there will be no winner. We realize that we must begin to prepare for peace if we want a future for our children.

DAISY ZAMORA (NICARAGUA)

SONG OF HOPE

Some day the fields will be always green
and the earth will be black, sweet and damp.
On it, our children will grow tall,
and the children of our children.

And they will be free, like the trees
of the mountain, like the birds.
Every morning they will wake up happy
to be alive, and they will know that the earth
was reconquered for them.

Some day . . .

Today, we cultivate parched fields,
but every furrow is dampened with blood.

(Translated by Jane Glazer and Elizabeth Linder)

WHEN WE GO HOME AGAIN

When we go home again to our old land
the one we never knew
and we talk of all those things
that have never happened

We'll go on our way leading by the hand
children that have never existed

We'll listen to their voices and we'll live
the life we've talked about so much
and have never lived.

(Translated by Miriam Ellis)

Notes on Selections and Authors, Part IV:

BELLA ABZUG (b. 1920) is a former congresswoman to the U.S. House of Rep-
representatives from New York City. She was founder of Women USA,
and author of *Gender Gap*. In December of 1987, during the Gorbachev and
Reagan Summit Meeting in Washington, D.C., she helped to organize and
participated in an International Conference of Women from twenty-six nations who gathered for their own summit in a further expression of the yearn-
ing for world peace, voiced by thousands of participants in the landmark UN
Decade of Women Conference at Nairobi, 1985. The five-day conference was
attended by Women's Mobilization for Survival, World Women Parliamentarians for Peace, and the U.S. Women's Foreign Policy Institute.

JANE ADDAMS (1860–1935) was a social worker and founding president of
the Women's International League for Peace and Freedom. Her work at Hull
House, begun in 1889 as the first settlement house, among Chicago's poor
working classes is legendary. At a time when many feared the influx of immi-
grants, Jane Addams welcomed the cultural diversity they brought with them
to their new land. She attracted other capable women to her work, among
them Julia Lathrop, Florence Kelley, and Alice Hamilton. Hull House as a
center for activism began to have an influence in the state legislative battles
for child labor laws, industrial safety, immigrant protection, and labor rights.
When World War I broke out, Addams turned all her energies to the movement for peace and was chosen president of the Congress of Women at The
Hague. She helped in organizing the National Association for the Advancement of Colored People and the American Civil Liberties Union. In 1931,
she was awarded the Nobel Prize for Peace. These excerpts from various
speeches are just a small introduction to her inspirational oratory.

SIBILLA ALERMO (1876–1960) was an Italian poet who was raped as a young
woman and forced to marry her rapist because she was pregnant by him.
She suffered under the yoke of a domestic war. Courageously, she ran away in
1902 to Rome. There, a woman alone, she wrote and published the first
feminist novel of Italian literature, *Una Donna*, describing the imprisonment
of a wife by her husband's violent will. The novel became an international
success. Alermo worked hard to alleviate the labor conditions of Roman
workers. She wrote several more novels and in 1921 began to publish poetry.

SVETLANA ALLILUYEVA (b. 1926) is the daughter of Joseph Stalin, but her
sensibility could not have been more different. She escaped as a dissident to
the West, only to return to her homeland, and then travel West again. In her
book titled *Twenty Letters to a Friend* she explained how her life and her
mother's were devastated by her father's reign of terror, and how she hardly
knew him. A governess, a family servant, whose love and attention meant
more to her than anyone's, was her salvation as a child.

MILA D. ANGUILAR (see p. 169).

ANGELICA BALABANOFF (1878–1965) was born to a wealthy Jewish family
in the Ukraine. A true internationalist, she was one of the best-known figures
of European socialism in the first two decades of the century. Like Rosa
Luxemburg (see p. 174) and Alexandra Kollantai, she was one of hundreds
of rebellious, independent-minded women who sought to correct the poverty
and injustice they saw. Her primary achievements were in Italy, for which
she felt "a mystical attraction." Her involvement in the Italian Socialist

party was the central formative experience of her life. In Italian society, Balabanoff said she was spared the humiliating xenophobia that Rosa Luxemburg endured in Germany. After the Bolsheviks took power she returned to Russia. For many years she traveled and lived throughout Europe working for international accord.

NORMA BECKER (b. 1930) is an American educator who has been involved with nonviolent activism since the early sixties civil rights movement. She conducted a United Federation of Teachers Freedom School Project in Virginia in 1963 and a similar project in Greenville, Mississippi, in 1964. As an avid antiwar activist, she organized the Teachers' Committee for Peace in Vietnam in 1965. Chairperson of the War Resisters League in New York from 1976 to 1982, she was instrumental in 1977 in organizing National Mobilization for Survival, now an important networking group.

ELENA BRUSKOVA (b. c. 1935) is a contemporary Soviet citizen who wrote this article for *Soviet Literature Today* which publishes an English-language edition in Moscow. The magazine can be found in many U.S. libraries.

HELEN CALDICOTT (b. 1939), a citizen of Australia, has spoken more effectively than any other disarmament leader and activist on the issues of the nuclear threat. Founding member and president emeritus of Physicians for Social Responsibility, who was a teacher of pediatrics at Harvard Medical School, a winner of the British Medical Association Prize for Clinical Medicine and Surgical Anatomy, and founder of Women's Action for Nuclear Disarmament in Cambridge, Massachusetts. Making the rounds of hospitals and medical schools, she converted over 25,000 physicians to the cause of nuclear disarmament—adding credibility and ethos to the movement worldwide. Among the many awards for her international work are the Gandhi Peace Prize and the American Association of University Women Peace Award. She has published two books, *Nuclear Madness, What You Can Do,* and *Missile Envy.* Dr. Caldicott's husband, Dr. William Caldicott, resigned as a professor of pediatric radiology at Harvard Medical School in 1984 in order to devote his time to speaking on the nuclear issue. Together the Caldicotts have toured the United States, Bonn, Berlin, Munich, Amsterdam, The Hague, London, Glasgow, Edinburgh, and Dublin, as advocates of nuclear disarmament, as well as Tokyo, Kyoto, Hiroshima, and Nagasaki as participants in the fortieth anniversary observances of the bombings. A documentary film featuring Dr. Caldicott, titled *If You Love This Planet,* produced by the National Film Board of Canada, has received many international awards, including the World Peace Council Prize at the International Short Film Festival in Leipzig, and an Oscar in Hollywood for "Best Achievement for a Short Documentary Film." (See p. 69).

CH'IU CHIN (1879–1907) of China was a revolutionary activist and poet. She went to Japan to study—after her early marriage and the birth of her first child. There, she joined Sun Yat-sen's democratic party and soon became a leader along with the social reformer who sought to overthrow the Manchu dynasty. Back in China, in 1906, she founded a Shanghai newspaper concerned with women's rights and taught in a school which served as a secret headquarters for the revolutionary army. She was arrested by the Manchu government, which used her poems as evidence against her in her trial, and she was beheaded five years before the overthrow. Known throughout her land, she is venerated as a peoples' martyr.

JANE COOPER (b. 1924) is an American poet whose latest book is titled *Scaffolding.* She served for many years as a professor of writing at Sarah

Lawrence College in Bronxville, New York. She grew up in Jacksonville, Florida, and attended Princeton University in New Jersey. Her first collection of poetry won the Lamont Award of the Academy of American Poets in 1968. She is known for her long poem on the life of Rosa Luxemburg, titled *Threads of Rosa Luxemburg from Prison,* which she published to benefit the Washington Eleven, a group of nonviolent antinuclear protestors of the War Resisters League.

ARGENTINA DALEY (b. ?) is a Honduran poet who lives in Seattle, Washington. Her poetry has been published in the United States and Canada. Her mother's family lives in Puerto Cortés, giving her continuing ties with her homeland—one of the poorest nations on earth. Honduras suffers from one of the highest rates of prostitution in the world. Many refugees from the war at the border of Nicaragua, predominantly women, are housed in shantytowns around the military bases and throughout the cities of Honduras.

BARBARA DEMING (1917–1984) was an American writer, author of *We Are All Part of Each Other,* and a film historian. Arrested many times for nonviolent civil disobedience in the fight against racism and the war in Vietnam, among other causes, she offered this important observation toward the end of her life. She is the author of several books and papers on nonviolent protest.

BARBARA EHRENREICH (b. 1941) is a leading socialist thinker who has written extensively on the feminization of poverty. She is an American journalist and political satirist who writes regularly for a California-based magazine, *Mother Jones,* named after Mary Harris (1830–1930) an orator, union organizer, and political activist. Ehrenreich's article first appeared in June 1986, as a response to President Reagan's announcement of what is called the Strategic Defense Initiative. She is a leading spokeswoman of today's movement for economic justice for third world women.

ORIANA FALLACI (see p. 171), internationally known Italian journalist, is one of a generation of dedicated and courageous newspaperwomen and war correspondents who have risked their lives in places like San Salvador, Managua, Beirut, and Iraq. Frances FitzGerald, Brigette Friang, Marguerite Higgins, Gloria Emerson, Catherine Le Roy, and many others are among them.

ANNE FRANK (1929–1945) was a young Jewish Dutch girl who died in a Nazi concentration camp during the Holocaust. She and her family and friends were hidden in an attic in Amsterdam, helped by Dutch friends during a long and tedious confinement—before being discovered by Hitler's police and dragged away to the death camps.

MATRICE GRICE (b. 1949) is one of the women from Italy, Holland, Denmark, Switzerland, West Germany, Britain, Ireland, and the U.S.A. who gathered at Comiso, Sicily, to celebrate International Women's Day and voice a determined opposition to the increasing militarization of Europe and the deployment of cruise missiles from U.S. arsenals. A sit-in protest for peace at the Magliocco airport, where 112 cruise missiles were due to arrive, started in August of the same year. Days later, making history, 600 other women marched to the U.S. military base in Signonella, where some 1,500 U.S. technicians and soldiers are employed. Undaunted protestors, both men and women, continued to camp at Comiso, pursuing their cause through the courts and on the streets as well as at the base. In early August of 1983, police clashed with nuclear disarmament activists at a mass rally. They injured seventy citizens—including four members of the Italian parliament among the nonviolent protestors. Here Matrice Grice describes what happened after the opening ceremonies of March 6th International Women's Day Celebration peace walk.

DOROTHY CROWFOOT HODGKIN (b. 1910) is a world famous crystallographer who won the Nobel Prize for Science in 1964. She is a British citizen and among the renowned scientists of the world to speak out against the insanity of what is now called, by those who know, the Strategic *Offense* Initiative. Here she was interviewed collectively with Yevgeni Velikhov, Peter Starlinger, Albert Jacquard, and Dr. Allan Din, of the U.S.S.R., the United States, France, and Sweden.

LINDA HOGAN (b. 1947) is a poet of Chickasaw Native American descent. The Chickasaws were indigenous to the area now known as Oklahoma. She lives with her family in the Colorado mountains and has published volumes of poetry and fiction.

JESSIE WALLACE HUGHAN (1876–1955) was an American pacifist organizer who worked for forty years to unite all people who believed that war was a crime against humanity. She attained a Ph.D. in political science from Columbia University where with Jack London, Upton Sinclair, and Harry Laidler, she founded the Inter-Collegiate Socialist Society in 1905. She was an educator and a labor organizer who served with the League of Industrial Democracy. Her writings include *American Socialism of the Present Day*, and *Study of International Government*. As a member of the Fellowship of Reconciliation, she believed wholeheartedly in true democracy and was an instrumental force in the founding of the War Resisters League—now an international organization with offices in major cities all over the globe.

PETRA KARIN KELLY (b. 1947) is a West German political scientist who is an internationally known and leading member of the Green party. She has studied world politics and international relations at the American University in Washington and political science and European integration at the University of Amsterdam. She also worked as a research assistant at the Europa Institute. She was appointed administrator in the Secretariat of the Economic and Social Committee, dealing with the questions of environmental protection, health, and education in 1973 at the European Economic Community in Brussels. While in the United States she demonstrated against the Vietnam War and nuclear weapons. When her ten-year-old sister died of cancer, she founded the Grace P. Kelly Association for the Support of Research into Children's Cancer which includes in its work an investigation of the causes of cancer in children living in the vicinity of chemical and nuclear installations. In 1972, she joined the West German Association for Environmental Protection Actions Groups and from 1979 helped to found the Greens, becoming their leading national candidate. Following the West German elections in 1983, Petra Kelly was one of the twenty-seven Greens elected to the Bundestag. There she was elected one of the Greens' three parliamentary speakers. She has been awarded the Alternative Nobel Prize, established by Jahob von Uexküll, in Stockholm, in 1982. In 1983, the Women's Strike for Peace, a U.S. organization, named her Peace Woman of the Year. She has written several books and articles on feminism, children's cancer, disarmament, and Hiroshima, the best known being the collection titled *Fighting for Hope*.

VERA KISTIAKOWSKY (b. 1928), professor of physics at Massachusetts Institute of Technology, addressed these words to a gathering of women from around the globe—concerned with peace and nuclear disarmament. Her point of view is echoed by experts such as Lall, Forsberg, and Hodgkin, and books such as *Star Warriors*, which received the Olive Branch Award from the Writers' and Publishers' Alliance for Nuclear Disarmament in 1985.

ALEXANDRA KOLLANTAI (1872–1952), the famed Russian revolutionary, worked to achieve decent living conditions, health- and child-care centers for the workingwoman. Though born to comfort, wealth, and culture, like Angelica Balabanoff, her contemporary (see p. 361), she chose to labor for peace and social justice at great cost to her well-being. "We no longer will have before us the 'little woman'—the pale shadow of the man—what we will have is the personality of the woman as an individual," she declared. Toward the end of her life she worked as ambassador to Sweden where she did what she could, under compromising conditions and threats of death from Stalin's regime, to help the cause of world peace. In 1939 when she was ill in a hospital and recuperating, despite many reasons for disillusionment, Alexandra Kollantai wrote these words of hope to her lifetime friend, the Swedish physician, Dr. Ada Nilson.

KÄTHE KOLLWITZ (1867–1945), the renowned German artist, more than any other artist of the century, was concerned with expressing the need for social justice among the poor, the laborers, and the sufferers of war. Born Käthe Schmidt to Lutheran parents with progressive ideals, she married Karl Kollwitz, a physician who set up a practice geared to the poor of Berlin. They lost their son in World War I and grandson in World War II. No one has more poignantly and profoundly portrayed the grief of parents who lose their children to the violence and famine of war. Educated in art and feminine independence from an early age, Käthe Kollwitz worked with determination, and her work rose to a position of prominence in the early 1920s. She became the first female professor of the Prussian Academy of Arts in 1919. Soon after the onset of World War I, Kollwitz became and remained, throughout her life, an uncompromising pacifist. During her later years, when the Nazi regime came to power, because of her sympathies with the followers of such labor leaders as Karl Liebknecht for whom she created memorial graphics, she was forbidden to exhibit her work and was dismissed from her teaching post at the academy. Her final print, created three years before her death, *Seeds for Sowing Shall Not Be Milled,* begins Part 1 of the text, and three other examples of her drawings follow at the part divisions.

LA PASIONARIA (b. 1895) born Dolores Ibarruri, in the Basque region of Spain, was known the world over for her devotion to the working classes of Spain's mining towns—where she grew up as a girl. Celebrated for her passionate oratory, she was a leader of the Spanish Civil War, 1936 to 1938. The government it managed to establish at great cost was quickly overthrown by Hitler. As an elderly woman, La Pasionaria, still remembered and loved by the people, was able to return to Spain from where she lived in exile—to serve in parliament—after the death of Franco. She had become an eternal symbol in the continuing struggle for democracy.

FRANCES MOORE LAPPÉ (b. 1944) is cofounder of Food First—the Institute for Food and Development Policy. She is currently working on a book about American values and the meaning of freedom and democracy. Many Americans recognize her by the title of her classic book *Diet for a Small Planet.* What Frances Moore Lappé offers here is from *The Mobilizer,* an important newsletter of the U.S.–based citizens' organization, Mobilization for Survival.

LOLITA LEBRON (b. 1919) is a living symbol of the struggle for survival by indigenous peoples, according to Gloria Waldman in her essay, "Affirmation and Resistance: Women Poets of the Caribbean," published in a two-volume series, *Contemporary Women Authors of Latin America* (see bibliography). Lebron spent twenty-five years in the women's prison of Alderson, West Virginia, for leading and participating in a desperate act of national affirmation in 1954—the attack against the U.S. House of Representatives. Her charisma, at once mystical and political, is communicated through her poetry. Her poem from *Sandálo en la Celdá (Sandalwood in the Cell)* was written in prison. Her poems are frank and passionate and concern themes of loneliness, her longing for her homeland of Puerto Rico, and her deep religious faith. She was released from prison in 1979.

MERIDEL LE SUEUR (b. 1900) was the best-known woman among the "proletarian" writers of the 1930s in the United States. Blacklisted during the infamous McCarthy years after World War II, her work fell into obscurity. Now there is a renaissance of her writing. Carl Sandburg said that Le Sueur's work is infused with "a rather rare quality of reverence for humanity and of intimacy and pride regarding women and motherhood." Here, from a collection of her work titled *The Ripening*, is an essay written in Minneapolis in the 1930s.

DENISE LEVERTOV (b. 1923) is a native of England, but has lived in America since World War II. Author of several volumes of verse, she is known among American readers for her opposition to the Vietnam War and her many poems on the subject published in the late sixties. She has written much, too, on the threat of nuclear war and has worked as an activist with various peace and antiwar groups. She manages in her work to seam the personal with the political in a crafted lyricism. These poems come from her latest books, *Candles of Babylon* and *Breathing the Waters*.

MAIREAD CORRIGAN MAGUIRE (b. 1944) shared the Nobel Prize for Peace in 1976 with BETTY WILLIAMS of Northern Ireland for their nonviolent activism. They were the first women to receive the prize since it was given to Emily Greene Balch, in 1946, who had followed Jane Addams into the presidency of the Women's International League for Peace and Freedom. Since, Mother Teresa born in Yugoslavia, and Alva Myrdal of Sweden have received the Peace Prize. Considered to be "Homey women next door," Betty Williams and Mairead Corrigan—two "housewives"—have offered inspiration to all "ordinary citizens" in the cause of nonviolence. In 1975, they were awarded the Norwegian People's Peace Prize and a gift of $340,000 sponsored by Norwegian newspapers and civic groups. They were also recognized by Amnesty International with a prize in 1977. They had launched their peace crusade in Belfast, and like Martin Luther King or Gandhi, they had risked death leading many marches of nonviolent protest through the streets. Mairead wrote this letter, printed in the monthly newsletter of the Peace People, *Peace by Peace,* to her young son, Luke, in 1986. He was fifteen months old at the time.

GOLDA MEIR (1898–1978) was for many years the leader of Israel. Intelligent, strong-minded, diplomatic, and earthy, she had the following thoughts to offer Oriana Fallaci—when, toward the end of her life, she was interviewed for *L'Europeo* in Milan.

NANCY MOREJÓN (b. 1944) is a Cuban poet. She earned her diploma as a teacher of English and was graduated from Havana Institute with a degree in art in 1961. She has said, "As a black woman, I would not be a poet at all if it were not for La Revolución." Nancy Morejón has won the top prizes of

Cuba for her poems and has published several collections, plus an ethnic history, *The Tongue of a Bird,* of the mining town of Nicaro where peasant laborers were exploited by foreign corporations.

ALVA MYRDAL (1902–1985) was a Swedish activist known throughout the world peace movement. A constant crusader throughout her lifetime in the cause of population control, family welfare, and women's rights, she won the Nobel Peace Prize in 1982. She served as a director of UNESCO and then became deeply involved in nuclear disarmament as a member of the Swedish delegation to the United Nations General Assembly. Her profound commitment to the goals of disarmament and her intensive study of the science and technology of the arms race made her a leader in the cause among the non-aligned nations.

MARGARITA CHANT PAPANDREOU (see p. 176) here introduces the theme of Global Sisterhood Toward the Year 2000 of World Women Parliamentarians for Peace.

MURIEL RUKEYSER (1913–1980) was an American poet and advocate of women's rights and civil rights. She served as a president of the American Pen Center. During her last years she traveled to Hanoi in protest of American bombings and involvement in the Vietnam War. Her poem is only one of many she composed on such themes, but it attempts to make peace tangible and define it as more than the absence of war, a theme common to Jane Addams and traditional to the international women's movement for peace.

MOLLY RUSH (b. 1935), American nonviolent peace activist, a member of Father Daniel Berrigan's Ploughshares action (see p. 314), wrote the following letter home to her children as she served time in jail. Her husband, Bill Rush, understood that she was trying to help save the lives of her children. While she was in jail, he asked her, "Why . . . ?" She simply answered, "Because I know." Parents who work for nuclear disarmament are known by psychologists to instill a better sense of future and hope of survival in their children. Rush has been a staff member of the Thomas Merton Center for Peace and Social Justice and currently serves with the River City Nonviolent Resistance Campaign in Pittsburgh. She has six children and four grandchildren.

NELLY SACHS (1891–1970) was born in Berlin in 1891. She fled from Germany to Sweden in May of 1940, with her mother, to escape persecution as a Jew. She won the Nobel Prize for Literature in 1966. When the prize was awarded to her, Anders Osterling of the Swedish Academy explained her work with these words: "With moving intensity of feeling, she has given voice to the worldwide tragedy of the Jewish people, which she has expressed in lyrical laments of painful beauty and dramatic legends. Her symbolic language boldly combines an inspired modern idiom with echoes of ancient biblical poetry. Identifying herself totally with the faith and ritual mysticism of her people, Miss Sachs has created a world of imagery which does not shun the terrible truth of the extermination camps and the corpse factories, but which at the same time rises above all hatred of the persecutors, merely revealing a genuine sorrow at man's debasement."

ELEANOR CUTRI SMEAL (b. 1939) is a North American who has served as president of the National Organization of Women and is founder of the Gender Gap Project. She has led marches on Washington, D.C., in her support of women's reproductive rights. Even as a Catholic, she believes in the right of individual choice. The reproductive rights issue relates to war as Olive Schreiner explained (see p. 162).

SAMANTHA SMITH (1973–1985) was a young American girl from Maine of ten years old who was worried about nuclear war and found the whole thing "very stupid." So, she did something very unsophisticated. She wrote to Yuri Andropov, then premier of the Soviet Union, and simply asked: "I've been worrying about Russia and the United States getting into a nuclear war. Are you going to vote to have a war or not? If you aren't please tell me how you are going to help to not have a war." Andropov wrote back with an answer and invitation. "Come," said Andropov, "see for yourself. . . ." So she did. In 1983, Samantha Smith went to the Soviet Union, accompanied by parents and photographers, tracked by commentators and columnists. As Ellen Goodman, columnist for the *Boston Globe,* pointed out, everyone made a fuss. Some accused her of being used by propagandists. Others thought she was made too much of a fuss over. And still others let her express the hope and dream of peace that they feared they'd seem too naive in expressing. Samantha Smith died in a mysterious plane crash at the age of only thirteen years, but she had dreams and plans of starring in a TV show about making friends with Russian children. Her mother, Jane Smith, in October of 1985, established the Samantha Smith Foundation to encourage friendship among the world's young people and to educate people everywhere about peace. The foundation has sponsored exchanges between U.S. and U.S.S.R. students.

ANN SNITOW (b. 1943) is a writer living in New York City who coedited *Powers of Desire: The Politics of Sexuality.* She teaches women's studies and literature at the Eugene Lang College of The New School for Social Research. Greenham Common Peace Encampment in England, about which she writes here, is known worldwide as a symbolic women's action in opposition to nuclear armaments and the computerized death machine. Peace camps like it have become an international phenomenon from Comiso, Italy, to Seneca Falls, New York, to Puget Sound, or Kent, Washington. Others have taken root in West Berlin, Japan, Scotland, Northern Germany, Norway and Sweden, Tucson, Arizona, or Clam Lake in Madison, Wisconsin, or on the Savannah River in Aiken, South Carolina. Such makeshift camps as symbols of people's nonviolent resistance are reminiscent of "Resurrection City" built by civil rights activists in the 1960s or Crossroads Camp outside Cape Town, South Africa. In 1980, several hundred women and men set up an "environmental camp" on the proposed site of a nuclear waste dump recycling factory in Gorleben, West Germany. They stayed until plans for the factory were abandoned.

SHARON SPENCER (see p. 72).

MOTHER TERESA (b. 1910) has become legendary in our time for her work among the poorest of the poor. From Calcutta, India, to Bedford Stuyvesant in Brooklyn, New York, she and her Catholic Sisters of Charity have founded centers and hospitals for the most downtrodden people. Born Agnes Gonxha Bojaxhiu, she is an Albanian from Skopje, Yugoslavia. Winner of the Nobel Prize for Peace in 1979, Mother Teresa is known for the direct simplicity of her speech.

SOJOURNER TRUTH (c. 1797–1883) was an abolitionist and a freed slave originally called Isabella. Born in Ulster County, New York, she left domestic employment in New York City in 1843, named herself Sojourner Truth, and traveled throughout North America preaching emancipation and women's rights with great eloquence, despite her lack of schooling.

GRACE KENNAN WARNECKE (b. 1932), consultant on U.S.–Soviet Affairs; associate producer of a Public Broadcasting Service documentary, "The First

Fifty Years: Reflections on Soviet and U.S. Relations," had this to say at a Women's International Peace Conference held in Washington, D.C., by the Center for Defense Information.

JOANNE WOODWARD (b. 1930), well-known Hollywood actress and peace activist, spoke these words when she served as master of ceremonies at a national conference of women held in Washington, D.C. The conference was sponsored by the Center for Defense Information, a nonprofit organization founded by Rear Admiral Gene La Roque and other retired top U.S. Navy brass, to educate the public on the lack of the necessity for nuclear overkill and to give ethnos and credence to the absolute need for nuclear disarmament. CDI, with Ms. Woodward's and her husband Paul Newman's help, has done much to expose the disaster to U.S. strength and economy caused by the military-industrial complex. Despite recent disarmament agreements which do not address the constantly growing tactical arsenals of annihilation, the situation, according to the Union of Concerned Scientists, is as charged today as it was in 1984 when Woodward delivered her public address.

DAISY ZAMORA (b. 1959), of Nicaragua, was director of programming for the Sandinista radio during the years that her people struggled to free themselves from the violent oppression of Somozo—a notoriously cruel dictator. Since 1979, she has served as vice president of culture. Her poems, published internationally, have won the National Poetry Prize of her homeland. Her book of verse, written from 1968 to 1978, was titled *La Violenta Espuma*.

PART I

Words Spoken by Pasternak During a Bombing by Bella Akhmadulina, tr. Daniela Gioseffi, © 1988.

Freedom Sloganeering as an Excuse for War by Hannah Arendt, from *On Revolution*, © 1963, Viking Penguin, Inc., New York.

Guatemala, Your Blood by Alenka Bermúdez, tr. Sara Miles.

Omnicide by Rosalie Bertell, © 1986, The Women's Press, London.

Wars Past and Wars Present by Lady Borton, © 1988, *The New York Times*, New York. Reprinted by permission of the author.

The Progress by Gwendolyn Brooks, © 1971 from *Blacks*, The David Company, Chicago. Reprinted by permission of the author.

The End of the World Could Still Come Next Year by Helen Caldicott, © 1985. Reprinted by permission of the author and the Woman's Alliance for Nuclear Disarmament, Arlington, MA. 08174.

At Ground Zero in Hiroshima . . . by Ann Druyan, © 1988. Reprinted by permission of the author.

Letters to an Open City by Carolyn Forché, © 1988. From the December/January issue of *The American Poetry Review*. Reprinted by permission of the author.

World War III Is Here in Our Bodies by Dara Janekovic, tr. Daniela Gioseffi with Ivana Spalatin, © 1988. Originally published in Yugoslavia by *Globus*, Zagreb, 1964.

To the Soldiers of El Salvador Who from 1931–1980 Have Ruled the Country Through a Military Dictatorship by Lilliam Jiménez, tr. Mary McAnally.

Last Flash by Erica Jong, © 1983. Reprinted by permission of the author from *Ordinary Miracles*, New American Library, New York.

Nuclear Bomb Testing on Human Guinea Pigs by Darlene Keju-Johnson, from *Pacific Women Speak: Why Haven't You Known?*, © 1987, Green Line, Oxford, England.

The Nightmare Factory by Maxine Kumin, © 1970, from *The Nightmare Factory*, Harper & Row, New York. Reprinted by permission of the author.

The Nuclear Threat: A Woman's Perspective by Betty Lall, © 1986, from *Choices*, vol. 6, Women's Medical Center, New York. Reprinted by permission of the author.

Women's Active Role by Tat'yana Mamonova, quoted from *Soviet Sisterhood* by Barbara Holland, © 1985, University of Indiana Press, Bloomington, Ind.

Political Activism and Art by Lenore Marshall, © 1985, The Marshall Fund, Arizona. From *Invented a Person*, edited by Janice Thaddeus, Horizon Press, New York.

O Earth, Unhappy Planet Born to Die by Edna St. Vincent Millay, from *Collected Poems*, by Edna St. Vincent Millay and Norma Millay Ellis, Harper & Row, New York. © 1934, 1962.

They Followed Us into the Night by Michele Najlis, tr. Amina Munoz-Ali.

That Year by Grace Paley, © 1985, from *Leaning Forward*, Granite Press, Penobscot, Maine.

370

Among Tall Buildings by Molly Peacock, © 1984, from *Raw Heaven*, Random House, New York. Reprinted by permission of the author.

My Spoon Was Lifted by Naomi Replansky, © 1952, from *Ring Song*, Scribners, New York. Reprinted by permission of the author.

The Fifties by Wendy Rose, © 1986, from *Nuke Chronicles*, Contact II Publications, New York, 1985.

Love & War & the Future & the Martians by Libby Schier, © 1986, from *Second Nature*, Coach House Press, Ontario, Canada. Reprinted by permission of the author.

A Mayan Prophecy by Sharon Spencer, © 1985, first published in *Footwork*. Reprinted by permission of the author.

Stockpiles Are Used by Bertha von Suttner, quoted from *The Lady Laureates*, © 1986, Olga S. Opfell, The Scarecrow Press, Inc., New Jersey and London.

Children of the Epoch by Wisława Szymborska, tr. Austin Flint, © 1986, from *The Quarterly Review of Literature, Poetry Series*, vol. xxii, Princeton, New Jersey.

Never Before: A Warning by Maj. Britt Theorin, excerpted from a speech given at an International Women's Conference for Peace and Nuclear Disarmament, published, © 1984, (Newsletter, Vol. 13, No. 8), The Center for Defense Information.

Women's Peace Platform for the Summit by Women for a Meaningful Summit, courtesy of Women for a Meaningful Summit, Athens, Greece.

Mother Earth by Susan Yankowitz, a monologue from a play titled *Alarms*, © 1987 by Susan Yankowitz. Reprinted by permission of the author.

The Star Obscure by Gueni Zaimof, © 1985, from *The Star Observer*, International Publications, Euroeditor, Luxembourg.

PART II

Friend and Foe and *To One in Beirut* by Karen Alkalay-Gut, © 1986, from *Mechtiza*, Cross-Cultural Communications, Stanley Barkin, Merrick, N.Y.

Africa and *America* by Maya Angelou, © 1975, from *Oh Pray My Wings Are Gonna Fit Me Well*, Random House, New York.

Damn the Dictatorship and *To a Foreigner* by Mila D. Anguilar, © 1984, 1985, 1987, from *A Comrade Is as Precious as a Rice Seedling*, Kitchen Table: Women of Color Press, Latham, N.Y.

Testimony by Anonymous Afghan Woman, tr. Daniela Gioseffi, © 1988.

Bread by Margaret Atwood, © 1983, from *Murder in the Dark*, Coach House Press, Ontario, Canada. Reprinted by permission of the author.

The Blood of Others by Gioconda Belli, tr. Elinor Randall.

Sex and Death and the Rational World of Defense Intellectuals by Carol Cohn, excerpted from an article in *Signs* (summer issue), © 1987, University of Chicago Press, Chicago, Ill.

Stockpiling by Jane Cortez, © 1985, from *Coagulations*, Thunder's Mouth Press, New York. Reprinted by permission of the author.

A Miskito Woman of Nicaragua Testifies by Myrna Cunningham, © 1985, from an interview, *Women of Nicaragua*, The Women's International Resource Exchange, New York.

This Filthy, Rotten System by Dorothy Day, from a public speech.

We Must Share the Crime by Marguerite Duras, © 1986, from *The War*, tr. Barbara Bray, Pantheon Books, Random House, New York.

The Hamptons by Kathy Engel, © 1987, from *Banish the Tentative* by Kathy Engel. Reprinted by permission of the author.

Acknowledgments

A Man by Oriana Fallaci, © 1979, original Italian, Rizzoli Editore Milano, Sp.A., tr. © 1980, Simon and Schuster, New York.

Behind the Facade: Nuclear War and Third World Intervention by Randall Forsberg, © 1982, from a speech delivered at M.I.T., published in full in *The Deadly Connection,* © 1983, American Friends Service Committee, Cambridge, Mass. Reprinted by permission of the author. Now available from New Society Publishers, Berkeley, Calif.

The Son of Man by Natalia Ginzburg, from *The Little Virtues,* tr. Dick Davis, © 1985, Seaver Books, New York, 1986. Also © 1983, Carcanet, London.

The Exotic Enemy by Daniela Gioseffi, © 1988.

Patriotism as a Cause of War by Emma Goldman, public domain.

Burger's Daughter by Nadine Gordimer, © 1979, from *Burger's Daughter,* Russell & Volkening, London. Also Jonathan Cape, London. Reprinted by permission of the author.

Cain and Abel by Margherita Guidacci, tr. Ruth Feldman, © 1987. Reprinted by permission of the translator and author.

The Struggle Of the Palestinian People for Peace by Jehan Helou, from a public speech.

Yankees by Renya Hernández, tr. Zoe Anglesey.

We the People . . . by Helen Keller, from a public speech.

The Judgment of History Will Show by Coretta Scott King, excerpted from a speech given at an International Women's Conference for Peace and Nuclear Disarmament, published © 1984 (Newsletter, Vol. 13, No. 8), The Center for Defense Information.

Letter From Prison by Jong Ji Lee, tr. Daniela Gioseffi, © 1988.

The Catastrophe in Afghanistan by Doris Lessing, © 1987, quoted from *The Wind Blows Away Our Words,* Random House, New York. Also Jonathan Clowes, Ltd., London.

Militarism as a Province of Accumulation by Rosa Luxemburg, tr. Daniela Gioseffi, © 1988.

Despair and Personal Power in the Nuclear Age by Joanna Macy, excerpted from a speech given at an International Women's Conference for Peace and Nuclear Disarmament, published, © 1984 (Newsletter, Vol. 13, No. 8), The Center for Defense Information.

"A Way of Looking at Killing" by Karen Malpede, excerpted from a speech given at a Women's Conference on Nonviolence, © 1982, from *Reweaving the Web,* New Society Publishers, Philadelphia, Pa.

Creating the Enemy with a Name by Lenore Marshall, © 1985, The Marshall Fund, Arizona, from *Invented a Person,* edited by Janice Thaddeus, Horizon Press, New York.

False Heroes by Margaret Mead, from a public speech.

Hatred by Maire Mhac an tSaoi, © 1959, Dolmen Press, and © 1987, from *An Cion Go dlí Seo,* Sait Seal O Marcaigh, Ita, Dublin.

"*Once Upon a Time . . .*" by Nicholasa Mohr, © 1985, from *El Bronx Remembered,* Harper & Row, New York.

A Science of Peace by Maria Montessori, from a public speech.

The Colonization of the Mind by Bharati Mukherjee, © 1975, from *Days and Nights in Calcutta* by Bharati Mukherjee and Clark Blaise, Viking Penguin, Canada. Reprinted by permission of the author.

Calypso Woman by Elizabeth Nunez-Harrell, © 1986, from *When Rocks Dance,* G. P. Putnam's Sons, New York. Reprinted by permission of the author.

Free Spirits: Annals of the Insurgent Imagination by Alanis Obamsawin, © 1982, City Lights Books, San Francisco.

The Colonization of Our Pacific Islands by Chailang Palacios, from *Pacific Women Speak: Why Haven't You Known?*, © 1987, Green Line, Oxford, England.

Anxiety by Grace Paley, © 1985 and 1987, from *Later the Same Day*, Farrar, Straus & Giroux, New York.

Causes and Cures of Anti-Americanism by Margarita Papandreou, © 1986 (March 22 issue), *The Nation*, The Nation Co. Inc., New York.

Memory Says Yes by Margaret Randall, © 1982, with acknowledgment to *Nuke Rebuke*, The Spirit That Moves Us Press, 1984. Reprinted by permission of the author from *Memory Says Yes* by Margaret Randall, © 1988, Curbstone Press, Conn.

Borders by Rochelle Ratner, © 1987. Reprinted by permission of the author. First appeared in *Minnesota Review*, Spring 1987.

A Challenge for the West by Eleanor Roosevelt, public domain.

Why Is There So Much Appalling Cruelty in the World? by Dorothy Rowe, © 1985, from *Living with the Bomb*, Routledge and Kegan Paul, London. Reprinted by permission of the author.

Poem by a Yellow Woman by Sook Lyol Ryu, © 1986. Reprinted by permission of the author.

Fifty Thousand Puerto Rican People Demonstrate Against U.S. Nuclear Proliferation by Yolanda Sanchez, excerpted from a speech given at an International Women's Conference for Peace and Nuclear Disarmament, published © 1984 (Newsletter, Vol. 13, No. 8), The Center for Defense Information.

Bearers of Men's Bodies by Olive Schreiner, from Women and Labour, © 1911, and since by Virago Press, London.

Poverty, Refugees, The Vote and *Government* by Joni Seager and Ann Olson, © 1986, from *Women in the World*, Touchstone Books, published by Simon & Schuster Inc., New York.

The Enemy by Layle Silbert, © 1981, with acknowledgment to *Cottonwood*, No. 24, Lawrence, Kansas. Reprinted by permission of the author.

Worldwide Military Priorities Leave Social Programs in the Dust by Ruth Sivard, from *Christian Science Monitor*, © 1987.

Verses to Chekhia, 1938 by Marina Tsvetayeva, tr. Daniela Gioseffi, © 1988.

Politicians and Television by Barbara Tuchman, from *The New York Times*, 1987.

Bread and Bombs by Christa Wolf, from *Cassandra*, tr. Jan van Heurk, © 1984, Farrar Straus Giroux, New York. Originally published in German by Herman Luchterhand Verlag GmbH & Co KG, Darmstadt and Neuwied. Published in Canada by Collins, Toronto.

As a Woman, My Country Is the Whole World by Virginia Woolf, from *Three Guineas*, © 1938.

PART III

War Is Not a Natural Activity by Jane Addams, public domain.

Reflection by Mona Elaine Adilman, © 1986, from *Piece Work*, a collection of poems by the author, Borealis Press, Canada.

The First Long Range Artillery Fire on Leningrad by Anna Akhmatova, tr. Daniela Gioseffi, © 1988.

Evasion by Claribel Alegria, tr. Lynne Beyer.

The Hour of Truth by Isabel Allende, tr. Magda Bogin, © 1985, from *House of Spirits*, Alfred A. Knopf, Random House, New York. Reprinted by permission of the author.

Gang-Bang, Ulster Style by Linda Anderson, © 1987, from *Pillars of the House: An*

ACKNOWLEDGMENTS

Anthology of Irish Women's Poetry, edited by A. A. Kelly, Wolfhound Press, Dublin.
Melting by Marjorie Appleman, © 1979. Reprinted by permission of the author.

Haiti by Emily Greene Balch, from *Occupied Haiti,* © 1972, Garland Press.

Reports from the World Tribunal on Vietnam by Simone de Beauvoir, © 1974. Quoted from *All Is Said and Done,* G. P. Putnam's Sons, New York. Tr. Patrick O'Brian. Original French edition, © 1972, *Tout Complet Fait,* Gallimard, Paris.

A Cruel Whipping by E. Brown, from *The Autobiography of a Female Slave,* public domain.

On a Japanese Beach by Nina Cassian, tr. Daniela Gioseffi with the author, © 1987. Original Romanian © by Nina Cassian.

The Grand Commander, 1916 by Vinnie-Marie D'Ambrosio, © 1971, from *The Life of Touching Mouths,* New York University Press, New York.

Flags Vex a Dying Face by Emily Dickinson, Amherst College and Harvard University. *Lament to the Spirit of War* by Enheduanna, public domain.

From *Greek Women of the Resistance* by Eleni Fourtouni, © 1986, Thelphini Press, New Haven, Conn.

The Night After the Day After by Vera Gancheva, courtesy of Bulgarian PEN.

The Parachutist's Wife by Sandra M. Gilbert, © 1988, from *Blood Pressure,* W. W. Norton, New York. First printed in *Field.*

News Photos of Bombed Children by Rose Graubart, © 1988, from *The Unpublished Journals of Rose Graubart.* Reprinted by permission of the author.

The Bath by Kimiko Hahn, © 1987, first printed in *Jes'Grew.* Reprinted by permission of the author.

Dream of the Hair Burning Smell by Jana Harris, © 1986. Reprinted by permission of the author.

Hellish Years After Hellish Days by Toyomi Hashimoto, from *Cries for Peace,* © 1978, edited by Richard L. Gage and compiled by the Youth Division of Soka Gahkai, Anti-War Publication Committee, *The Japan Times,* Ltd., Tokyo.

The Murdered City by Anne Hébert, tr. Al Poulin, Jr., from *The Selected Poems of Anne Hébert,* © 1987, by Al Poulin, Jr., Boa Editions, Ltd., Brockport, N.Y.

Songs of Bread and *An Armenian Looking at Newsphotos of the Cambodian Deathwatch* by Diana der Hovanessian, © 1986. First printed in *Graham House Review* and *Nantucket Review.* Reprinted by permission of the author.

Moving Towards Home by June Jordan, © 1986, from *Living Room,* Thunder's Mouth Press, New York. Reprinted by permission of the author.

Exhumation by Zoe Karelli, tr. Rae Dalven, © 1986. First printed in the April issue of The Newsletter of The Friends of the Jewish Museum, Greece.

Murder by Gertrude Kolmar, tr. Henry A. Smith, © 1975, from *Selected Poems of Gertrude Kolmar,* The Continuum Publishing Company, New York.

America's Concentration Camps by Foumiko Kometani, a brief quote from a review, © 1987, *The New York Times Book Review,* The New York Times Company, New York.

Women Under Apartheid by Margaret MacKay, © 1985, *The Peoples' Daily World,* March 7 issue, New York.

Antigone by Ileana Malacioui, tr. Daniela Gioseffi, © 1988.

No Human Being Can Take Such Humiliations by Winnie Mandela, © 1984, from *Part of My Soul Went with Him,* W. W. Norton & Co. Originally published by Rowohlt Taschenbuch, Verlag GnbH, Reinbek bei, Hamburg, West Germany.

Finnish Champion by Gabriela Mistral, tr. Doris Dana, from *Selected Poems of Gabriela Mistral,* © 1961, 1964, 1970, 1971, Johns Hopkins University Press, Baltimore, Md.

374

Sunday Evening by Elsa Morante, tr. Ruth Feldman and Brian Swann, © 1979, from *Italian Poetry Today,* New Rivers Press, St. Paul, Minn.

Recollections by Yunna Petrovna Moritz, tr. Thomas P. Whitney, © 1987. Original Russian from *Oktyabr,* no. 6, 1986, U.S.S.R.

Sula by Toni Morrison, © 1973, Alfred A. Knopf, Random House, New York.

Between the Crosses by Hope Morritt, © 1988, Reprinted by permission of the author. *The Time Has Not Come* by Lucretia Mott, public domain.

Viet Minh and *Famine* by Tran Thi Nga, © 1986, from *Shallow Graves,* Random House, New York.

When by Sharon Olds, © 1987, from *The Gold Cell,* Alfred A. Knopf, Random House, New York.

The War and *The Ballad of Deceived Flowers* by Vesna Parun, tr. Daniela Gioseffi with Ivana Spalatin, © 1987. Original Yugoslavian, 1964, by Vesna Parun (Pjesme), Matica Hrvatska, Zagreb.

Report from Vietnam for International Women's Day by Minerva Salado, tr. Daniela Gioseffi with Enildo Garcia, © 1987. Original Spanish © 1985, Letras Cubanas, Havana, Cuba.

They Carried Their Truth to the Ditch Where They Were Thrown by Christian Santos, tr. Anna Kirwan Vogel and Isabella Halsted.

To an Army Wife in Sardis by Sappho, public domain.

The Spoils of War by Lynne Sharon Schwartz, © 1985, The New York Times Company. Reprinted by permission.

Gallup, New Mexico by Leslie Mormon Silko, from *Ceremony* by Leslie Mormon Silko, © 1977, Viking (Richard Seaver Books), New York.

The Situation in Soweto . . . by Mavis Smallberg, © 1987. Reprinted by permission of the author.

Torture by Wisława Szymborska, tr. Austin Flint, © 1986, *The Quarterly Review of Literature, Poetry Series,* vol. xxii, Princeton, N.J.

I'm Your Horse in the Night by Luisa Valenzuela, © 1985, tr. Deborah Bonner, from *Other Weapons,* Ediciones del Norte, Hanover, N.H. Original Spanish, © 1982 and 1987, *Cambio de armas,* also by Ediciones del Norte.

Only Justice Can Stop a Curse by Alice Walker, © 1982, from *In Search of Our Mothers' Gardens,* Harcourt Brace Jovanovich, San Diego, Calif.

From: *The Iliad: Poem of Force* by Simone Weil, excerpted by Daniela Gioseffi, translation © 1957 from *Intimations of Christianity Among the Ancient Greeks,* Routledge and Kegan Paul, London and New York. Original French, © Gallimard, Paris. First published in *Cahiers du Sud,* December 1940 and January 1941, Marseilles.

Wounds by Harriet Zinnes, © 1986. Reprinted by permission of the author.

PART IV

The Issue Is Survival by Bella Abzug, excerpted from a speech given at an International Women's Conference for Peace and Nuclear Disarmament, published, © 1984 (Newsletter, Vol. 13, No. 8), The Center for Defense Information.

Maturing Concepts of Peace by Jane Addams, public domain.

Yes to the Earth by Sibilla Alermo, tr. Muriel Kittel, © 1986, from *The Defiant Muse: Italian Feminist Poems from the Middle Ages to the Present,* edited by Beverly Allen, Muriel Kittel, and Keala Jane Jewel, The Feminist Press at The City University of New York, New York.

Twenty Letters to a Friend by Svetlana Alliluyeva, © 1967, Harper & Row, New York.

My Son Asks by Mila D. Anguilar, © 1984, 1985, 1987, from *A Comrade Is as Precious as a Rice Seedling,* Kitchen Table: Women of Color Press, Latham, N.Y.

The Truth Was Never More Necessary by Angelica Balabanoff, from *My Life as a Rebel* by Angelica Balabanoff, © 1938, Harper & Row, New York.

Strategies for Peace by Norma Becker, © 1983, from *The Deadly Connection,* American Friends Service Committee, Boston. Reprinted by permission of the author.

The Soviet Peace Fund by Elena Bruskova, reprinted by permission from *Soviet Literature Today,* © 1987, No. 7, Moscow.

Eradicate Nuclear Weapons from the Face of the Earth by Helen Caldicott, © 1985. Reprinted by permission of the author and the Women's Alliance for Nuclear Disarmament, Arlington, MD. 08174. Excerpted from a film, *If You Love This Planet,* The Canadian Film Association, and from *Missile Envy,* © 1986, William Morrow, New York, N.Y.

Free Women Blooming Like Fields of Flowers by Ch'iu Chin, tr. Kenneth Rexroth and Ling Chung, © 1972, from *Women Poets of China,* New Directions Publishing Corporation, New York.

The Blue Anchor by Jane Cooper, © 1984, from *Scaffolding: New and Selected Poems,* Anvil Press Poetry, London. Reprinted by permission of the author.

On Hearing Peace Has Been Declared by Argentina Daley, tr. Susana Settri.

The Challenge of Nonviolence by Barbara Deming, courtesy of New Society Publishers, Calif., and The War Resisters League.

Blocking the Gates to Heaven by Barbara Ehrenreich, © 1986. First printed in *Mother Jones,* June 1986 issue. Reprinted by permission of the author.

Interview with History by Oriana Fallaci, from *An Interview with History.*

Anne Frank: The Diary of a Young Girl by Anne Frank, © 1952, Doubleday, New York.

The March at Comiso: The Air Was Filled with Optimism by Matrice Grice, Italy.

Star Wars Can't Work by Dorothy Crowfoot Hodgkin, from a public speech.

Black Hills Survival Gathering, 1980 by Linda Hogan, © 1984, from *Songs from This Earth on Turtle's Back,* edited by Joseph Bruchac, The Greenfield Press, Ithaca, N.Y. Reprinted by permission of the author.

The Strength of War Resistance: Patriotism in Its Highest Significance by Jessie Wallace Hughan, from a public speech.

Women and Ecology and *The Power of Non-violence* by Petra Kelly, tr. Marianne Howarth, © 1984, from *Fighting for Hope,* South End Press, Boston. Also Chatto & Windus, The Hogarth Press, London.

No to Weapons in Space by Vera Kistiakowsky, excerpted from a speech given at an International Women's Conference for Peace and Nuclear Disarmament, published, © 1984 (Newsletter, Vol. 13, No. 8), The Center for Defense Information.

The Letters of Kollantai by Alexandra Kollantai, tr. Daniela Gioseffi, © 1988.

A New Idea Will Arise by Kathe Kollwitz, from *The Diaries of Kathe Kollwitz,* tr. Daniela Gioseffi, © 1988.

A New Beginning by La Pasionaria, Dolores Ibarruri, © 1966, from *They Shall Not Pass,* International Publishing Co., New York.

For the Future, a quote from an article by Frances Moore Lappé, © 1988, *The Mobilizer,* January Newsletter from National Mobilization for Survival, New York.

I Have All the Passion of Life by Lolita Lebron, tr. Gloria Waldman, © 1984. First printed in *Voices of Women: Poetry by and About Third World Women,* The Women's International Resource Exchange. Reprinted by permission of the translator.

Women Know a Lot of Things by Meridel Le Sueur, © 1957, 1982, from *The Ripening,* The Feminist Press at The City University of New York, New York.

Making Peace, © 1987, from *Breathing the Waters* and *What It Could Be*, © 1982, from *Candles in Babylon*, by Denise Levertov, New Directions Publishing Corporation, New York.

Dear Son: Letter to Luke by Mairead Corrigan Maguire, © 1986. First printed in *Peace by Peace*, the monthly newspaper of the Peace People, February 1986 issue, Northern Ireland.

An Evolution That Includes Democracy by Golda Meir, from *An Interview with History*, Oriana Fallaci,

Black Woman by Nancy Morejón, tr. Daniela Gioseffi with Enildo Garcia, © 1987. The original Spanish © 1985, Letras Cubanas, Havana, Cuba. Reprinted by permission of the author.

Peace Is Our Only Hope by Alva Myrdal, from a public speech.

Global Feminism for the Year 2000 by Marguerita Chant Papandreou, courtesy of the author.

It Is There by Muriel Rukeyser, © 1973, from *Breaking Open*, Random House, New York. Reprinted by permission of I.C.M., The Muriel Rukeyser Literary Estate.

Letter from Jail by Molly Rush, © 1981, *The Ploughshares & Support Committee*, Trinity Church, New York.

Chorus of the Dead and *Machines of War* by Nelly Sachs, tr. from the German by Ruth and Matthew Mead, © 1978, from *The Seeker*, Farrar, Straus & Giroux, Inc., New York. Reprinted by permission.

A Political Focus on Military Profiteery: The First Step to Peace by Eleanor Cutri Smeal, excerpted from a speech given at an International Women's Conference for Peace and Nuclear Disarmament, published, © 1984 (Newsletter, Vol. 13, No. 8), The Center for Defense Information.

Nothing Could Be More Important by Samantha Smith, courtesy of the Samantha Smith Foundation.

Holding the Line at Greenham Common: Being Joyously Political in Dangerous Times by Ann Snitow, © 1985, from *Mother Jones*, February/March 1985 issue. Reprinted by permission of the author.

Invocation to the Mayan Moon Goddess by Sharon Spencer, © 1985. Reprinted by permission of the author.

Works of Peace by Mother Teresa, from a public speech.

Women by Sojourner Truth, public domain.

What About the Russians? by Grace Kennan Warnecke and *Seeds of Peace* by Joanne Woodward, both excerpted from speeches given at an International Women's Conference for Peace and Nuclear Disarmament, published © 1984 (Newsletter, Vol. 13, No. 8), The Center for Defense Information.

Song of Hope and *When We Go Home Again* by Daisy Zamora, tr. Jane Glazer, Elizabeth Linder, and Miriam Ellis, reprinted from *IXOK AMAR GO*, edited by Zoe Anglesey, © 1987, Granite Press, Penobscot, Maine.

AUSTRALIA:
War Resisters League
PO Box 697, Civic Square,
A62608 Canberra
Nuclear Free and Independent
Pacific Coordinating Committee
PO Box A 391/Sydney South
New South Wales 2000
AUSTRIA:
Arbeitsgemeinschaft für Zividienst
Gewaltfreibeit und Soziale
Verteidgung
Schottengasse 3a/St. 1/Tur 59
1010 Vienna
Begegnungsstätte für Aktive
Gewaltlosigkeit
St. Wolfgangerstr. 26,
4820 Bad Ischl.
BELGIUM:
Confédération Service Civile pour
la Jeunesse
35 rue van Elewyck
1050 Brussels
Internationale van
Oorlogstegenstanders
35 Van Elewyckstraat
1050 Brussels
MIR/IRG
35 rue van Elewyck
1050 Brussels
Mouvement Chrétien pour la Paix
rue du Trone 102
1050 Brussels
CANADA:
Union des Pacifistes du Québec
1264 rue St. Timothée
Montreal, Québec H2I 3NI
DENMARK:
Aldrig Mere Krig
Dronningrasgade 14
1420 Copenhagen
ENGLAND:
Aboriginal Land Rights

Support Group
19c Lancaster Rd
London W11 1QL.
CIMRA (Colonialism and
Indigenous Minorities
Research and Action)
Liverpool Rd.
London N1
Fellowship of Reconciliation
40 Harleyford Rd., Vauxhall
London SE11 5AY
Feminism and Nonviolence Study
Group
67b Landor Road London SW9
Friends of the Earth
(National Office)
City Road, London EC1
Green Party
(National Office)
36-38 Clapham Road
London SW9
Greenpeace (London)
6 Endsleigh Street
London WC1 oDX
Housmans Bookshop
5 Caledonian Road, Kings Cross,
London N1 9DX
Peace News
8 Elm Avenue
Nottingham 3
Peace Pledge Union
6 Endsleigh Street
London WC1 oDX
War Resisters' International
55 Dawes Street
London SE17 1EL
FINLAND:
Union of COs
Peace Station
Veturitori, SF 00520
Helsinki 52
World Peace Council
Linnankoskenk 25A6

* This compendium can only suggest the numerous organizations worldwide for global peacemaking. It is recommended that each country in which this book is published expand its own indigenous list of resources, placing them at the end of the international listings, as here.

00250 Helsinki
FRANCE:
Association de Soutien aux
Objecteurs de Conscience (ASOC)
B.P. 176
57104 Thionville cedex
Mouvement des Objecteurs de
Conscience (MOC)
24 rue Crémieux
75012 Paris
Mouvement International de la
Reconciliation
c/o Yves Poulain Le Meyran
Bd. Gérard Philippe
13500 Martigues
Union Pacifiste de France
4 Rue Lazare Hoche
92100 Bologne sur Seine
Femmes pour la paix
68480 Biederrthal
Les Jerts
GERMAN FEDERAL REPUBLIC:
Deutsche Friedengesellschaft/
Internationale der
Kriegsdienstgegner
Jungfrauenthal 37/2E
2000 Hamburg 13
Deutsche Friedensgesellschaft/
Vereingte Kriegsdienstgegner
Schwanenstr. 16
5620 Velbert 1
Föderation Gewaltfreier
Aktonsgruppen-
Graswurzelrevolution
Scharnhort Str. 6
5000 Cologne 60
Internationale der
Kriegsdienstgegner
Gneisenanstr. 2a, Mehringhof
1000 Berlin 61
Selbstorganisation der Zivildienstle.
Vogelbergstr. 17
6000 Frankfurt am Main 1
Societas Populorum Progressio
Hergenroeder Str. 15
6050 Offenbach
Women's International League for
Peace & Freedom, Germany
Witzlebensh. 16
1000 Berlin 19
INDIA:
Shanti Sena Mandal—War Resisters

International
Rajghat
Varanasi, U.P. 1
IRELAND:
Dawn
Box 1522
Dublin 1
ISRAEL:
International Movement of
Conscientious War Resisters
PO Box 28058
Tel Aviv—Jafo
ITALY:
Lega degli Obiettori di Conscienza
Corso Sempione no. 88
20754 Milan
Movimento Nonviolento
C.P. 201
06100 Perugia
Partito Radicale
Via di Torre Argentina 18
00186 Roma
JAPAN:
Nipponzan Myohoji—War Resisters
Board
7-8 Shinsen-Cho
Shibuya-Ku, Tokyo
WRI Group
2-12-2 Asahi-machi
Obeno-Ku, Osaka
New Japan Women's Association
& Japan Council Against the
A & H Bombs
Yasue Muramatsu
Reimei Bldg. 1-36
Kandajinbocho
Chiyoda-ku, Tokyo
International Liaison Committee
c/o Gensuikyo
6-19-23 Shinashi
Minato-ku, Tokyo
NETHERLANDS:
Vereniging Dienstweigeraars
Postbus 4802
Amsterdam
't Kan Anders
Postbus 385
Amsterdam
NEW ZEALAND:
Christian Pacifist Society of New
Zealand
29 McGregors Ave.

Christchurch 1
Pacific Peoples Anti–Nuclear
Action Committee (PANAC)
Box 61086
Otara, Auckland
Aotearoa (New Zealand)
New Zealand Foundation
for Peace Studies
c/o Katie Boanas
35 Rata St.
Box 4110, Auckland
Christchurch 481-353
Te Whanau A Matariki
P.O. Box 1375
Otepoti (Dunedin)
Aotearoa (New Zealand)
NORWAY:
Folkereisning Mot Krig (FMK)
Rosenkrantzgate 18
0160 Oslo 1
Kampanjen mot Verneplikt
Postboks 8248, Hammersborg
Oslo 1
The Norwegian Peace Society
Oslo
The Peace Center
Oslo
PHILIPPINES:
Third World Movement Against
the Exploitation of Women
c/o Mary Soledad Perpinan
Good Shepherd Convent
1043 Aurora Boulevard
Quezon City
Cable: GODSHEPCON Manila
The Campaign Against Military
Prostitution (Camp International)
Tw-Mae-W
P.O. Box SM 366
Manila
SOUTH PACIFIC:
Fiji Anti-Nuclear Group (FANG)
P.O. Box 13861
Suva Fiji, South Pacific
SPAIN:
Asamblea Andaluza de Noviolencia
Pasaje Pezuela 1-7
29010 Málaga
Movimiento de Objectores de
Concienza
Desengaño 13, 1° Iza
Madrid 28004

SRI LANKA:
Nonviolent Direct Action Group
PO Box 2
Chavakachcheri
SWEDEN:
Göteborgs Lokala Samorganisation
Folkets Hus, Järntorget 1 Str.
41304 Göteborg
Kristna Fredsroerelsen
Karlsrogatan 10
S-75238 Uppsala
Swedish Peace and Arbitration
Society
Brannkyrkagatan 76
117 23 Stockholm
Vapenvagrarforbundet (VVF)
Brannkyrkagatan 76
117 23 Stockholm
SWITZERLAND:
Gruppe Schweli Ohne Army
Postfach 261
5026 Zurich
UNION OF SOVIET SOCIALIST
REPUBLICS:
Soviet Women's Committee
Neirovich-Danchenko St.
Moscow
Soviet Peace Committee
Prospect Mira, 36
Moscow
The Institute of U.S.A. & Canada
Studies Academy of Sciences of
the U.S.S.R.
Khelbny per., 2/3
Moscow 121069
INTERNATIONAL:
International Fellowship of
Reconciliation
Hof van Sonoy 15-17
N-1811 LD Alkmaar
Netherlands
Women for a Meaningful Summit
International Liaison Office
c/o Women's Union of Greece
8. Ainianos Str.
Gr. 104 34 Athens, Greece
Women's Union of Greece
Margarita Papandreou, President
146 71 Kastri, Athens, Greece
Tel. 884-3202 or 884-3859
World Women Parliamentarians
for Peace:

c/o Silvia Hernández, Senator
Xicotencatl 9, Centro
Mexico, D.F.
Tel. 521-3418
c/o Eleonore Romberg
Soldnerwegz 80
8000 München
Federal Republic of Germany
Tel. 089-982102
c/o WILPF
Rue de Varembe 1
Geneva, Switzerland
*UNITED STATES OF
AMERICA:
*Jane Addams Peace Association,
Inc.*
777 UN Plaza
New York, NY 10017
Tel. (212) 682-8830
A. J. Muste Institute
339 Lafayette St.
New York, NY 10012
*American Association of University
Women*
2401 Virginia Ave., NW
Washington, DC 20037
American Civil Liberties Union
132 West 43rd St.
New York, NY 10036
American Committee on Africa
198 Broadway
New York, NY 10038
*American Friends Service
Committee*
1501 Cherry St.
Philadelphia, PA 19102
*American Peace Test
Clearinghouse*
33 State St.
Salem, OR 80002
Amnesty International
322 Eighth Ave., 10th floor
New York, NY 10001
Boise Peace Quilt Project
Box 6469
Boise, ID 83707
Brandywine Peace Community
PO Box 81
Swarthmore, PA 19081
Catholic Peace Fellowship
339 Lafayette St.
New York, NY 10012

The Catholic Worker
36 East First St.
New York, NY 10003
Center for Defense Information
600 Maryland Ave. SW
Washington, DC 20024
Center for Economic Conversion
222C View St.
Mountain View, CA 94041
Center for Nonviolent Action
RFD 1, PO Box 430
Voluntown, CT 06384
*Center for Peace and Conflict
Studies*
5229 Cass Ave., Room 101
Wayne State University
Detroit, MI 48202
*Center for Psychosocial Studies
in the Nuclear Age*
1493 Cambridge St.
Cambridge, Mass. 02139
Center for War/Peace Studies
218 East 18th St.
New York, NY 10003
Center on Law and Pacifism
PO Box 308
Cokedale, CO 81032
*Central Committee for
Conscientious Objectors*
2208 South St.
Philadelphia, PA 19146
*CCCO: An Agency for Military
and Draft Counseling*
Philadelphia, PA 19146
*Church of the Brethren World
Ministries*
1451 Dundee Ave.
Elgin, IL 60120
Clergy and Laity Concerned
198 Broadway
New York, NY 10038
*Coalition Against Registration
and the Draft (CARD)*
731 State St.
Madison, WI 53703
*Coalition for a New Foreign
and Military Policy*
120 Maryland Ave. NE
Washington, DC 20002
*Committee in Solidarity with the
People of El Salvador (CISPES)*
930 F St. NW, No. 720

Washington, DC 20004
*Community for Creative
Nonviolence*
1345 Euclid St. NW
Washington, DC 20009
Committee for National Security
1601 Connecticut Ave., NW
Washington, DC 20009
*Consortium on Peace
Research, Education and
Development (COPRED)*
University of Illinois
911 West High St.
Urbana, IL 61801
Continuing the Peace Dialogue
Box 1710
Carmel Valley, CA 93924
Council for a Livable World
100 Maryland Ave. NE
Washington, DC 20002
Council on Economic Priorities
30 Irving Place
New York, NY 10003
*Critical Mass Energy Project/
Public Citizen, Inc.*
215 Pennsylvania Ave. SE
Washington, DC 20003
Earth First!
PO Box 5871
Tucson, AZ 85703
Educators for Social Responsibility
23 Garden St.
Cambridge, MA 02138
Environmental Action
1525 New Hampshire Ave. NW
Washington, DC 20036
Environmental Defense Fund
1616 P St. NW, Suite 150
Washington, DC 20036
Episcopal Peace Fellowship
Hearst Hall
Wisconsin Ave.
at Woodley Rd. NW
Washington, DC 20016
Fellowship of Reconciliation
PO Box 271
Nyack, NY 10960
Forum Institute
2001 S St. NW, Suite 430
Washington, DC 20009
*Friends Committee on
National Legislation*

245 Second St. NE
Washington, DC 20002
Friends of the Earth
530 Seventh St. SE
Washington, DC 20003
Friends of the River
Fort Mason Center,
Building C
San Francisco, CA 94123
Girls Club of America, Inc.
1030 15th St., NW
Washington, DC 20005
Grandmothers for Peace
2708 Curtis Way
Sacramento, CA 95818
Greenpeace
1611 Connecticut Ave. NW
Washington, DC 20009
Ground Zero
PO Box 19329
Portland, OR 97219
*Ground Zero Center for
Nonviolent Action*
16159 Clear Creek Rd. NW
Poulsbo, WA 98370
Highlander Center
Route 3, PO Box 370
New Market, TN 37820
Humanitas International
Box 818, Menlo
Park, CA 94206
INFACT/GE Boycott
186 Lincoln St., Room 203
Boston, MA 02111
In Our Own Way
2437 15th St., NW, Suite 400
Washington, DC 20009
Institute for Community Economics
151 Montague City Rd.
Greenfield, MA 01301
*Institute for Defense and
Disarmament Studies*
2001 Beacon St.
Brookline, MA 02146
Institute for Policy Studies
1901 Q St. NW
Washington, DC 20009
*Interfaith Center on
Corporate Responsibility*
475 Riverside Drive, Room 566
New York, NY 10115

Interhelp
PO Box 331
Northampton, MA 01061
International Physicians for the
Prevention of Nuclear War
225 Longwood Ave.
Boston, MA 02115
International Seminars on
Training for Nonviolent Action
(ISTNA)
PO Box 38
Boston, MA 02127
Jewish Peace Fellowship
PO Box 271
Nyack, NY 10960
Jobs with Peace
220 1st St. NE
Washington, DC 20002
Jonah House
1933 Park Ave.
Baltimore, MD 21217
Jubilee Partners
PO Box 68
Comer, GA 30629
Koinonia Community
Route 2
Americus, GA 31709
Martin Luther King, Jr.
Center for Social Change
449 Auburn Ave. NE
Atlanta, GA 30312
Mennonite Central Committee
21 South 12th St.
Akron, PA 17501
Midwest Academy
600 West Fullerton
Chicago, IL 60614
Mobilization for Survival
853 Broadway
New York, NY 10003
Movement for a New Society
PO Box 1922
Cambridge, MA 02238
National Action/Research on the
Military Industrial Complex
(NARMIC)
1501 Cherry St.
Philadelphia, PA 19102
National Association for the
Advancement of Colored People
4805 Mt. Hope Drive
Baltimore, MD 21215

National Center for Policy
Alternatives
2000 Florida Ave. NW
Washington, DC 20009
National Council of Churches
of Christ
475 Riverside Drive
New York, NY 10015
National Inter-Religious Service
Board for Conscientious Objectors
800 18th St. NW, Suite 600
Washington, DC 20006
National Organization for Women
1401 New York Ave. NW, Suite 800
Washington, DC 20005
National Rainbow Coalition
2100 M St. NW
Washington, DC 20037
National Resistance Committee
P.O. Box 40428
San Francisco, CA 94142
National War Tax Resistance
Coordinating Committee
P.O. Box 2236
East Patchogue, NY 11772
Nuclear Information Resource
Service
1616 P St. NW, Suite 160
Washington, DC 20036
Nuclear Weapons Freeze Campaign
220 I St. NE, Suite 130
Washington, DC 20002
Pax Christi
348 E. Tenth St.
Erie, PA 16503
Peace Fleece
RFD 1, Box 57
Kezar Falls, ME 04047
Peace Links
747 Eighth St. SE
Washington, DC 20003
Peacemakers
P.O. Box 627
Garberville, CA 95440
Pendle Hill
338 Plush Mill Rd.
Wallingford, PA 19086
Physicians for Social Responsibility
639 Massachusetts Ave.
Cambridge, MA 02139
Psychologists for Social
Responsibility

1841 Columbia Rd. N.W., Suite 209
Washington, DC 20009
Pledge of Resistance
P.O. Box 53411
Washington, DC 20009
Progressive Student Network
P.O. Box 1027
Iowa City, IA 52244
Prisoner Visitation and Support
1501 Cherry St.
Philadelphia, PA 19102
Religious Task Force
85 South Oxford St.
Brooklyn, NY 11217
Resource Center for Nonviolence
P.O. Box 2324
Santa Cruz, CA 95063
Riverside Disarmament Program
490 Riverside Dr.
New York, NY 10027
Rocky Flats Conversion Project
1660 Lafayette St.
Denver, CO 80218
SANE/Committee for a Sane Nuclear Policy
711 G St. SE
Washington, DC 20003
SANE/Freeze
220 1st St. NE, Suite 130
Washington, DC 20002
SANE/FREEZE INTERNA-TIONAL
777 United Nations Plaza
New York, N.Y. 10017
Sierra Club
330 Pennsylvania Ave. SE
Washington, DC 20003
Sojourners
P.O. Box 29272
Washington, DC 20017
Southern Christian Leadership Conference
334 Auburn Ave. NE
Atlanta, GA 30303
Southwest Research and Information Center
P.O. Box 4524
Albuquerque, NM 87106
Syracuse Peace Council
924 Burnett Ave.
Syracuse, NY 13203

TransAfrica/Free South Africa Movement
545 Eighth St. SE
Washington, DC 20003
Traprock Peace Center
Woolman Hill, Keets Rd.
Deerfield, MA 01342
Union of Concerned Scientists
26 Church St.
Cambridge, MA 02138
United Farm Workers
P.O. Box 62
Keene, CA 93531
US Corporation and Foundation Women
1133 Ave. of the Americas
New York, NY 10022
USA-USSR Citizens Dialogue, Inc.
777 United Nations Plaza
New York, NY 10017
Veterans for Peace
P.O. Box 3881
Portland, ME 04104
Vietnam Veterans of America
2001 S St. NW, Suite 700
Washington, DC 20009
War Resisters League
339 Lafayette St.
New York, NY 10012
Witness for Peace
515 Broadway
Santa Cruz, CA 95060
Women's Action for Nuclear Disarmament (WAND)
691 Massachusetts Ave.
Arlington, MA 02174
Women Strike for Peace
145 South 13th St.
Philadelphia, PA 19107
Women's International League for Peace and Freedom
1213 Race St.
Philadelphia, PA 19107
World Policy Institute
777 United Nations Plaza
New York, NY 10017
World Priorities
P.O. Box 25140
Washington, DC 20007
World Without War Council
1730 Martin Luther King Jr. Way
Berkeley, CA 94709

Bibliography for Further Reading

Asterisk (*) = the author/book is quoted in the text. See Table.
Plus-sign (+) = books dealing with psychological health in the nuclear age.
Double plus-sign (++) = books for young people.

I. Sociopolitical Fact, Theory, History, Experience

*Addams, Jane. *A Centennial Reader*. Edited by Emily Cooper Johnson. New York: Macmillan, 1960.

Balch, Emily Greene. *Occupied Haiti*. New York: Garland, 1972.

Balser, Diane. *Sisterhood and Solidarity: Feminism and Labor in Modern Times*. Boston: South End Press, 1987.

Barash, Carol, ed. An *Olive Schreiner Reader*. London: Routledge & Kegan Paul, 1987.

Beard, Mary Ritter. *Woman as Force in History*. 1946. Reprint New York: Persea Books, 1987.

Beauvoir, Simone de. *The Second Sex*. Translated by H. M. Parshley. New York: Random House, 1953.

———. *The Ethics of Ambiguity*. Secaucus, N.J.: Citadel, 1962.

———. *All's Said and Done*. Paris: Gallimard, 1971; New York: Putnam, 1972.

———. *The Coming of Age*. New York: Putnam, 1972.

Berkin, Carol R., and Lovett, Clara M., eds. *Women, War, and Revolution*. New York and London: Holmes & Meier, 1980.

Brown, Wilmette. *Black Women and the Peace Movement*. From International Women's Day Convention, July 1983. Available from King's Cross Women's Centre, 71 Tonbridge St., London, WC1, England.

*Caldicott, Helen. *Missile Envy: The Arms Race and Nuclear War*. New York: Morrow, 1984; Bantam, 1986.

Cataldo, Mima; Putter, Ruth; Fireside, Byrna; and Lytel, Elaine. *Women's Encampment for a Future of Peace and Justice*. Boston: South End Press, 1983.

Comiso, Ellen Turkish. *Workers' Control Under Plan and Market*. New Haven, Conn.: Yale University Press, 1988.

Cooney, Robert and Michalowski, Helen. *The Power of the People: Active Nonviolence in the United States*. Philadelphia: New Society Publishers, 1987.

Crolle, Elisabeth. *Women's Rights in Government Policy in China Since Mao*, Zed Press, London, 1983.

Cultural Survival, Inc. (a nonprofit study group). *Indigenous Peoples: A*

Global Quest for Justice; The Spoils of Famine: Ethiopian Famine Policy and Peasant Argiculture; Indigenous Peoples and Tropical Forests, 1987–88. Other pamphlets also available from Cultural Survival, Inc., 11 Divinity Ave., Cambridge, Mass. 02138.

Deming, Barbara. *We Are All Part of One Another: A *Barbara Deming Reader.* Edited by Jane Meyerding. Philadelphia: New Society Publishers, 1984.

Elshtain, Jean Bethke. *Women and War.* New York: Basic Books, 1987.

Enloe, Cynthia. *Does Khaki Become You? The Militarization of Women's Lives.* Boston: South End Press, 1983.

Everett, Melissa, ed. *Bearing Witness, Building Bridges: Interviews with North Americans Living and Working in Nicaragua.* Philadelphia: New Society Publishers, 1986.

Frederikse, Julie. *South Africa: A Different Kind of War.* Boston: Beacon Press, 1987.

Fitzgerald, Frances. *Fire in the Lake: The Vietnamese and the Americans in Vietnam.* Boston: Little, Brown, 1972.

———. *America Revised.* Boston: Atlantic Monthly Press, 1979.

Fuentes, Annette, and Ehrenreich, Barbara. *Women in the Global Factory.* Boston: South End Press, 1983.

George, Susan. *Ill Fares the Land: Essays on Food, Hunger, and Power.* Washington, D.C.: Institute for Policy Studies, 1987.

George, Susan, and Bennett, Jon. *The Hunger Machine.* Washington, D.C.: Institute for Policy Studies, 1987.

Giddings, Paula. *When and Where I Enter: The Impact of Black Women on Race and Sex in America.* New York: Morrow, 1984.

*Glendinning, Chellis. *Waking Up in the Nuclear Age: The Book of Nuclear Psychotherapy.* New York: Morrow, 1987.

Goldman, Emma. *Anarchism and Other Essays.* Reprint Mineola, N.Y.: Dover, 1970.

*Gordon, Suzanne, and McFadden, Dave. *Economic Conversion.* Boston: Ballinger, 1984.

*Gould, Benina Berger: Moon, Susan; and VanHoorn, Judith. *Growing Up Scared? The Psychological Effects of the Nuclear Threat on Children.* Berkeley, Calif.: Open Books, 1986.

*Griffin, Susan. *The First and the Last: A Woman Thinks About War.* New York: Harper & Row, 1987.

Holland, Barbara, ed. *Soviet Sisterhood.* Bloomington, Indiana: Indiana University Press, 1985.

Hooks, Bell. *Ain't I a Woman? Black Women and Feminism.* Boston: South End Press, 1981.

Jensen, Joan M. *With These Hands: Women Working the Land.* New York: The Feminist Press of the City University of New York, 1986.

Kelly, Petra. *Fighting for Hope.* Boston: South End Press; London: Chatto & Windus, The Hogarth Press, 1984.

Keon, Susan, and Swaim, Nina. *A Handbook for Women on the Nuclear Mentality: Ain't Nowhere You Can Run.* Arlington, Mass.: Women's Alliance for Nuclear Disarmament, 1980.

Király, Béla K., and Rothenberg, Gunther E. *War and Society in East Central Europe.* Vol. 1. Brooklyn, N.Y.: Brooklyn College Press, 1979.

———. *War and Society in East Central Europe.* Vol. 4 of *East European Quarterly.* Lanham, Md.: University Press of America, 1984.

Kollantai, Alexandra. *Selected Writings of Alexandra Kollantai*. Edited by Alix Holt. Westport, Conn.: Lawrence Hill, 1977.

*Lappé, Frances Moore. *Diet for a Small Planet*. New York: Ballantine Books, 1972.

Lappé, Frances Moore, et al. *Betraying the National Interest*. New York: Grove, 1987.

*Larson, Jeanne, and Micheels-Cyrus, Madge, eds. *Seeds of Peace: A Catalogue of Quotations*. Santa Cruz, Calif.: New Society Press, 1987.

Laska, Vera, ed. *Women in the Resistance and in the Holocaust: The Voices of Eyewitnesses*. With a foreword by Simon Wiesenthal. Westport, Conn.: Greenwood, 1983.

Lessing, Doris. *The Wind Blows Away Our Words*. New York: Random House, Vintage Books, 1987.

*Luxemburg, Rosa. *The Accumulation of Capital*. Translated by Agnes Schwarzschild. New Haven, Conn.: Yale University Press, 1951.

———. *Reform or Revolution*. 1899. Reprint New York: Pathfinder Press, 1986.

+McAllister, Pam, ed. *Reweaving the Web of Life*. Santa Cruz, Calif.: New Society Publishers, 1982.

+Macy, Joanna Rogers. *Despair and Personal Power in the Nuclear Age*. Philadelphia: New Society Publishers, 1983.

*Mansfield, Sue. *The Gestalt of War: An Inquiry into the Origin and Meaning as a Social Institution*. New York: Dial Press, 1982.

Marx, Eleanor. *Marx's Theories of Surplus Value; Karl Marx: A Biography; The Socialist Democrat*. Available in university libraries only. Published in *Progress, The Socialist Democrat,* etc., Dates of writings: 1884–1891.

Meeker-Lowry, Susan. *A Catalyst Guide to Socially Conscious Investing*. Santa Cruz, Calif.: New Society Publishers, 1987.

Miller, Alice. *For Your Own Good: Hidden Cruelty in Child-Rearing and the Roots of Violence*. New York: New American Library, Plume Books, 1983.

Morgan, Robin, ed. *Sisterhood Is Global: The International Women's Movement Anthology*. New York: Doubleday, Anchor Books, 1984.

Myrdal, Alva. *The Game of Disarmament: How the U.S. and Russia Run the Arms Race*. New York: Pantheon Books, 1982.

Obbo, Christine. *African Women: Their Struggle for Economic Independence*. London: Zed Press, 1980.

Pacific Women Speak: Why Haven't You Known?. Edited by Women Working for a Nuclear Free and Independent Pacific. Oxford, England: Green Line, 1987.

Pearce, Jenny. *Under the Eagle: U.S. Intervention in Central America and the Carribean*. Boston: South End Press, 1983.

Reardon, Betty. *Sexism and the War System*. New York: Teachers College Press, 1985.

Reed, Evelyn. *Woman's Evolution, from Matriarchal Clan to Patriarchal Family*. New York: Pathfinder Press, 1975.

Reilly, Catherine, ed. *Chaos of the Night: Women's Poetry and Verse of the Second World War*. London: Virago, 1984.

+Rowe, Dorothy. *Living with the Bomb*. London: Rutledge & Kegan Paul, 1985.

Russell, Diana E., and Van deVen, Nicole, eds., *Crimes Against Women: Proceedings of the International Tribunal*. East Palo Alto, Calif.: Frog in the Well, 1984.

Schecter, Susan. *Women and Male Violence.* Boston: South End Press, 1982.

Seager, Joni, and Olson, Ann. **Women in the World: An International Atlas.* New York: Simon & Schuster, Touchstone Books, 1986.

Sidel, Ruth. *Women and Children Last: The Plight of Poor Women in Affluent America.* New York: Viking-Penguin, 1986.

Simons, Margaret A., ed. *Hypatia.* Edwardsville, Ill.: Southern Illinois University Press, 1987.

Smedley, Agnes. *The Struggle to Liberate India from Britain.* 1923. Reprint New York: The Feminist Press at the City University of New York, 1984.

————. *Reports on the War Years in China, 1928–41.* Edited by Jan and Steve MacKinnon. New York: The Feminist Press at the City University of New York, 1985.

Stallard, Karin, and Ehrenreich, Barbara. *Poverty in the American Dream.* Boston: South End Press, 1983.

War Resisters League, Study Group. *Piecing It Together: Feminism and Non-Violence,* 1983 pamphlet; *Daring to Change,* 1987; and *We Are Ordinary Women,* 1983. Available from War Resisters League, 339 Lawayette Street, New York, N.Y. 10012. (Also ask for WRL Literature List/Catalog, including books/pamphlets by *Barbara Deming, *On Revolution and Equilibrium,* and others, such as Emma Goldman, Rosa Luxemburg, Simone Weil, Jessie Wallace Hughan, and the 1982 Collective Working Statement of The Women's Pentagon Action.

Warner, Gale, and Shuman, Michael. *Citizen Diplomat.* Foreword by Carl Sagan. New York: Continuum Press, 1987.

Waters, Mary-Alice, ed. *Rosa Luxemburg Speaks: 16 Speeches and Articles.* Reprint. New York: Pathfinder Press, 1988.

Weil, *Simone. *The Simone Weil Reader.* Edited by George A. Panichas. New York: David McKay, 1977.

Willenz, June A. *Women Veterans: America's Forgotten Heroines.* New York: Continuum Press, 1983.

Women: A World Report. Compiled by New Internationalist Public Staff. New York: Oxford University Press, 1986.

Women's International Resource Exchange. *Philippine Women: From Assembly Line to Firing Line,* 1987. *Nicaraguan Women and the Revolution,* 1982; *We Continue Forever: Sorrow and Strength of Guatemalan Women,* 1983: by The *WIRE Collective, Broadway, N.Y. 10025.

Women's Economic Agenda for Change. *Toward Economic Justice for Women.* Washington, D.C.: Institute for Policy Studies, 1987.

Zoryan Institute. *The Armenian Experience: Genocide.* (c) 1984, Cambridge, Mass.: Zoryan Institute, 1984.

II. Biography or Autobiography and Memoir Oral History

Bacon, Margaret Hope. *Valient Friend: The Life of *Lucretia Mott.* New York: Walker, 1980.

Balabanoff, Angelica. **My Life As a Rebel.* New York: Harper, 1938. Reprinted Westport, Conn.: Greenwood Press, 1968.

Baxandall, Rosalyn Fraad. *Words on Fire: The Life and Writing of Elizabeth Burley Flynn, Early Twentieth Century U.S. Social Activist and Labor Organizer.* New Brunswick, N.J.: Rutgers University Press, 1988.

Borton, Lady. *Sensing the Enemy: An American Woman Among the Boat People of Vietnam.* New York: Dial Press, 1984.

Brombert, Beth Archer. *Cristina.* Chicago: University of Chicago Press, 1977.

Cantarow, Ellen, with Susan Gushee O'Malley and Sharon Hartoman Strom. *Moving the Mountain; Women Working for Social Change.* New York: The Feminist Press at the City University of New York, 1980.

Claiborne, Sybil. *Climbing Fences: Grace Paley.* New York: War Resisters League, 1987.

Day, Dorothy. *The Long Loneliness.* Introduction by Father Daniel Berrigan. Boston: South End Press, 1984.

Duras, Margarite. *The War.* Translated by Barbara Bray. New York: Panetheon Books, 1986.

Durova, Nadezhda. *The Cavalry Maiden.* Translated and annotated by Mary Fleming Zirin. Bloomington: University of Indiana Press, 1988.

Florence, Barbara Moench, ed. *Lela Secor: A Diary in Letters, 1915–1922.* New York: Burt Franklin, 1978.

Fourtouni, Eleni. *Greek Women of the Resistance.* New Haven, Conn.: Thelphini Press, 1986.

Freedman, Dan, and Rhoads, Jacqueline, eds. *The Forgotten Vets: Nurses in Vietnam.* Austin: Texas Monthly Press, 1987.

Freeman, Lucy; La Follette, Sherry; and Zabriskie, George A. *Dear Heart: The Biography of Belle Case La Follette.* New York: Beaufort Books, 1986.

Galicich, *Anne. *Samantha Smith: A Journey from the US to the USSR for Peace.* Minneapolis: Dillon Press, 1987.

Glendenning, Victoria. *Rebecca West; A Life.* New York: Alfred A. Knopf, 1988.

Gluck, Sherna, ed. *From Parlor To Prison: Five American Suffragists Talk About Their Lives.* New York: Vintage Books, Random House, 1976.

Gluck, Sherna Berger. *Rosie The Riveter Revisited; Women, the War and Social Change.* New York: Twayne, 1987.

Goldman, *Emma. *Living My Life.* 2 vols. Civil Liberties in American History Series. Reprint of 1931 ed. 1976.

Ibarruri, Dolores. "La Pasionaria." *They Shall Not Pass.* New York: International Publishers, 1976.

Kearns, Martha. *Käthe Kollwitz: Woman and Artist.* New York: The Feminist Press at the City University of New York, 1976.

Larsen, Wendy Wilder, and Nga, Tran Thi. *Shallow Graves.* New York: Hill & Wang, 1986.

McAllister, Pam. *You Can't Kill the Spirit.* Santa Cruz, Calif.: New Society Publishers, 1988.

Mandéla, Winnie.* *Part of My Soul Went with Him.* New York: Norton, 1985; Reinbek near Hamburg, West Germany; Rowohlt Taschenbuch, Reinbek, 1984.

Marshall, Lenore.* *Invented a Person.* Edited by Janice Thaddeus. Foreword by Muriel Rukeyser. New York: Horizon Press, 1979.

Morhange-Beague, Claude. *Chamberet: Recollections from an Ordinary Childhood.* Translated by Austryn Wainhouse. New York: Marlboro Press, 1988.

Mullaney, Maria Marmo. *Revolutionary Women.* New York: Praeger, 1983.

Opfell, Olga S. *The Lady Laureates: Women Who Have Won the Nobel Prize.* 2d ed. Metuchen, N.J., and London: Scarecrow Press, 1982.

Saywell, Shelly. *Women in War.* New York: Viking-Penguin, 1985.

Sterling, Dorothy. *Black Foremothers.* 2d ed. New York: The Feminist Press at the City University of New York, 1987.

Szymusiak, Molyda. *The Stones Cry Out: A Cambodian Childhood.* Translated from the French by Linda Coverdale. New York: Hill and Wang, 1986.

Uglow, Jennifer S., ed. *The International Dictionary of Women's Biography.* New York: Macmillan, 1982.

Webb, Sheyann, and Nelsen, Rachel West. *Selma Lord Selma: Girlhood Memories of the Civil-Rights Days.* New York: William Morrow, 1980.

Young-Bruehl, Elisabeth. *For Love of the World: A Biography of *Hannah Arendt.* New Haven, Conn.: Yale University Press, 1982.

III. Fiction and Poetry on War and Cross-Cultural Literature

Akhmatova, *Anna. *The Poems of Akhmatova.* Translated by Stanley Kunitz and Max Hayward. Boston: Little, Brown, 1972.

———. *Poems.* Selected and translated by Lyn Coffin. New York: Norton, 1983.

Allende, Isabel. *The House of the Spirits.* Translated from the Spanish by Magda Bogin. New York: Knopf, 1985; Bantam, 1986.

Anderson, Jennifer, and Mumford, Theresa. *Chinese Women Writers.* Hong Kong: Janit Publishing, 1985.

Anglesey, Zoe. **Ixok Amar Go, Central American Women's Poetry for Peace.* Penobscot, Me.: Granite Press, 1987.

Bachman, Ingeborg. *The Thirtieth Year.* Translated by Michael Bullock. New York: Holmes & Meier, 1987.

Benedict, Ruth, ed. *Tales of the Cochiti Indians.* Albuquerque: University of New Mexico Press, 1981.

Bennett, Betty T. *British War Poetry in the Age of Romanticism.* London: Garland Publishers, 1977.

Emecheta, Buchi. *Second-Class Citizen.* New York: Braziller, 1985.

Fallaci, Oriana. **A Man.* New York: Simon & Schuster, 1980; Milan, Italy: Rizzoli Editore, 1979.

Forché, *Carolyn. *The Country Between Us.* Pittsburgh: Pittsburgh University Press, 1984.

Gordimer, Nadine. **Burger's Daughter.* New York: Viking, 1979.

Green, Rayna, ed. *That's What She Said: Contemporary Poetry and Fiction by Native American Women.* Bloomington: Indiana University Press, 1984.

Hurston, *Zora Neale. *I Love Myself When I Am Laughing . . . and Then Again When I Am Looking Mean and Impressive.* Edited by Alice Walker. New York: The Feminist Press, 1979.

Kumin, Maxine. *The Long Approach.* New York: Viking Penguin, 1986.

Lessing, *Doris. *The Good Terrorist.* New York: Vintage Books; London: Jonathan Cape, 1985.

Levertov, Denise. *Poems 1968–1972.* New York: New Directions, 1987.

*Morrison, Toni, *Beloved,* © 1987 and *Sula* © 1973, New York: Alfred A. Knopf.

Paley, Grace. **Later the Same Day: A Collection of Stories.* New York: Farrar, Straus & Giroux, 1986.

———.* Leaning Forward. Penobscot, Me.: Granite Press, 1986.

Paolucci, Anne, and Warwick, Ronald. *Review of National Literatures India.* Vol. 10. New York: Griffon House Press, 1987.

++Pirtle, Sarah. *An Outbreak of Peace.* With an afterword by Shelly Berman and Susan Jones, Educators for Social Responsibility. Santa Cruz, Calif.: New Society Publishers, 1987.

Rich,* Adrienne. *The Will to Change.* New York: Norton, 1971.

Tanaka, Yukiko. *To Live and To Write: Selections by Japanese Women Writers, 1913–1938.* New York: Seal Press, 1988.

Walker,* Alice. *Meridian.* New York: Harcourt Brace Jovanovich, 1976.

Washington, Mary Helen, ed. *Invented Lives: Narratives of Black Women, 1860–1960; by Harriet Jacobs, Zore Neale Hurston, Gwendolyn Brooks, and Others.* Garden City, N.Y.: Doubleday, Anchor Press, 1987.

Wolf, Christa. *Cassandra.* Translated from the German by Jan Van Heurck. New York: Farrar Straus & Giroux, 1984.

Woolf, Virginia. *Three Guineas.* 1938. Reprint. New York: Harcourt Brace Jovanovich, 1966.